their misguided efforts to help and heal. So-called clinical depression and the wholly iatrogenic disorders Multiple Personality Disorder (MPD) and Attention Deficit Disorder (ADD) have become the new, in vogue "illnesses" of the decade. Baker clearly demonstrates, however, that these "ailments," if they are present at all, are the creations of overzealous, misinformed therapists eager to slap medical labels on unsuspecting patients with emotional (not medical) problems.

In our present era of the "Physician–Insurer–Drug Company Complex" and unaffordable health care, we must learn to take steps to help ourselves and give up entirely our delusion that psychiatry can provide some kind of magic cure for the anxieties and depressions common to everyday life. *Mind Games: Are We Obsessed with Therapy?* gives us concrete ways to do so.

ROBERT A. BAKER, PH.D. is professor emeritus of psychology at the University of Kentucky in Lexington and is a Fellow of the American Psychological Association and the Committee for the Scientific Investigation of Claims of the Paranormal (CSICOP). He has authored over a dozen books, including *They Call It Hypnosis* and *Hidden Memories*, and his professional career as a military, industrial, forensic, and clinical psychologist has spanned forty years.

mind
games

ARE WE
OBSESSED
WITH
THERAPY?

mind
games

ROBERT A. BAKER, Ph.D.

 Prometheus Books
59 John Glenn Drive
Amherst, New York 14228-2197

Published 1996 by Prometheus Books

00 99 98 97 96   5 4 3 2 1

Library of Congress Cataloging-in-Publication Data

Baker, Robert A. (Robert Allen), 1921–
      Mind games : are we obsessed with therapy / Robert A. Baker.
            p.   cm.
      Includes bibliographical references and index.
      ISBN 1–57392–071–1 (cloth)
      1. Antipsychiatry. 2. Psychiatric errors. 3. Psychotherapy—Moral
and ethical aspects. 4. Psychotherapy patients—Abuse of. 5. Consumer
education. I. Title.
RC437.5.B35   1996
616.89'14—dc20   96–3035
                                                           CIP

Printed in the United States of America on acid-free paper

"I never write on any subject unless I believe the opinion of those who have the ear of the public to be mistaken and this involves as a necessary consequence that every book I write runs counter to the men who are in possession of the field."

Samuel Butler
Quoted in R. V. Sampson, *The Psychology of Power,*
(New York: Pantheon, 1966), p. 40.

"The object of life is not to be on the side of the majority, but to escape finding oneself in the ranks of the insane."

Marcus Aurelius

Acknowledgments

I would like to thank Joe Nickell, Philip J. Klass, Phil Dare, Newton Joseph, William Cone, Joel Carlinsky, Dr. Andrew Reisner of Mansfield, Ohio, and Henry Palka of Hartford, Connecticut, for some of the material included. Also, Ed and Donna Bassett, Richard Franklin, Dennis Biddle, Dr. John H. Parks, Janet Timberlake, and Nancy Collins for services rendered. For support and encouragement and unflagging belief in the value of this project, I am also indebted to Paul Kurtz; Steven Mitchell; and Charlotte Taraba, whose patience emulates that of Job.

Dedication

This book is dedicated to all of those psychotherapists who for many years now have been engaged in an ongoing battle with the proponents of "the Psychotherapeutic State" earlier identified in 1963 by Dr. Thomas Szasz as "the Therapeutic State." As noted by Dr. David Cohen, this state "includes a vast array of connected ideas and theories, legal codifications and moral justifications, therapeutic practices and helping professions, institutional loci, supporters and proponents." Moreover this state does not seek merely to eliminate or control "mental illness" but also to manage every aspect of our social lives. Of all the various mental health professions psychiatry is the most powerful and dominant member and has headed the Therapeutic State from its inception. With its current emphasis on biological theorizing and genetic speculation and its use of the "medical" model for dealing with every aspect of human behavior, it has been the prime mover in the "diseasing," "shrinking," and "tranquilizing" of the American public and the primary reason why we are currently "a nation of victims." Rather than succeeding in their avowed aim of producing and maintaining "mentally healthy citizens" the "professionals" have created instead a nation of whining, self-pitying, and irresponsible "psychiatric-drug" and "therapy" addicts totally incapable of living free, independent, and spontaneous lives, which is, paradoxically, the therapeutic goal! This book is dedicated to all of those who have seen this problem and have fought it tooth and nail, primarily:

Dr. Thomas Szasz
Dr. R. D. Laing
Dr. Jonas Robitscher
Dr. Peter Breggin
Dr. Theodore Sarbin
Dr. Seth Farber
Dr. Stanton Peele
Dr. David Hill
Dr. Garth Wood
Dr. Ronald Leifer
Dr. Lee Coleman
Dr. David Cohen

Dr. Eileen Walkenstein
Dr. George Albee
Dr. Dorothy Tennov
Dr. Bernie Zilbergeld
Dr. Walter Fisher
Dr. Jeffrey Masson
Dr. Lesley Hazleton
Dr. Theodore Lidz
Judi Chamberlin
Leonard Frank
John Modrow
Dr. E. M. Thornton

and other noble therapeutic soldiers too numerous to mention.

Contents

Introduction

SHRINKAGE

Upon visiting a mental institution, it would not be surprising to observe that many patients are "out of touch with reality," failing to perceive discrepancies between their beliefs and external events. But it would be amazing, indeed, to discover that a large number of the professionals concerned with the "mentally ill" (psychiatrists and psychologists, for example) manifest such a perceptual deficit. We have been amazed.[1]

Before beginning this book a number of definitions are in order. First, it is important to know that people whose profession and occupation is that of psychotherapy are often referred to as "headshrinkers" after those primitive tribes in the Amazon basin who do, quite literally, kill others, cut off their heads and shrink them to the size of the average man's fist. When the term "shrink" is applied to a psychotherapist it is seldom a compliment. Instead, most people feel vaguely uncomfortable around such therapists and, whether true or not, they feel their self-esteem and ego threatened and believe that all therapists—especially psychiatrists—can read their minds and know all their hidden secrets. The term "shrink" is, therefore, usually derogatory. As for the term "shrinkage," it refers to both the psychological as well as physical damage done by the psychotherapist to patients or clients. One

13

usually assumes that any and all trips to a licensed, certified, or trained and experienced therapist are bound to have a favorable and positive outcome—especially if one goes to a psychiatrist who is also a medical doctor. Doctors treat you and make you well; seldom do they do you harm or make you sicker. Most of the time this is true, thank heaven. Unfortunately, as you will discover in the following pages, it is not always true that psychiatrists, clinical psychologists, counselors, psychiatric social workers, family therapists, and pastoral counselors—all those calling themselves psychotherapists—are able to treat you successfully and effectively. Instead of helping you they may do you harm—intentionally or unintentionally. It is important to recognize at the outset that psychotherapy is a hazardous undertaking. It is definitely not, despite many efforts to make it so, a scientific discipline. This is true in the middle 1990s, it has always been true and it will probably be many years into the twenty-first century before psychotherapy ever becomes an empirically founded, fully developed, scientific discipline based upon experimentally validated research. But just what is *psychotherapy* anyway?

PSYCHOTHERAPY: THE PRETENTIOUS PROFESSION

Individual psychotherapy may be defined as an exploratory technique through which one person helps another find relief from emotional pain. Its success depends on the therapist's ability to understand the patient and on the patient's use of the therapists' help to make decisions and changes that will reduce the pain. The psychotherapists' major task is learning about the patients and their needs and providing the assistance that is needed. The clients' task is to help the therapist help them. Another common definition is, simply, the treatment of mental or emotional disorders or of related bodily ills by psychological means. Psychological means include giving advice or information verbally; prescribing medication; using physical techniques such as electroconvulsive shock treatment, hypnosis, or relaxation and guided imagery and suggestive techniques; as well as literally hundreds of other techniques and procedures designed to bring about a change in the clients' thinking and feeling. As Engler and Goleman define the term in their *Consumer's Guide to Psychotherapy,* "psychotherapy is the general name for a variety of psychological interventions designed to help people resolve emotional, behavioral, or interpersonal personal problems of various kinds and improve the quality of their lives."[2] They also add that no single definition of psychotherapy is accepted by all so-called therapy experts or by the many different schools of therapy. Many see it as a kind of re-education or relearning how to live. Others see it as a way of overcoming internal conflicts stemming from early traumatic experiences while others see it as a way of bringing about more effective ways of thinking, feeling, and coping with the world we inhabit. Still others view it as a way to change dysfunctional behavior patterns in our social intercourse with husbands, wives, children, and all other human beings we encounter into more functional an effective ones.

Despite differences about the definition, all psychotherapy involves a special kind of interpersonal relationship between the client and therapist. If this special relationship is effective, then the therapy will be effective; if this relationship fails, then the therapy will fail. The goal of all psychotherapy is *change*: change in the individuals', couples', or families' feeling, thinking, and behavior. The primary differences among therapists consist of views on the best way to bring about this change and exactly what it is that needs to be changed. If the therapy is to be successful—no matter what form it may take—there should be an alliance between the therapist and client that is focused exclusively on the client's welfare; there should be a feeling of trust and confidence between the therapist and client; the therapist must offer a different way of seeing and interpreting the client's world and a way for the client to make sense out of what is bewildering and confusing; and, finally, the therapist must provide specific ways and means for the client to take action that will lead to more effective ways of thinking, feeling, and acting and an end to discomfort, distress, and suffering.

Another fundamental assumption underlying all psychotherapy, one that is often overlooked, is that your problem, whatever it may be, is within your capacity to affect or change. If there is absolutely nothing you can do that will affect or change what is distressing you, no therapy on earth will help. A second assumption essential to psychotherapy is that our behavior; our feelings and emotions; our thoughts, beliefs, and attitudes; as well as our self-esteem and self-image are all learned and are due to our experiences in life. If our problem is due to some physical or biochemical or hereditary defect, psychotherapy has little to offer. Moreover, if people are forced into therapy because of legal difficulties, political oppression, family pressure, and so on, therapy is usually of little help. The third major assumption is that each and every one of us has the ability and the capacity to grow and develop and change ourselves for the better. We *can* solve our problems and overcome almost any obstacle no matter how hopeless or forlorn we may feel at the outset. Change is, of course, the key to all psychotherapy, since the goal of psychotherapy is to help you take charge of your life and gain freedom from fear and pain and gain greater self-esteem. When Matthew Dumont, the eminent psychotherapist, was asked for his definition of mental health he replied, "Freedom."[3]

Your freedom is maximized when you have taken active and effective charge of your life and you become a human being capable of acting in your own behalf. Despite what many people think, the goal of therapy is not to advise, direct, or tell you what to do—even though most therapists will offer that when you are in a crisis situation and are unable to act on your own. It is most important to realize that the therapists' function, and their most important role and obligation, in fact, is to *set you free* to act and think for yourself. If they behave otherwise they violate the therapeutic relationship and make a serious therapeutic error. Beware of any therapist who keeps you dependent upon his advice or pseudowisdom for very long. Learning to trust your therapist is a very important task on your part and, if for some reason, you find such trust and confidence is not there, you should change therapists immediately.

Although you may have believed otherwise, a therapist doesn't *do something to you,* even though it is often referred to as "treatment." Most people go into therapy wanting the therapist to do something to them, such as giving them a magic pill to cure their problems, just as a doctor's pill cures a sore throat. From its outset psychotherapy has suffered from this medical analogy despite the heroic efforts of Thomas Szasz and others to point out there are no bacilli or viruses that cause mental illness. Mental illness is, in fact, a myth. So is psychotherapy, as we shall see a little later. As for psychotherapy, it is designed not to change you but, rather, to help you change yourself. The psychotherapist is not a doctor in the medical sense of the term (unless he is, of course, a psychiatrist). He is, rather, an agent for change, like a teacher or a parent who can only help you change yourself. Psychotherapists do not give you anything nor do they do anything to you that will cure you or fix what ails you and they do not solve your problems for you. *This you must do yourself.* They can only help you help yourself, nothing more. They help you look into your past and discover what has caused your present problems or emotional difficulties and what needs to be done about your thinking and behavior to end your present discomfort.

If your psychotherapist is a psychiatrist and a *biological* psychiatrist, he will attempt to cure you or alleviate your emotional problems and difficulties by giving you *medication,* since he believes all psychological problems are biological in nature and should be treated not with talk but with medication. Patients with purely psychological problems falling into such hands will not be helped, they will merely be tranquilized. The medication will suppress and cover up the symptoms, but will not affect the underlying disorder. If this is what you want, medication will supply it. You will, however, have to pay the price: possible addiction to the drugs prescribed and a number of side effects, since no drug is free from side effects. Long-term maintenance on many of the neuroleptics (drugs, including many antipsychotic agents, which produce analgesia, sedation, or tranquilization) can also cause permanent physical and mental damage in many patients.

Other psychologists and psychiatrists practice what is known as *psychodynamic* therapy and use words instead of drugs, that is, talk therapy, as well as behavior modification and other approaches and techniques. Again, the purpose is an attempt to change your thinking and behavior in ways that will restore your feelings of happiness, security, and self-esteem. This re-education is the only thing that psychotherapists can really do to help. Unfortunately, as every teacher knows, even the best efforts often go astray and are never as effective as hoped or desired. Teachers can only guide and inform. The real changes can only be made by the students themselves. Does biological psychiatry re-educate? No! Does medicine guide, lead, or inspire? Again, No!

The problem we face is that most of the major "mental diseases" are not diseases at all. Schizophrenia, depression, addictions, anxieties, and compulsions are *psychological* and *social-interpersonal*. They are emotional problems not *biological* or medical problems. Such problems will never be solved or even alleviated by a purely medical or organic approach. Medication only covers the problem and delays cure and recovery. Rather than less psychology in psychiatric training, much more psychology in needed. Many psychiatrists are, unfortunately, neither scientists nor psychologists. Instead, they are actually poorly trained medical technicians who, at the moment, are incapable of dealing adequately with many—if not most—of the various psychological disorders experienced by the public. Today, as in the past, psychiatrists receive little or no training in psychotherapy per se.

Another equally serious issue is the current psychiatric assumption that an abandonment of biological psychiatry leaves one with no choice but Freudian theory—an approach even more seriously flawed, fallacious, and inadequate than the medical model. (Freud's theories are discussed in detail in chapter 3.) Today, for the most part, psychiatrists are either pill-pushers or analysts. Neither approach is either effective or relevant in the care and treatment of any of the major human behavioral problems. As I will demonstrate throughout this book, at present, a strong case can be made that psychiatric treatment, "shrinkage," across the board is doing more harm than good. If no primary or actual damage is done to the patients by the biomedical or organic treatment, secondary harm is done by depriving or delaying them from receiving the psychological treatment they really deserve.

These statements also apply to those clinical psychologists and other therapists who are convinced of organic (i.e., physical) causation or sincerely believe that the application of Freudian-based treatment can heal and cure. That they are called psychologists or psychotherapists in no way guarantees that they have the training, knowledge, and skills necessary for the effective treatment of the various emotional and behavioral disorders. They may or may not.

To reiterate, just because something is done in the name of psychotherapy is no guarantee that what is done is effective, proper, worthwhile, or the best thing that *can be* done. In fact, too often what is done is the *worst* thing that could be done. Most of the time, fortunately, what is done in the name of psychotherapy is fairly harmless and innocuous or even, on rare occasions, of some help. But the occasions in which the fundamental principle of medicine, "first do no harm," is violated are much too frequent for either public comfort or individual complacency.

For much too long the public has been bedazzled by the charisma surrounding the medical profession and its practitioners and, as a result, has assumed that psychiatry, as a branch of medicine, is like the other medical specialties, capable of performing miraculous cures or at least bringing quick relief for discomfort and pain. In this regard the shrink has in no way disappointed his public. Pills by the trillions have been dispensed and nerves by the zillions have been calmed and deadened. The axiom: Got a pain, pop a pill! has been reinforced and sustained. Temporary relief has been obtained, but the needed change in emotional behavior, the "cure," has been delayed indefinitely.

TYPES OF PSYCHOTHERAPY

According to Richie Herink, editor of *The Psychotherapy Handbook: The A to Z Guide to More Than 250 Different Therapies in Use Today,* the actual number of therapeutic systems and techniques of psychotherapy in existence is not only unknown but unknowable. Why? Because the term "psychotherapy" itself is so inclusive that anything a therapist does to improve his client's well being is called therapy. As anyone would expect, the possibilities are endless and what has been used and is being used by therapists to help their patients is mind boggling. Herink's handbook, for example, describes over 250 separate types of psychotherapy. Most are self-explanatory, but some are real stunners. For example, it is easy from the name alone to determine just what is or is not done by the therapist if he uses these particular therapeutic approaches:

Cooking Therapy   Poetry Therapy
Computer Therapy Puppet Therapy
Dance Therapy   Writing Therapy
Pet Therapy

In other types of therapy the name provides no clue whatsoever as to what the therapist does. For example:

- Bioplasmic Therapy: Based on the occultist Rudolf Steiner's notion of etheric forces in living matter. To get the etheric energy flowing, needles and electricity are applied to the body.
- Exaggeration Therapy: Exaggerate all your complaints until they become funny!
- Kinetic Psychotherapy: Physical interaction games arouse emotions and conflict resolution.
- Mirror Image Therapy: Watch yourself in the mirror as you talk and act to see yourself as others do.
- Neurotone Therapy: Electrosleep. Use of electricity to induce sleep and relaxation.
- New Identity Process: Clients scream and express emotion until they feel better and become new persons.
- Paroverbal Therapy: Therapist uses bells, drums, balls, jump ropes, etc. to get patients', usually children's, attention and to get them to open up and communicate better.
- Soap Opera Therapy: Watch soap operas and discuss them. A tool, not a therapy—gets at unconscious problems.
- Via-Erg Therapy: Makes catatonic ward patients work and care for themselves.[4]

In fact just about anything and everything under the sun can be used and pressed into service under the name of therapy, and it probably already has been. As long as someone can convince a sufferer that he has the cure, we will see yet another therapy promoted and adopted. Recently we have seen "finger-waving," "mirror-staring," and "repeat-after-me-and-say-it-again" procedures supported by psychotherapists and hailed as cure-alls. And with only a little thought I am confident that other therapies will soon arise. I have in mind at the moment a few sure things: Bart Simpson Therapy, Rush Limbaugh Therapy, and Therapyless Therapy!

What is truly remarkable is how professional therapists, in only a few decades, have managed to transform the ordinary behaviors of ordinary persons into a veritable pantheon of extraordinary and awe-inspiring symptomatologies and mental disorders. In his *Myth of Psychotherapy,* Thomas Szasz noted that just about everything conceivable has been given the name of therapy, including nudity, sexual intercourse, dancing, poetry, music (all sorts), going to the movies, drawing and painting, camping, screaming, friendship, shopping, physical stimulation of the rib cage area, rubbing a stone with one's thumbs, pet possession, sailing, skydiving, talking on the phone, and just about anything and everything else.[5]

According to Szasz, there are three broad classes of psychiatric treatment: institutional, physicochemical, and rhetorical. The conventional "institutional" method is involuntary mental hospitalization, while the standard "physicochemical" method is the use of drugs or electroshock, and the usual "rhetorical" method is conversation. These procedures came into being not so much because they work—although, depending on one's expectations, of course, they all do or they all fail—but rather because they satisfy needs in the mental patient or those he disturbs and in the person who treats him or her.

Disease, however, in Szasz's view, means and should only mean a disorder of the body. Similarly, treatment means, and should only mean, a physical-chemical intervention in the structure and function of the body aimed at combating or curing disease. The term "psychotherapy," insofar as it is used to refer to two or more people speaking and listening to each other, is a misnomer, and a misleading category for treatment as well. Simply because it may help people, psychotherapy may be thought of and said to resemble regular medical treatment, but it is no such thing.

> There is, properly speaking, no such thing as psychotherapy. Like mental illness, psychotherapy is a metaphor and a myth. Hypnosis, suggestion, psychoanalysis, whatever the so-called psychotherapy might be labeled, are names we give to people speaking and listening to each other in certain ways. By calling some types of human encounters "psychotherapy," we only impede our capacity to understand them.[6]

If Szasz is correct, and we will see that there are sound logical and persuasive reasons to believe that he is, the conditions psychotherapists seek to cure are not diseases, and consequently the procedures they use are not genuine treatments. Moreover, if such procedures are imposed on people against their will, they are abuses, not treatment. Finally, if the psychotherapeutic procedures consist of nothing except listening and talking, they constitute a type of conversation which can be considered "therapeutic" in a metaphorical sense only (as opposed to medication or surgery). The problem at the core is that for much too long we have suffered from a powerful tendency to view each and every attempt on the part of one person to influence another through the pseudomedical spectacles of psychiatry and to relabel them as psychotherapies. The result has been that everyone now believes that magic, faith-healing, witch-doctoring, prayer, electrotherapy, hypnosis, and all of the other human activities listed previously are actually different forms of psychotherapy used to treat and cure sick minds. This form of psychiatric mythology has for far too long been used to disguise deception and to conceal coercion by those with various sorts of axes to grind and causes to promote.

Therapies, of course, vary in their effectiveness. Several years ago in the *Journal of Canadian Psychology,* Dr. Robert F. Morgan gave the details of one of the greatest therapeutic inventions of all time: Balloon Therapy. Issuing from Dr. Morgan's personal worldview known as "contemporary fragmatism," balloon therapy requires that the suffering client fasten a large, helium-filled balloon to each of his ears. In the event of only one ear, use only one balloon. The shape, filling, color, and design of the balloons, of course, will vary with the therapist's preference. If the therapist has a favorite verbal prescription or therapeutic message this must be securely fastened to the balloon. It is important, however, that the message not exceed the vocabulary of the people likely to be encountered. The client must wear the fastened balloons twenty-four hours per day for an entire week. At the end of the week, Morgan states, the client returns to the therapist and the balloons are removed.

According to Morgan the benefits are

1. Relief of depression: client feels elation at no longer having balloons on ears.
2. Bolstering of self-confidence: client, having survived this, can survive anything.

3. Advertising: few clients completing this procedure will fail to rationalize it as extremely beneficial (the alternative to be defended against is that they are, to some infinite extent, gullible) and the technique itself draws notice.
4. Reducing social isolation and withdrawal: not only are balloons a conversation piece but they would immediately identify anyone else undergoing this therapy (without breaching confidentiality, clients would be able to recognize each other anywhere).
5. Relieves anxiety neuroses: everything relieves anxiety neuroses.

Points of Therapeutic Expertise:

1. Deciding on characteristics of balloon (see Method).
2. Choosing between glue, clip, tape, magnetic, or natural honey fastenings.
3. Selecting the best point of attachment for the balloons—using body parts other than the ears may be appropriate with several types of clients.
4. Matching lengths of strings to client characteristics.

Contraindications:

This technique is not recommended when the client has a poor sense of humor, combat experience, an attorney, or is financially insolvent.[7]

Morgan also tells a fascinating story about a woman named Elsa who in 1947 was discovered in a railway station in Kingston, Ontario. With millions of soldiers rushing home from World War II and hundreds of others vying for tickets, looking for loved ones, and trying to catch trains, confusion and bedlam reigned. In the middle of this was a bewildered and frightened woman who would periodically look up at a stranger, babble some incoherent sounds, and consequently be ignored. After she began to cry she drew a policeman's attention. When he tried to intervene Elsa continued to babble and cry. Unable to understand her, the officer became irritated. Elsa, sensing his anger, became more frightened and started weeping hysterically. The officer decided she was insane and took her to the local sanitarium.

Initially Elsa was diagnosed as a psychotic and over a period of time was given a variety of drugs. Although the drugs calmed her, she continued to cry, talk incoherently, and become depressed. This led a new therapist to recommend shock treatments. She became increasingly more upset and then withdrew totally into herself. She was rediagnosed as catatonic. As years passed, other psychotherapies were tried without success. The frustrated psychiatrists then classified her as suffering from an extreme form of dementia and consigned her to a ward for the chronic and incurable. In 1970, a new attendant was assigned to Elsa's ward. One day he heard her babbling and slowly walked over to listen. He smiled and began to babble back to her. After a moment Elsa opened her eyes, looked up at the smiling face, jumped to her feet, grabbed the attendant, and began to hug him. A group of doctors standing nearby rushed over and separated the two. One demanded, "What's going on here? What do you mean by babbling at this patient and exciting her?" The completely nonplussed attendant replied, "Sir, we weren't babbling, we were speaking Polish."[8]

Morgan tells us this, unfortunately, is a true story. Sadly enough, Elsa's story is not unique. A number of similar cases showing that the total lack of communication and understanding of human problems on the part of the shrinks led to monstrous tragedies that could have and should have been avoided. In February 1994, reporter Gary L. Wright told the story of Junius Wilson, a ninety-six-year-old who was released from a North Carolina state mental hospital after sixty-eight years of having been assumed to be mentally ill. What happened to Wilson was kept a secret for more than six decades. Wilson was twenty-eight when he was jailed for assault, declared insane, and committed to the state asylum for blacks. Wilson was never convicted of the criminal charge and it was eventually dropped. In the 1970s hospital officials wanted to release him, but there was no one available to help since his family could not be located. Nothing further was done until the state appointed a guardian in 1991. John Wasson, Wilson's guardian, then discovered Wilson was deaf—not mentally ill. The state is now committed to making Wilson's life as comfortable as possible during his remaining years. "We can't repay those years Mr. Wilson has been locked up. Nobody can," a hospital spokesman said. "We're very sorry."[9]

TYPES OF PSYCHOTHERAPISTS AND TRAINING

Certainly we would expect that anyone put into the position of solving all the mental problems to which the human brain is heir, and especially because of the extraordinary complexity of mental phenomena, would spend years of intensive training in every possible aspect of human psychopathology, diagnosis, and the treatment of behavioral aberrations. One would assume that many long years of study, clinical experience, and practice in some particular field of specialization would be paramount if one was truly to become an expert. Just how *are* our doctors of psychiatry and psychology trained, and precisely *how* do they acquire their status as experts?

Psychotherapists fall into five major groups: psychiatrists, who are graduate physicians with M.D. degrees; clinical psychologists trained in psychology who usually have a Ph.D. degree; psychiatric social workers, who have a Master's degree in social work; psychiatric nurses; and marriage and family therapists.

Psychiatrists

The typical psychiatrist has received a basic education in medical science, including subjects like anatomy, physiology, pathology, bacteriology; and supervised experience in the clinical specialties, including medicine, neurology, surgery, and obstetrics, among others. Normally there are two years of basic science courses followed by two years of training and supervised, apprenticelike experience in the clinical fields. The basic four-year programs are common to all M.D.s, including the psychiatrist. He spends the same amount of time studying chemistry, anatomy, and physiology as all other physicians in all the medical specialties. Since medical school preparation usually begins at the undergraduate level, the doctor-to-be usually has had premed training in chemistry, physics, and other sciences before entering medical school. The amount of instruction and exposure to general human psychology, and particularly to psychopathology, he received during the two preclinical years will depend upon which medical school he attended. It may be as little as twenty hours, and rarely exceeds 180 hours of instruction. As for anatomy, he may well have had as much as five hundred hours.

After medical school the would-be psychiatrist completes a one-year internship in an accredited hospital in which his clinical, diagnostic, and therapeutic skills are further honed and polished, not in psychopathology, but over the full range of medical maladies. Following this internship he is now qualified for the practice of medicine; to be a psychiatrist he must now undertake specialized training in psychiatry. This training is known as a *residency* and includes a three-year period of instruction and supervision by the staff of an accredited psychiatric hospital. As a psychiatric resident he is exposed to some formal instruction on the subjects of psychopathology, interviewing techniques, special diagnostic procedures, classification of disorders, special therapies such as electroshock and drugs, and in the past, principles of psychotherapy. The amount of formal instruction he receives will depend upon the particular psychiatric staff responsible for his training. Whether his theoretical orientation is psychoanalytic (based on Freudian theory), behavioral (based on the theories of Watson and Skinner), or eclectic (a mix of both) will depend upon who provides the training and where it is received. Over the course of the three years he is usually exposed to a wide variety and a large number of patients—both hospitalized and out-patient—for whose treatment he is responsible. In sum, the residency is an intensive and extensive apprenticeship in the diagnosis and treatment of people with emotional disorders.

Nevertheless, as E. Fuller Torrey and many other psychiatrists have noted, one of the more curious things about psychiatrists as doctors is that they really do not need to be trained in medicine: "Individuals who have not been so trained appear to get about the same results as the psychiatrists do in their practice of 'psychotherapy.' This fact has been revealed in gradual stages over the past 25 years."[10]

If they don't need to be trained as doctors to do their job, then what kind of training do they need? Optimally what they need is the sort of education that increases their insight into people's problems, and the ability to help other people change their behavior. In a word, training in the behavioral sciences, not in medicine. In Torrey's words,

"Psychiatrists then, who turn out to be good 'psychotherapists' do so, in spite of, not because of, their medical training."[11] Psychiatrists who still insist that medical training is essential, or very important at least, argue that: (1) psychotherapy is based on science and thus practitioners need the science training; (2) since medical diseases often contribute to mental diseases, then the person had better be a doctor so he can recognize the medical aspects; and (3) only doctors really understand how to take responsibility for another human being.

All three of these rationales are either fallacious or half-truths. Techniques used by psychiatrists are no more scientific than those used by medicine men or witch doctors, or chemists, geologists, psychologists, or any other professional group. Psychotherapy is, if anything, more of an art than a science. As for the second point, Torrey points out that for screening purposes the signs and symptoms of possible organic brain disease can be taught to a nondoctor in one or two weeks. And, medical disorders contribute to many things besides mental diseases, yet the same conclusion isn't drawn. Injuries and diseases are important to a football team, but no one requires that the coach be a doctor. As for the third argument, the taking of responsibility more than likely has little or nothing to do with training but rather is a personality trait. Responsibility for others is not a commodity on which medicine has cornered the market.

Psychiatrists who wish to practice Freud's specialized form of therapy called "psychoanalysis" should go through analytic training and should themselves be analyzed and learn analytic and psychodynamic techniques at a training institute. Legally, however, anyone can call himself a psychoanalyst.

Clinical Psychologists

The clinical psychologist has a Ph.D. in psychology, which means that he has completed a minimum of three years of graduate study in clinical psychology from an accredited university training program. Prior to admission he must have completed a four-year undergraduate major, usually in psychology. Graduate study usually includes courses in personality theory, abnormal psychology and psychopathology, psychological measurement (measuring traits and abilities), statistical methods and research design, clinical diagnostic tests and measures, interviewing techniques, and theories and methods of psychotherapy. This is his major program and is usually supplemented with a minor program of studies in a related or allied field such as sociology, criminology, anthropology, physiology, or biology. The graduate program includes both didactic instruction as well as supervised clinical practice in interviewing, testing, diagnostics, and the like. The student must also design and write up an original research investigation in an appropriate clinical problem area of psychology. Finally, he must complete a full year's internship in an approved psychiatric facility having a full complement of professionals qualified to provide appropriate supervision and training. This total program normally requires anywhere from five to eight years after the bachelor's degree. Most programs also require that the clinical student complete a Master's degree with a thesis by the end of his second year. This is considered to be excellent preparation for the Ph.D. program.

Psychiatric Social Workers

Psychiatric social workers (PSWs) typically hold the Master of Social Work (M.S.W.) degree which means that in addition to a four-year undergraduate degree they have completed a two-year course of study in a recognized school of social work. M.S.W.s usually have an undergraduate major in psychology, sociology, human development, or the family. At the graduate level, they receive formal instruction in personality development, psychopathology, community organization, social welfare programs and agencies, and principles of social case work. Candidates may also be required to complete a thesis or research project, or a group project. In the first year of study students usually complete a sequence of intensive field work experience—usually with a family or children's service unit. Then, in the second year they are placed in a psychiatric clinic or hospital where on-the-job orientation and training is administered by a qualified PSW who provides close case-by-case supervision. Normally the budding M.S.W.s accumulate the equivalent of one year of full-time supervised experience in interviewing patients and families, collecting and integrating case material, contacting relevant community agencies, and communicating the findings to other members of the staff. In the field work trainees are required, under very close supervision, to engage several patients in therapeutic conversations. In areas where the demand for psychotherapeutic services is great, many social workers are in private practice. In most cases, in practice the PSWs' work is overseen or supervised by a psychiatrist, and although it is called "case work" it is difficult to distinguish from that which is generally termed "psychotherapy."

It should also be noted that both psychiatry and clinical psychology have specialty or licensing boards which examine and award licensing or certification in their respective specialties. Eligibility requirements are two years of appropriate experience after the residency for psychiatrists, and four years after the Ph.D. for psychologists.

Other Therapists

There are also counseling psychologists, pastoral counselors, psychiatric nurses, and psychotherapists who receive little or no training of any sort.

The counseling psychology training program is almost identical to that of the clinical psychologists' program with the exception that the emphasis is primarily on counseling technique and less on psychopathology. Pastoral counselors are ministers and theologians who receive specialized counseling training. The pastoral counseling training, again, is almost identical with that of the regular counseling and clinical psychologists except they specialize in the kinds of problems most frequently encountered among their parishioners. Psychiatric nurses are registered nurses who have specialized in dealing with patients normally confined to mental hospitals and other psychiatric institutions. The title itself, however, does not indicate any training or competence in psychotherapy.

Marriage and family therapists are now licensed in more than thirty states but are not regulated at all in those states which do not require licenses. Most licensed therapists have completed a two-year Master's program mainly oriented toward the therapy of couples and families, followed by two to three years of clinical practice under supervision. They have also passed a state licensing exam. Typically they specialize in problems arising in couples or among family members.

There are numerous other individuals who use the title "psychotherapist" other than those listed above. Most call themselves by the name of their specialty, for example, hypnotherapist, biofeedback therapist, relaxation therapist, child psychotherapist, or sex therapist. Be warned, many of the people using such titles are neither trained nor regulated and many therapists claim expertise who do not have it. Make sure that you check on the training, experience, and competence of any and all those who use these titles. Some human problems, like sexual problems for example, should never be treated by amateurs since some people may exacerbate the clients' problems and difficulties. Your best bet is always to look for a licensed professional.

As for the hordes of untrained and unqualified psychotherapists, hypnotherapists, etc., they need do nothing more than rent an office, hang out a shingle, announce they are in the therapy business, and go to work. For those practitioners who want a certificate to hang on their office walls, a large number of degree and diploma mills will supply these for a modest fee. If the therapist is even honest enough to "go through the motions" of formal or legitimate training there are a number of pseudotraining programs available to meet these needs. Advertisements for these are easily found in the pages of popular periodicals like *OMNI, Psychology Today, New Age,* and other such magazines.

What is most difficult for the average layman to understand is why it is that the profession of psychotherapy is so poorly and inadequately regulated. In their *Consumer's Guide to Psychotherapy,* Engler and Goleman state the following:

> No regulatory body at any government level oversees certification and maintenance of professional standards for the practice of psychotherapy *as such,* though standards exist for psychiatry and the other professions most psychotherapists belong to. Legally, anyone can call him or herself a "psychotherapist."
>
> The absence of an independent profession of psychotherapy has had several unfortunate consequences. One is the lack of universally accepted clinical or legal standards for practicing psychotherapy.

Even professional training in one of the allied professions does not by itself qualify a professional to be a psychotherapist. Psychiatrists, psychologists, social workers, or nurses may be qualified to practice their profession but still not have received the specific training and supervision needed to practice therapy.

The absence of licensing and regulation of therapy as a separate profession means that many people can—and do—practice therapy without adequate training as therapists, even among licensed professionals. It is important that you, as a consumer, be well-informed in making choices about something as important as therapy. The old adage applies here as elsewhere: "Let the buyer beware." . . .

Nevertheless, for a therapist to be licensed as a member of a regulated profession has two important implications for you as a consumer. It means they have received a certain level of professional training and supervision in a major mental health discipline, which includes several thousand hours of supervised work in the field, some of which will probably have been in psychotherapy. They have demonstrated an acceptable level of professional competence and have passed a national certifying examination in their discipline.

Second, it means they are legally bound to specific standards of professional and ethical practice in their field, including continuing education, and are legally accountable to a state licensing board for maintaining these standards in their practice, *including their practice of psychotherapy.* It also means they are subject to annual review and recertification by the licensing board. Both professional training and licensing offer important protection to the consumer, though they still are not a guarantee of competence in therapy. [Emphasis in original.][12]

As noted above, the fact of training and experience does not, in and of itself, guarantee that the therapy you receive will be what you need or that the licensed and trained "professionals" can and do make more accurate clinical judgements than untrained or lay persons.[13] While some studies have shown a slight professional advantage, others have favored the layman and, most often, both groups perform alike. Another study concerning the visual-motor productions of normal versus brain-damaged individuals on a commonly used screening test showed that professional psychologists performed no better than office secretaries in analyzing the results.[14] A second study revealed that lay interviewers using standardized questions produced information of equal or greater validity than psychiatrists conducting interviews in their preferred manner.[15] Another study found that high school students and professional clinicians working from a common data base experienced comparable difficulty predicting violent behavior and weighed the data in a similar fashion. This similarity in interpreting the data suggests that both groups relied on common assumptions about potentially violent individuals, or they shared the same cultural stereotypes.[16]

With regard to clinicians making judgments about *prior* and *future* states of their clients, such studies that compare clinicians' predictions against objectively determinable hard data commonly show that the error rate exceeds the accuracy rate.[17]

In another study a series of military recruits was retained in service despite psychiatrists' recommendations that they be discharged because of severe psychiatric problems. Yet after two years most of these individuals had not only remained on active duty, but their overall rate of success and adjustment was not substantially different from that of matched controls initially judged to be free of pathology.[18] Faust and Ziskin, in a very important article dealing with the use of psychiatrists and psychologists as expert witnesses in the courtroom have also pointed out that clinicians generally overvalue evidence supportive of pathology, and undervalue evidence against it. They also note that "in psychology, the selective pursuit of supportive evidence is especially pernicious."[19] It is important for us to remember that individual human behavior is highly variable across time and situation, and there is tremendous overlap across criteria for various psychiatric disturbances, as well as between the characteristics of aberrant and normal individuals. We must never forget that the lives of normal individuals commonly contain the full range of trauma, stress, and turmoil found among the mentally disabled and disordered. At times everyone engages in thoughts and actions that are radically different from their routine everyday behavior. This does not indicate, however, they are in need of either medication, confinement, or psychiatric care.[20]

It's little wonder, then, that laymen as well as many therapists are totally confused upon encountering apparently "normal, mentally sound" individuals who maintain they have lived before or that they receive phone calls from dead relatives, or have been abducted by aliens in UFOs, or are possessed by demons. In such encounters, therapists, like the general public, tend to split into two groups. The first and larger group assumes pathology, that is, the claimant is mentally disturbed. The minority group of both the public and—we regret to say—the therapists, assume the claimant is telling the truth. Unfortunately, there is gross error in both of these positions. Regarding the first mistake, clinicians typically expect to find something abnormal, and as Faust and Zisken state, "a search for supportive evidence will almost always 'succeed' regardless of the examinee's mental health."[21] In a study by Temerlin and Trousdale, every psychiatrist who heard a script portraying a well-adjusted individual nevertheless diagnosed a mental disorder.[22] This tendency to assume the presence of abnormality, Faust and Zisken aver, and then to seek supportive evidence for it fosters a mindset that "overpathologizes," that is, frequently misidentifies or misdiagnoses individuals as abnormal.[23] Whenever the general public does this, nothing of consequence comes of it, but this is not true in the case of our psychotherapists. At the other extreme the proclivity with which clinicians are eager to believe every deluded statement of an apparently normal individual is equally reprehensible. Fortunately the number of therapists who are so credulous and gullible are few in number, yet even these few can cause or promote grievous harm to both their clients and our society.

Both Wood and Torrey have expressed considerable dismay at the fact that most psychiatrists are in private practice tending the needs of the people who need their service the least, "the worried well," in preference to the more disturbed patients found primarily in the state-supported mental hospitals who are in far greater need of their services. Wood, in his book *The Myth of Neurosis,* argues that not only is the concept of "neurosis" a myth, but that its bogus status as an illness has stigmatized millions of perfectly normal people whose chief deficiency is their inadequate approach to problems, and their unrealistic expectations of what life should give them. By the damaging "illness excuse" the clinicians not only promote the illusion that patients are not responsible for their predicament and are, therefore, powerless to help themselves, but also encourage them to commit themselves to lengthy and expensive care.[24]

Torrey, in his book *Nowhere to Go,* shows that over the years from 1954 to 1984 there was a steady decrease in the number of psychiatrists working in state mental hospitals and in the comprehensive mental health centers (CMHC). Despite the fact that billions of dollars were spent by the National Institute of Mental Health to train mental health professionals to treat the seriously mentally ill, "the program appeared to be having the opposite effect."[25] There were many reasons why psychiatrists trained under federal dollars eschewed the seriously mentally ill for private practice. Money was, of course, part of the reason, but with increasingly liberal insurance benefits it was easy for psychiatrists to fund private patients and make more money than they could in the public sector. More important even than money, however, was the prestige of psychotherapy. Leaders of the profession saw public sector work as beneath their dignity. Anyone accepting a state mental hospital position between 1950 and 1980 was accepting the lowest status job in the entire psychiatric hierarchy. It was for this reason that most of the state mental institutions were, and still are, staffed with foreign psychiatrists. During the 1960s psychiatrists moved en masse to the economically affluent areas and the psychologists and PSWs migrated with them. Thus by 1980 all three professional groups were concentrated in areas of the United States where higher income, higher education, more urbanization, and more insurance dollars were concentrated. It was apparent by then to anyone who looked that all the mental health professionals were selectively avoiding those patients with serious mental illnesses. Today, in the 1990s, they still are selectively avoiding the seriously disturbed who need their help the most.

KINDS OF PROBLEMS PSYCHOTHERAPISTS TREAT

It is generally agreed that psychotherapists are asked to deal with problems in three areas: problems in everyday living; problems of personal growth; and emotional and behavioral problems. With regard to the first broad area, most of our problems in living stem from such things as interrelationship problems: finding a mate, parental conflict, marital problems, school or employment difficulties, financial problems, illness or disability, retirement, death, divorce, having a baby, and so on.

Many people seek therapy in order to improve the quality of their lives. They want to get more joy, happiness, and satisfaction out of life. They look for meaning in their lives and maybe for a more spiritual way of life or they seek to develop the more creative aspects of their personalities. Therapy can be of significant help to understand yourself better if this is what you want and you can afford it in terms of both time and money.

For the more serious sorts of human problems—emotional and behavioral disorders—psychotherapy is most frequently called upon for help. These are the things that can become so serious that your life and future are in danger. Examples include excessive drug and alcohol abuse, anxiety and panic attacks, and unreasonable fears and phobias that interfere with daily living. Disturbances in feeling, thinking, and physical functioning also require attention whenever they interfere with one's daily behavior. Serious debilitative emotional and mental disturbances like the psychoses (schizophrenia, manic-depression, borderline personality disorders, and the post-traumatic stress syndrome) must also be attended to. All of these require varied and different therapeutic approaches and success usually entails more than one kind of approach. In fact, just about anything that *can* go wrong with a human life *will* go wrong and because these "wrongs" are so painful we are all called upon to do something about them.

Although each human disorder is usually marked by a number of specific symptoms, many different disorders may have common symptoms (such as anxiety and depression) which show up in nearly all human problems. We must also consider the fact that psychological factors play an important role in strictly physical disorders and medical diseases. Conversely, many physical problems have psychological complications. For example, many patients suffering from panic disorder will behave in ways the therapist is certain are due to psychological factors when in reality the panic attacks may be due to brain dysrythmias (i.e., the misfiring of brain cells). Similarly, heart by-pass surgery can sometimes cause severe clinical depression in patients.

In general, however, most human problems that wind up in therapist's hands are in no way life-threatening. Most are what therapists refer to as problems of "the worried well," that is, people who are not really ill but worry too much. Many years ago in *The Art of Selfishness* David Seabury cataloged a thousand cases looking at the reasons why people sought therapeutic help. In well over half of the cases the reasons were due to extreme self-centeredness. The presenting problems in 849 cases were loneliness, egocentricity, and self-absorption. In another 827 cases they were personal, money, and financial problems; in 627 cases the problem was hedonism and self-indulgence; and in another 582 boredom and cynicism about life was the cause. (Many individuals, of course, had more than one problem.) As for the remainder, most were due to interpersonal difficulties of one sort or another, such as sexual and marital problems, parental disputes, inability to get along with others, emotional immaturity, general depression and dissatisfaction, indecision, and social isolation.[26]

Before you decide to seek out the help of a therapist you should ask yourself: Am I capable of handling and dealing with this on my own? Is my current level of pain and distress so high I can't handle it anymore? Is this problem interfering with my work, my relations with my family and friends, and affecting my ability to function? If you can honestly answer the first question affirmatively, you *will* be better off doing it yourself. If you answer the second and third questions with a "yes," then you should seriously consider taking therapeutic steps.

Even here, however, there are some alternatives to professional help. Perhaps the first and best resource—depending upon the nature of the problem of course—is your own family and friends or your pastor or minister. Nearly every community now provides crisis intervention services and twenty-four-hour-a-day hot lines to help in the event of rape, poisoning, suicide threat, child abuse, drug and alcohol problems, etc. There are also numerous community self-help and support groups that can offer acceptance, understanding, advice, and wisdom since they've faced and solved problems like yours. Alcoholics Anonymous is, perhaps, the most famous of all such groups. Similar groups now exist for drug addiction, gambling, single parents, and so on.

You should also determine if your problem is one that you can solve yourself by acquiring new living skills. Nearly every community has a number of educational institutions and community services that offer a wide variety of programs for all sorts of human problems. Free programs in relaxation training and stress management, assertiveness training, health maintenance, bereavement, dealing with old age or emotional crises, etc., are made available by churches, YMCA and YWCA organizations, local schools, and other interest groups. All of these can help you acquire the living skills that will make you and your life more effective and efficient.

All of these organizations will also extend the range and number of your friendships, which alone will oftentimes give you all the relief you need, as well as provide you with moral stamina and self-confidence to carry on.

Never underestimate the ability and healing powers of your friends. In fact, years ago William Schofield called psychotherapy the "purchase of friendship," an analogy not too far from the truth.[27] Engler and Goleman in *The Consumer's Guide to Psychotherapy* argue that complete self-disclosure is awkward with a friend and that you will hold back deep feelings and emotional secrets with a friend that you wouldn't with a therapist. Friends also might not respect your confidence whereas a therapist is ethically and legally bound to do so. Friends may feel burdened by your truth and confidence. A therapist would not. Friends are not trained to listen and respond appropriately and may let your friendship color what they do and do not tell you. Therapists are trained, allegedly, in methods and techniques that address specific emotional and interpersonal problems whereas friends are not.[28]

On the other hand, you may also find it difficult to relate successfully to and trust your therapist. Moreover, your therapist cannot ever be expected to know and understand you as deeply and as well as a lifelong friend in only a few hourly sessions scattered over many weeks. Moreover, the therapist is never as deeply concerned about your future and your welfare as your friends who care about you and have cared about you sometimes for years. It is also true that for many personal problems, issues, and crises it is much easier to talk with a friend than it is with a stranger no matter how degreed or credentialed. In fact, the therapist's scientific detachment can be very "off putting." Friends may be more likely than therapists to put your best interests first and to advise you more wisely because they understand you much better than a therapist ever will since they know your past history, likes, and dislikes much better than anyone else. Friendship in many instances provides a personal advantage no therapist can ever have. Regarding specific therapeutic methods and techniques, as noted earlier there are hundreds of methods and techniques varying from prayer to group bathing in the nude. What all of the truly effective approaches have in common is an emphasis on personal growth and improvement in the individual's interpersonal relations. Psychotherapy is essentially re-education with an emphasis on growth or change.

As for the need for professional training in psychotherapy, except in cases of extreme psychopathology (which are really quite rare), it seems hardly necessary to have any professional level courses at all in order to be an effective psychotherapist. Schofield has seriously questioned whether any differences—other than semantic and economic—actually exist among what M.D.s, Ph.D.s, M.A.s, and M.S.W.s actually do in psychotherapy.[29] Nor is there any empirical evidence to support the contention that psychiatrists are superior therapists to other professionals. Differences between psychiatrists in different clinics are probably greater than differences between disciplines in the same clinic. According to Schofield, J. S. Wherry, himself a psychiatrist, has written that he refuses to honor what is, in reality, no more than semantic and social gobbledygook.[30]

Recent evidence also suggests that prespecialization training for psychotherapy, formal schooling for the M.D., Ph.D., M.S.W., and M.A. degrees, is largely irrelevant and only actual clinical experience is important.[31] The old assumption that all the required courses of professional training can't help but make one "a good therapist" is naive. In 1960 Whiteborn and Betz of Johns Hopkins demonstrated clearly that psychiatrists fell, by personality, into two categories, one of which was much more successful as psychotherapists than the other. Those doctors who were more often humane and caring were much more successful than those who were more formal, reserved, and scientifically objective and detached.[32] The distinguished psychiatrist Morton Prince and Torrey have both reported that the quality of psychiatric care given by the Nigerian medicine man is almost as good as that given by Western psychiatrists, and this without the benefit of our highly specialized psychiatric training.[33] Many people other than the traditional therapists can also do effective psychotherapy. Several studies have shown that selected, untrained college students were just as effective as the most highly trained psychiatrists in group-psychological treatment of severely regressed and chronic psychotics. Given a few hours of orientation and instruction, mature housewives can also become effective psychotherapists.[34] What is obvious here is that there is some personality factor in the therapist that seems to be more vital than any sort of professional training. That factor seems to be, without any doubt, the quality of *humaneness* or sincere *caring*. Except in cases of extreme psychopathology, long and intensive professional psychological training is not necessary in order for one to be an effective psychotherapist. What is critical is that one be a sincere, warm, loving human being *who cares—sincerely cares*—about his fellow human beings. To the psychiatric profession this is, of course, sheer heresy. Perhaps it is now high time for heresy and lots of it. The need for a public revolution in the area of mental health care could not come too soon, especially in a time when health care costs are about to destroy us financially.

Since research indicates no one psychotherapeutic technique is superior to another it seems silly to worry about teaching technique. Yet, it is easier to teach technique and theory than it is to teach humaneness and personality, so the schools and faculty teach what they know. Humanistic therapies, those which increase the therapist's sensitivity to the feelings of others and that emphasize therapeutic openness, flexibility, and concern, *should* be the training goals.

TYPES OF THERAPEUTIC ABUSE

Sadly, much too often nowadays, rather than finding the caring, sensitive, and humane therapist one deserves and expects, one finds oneself much worse off after therapy than before. Since psychotherapists are also human, they are prone to the ills and weaknesses all other human beings endure. The result is that we find in this profession the same problems and difficulties one encounters in all professions and among all professionals: incompetence; misdiagnosis and mistreatment; neglect; and even criminal behavior including, believe it or not, murder, rape, kidnapping, assault, and theft. Less serious offenses peculiar to unnecessary psychotherapy in particular include prescribing the wrong, unnecessary, or damaging treatments; refusing to discharge patients who are not being helped; violating the patient's person and his legal rights; confining, imprisoning, and drugging patients who are not mentally ill; having sex with patients in treatment or those formerly in treatment; betraying the patient's confidence; failure to monitor dangerous drugs and prescribed medications; and creating various sorts of iatrogenic (i.e., therapist-caused) disorders that are more serious than the patient's original complaint. Even more common nowadays are gross and flagrant examples of excessive greed showing up in Medicare and Medicaid fraud as well as conspiratorial arrangements among mental hospitals, drug companies, and insurance carriers that result in cozy profits for all except those paying the bill.

Quite recently a new form of fraud, which is defined as the receipt of something of value as a result of false pretenses, has appeared on the medical scene. Known as benevolent misdiagnosis, this particular form of widely practiced deception is apparently very common in the psychological professions. As described by Pallone and Hennessy, this form of deceit typically occurs to protect the reputation and "name" of VIPs whose public embarrassment could cause financial damage or harm to large organizations.[35]

For example, suppose a senior executive officer of a large corporation is caught in a motel room with an underage female. Moreover, this is not a first offense. This incident leads to the executive's arrest and appearance before a judge. The judge agrees to lay aside the charges provided the executive agrees to undergo professional mental health treatment. Since the executive is well insured for mental health treatment, he hires an expensive private psychiatrist. To make sure his services qualify for payment under the executive's health insurance plan, the psychiatrist is legally required to state on the insurance claim form a diagnosis taken directly from the American Psychiatric Association's *Diagnostic and Statistical Manual III, Revised* (DSM-III-R) or the new DSM-IV. In this Bible, however, the proper diagnosis should be something like "focused pedophilia, opposite sex, nonexclusive."

Fine, except when the executive sees the therapist's completed form he is ready to faint. This form will have to be processed by people in his firm's personnel department and there is no way on God's green earth that he can keep his little sexual peccadillo from spreading from one end of his corporation to the other. The executive, in other words, is in deep doo doo. Unless . . . After a few words with his therapist, a new, revised claim form is filed with a benign and indefinite diagnosis stating something like "adult adjustment disorder with behavioral complications." While it may not end speculation it certainly protects both the executive and the organization's name and reputation.

Many, unfortunately, do not see this pathologizing of obvious criminal behavior as anything to get excited about. They would argue a greater good has been done and a better end has been met. The patient has been protected—no possible therapeutic good could come from his shame and public humiliation. Moreover, the company's economic welfare has also been served and the jobs and income of all have been protected.

Unfortunately, there are also a number of overlooked and subsequent consequences that must be taken into account. An "adjustment reaction" by definition is usually transitory. Should extended treatment be required or should the executive have a relapse and require medication, then a pharmacist enters the picture and may be caught in the "benevolent collusion." In Pallone and Hennessy's words:

> In the most extreme scenario, a pharmacist, mindful of the ethical canons of his profession no less than of federal and state regulations governing the dispensing of psychotropic [mind-altering] medication, may simply refuse to fill a prescription for a drug that is contra-indicated for a benign and transient condition. Nor can one reasonably predicate a willingness to disregard the canons governing the ethical practice of medicine to all those empowered to write prescriptions, but instead insist that a dead-accurate diagnosis be recorded on the claim form filed with the same insurance carrier. If the scenario unfolds in that direction, the insurance carrier is now faced either with data that cannot be interpreted in any meaningful way or with presumptive evidence of collusion.[36]

In active practice, when a demurrer to payment for prolonged treatment of a relatively benign and short-lived disorder is fielded by a third-party payer, the inventive clinician and the patient merely collude to provide yet another euphemistically, but benevolently, inaccurate diagnosis—perhaps even colluding to suggest that the "new" disorder has arisen sequentially to and independently of, the initial condition to which a euphemistically inaccurate diagnosis had been benevolently applied.[37]

Lest one assume this is a rare and unusual occurrence, Pallone and Hennessy state that they

> can with some confidence multiply our pedophilic senior executive by hundreds of thousands of cases per year. . . . Some studies have reported that the prevalence of misdiagnosis (not necessarily conscious, deliberate, or benevolent) hovers near 75 percent in the caseloads of even highly experienced mental health clinicians. Unless we are willing to accept an explanation that veers in the direction of gross incompetence among members of the mental health professions, it would be foolhearted to discount consciously inaccurate diagnoses by benevolence and/or euphemism as a major contributing factor.[38]

There can be little doubt that this behavior encourages the general public to see very clearly that mental health diagnoses are driven by economics rather than by any concern for science or accuracy. As Pallone and Hennessy conclude, it is clear that the clinician is "little more than a hired gun."[39]

Specific examples of "shrinkage" in all of its many and varied manifestations on the modern scene are provided in chapter 3, which discusses victims.

WARNING: CAVEAT EMPTOR!

Psychotherapy as currently practiced may be hazardous to your health! This is particularly true of therapy provided by psychiatrists who call themselves "biological psychiatrists," those who practice "recovered memory" therapy or who ally themselves with or identify with the

"New Age," and those who specialize in codependency and the recovery movement or, as it is often referred to, "Talk Show Therapy."

Biological psychiatrists do not practice psychotherapy or "talk therapy," since they are not trained to do so and do not believe in it. Instead, they prescribe medications and other sorts of physical treatments such as electroconvulsive shock therapy (ECT), hospitalization, physical isolation, and restraint, all designed to cure you of your mental disease. The fact that there is no such thing as a "mental disease" or "mental illness" never gets in their way of curing you of something that doesn't ail you.

Recovered memory therapists use such procedures as hypnosis, guided fantasy, support groups, suggestion, interpersonal pressure, and propaganda to create fictions and fantasies in your mind and then convince you that horrible things happened to you as a child—usually some form of sexual molestation. Therapists ("the rapists") of this persuasion do not understand how the human memory works nor are they qualified to use hypnosis or suggestion in a helpful rather than harmful way. They succeed only in convincing many helpless and unsuspecting clients that their parents raped them when they were little, they were abused by horrible satanic cults, or that they have been abducted and sexually abused by extraterrestrials.

Those therapists who specialize in codependency, New Age, or talk show therapy consider everyone on Earth a victim, mentally dysfunctional, and in need of their expensive and covertly authoritarian ministrations. *Do not, under any circumstances, put yourself in the hands of any of these individuals or surrender your willpower and freedom, no matter how attractive or persuasive their promises may appear.* All of these "doctors" believe that they and they alone know what is best for you. They do not and they cannot. None of them, no matter how well and how long you know them, will ever know you and what is best for you as well as you do. They are only hired help and advisors. No matter how sane, wise, and sensible such advice may seem, you and you alone should make the final decision to accept or reject it.

Just as you would not, under any circumstances, undergo major and possibly life-threatening surgery without seeking expert second— even third—professional opinions, it is even more urgent that you do this before following psychotherapeutic advice of any sort. All psychotherapists, no matter how prestigious or credentialed they may be, carry their own hidden and biased agenda. It is paramount that you, before you go to them for counsel and advice, determine precisely what their beliefs, attitudes, and values may be. It is always *your* mind, *your* body, and *your* personal problem. They are paid only to advise and recommend and if you are to get your money's worth you had best make certain that the therapists' values, beliefs, and attitudes parallel—or are in harmony with—your own.

In the case of psychiatrists, there is another much more grave danger: these individuals have been given the legal powers—because of their supposedly "medical" expertise—to institutionalize you against your will. This is, itself, a serious flaw in our current legal system that the public should immediately correct. It is, therefore, particularly urgent that you be very careful about what you disclose to a professional psychiatrist. They have the power to legally confine you to a mental institution (literally a prison), to drug you into insensibility, and if you resist, to actually destroy you mentally and physically with electroconvulsive shock and brain operations. Difficult as it may be to believe, many psychiatric therapies currently in use actually do physically *shrink the brain,* thereby destroying your mind, your personality, your memory, and your sense of self.

The book that follows supports and documents the above statements and offers specific and detailed advice for what you should and should not do if you find yourself overwhelmed with anxiety, sadness (depression), persistent and unwelcome thoughts and behaviors (obsessions), insomnia, or any other mental problems brought on by troublesome beliefs (delusions) or hallucinations. Never forget, no matter how it is characterized, described, or glamorized, psychotherapy is, in the final analysis, nothing more than the *purchase of friendship.* And friendship, as you well know, is something that should never have to be purchased.

A NOTE FOR OFFENDED THERAPISTS

Like all human traits in all human professions, incompetence, stupidity, perversity, greed, and malfeasance are normally distributed. This is true as well for the professions of psychiatry, clinical psychology, counseling, psychiatric nursing, pastoral counseling, and other human service careers. This book is not intended to malign or belittle the work, efforts, and invaluable service performed by the majority of knowledgeable and dedicated therapists who do provide essential and invaluable aid and comfort to people in psychic pain which can equal or exceed physical discomfort. Therefore, as a professional therapist you should not take offense at the indictments or damning statements aimed at the invidious members of your profession, at the crimes and misdemeanors of the warped, or at the sins of both omission and commission perpetuated by the "bad apples" in your professional barrel. You are, perhaps, more aware than I will ever be who the good guys are and what is wrong within your professional area of theory and practice. So, in reading the ensuing pages, keep foremost in mind that ancient axiom: if the shoe fits, wear it; if it does not, try on another shoe. Please refrain from damning the shoemaker!

As Dr. Anne Boedecker, a private practitioner, noted recently in the *National Psychologist*, "as a profession we have let 'therapy' grow unchecked and unregulated."[40] And, more specifically, a number of factors have led psychotherapy into the present era of managed care. Boedecker cites a number of very serious problems and flaws in current psychotherapeutic practice:

1. Despite calling ourselves a scientifically-based enterprise, most therapy works from theory, not research. Some of our methods have no more justification than faith-healing. (And some of our methods are faith-healing, and we ought to be honest about that and demonstrate how faith-healing works.)
2. Psychology has spawned so many diverse theories that practically anything can be justified by one theory or another. Therapists used to justify sexual involvement with clients from a theoretical point of view, and get away it! And we still use and teach anachronistic theories that have no research to back them up.
3. Therapy has become encased in its own value system, its own language. We define (vaguely) "codependency" and attempt to cure people of it. We treat "complexes" and "core issues" and all sorts of things nobody ever complained about before.
4. From graduate school admissions to the licensing/certification

process, there is no real screening process for preventing destructive people from becoming therapists. You'd think we ought to be able to keep seriously disturbed people out of the profession. But no group of mental health professionals would be able to decide on what criteria to use, or how to assess them.

5. Only recently have we begun to enforce standards and eliminate blatantly unethical practitioners. The present system still depends on consumer complaints—someone has to get hurt—often badly—before anything is done.

6. We still have very little in the way of standards of practice. There's no consensus on the best methods for treating different conditions or populations or even length of treatment for different diagnoses. And we have been unable to define quality care.

7. We paid no attention to cost-effectiveness of treatment before managed care [supervision decreed by insurance providers]. We have been "process-oriented," not outcome-oriented. We'll take our time "building rapport," "working through resistance" for weeks on end, and let the "uncovering process" take us wherever it goes. How many therapists wrote up treatment plans, set goals and objectives, and assessed progress periodically before managed care?

8. The mental health field in general has been poorly regulated. In our attempt to keep other mental health professionals out of the insurance-reimbursement market, we tolerated a situation where anyone could call themselves a counselor or therapist. This only increases the potential for harmful therapy, and decreases the avenues for eliminating the bad apples.

9. Our interdisciplinary relationships have been testy at best. [New Hampshire] Congressman Dick Swett recently addressed a group of psychologists about health care reform and the need for mental health professionals to work together for the inclusion of mental health benefits. Unless the mental health community can learn to speak as one voice anything we say will be discounted. Historically, psychology itself has had difficulty finding one voice.

10. Last but not least, we have sorely neglected our public image. Most "ordinary people" don't even know the difference between a psychologist and a psychiatrist, much less the difference be-

tween a psychologist and a psychotherapist. And we have done little to dispel the notion that psychologists are greedy, self-centered professionals. Psychologists' level of community involvement is not what it could be.

If you take all this into consideration, it's no wonder that mental health benefits are an easy target for managed care. We need serious reforms in our profession if we are to survive into the 21st century.[41]

In case anyone doubts the accuracy and honesty of Dr. Boedecker's assessment, they have but to read Robyn Dawes's *House of Cards* or Terence Campbell's *Beware the Talking Cure: Psychotherapy May Be Hazardous to Your Mental Health.*[42]

NOTES

1. Benjamin M. Braginsky, Dorothea D. Braginsky, and Kenneth Ring, *Methods of Madness: The Mental Hospital as Last Resort* (New York: Holt, Rinehart & Winston, 1969), p. vii.

2. Jack Engler and Daniel Goleman, *Consumer's Guide to Psychotherapy* (New York: Simon & Schuster, 1992), p. 15.

3. Matthew P. Dumont, *The Absurd Healer: Perspectives of a Community Psychiatrist* (New York: Science House, 1968), pp. 49–50.

4. Richie Herink, *The Psychotherapy Handbook: The A to Z Guide to More Than 250 Different Therapies in Use Today* (New York: Meridian Books, 1980), pp. vi-xiii.

5. Thomas Szasz, *The Myth of Psychotherapy: Mental Healing as Religion, Rhetoric and Repression* (Garden City, N.Y.: Anchor Press, 1978), p. xviii.

6. Ibid., p. 16.

7. Robert F. Morgan, "Balloon Therapy," *Canadian Psychology* 23 (1982): 45–46; reprinted in *The Iatrogenic Handbook*, ed. Robert F. Morgan (Toronto: IPI, 1983), pp. 446–47.

8. Ibid., p. 447.

9. Gary L. Wright, "NC Mental Ward Frees Deaf Man Held since 1925," *Lexington Herald Leader*, 5 February 1994, p. A3.

10. E. Fuller Torrey, *The Death of Psychiatry* (Radnor, Penn.: Chilton Book Co., 1974), pp. 64–65.

11. Ibid., p. 65.

12. Engler and Goleman, *Consumer's Guide to Psychotherapy*, pp. 73–74.

13. J. Ziskin and D. Faust, *Coping with Psychiatric and Psychological Testimony*, vols. 1–3 (Venice, Calif.: Law and Psychology Press, 1988).

14. L. R. Goldberg, "The Effectiveness of Clinician's Judgement," *Journal of Consulting Psychology* 23 (1959): 25–33. See also Andrew Christensen and Neil S. Jacobson, "Who (Or What) Can Do Psychotherapy: The Status and Challenge of Nonprofessional Therapies," *Psychological Science* 5, no. 1 (January 1994): 8–14.

15. L. N. Robins, "Epidemiology: Reflections on Testing the Validity of Psychiatric Interviews," *Archives of General Psychiatry* 42 (1985): 918–24.

16. Van O. Leirer et al., "Predictions of Violence by High School Students and Clinicians," Paper presented at Oregon Psychological Association Conference, Newport, Ore., Spring 1984. See also Christensen and Jacobson, "Who (Or What) Can Do Psychotherapy?"

17. Ziskin and Faust, *Coping with Psychiatric and Psychological Testimony*.

18. J. A. Plag and R. J. Arthur, "Psychiatric Reexamination of Unsuitable Naval Recruits: A Two-Year Follow Up," *American Journal of Psychology* 122 (1965): 534.

19. D. Faust and J. Ziskin, "The Expert Witness in Psychology and Psychiatry," *Science* 241 (July 1988): 31–35.

20. H. Renaud and F. Estes, "Life History Interviews with 100 Normal American Males: Pathogenicity of Childhood," *American Journal of Orthopsychiatry* 31 (1961): 786–95.

21. Faust and Ziskin, "The Expert Witness."

22. M. R. Temerlin and N. W. Trousdale, "The Social Psychology of Clinical Diagnosis," *Psychotherapy, Theory, & Practice* 6 (1964): 24–29.

23. Faust and Ziskin, "The Expert Witness."

24. Garth Wood, *The Myth of Neurosis* (New York: Harper & Row, 1987).

25. E. Fuller Torrey, *Nowhere to Go* (New York: Harper & Row, 1988), p. 164.

26. David Seabury, *The Art of Selfishness* (New York: Conerstone Library, 1937).

27. William Schofield, *Psychotherapy: The Purchase of Friendship* (Englewood Cliffs, N.J.: Prentice Hall, 1969).

28. Engler and Goleman, *Consumer's Guide to Psychotherapy*, p. 47.

29. Schofield, *Psychotherapy: The Purchase of Friendship*, p. 19.

30. Ibid. See also J. S. Wherry, "Psychotherapy: A Medical Procedure?" in *Going Crazy*, by H. H. Ruitenbeek (New York: Bantam Books, 1972), pp. 167–75.

31. Christensen and Jacobson, "Who (Or What) Can Do Psychotherapy?"

32. J. C. Whiteborn and Barbara J. Betz, "Further Studies of the Doctor as a Crucial Variable in the Outcome of Treatment with Schizophrenia Patients," *American Journal of Psychiatry* 17 (1960): 215–23.

33. E. Fuller Torrey, *The Mind Game* (New York: Bantam Books, 1973).

34. Margaret Rioch et al., "NIMH Pilot Study in Training Mental Health Counselors," *American Journal of Orthopsychiatry* 33 (1963): 678–723.

35. N. J. Pallone and J. J. Hennessy, "Benevolent Diagnosis," *Society* 31, no. 2 (March/ April 1994): 11–17.

36. Ibid., p. 15.

37. Ibid., p. 16.

38. Ibid., p. 17.

39. Ibid.

40. Anne Bodecker, "My View," *The National Psychologist* 3, no. 3 (May/June 1994): 14.

41. Ibid.

42. Robyn Dawes, *House of Cards: Psychology and Psychotherapy Built on Myth* (New York: Free Press, 1994). See also Terence Campbell, *Beware the Talking Cure: Psychotherapy May Be Hazardous to Your Mental Health* (Boca Raton, Fla.: Upton Books, 1994).

1

Life in the Modern
Psychotherapeutic State

*Doctors pour drugs of which they know little, to cure diseases of which they
know less, into human beings of whom they know nothing.*

Voltaire

Over the last forty years the United States has seen the birth and development of what many astute social critics have termed "the Therapeutic State." More than likely it began in the early 1950s with the large
gains in political power by the psychiatric profession as chronicled by
Jonas Robitscher's *The Powers of Psychiatry* and David Hill's *The Politics
of Schizophrenia*.[1] Shortly thereafter was seen the rise of other interlock-
ing supportive professional disciplines, including clinical psychology,
psychiatric social work, psychiatric nursing, and so on. Added to that
was the establishment of a therapeutic hierarchy with medicine on top,
supported by a retinue of hospitals, drug companies, medical administrators, training programs and research personnel, state and local
politicians, and an overwatching but supportive federal bureaucracy of
health. All of this is, of course, supported by a pervasive and well-orga-
nized media propaganda machine of medical publishers, professional
journals, newspapers and popular magazines, TV and radio mental
health programs, and public information pamphlets. With the onset
and propagation of the Community Mental Health Center System
established by the Kennedy administration to deliver comprehensive

mental health care services on a nationwide basis, the work was finished and the "shrinking,"[2] "diseasing,"[3] and "tranquilizing"[4] of America was well under way. The preparatory work for mass victimization—all in the name of fighting mental illness—was now complete.

To obtain full public cooperation, however, the masses had to be convinced that they were indeed mentally ill. To do this effectively, a propaganda campaign had to be launched, one carefully designed to convince even the healthiest and most reluctant of our citizens that something was terribly wrong with their lives and the way they lived them. In the late 1980s and early 1990s the media began their systematic attack on our national feeling of being sanely normal.

First, according to the *New York Times* in a March 17, 1993 story by Daniel Goleman, "While approximately 52 million adults in the United States—more than one in four—suffer from a mental disorder at some point during a year, only 28 percent of them seek help according to the most comprehensive study of the nation's mental health ever conducted."[5] According to Dr. Darrel A. Regier, director of the Division of Epidemiology and Services Research at the National Institute of Mental Health—the man who directed the study—approximately 9 million citizens develop a mental problem for the first time in any given year, another 8 million suffer a relapse and the remaining 35 million suffer continuing symptoms. Approximately 28 percent of the total population is affected.[6] "Though the figures sound high at first," says Dr. Myrna Weissman, a psychiatric epidemiologist at Columbia University, "Just think about the people you know."[7] The pollsters were candid enough to admit, however, that not all the diagnosable mental disorders described in the study required treatment. "Many people with mental disorders have relatively brief, self-limiting illnesses and don't have enough disability to warrant going in for care," Dr. Regier confessed. Certainly! If problems of everyday living are perceived as sickness or an illness, then everyone is sick—at least to some degree or another. Ah, but also discovered was the fact that "mental illness goes untreated in 7 out of 10 cases, and that general physicians rather than psychiatrists or other psychotherapists treat the bulk of the mentally ill people who seek help."[8] The solution? Obviously everyone should seek the help of a professional psychiatrist or psychotherapist! Shocking? Wait, there's more!

A year later the public was slapped with an even more impressive set of figures. Ronald C. Kessler, a sociology professor at the University of Michigan, published a study in the *Archives of General Psychiatry* revealing that almost 50 percent of the American population experience mental illness at some time in their lives and almost one-third are afflicted in any one year. "It shouldn't be scary to say half the population has suffered from some mental disorder. That's part of life," says Kessler.[9] Kessler interviewed 8,098 people aged fifteen to fifty-nine nationwide between September 1990 and February 1992 and found 48 percent of his respondents had suffered from at least one mental disorder at one time or another during their lives. Twenty-nine-and-a-half percent had suffered in the previous year. Most common were depressions, alcohol dependence, and social and simple phobias (fear of people or "social" situations, such as crowds or assault; and fear of items, such as dirt, dogs, or cats; respectively). Incredibly, Dr. William Narrow opined that Kessler's study underestimated the prevalence of mental illness because some ailments—like borderline personality disorder, for example, which can't be diagnosed via interviews—were not covered by the survey.[10]

But Narrow is only following in the footsteps of psychiatrists who have gone before in seeing mental illness everywhere they look. In the *American Journal of Psychiatry* in 1990, Drs. James J. Hudson and Harrison G. Pope, Jr., published an article stating they were able to specify and identify a new illness—one they have called the "affective spectrum disorder," which according to these psychiatrists' predictions is "one of the most widespread diseases of mankind" affecting approximately one-third of the world's population.[11]

Now if this doesn't persuade you that we are all mentally sick, another stratagem—perhaps even more effective on an individual basis—is the "diagnostic questionnaire." This clever device lists a number of common symptoms or behaviors in a checklist form to which you, the potential victim, are to respond. Following are examples of these diagnostic checklists plucked out of popular newspapers, magazines, and drug company publications:

ARE YOU DEPRESSED?

Do you . . .

_____ Find it easy to do the things you used to do?
_____ Feel hopeful about the future?
_____ Find it easy to make decisions?
_____ Find that you are useful and needed?
_____ Still enjoy the things you used to do?

If you answered "no" to any of the above questions, you may suffer from depression . . .[12]

Those whose overall written test scores indicated depression or severe depression were most apt to answer "no" to the above questions, says Harvard psychiatrist Douglas Jacobs. Almost *any* older, suggestible individual answering the above questions is likely to answer at least two of the questions no—and in no way does this either indicate or guarantee he is depressed! The checklist can, however, shove him into the hands of a psychotherapist because the questionnaire has persuaded him he's depressed.

Then in a daily newspaper, we found this beauty:

DO YOU SUFFER FROM MANIC DEPRESSION?

Some of the symptoms of depression are:

loss of energy   changes in appetite
feelings of hopelessness,   difficulty concentrating
   helplessness, or guilt   feeling bad or blue
changes in sleep patterns

For more information call _____[13]

While all of the above symptoms might suggest a diagnosis of manic depression, they also accompany a wide range of other disorders which are not in any way related to mental illness.

If you, perchance, happen to pick up any drug company or mental health literature, you might chance upon another gem such as the

Obsessive-Compulsive Checklist found in John Greist, James Jefferson, and Isaac Marbs's *Anxiety and Its Treatment: Help Is Available.*[14]

The checklist reads as follows:

People with [Obsessive Compulsive Disorder] usually have trouble with one or more of the activities listed below. Answer each question by giving it a score:

0   No problem with the activity, takes me the same time as an average person. I don't need to repeat or avoid it.

1   Takes me twice as long as most people or I have to repeat it twice or I usually avoid it.

2   Takes me three times as long as most people, or I have to repeat it three or more times, or I usually avoid it.

_____   Bathing or showering
_____   Washing hands and face
_____   Hair care (washing, combing, brushing)
_____   Brushing teeth
_____   Dressing, undressing
_____   Using toilet
_____   Touching others or being touched
_____   Handling trash or garbage
_____   Washing clothes or dishes
_____   Cleaning house
_____   Making the bed
_____   Turning lights on and off
_____   Doing arithmetic
_____   Writing or reading
_____   Mailing letters

And so on, listing many other daily activities. The above is only a partial list—a total of twenty-nine daily activities are included and, according to the authors, a score above ten raises a question about your obsessive-compulsive proclivity and a score above twenty suggests the possibility more strongly.

On the more esoteric side, according to clinical psychologist Dr. Edith Fiore, there are some common signs that can indicate your possession by demonic dead people and abduction by extraterrestrials. First, the ten most common signs of possession are:

1. Low energy level
2. Character shifts or mood swings
3. Inner voice(s) speaking to you
4. Abuse of drugs (including alcohol)
5. Impulsive behavior
6. Memory problems
7. Poor concentration
8. Sudden onset of anxiety or depression
9. Sudden onset of physical problems with no obvious cause
10. Emotional and/or physical reactions to reading her book *The Unquiet Dead*[15]

Apparently it never occurred to the good doctor that the above symptoms could also indicate something other than possession by the dead. Now as for the ten most common signs of abductions by extraterrestrials, we have the following:

1. Inability to account for periods of time
2. Persistent nightmares and/or dreams of UFOs and/or aliens
3. Sleep disorders
4. Waking up with unusual bodily sensations
5. Appearance of mysterious marks on the body
6. Feeling monitored, watched, and/or communicated with
7. Repeated sightings of UFOs
8. Vague recollections of a close encounter
9. Unexplained healing of ailments or afflictions
10. Reacting with fear of and/or anxiety about UFOs and/or extraterrestrials

These signs and symptoms were included in Dr. Fiore's 1989 book *Encounters.*[16]

Of late, we have the double-page spread, public service advertisements sponsored by the drug companies in popular magazines, informing the reader that Irma Lagonza from Anytown, USA, will never forget trying to cover up her crying jags for years until she finally confessed to her friendly physician who, thanks to the magnanimity of our blessed pharmaceutical companies, prescribed their magical pill and gave her her life back. She, of course, is undyingly grateful—the drug company says so.[17]

Not to be outdone by the drug companies, many psychiatrists have also discovered that it pays to advertise. One of the cheapest and most effective ways to do this is to write a book about a new, or old, or common mental problem in which you are an expert (it even helps if you confess that you too suffered from the disorder until you learned how to master it) and then tell your audience what to do about it—making sure, in the process, that you don't give too much away, to ensure that your audience seeks out the closest possible M.D. for treatment. Edward M. Hallowell, M.D., and John J. Rotey, M.D., authors of *Driven to Distraction* and psychiatrists who are specialists in *Recognizing and Coping with Attention Disorder from Childhood through Adulthood,* judging by the book's subtitle, both suffer from Adult Attention Deficit Disorder (AADD), which makes their advice on how to deal with it doubly valuable![18]

According to the good doctors, this is a problem of which millions of adults and children are unaware, because they think they are merely procrastinating, or having trouble concentrating, or having difficulty getting organized. Victims believe there's really nothing wrong with them! They are, Hallowell and Rotey assure us, very sick with Attention Deficit Disorder (ADD) and AADD and they don't even know it! How does one find out if one is sick? Ah, ha! The answer is easy. Just complete the handy dandy checklist, which is, of course, as broadly based and all-encompassing (and therefore as useless) as those we've seen previously.

If you manage to slip through the extensive screen, look for some other conditions that may accompany, resemble, or even mask ADD and AADD, including anxiety disorders, bipolar disorder or manic-depressive disorder, caffeinism, (excessive coffee or cola drinking), any sort of conduct disorder in children, depression, disorders of impulse control, chronic fatigue syndrome, and so on. And if none of these convinces you you're sick and need treatment, then, by God, as a last resort you damn well must be suffering from that comprehensive all-inclusive wastebasket category that makes all those hard to categorize: the Borderline Personality Disorder. You're sick. Why don't you admit it? You have a poor inner self-image, poor interpersonal relations, need lots of excitement and stimulation, are impulsive, get angry when frustrated, and have strong emotional needs. You're moody, under-achieving, and your substance abuse isn't uncommon. But doesn't everyone at times? No, you're in denial! Admit you're sick and let me therapize you! So it goes, day in and day out, year in and year out, in the modern therapeutic state. We soon will—if we haven't already—get the message.

THE MESSAGE

The message of the 1990s, just in case you missed hearing it (which is most unlikely), is that all of us are sick, dysfunctional, neurotic, addicted, maladjusted, depressed, compulsive, codependent, discon-nected, spiritually lost, disaffected, anxious, phobic, and so on. We are all victims of our time, our genetic inheritance, our parents, our schools, our environment. We are victims of mental and physical abuse; moral, sexual, economic, and emotional circumstances; of our neglected needs and of social and verbal abuse. We are bombarded daily by the media artillery pounding into us the message that we are all psychologically disturbed and teetering precariously on the brink of a nervous breakdown, or total mental and physical collapse. In all of this stygian atmosphere of gloom and doom, however, *there is a ray of light,* a hope of salvation, an answer to our pitiful prayers: psychother-apy! Today—no matter how trivial or serious our problems—there is the promise of a cure. For every mental ailment there is a psychother-apeutic antidote.

Such therapeutic promissory notes have been issued since the beginning of time. Modern medicine, we are told, has made such gar-gantuan strides in creating pills, potions, and panaceas—both physi-cal and mental—to placate and ease the pain of human anxiety, we should all consider it an honor and a privilege to become mentally ill. The medical priests and the psychological shamans backed up by their concrete temples of curative wonders (the hospitals) daily defeat the demons of death and human destruction and stave off madness with their powerful potions. Got a pain or problem in this day and age? Pop a pill! With the help of the pharmaceutical industry our contemporary shrinks have managed to mute human misery by inventing a pill for every problem or pain, physical or mental. Hovering over our heads from the moment we pop from the womb until we sink into the tomb is the caring, concerned (and expensive), visage of the medicine man slapping us into the world and reminding us that physical and mental maintenance is an expensive proposition. This is a lesson we cannot forget—we are reminded much too often. Pills and potions, as well as words, have their price! Increasingly over the years this lesson in elementary economics has been so deeply inculcated that medical care and concern and how each of us pays for it is now the greatest single economic issue of the 1990s. Anyone harboring any doubt must read Robert Sherrill's "Medicine and the Madness of the Market."[19]

This first experience outside of the womb, enterprising psychodynamic psychotherapists tell us, is only the beginning of our victimization and continuing abuse. Since the abusing obstetrician is behind us and our doting sires in front of us we, of course, attribute our pain to our parents, the primal abusers. Being victimized from birth, none of us is immune and we all are, thus, potential customers for the ministrations of the psychological savants and patent mental medicine men. We cannot and will not ever win. The massive machine of modern medical care marches inexorably onward, grinding any and all opposition into the silent dust.

If we look at modern physical medicine it has, indeed, made marvelous strides in easing physical pain and saving and prolonging lives. Its achievements must not be mocked or ignored. On the other hand, in its dealings with the human mind and human behavior, medical care has little or nothing of which to be proud. Rather, the history of mental medicine, with the exception of neurology, of course (as we shall see in chapter 2), has been a disgrace and a continuing story of un- and antiscientific fumbling and bumbling; on occasion it has been marked by outright fraud and malpractice, as numerous critics have noted.[20] In many ways American psychiatry has gone backward rather than forward.

How did things come to such a sorry state? Well, we certainly can't say that we weren't warned! Over a decade ago psychologist Dr. Bernie Zilbergeld, in *The Shrinking of America,* warned us of the efforts of the psychotherapists to psychologize every aspect of contemporary existence to convince everyone we were mentally ill and then to sell therapy as the solution to all our problems.[21] What was not told us was the fact that therapy unfortunately does very little and there are relatively few problems it has ever been able to solve. Zilbergeld is at his best in proving beyond a doubt that significant psychological change —the goal of all psychotherapy—is a monumental myth and people seldom, if ever, really significantly change.

Nevertheless, in Zilbergeld's words:

> Our culture is strongly committed to the proposition that people are highly malleable. Three key assumptions of the present age are that human beings should change because they are not as competent or good or as happy as they could be; that there are few limits to the alterations they can make; and that change is relatively easy to effect. If only the right methods are used and the right attitudes are held, people can make significant changes and become almost whatever they want.[22]

Not only is this not true (nor has it ever been true) but it is part and parcel of the fantasy of the golden American dream that sees everything as not only possible but easily attainable. In a culture that believes every man or woman can be president, it is little wonder that the average citizen approaching a psychotherapist believes all things are possible. Zilbergeld does his best to throw cold water on these comforting dreams:

> It is a basic tenet of therapeutic ideology that people are not okay as they are; that's why they need therapy. In the therapeutic view, people are not regarded as evil nor as having done anything they should feel guilty about, but there is certainly something wrong with them. Specifically they are too guilty, too inhibited, not confident or assertive enough, not able to express and fulfill themselves properly, and without a doubt not as joyful and free from stress as they ought to be.[23]

If we were a wise and thoughtful people, Zilbergeld notes, we would recognize some of our basic limits and fundamental obstacles to personal change. Change may be difficult or impossible because of (1) physiology and heredity; (2) early learning and traumatic injury; (3) the severity and complexity of the problem; (4) lack of time and energy to deal with it; (5) learning difficulties; (6) unwillingness to carry out therapeutic and maintenance procedures; (7) lack of environmental support for change; (8) luck—chance, suffering, and evil are inherent parts of life; and (9) some things cannot and should not be changed—some problems are insoluble. Violence seems to be a way of life for some people and we have long known that suicide prevention centers do not lower the suicide rates.[24] Neither do cradle-to-grave welfare services prevent social problems and disasters. For people who believe nothing is impossible, Zilbergeld notes, these facts of life can be depressing, but such facts can be looked at differently. We can realize that "we are not nearly as bad off and in need of fixing as therapists tell us. Much of what we now think of as problems—things that ought to be altered and for which there are solutions—are not so much problems as [they are] unescapable limits and predicaments of life."[25]

Our current problem, Zilbergeld argues, is that we have swallowed whole a wide variety of psychotherapeutic myths. First and foremost is the notion that psychotherapy is the royal road to human health and happiness and that both the internal and external worlds we live in are best understood in psychotherapeutic terms. Corollary myths include the following:

1. There is *one best* therapy for our problem;
2. Counseling is equally effective for all problems. (No. It is best for phobias, anxiety, low self-esteem, marital and family problems, and some sexual difficulties. It is not effective at all for depression, addictions, criminal rehabilitation, schizophrenia, and sexual deviancy. Words can't change raw need and the power of addiction. Just saying "no" doesn't work!)
3. Behavior change is therapy's most common outcome. Therapy, like prayer, can be comforting.
4. Great changes are the rule. (No, changes achieved, if any, are very small.)

5. The longer the therapy, the better the results. (No, never.)
6. Therapeutic changes are permanent—or at least long lasting. (No, why should therapy do better than medicine or dentistry?)
7. At worst, counseling is harmless. (No, therapy makes many clients worse.)
8. One course of therapy is the rule for most clients. (No. Several courses of treatment are the rule.)
9. Only specially trained professionals can help people change. (Does systematic desensitization, a therapy which conquers patients' fears through gradual exposure to the feared object or situation, for example, require a high degree of skill? No, only common sense.)
10. Powerful methods for changing people—methods that therapists know and have mastered—exist. (No, they do not.)

Zilbergeld states,

In general, the change methods currently available are weak and seriously limited. I have already presented some of the evidence: the fact, for instance, that changes made by the presumably most sophisticated methods of therapy are usually modest and not much different from what people achieve on their own or with the help of friends.

There is also plenty of supporting evidence from elsewhere. Even when one has total control of the environment—as in prisons and mental institutions—the results hardly support the conclusion of tremendous effect.[26]

Even powerful brainwashing techniques such as those employed in the Korean War had only short term and limited effectiveness. Jerome Frank in his 1963 classic, *Persuasion and Healing*, states:

The main lesson to be drawn from thought reform is not its success in generating false confessions (fear) but its failure to produce permanent changes in attitude. . . . Adult belief systems are very resistant to change, and changes such as those produced by extreme environmental pressures tend to snap back once these are removed.[27]

Based on the work of Zilbergeld and others, we can confidently state that few, if any, schools of psychotherapy produce any fundamental personality change. This even applies specifically to long-term psychoanalysis.

Zilbergeld's messages in *Shrinking* are clear. First, "Whether you choose self-help, nonprofessional help, or professional treatment, you will serve yourself well by not burdening yourself and those you turn to with unrealistic expectations for change. You can have whatever fantasies you want, but counter them with the main message of this book: human beings and relationships are difficult to change and typically the alterations made are modest."[28] Zilbergeld feels you ought to know what the professional insiders know about therapy:

> Keep in mind the consensus that incompetence rather than competence is the rule (*among psychotherapists*) and also that there are no sure guidelines. Type of therapy and therapist reputation, experience, and training do not necessarily mean much. Therapist reputation is often based on showmanship, charisma, and number of publications, none of which has anything to do with clinical skill. There is no evidence that psychologists and psychiatrists who have the longest training and command the highest fees are more effective than social workers, marriage counselors, and other therapists. Even those who regularly refer to a certain therapist frequently have no idea of what kind of results are achieved. [Emphasis in original.][29]

This conclusion is well supported by the more recent research of Christensen and Jacobson. In a comprehensive survey of research on psychological interventions delivered by professional and paraprofessional therapists, they conclude that there is little doubt that "paraprofessionals or professionals with limited experience perform as well as or better than professionally trained psychotherapists. Professional training and clinical experience may not add to the efficacy of psychotherapy."[30] While in most professions it would be ludicrous to compare a trained and an untrained person, for example, surgeons or electricians, this is not the case with regard to "psychotherapy." Professional training contributes little to therapeutic effectiveness. It also is evident that self-administered self-help materials and treatments achieve therapeutic outcomes comparable to those of therapist-administered treatments. Similarly, self-help mutual-support groups seem to be as effective for some problems as the services provided by the professional therapist.

Incredible as it may seem, most talk-radio stations now have added a resident "shrink" who gives counsel on everything from anxiety to zoophobia with the heaviest emphases on sex, marriage, and romance. Those foolish enough to take such generalized advice seriously and to follow it religiously certainly deserve the fate they receive. If, however, it is taken with the recommended skeptical block of salt, it applies to your specific problem, and it helps provide insight and useful information, you will probably be no worse off listening to it than you would be if you had a $100-an-hour session with your friendly psychiatrist. *Caveat emptor.*

You do well to be very cautious in your choice of a therapist and in following your shrink's advice. Campbell has warned that too many psychotherapists fail to maintain familiarity with the current research literature, develop ill-conceived treatment plans, solicit the dependency of their clients, and often confuse them by creating imaginary problems.[31] When such negligence occurs, clients should file a malpractice suit. The fact that you do have legal recourse if necessary is, clearly, one significant advantage offered by the licensed therapist over the talk-radio shrink and other self-help sources.

JUST HOW SICK ARE WE?

According to Catherine Johnson in her book *When to Say Goodby to Your Therapist,* nearly 40 percent of all Americans will enter psychotherapy at some point in their lives, a figure that makes psychotherapy commonplace and a part of our everyday existence.[32] This is, in one sense, a rather extraordinary development: only a few years ago being in psychotherapy was seen as a clear sign of mental illness and being considered crazy was the very last thing on earth you wanted people to think. In the mid-seventies the comprehensive care centers (government-supported mental health clinics which provide comprehensive services regardless of one's ability to pay) had to have rear entrances so clients could come for service without being seen doing so. Clients were terrified of what people might think. The mere suggestion that any political candidate had received psychotherapy was more than sufficient grounds to disqualify him for office. In the 1990s, however, being in therapy is considered socially correct, prestigious, and a status symbol, since everyone is now proud to be a "victim."

But what, exactly, is the true size of the mental health problem in the nation today? Media estimates of the number of hospital beds occupied by mental patients range from one out of every four to one out of ten. The true number is difficult to assess since an accurate count will depend upon how "mental illness" is defined. Should, for example, old age mental debilitation fall into this category? Organic neurological disorders? Mental retardation? Alzheimer's? Alcoholism? The numbers will rise and fall according to the whims of the categorizer.

Findings from a recent National Institute of Mental Health (NIMH) survey stated that nearly 30 percent of Americans have symptoms of a psychiatric disorder at some time during any given year.[33] The majority of them receive no mental health treatment, however, either formal or informal. This study was carried out in the mid-1980s on sixteen thousand people living in five regions of the NIMH Epidemiological Catchment Area program, providing a representative sample of the adult national population. The researchers concluded that anxiety disorders, mood disorders, alcohol and drug abuse, schizophrenia, antisocial personality problems, somatization, and severe cognitive impairment were the most common complaints, and were suffered by 28.1 percent of the population. Interestingly enough, phobias proved to be the single most common behavioral problem affecting twenty million people or 10.9 percent of the population. The survey also revealed that 14.7 percent, approximately twenty-three million people, made some use of a mental health service.

Between 1975 and 1985 the proportion of the population seeing mental health professionals almost doubled, rising from 3.1 to 5.9 percent, despite the fact that more than two-thirds of the people with psychiatric disorders did not use even voluntary mental health services. For example, among the alcoholics and other drug addicts only 23.6 percent received any help. Most interesting was the finding that 45 percent of the people receiving mental health services, that is, about 10.4 million people, had no classifiable psychiatric disorder. Although the vast majority did have symptoms, they were not serious or persistent enough to warrant extended treatment. In sum, 22.8 million people paid a total of 326 million visits to a mental health practitioner or a mental health clinic.[34] This is a considerable amount of trouble and a whopping amount of business for the psychotherapists. And we have reason to believe this is only the tip of the psychotherapeutic iceberg.

None of the statistics includes any of the prolific "self-help" entrepreneurs who have made a fortune out of persuading members of the vast television audiences and bookstore-browsers that they are all either sick or victims of childhood abusers, and that their own particular brand of advice and/or self-help program can cure all of the disease and general malaise that modern civilized flesh is heir to. Members of this extensive self-help industry usually use one of three approaches to snare their victims: (1) organizing and leading self-help groups and workshops; (2) writing and selling self-help books, audio tapes, or videocassettes; (3) developing, manufacturing, and marketing self-improvement devices and products alleged to fine tune the brain and nervous system, raise one's intelligence, improve one's personality, energize the body, and so on. The entrepreneurial strategy is both straightforward and effective: first, you must take advantage of the normal trials and tribulations of living and convince your audience they are both sick and victims; then, persuade the ill that you have the answer to all their questions and the cure for whatever ails them. If, at the same time, you can tie all of this to the latent sense of spiritual yearning or religious belief in nearly everyone you are, indeed, on the threshold of worldly wealth.

One of the most successful of all of these entrepreneurs, for example, is former priest and current therapist John Bradshaw, who at one time had three nationally televised Public Broadcasting System series and three best-selling books on the market.[35] Bradshaw has successfully parlayed into a fortune the simple-minded notion that every adult secretly harbors an "inner child" and that we are all victims of a disastrous and crippling childhood. According to Bradshaw, nearly all of the middle-aged adults in the country were reared in dysfunctional families by parents who used "shame-based" tactics to control behavior. This and other, similar techniques caused deep and serious psychological wounds that only prolonged therapy can cure. To heal this serious emotional wound and one's "inner child," the original healthy personality that was driven into hiding by the unendurable childhood pain, we must attain recovery through Bradshaw's specific procedures. His technique of therapy is best illustrated in his book *Homecoming*.

In the early part of *Homecoming* Bradshaw informs us that the Wounded Child (WC) in each of us contaminates our lives and this is why our current lives aren't working. To show us that we need his ministrations Bradshaw presents us with a WC Questionnaire. Some items from it follow:

1. I experience anxiety and fear whenever I contemplate doing anything new.
2. I am a people pleaser with no mind of my own.
3. I am a rebel. I feel alive when I am in conflict.
4. In the deepest part of my secret self I feel that something is wrong with me.
5. I'm a hoarder. I have trouble letting go of anything.
6. I feel inadequate.
7. I have trouble starting things.
8. I have trouble finishing things.
9. My life is empty.
10. I don't know who I am.

And so on.[36]

If you answer yes to ten or more of the twenty-two items then you are in deep trouble and need this book and Bradshaw's program. A careful study of the items, however, will show that nearly everyone on earth could easily answer yes to at least ten of these misleading, ambiguous, and to a large extent contradictory statements, which are arranged so that if you don't answer yes to this one they'll get you on the next one!

In similar fashion Bradshaw has another questionnaire dealing with your development during your infancy. This questionnaire will yield what Bradshaw calls an "index of suspicion." This index will tell you at what development level you are fixated and where, supposedly, your parents did you the most harm. Every developmental level is covered by a questionnaire. Questions at the Infant level include the following (my comments are in parentheses following Bradshaw's questions):

1. Do you have an ingestive addiction such as overeating, drinking, or drugging? (Since infants are so concerned with food intake if as an adult you have such problems then you're still an infant!)
2. You find it hard to trust others.
3. You feel that you don't fit or belong.
4. You try to be helpful. (Who, pray tell, doesn't?)
5. You have an obsessive need to be valued and esteemed. (Who doesn't? And what is wrong with this if you do?)
6. Are you often gullible? (If you continue to read and believe this drivel you are!)
7. Do you stay alone a lot?
8. The more you say "yes" the worse off you are?[37]

We encounter more of the same inane questions at each subsequent development level (toddler, preschool, school age, and adolescence). The idea behind these queries is to get you to answer yes and then to sell you on the idea that you are, indeed, still an "inner child" who will never recover from your horrible treatment in your youth unless you re-educate your wounded inner child the way Dr. Bradshaw dictates. As the syndicated columnist John Rosemond noted:

Although there's no doubt that some of us did indeed have distinctly unhappy childhoods, Bradshaw's litany—since taken up by a significant number of "helping" professionals—has always struck me as less science than propaganda. As I travel the country, I witness frequent testimony to the effect that this rhetoric has alienated many an adult parent from an adult child. Not surprisingly, Bradshaw is often mentioned as having been a catalyst to these family feuds.[38]

To test his hypothesis Rosemond has been asking his audiences the question, "How many of you feel that you were raised by decent, well-meaning, moral parents, who despite whatever faults they might have brought to the task, managed to do an adequate job of instilling in you a good set of values?" Every time and without hesitation an over-whelming number of people raise their hand. While unscientific, Rosemond's polling procedure is more in line with the reality of the situation than Bradshaw's propaganda.

Wendy Kaminer, an investigative reporter and expert on the co-dependency and recovery movement, in her wonderful book *I'm Dys-functional, You're Dysfunctional,* also finds Bradshaw's brand of shrink-age offensive and distasteful. She remarks:

> There is something niggardly and mean-spirited in the passion with which some recovering codependents (*diseased adults*) point to them-selves as victims of abuse, laying claim to the crown of thorns. Adult Children Of Alcoholics (ACOAs) are like Holocaust survivors, suf-fering post-traumatic stress disorder, John Bradshaw writes offen-sively. Recovery gives people permission always to put themselves first, partly because it doesn't give them a sense of perspective on their complaints; parental nagging is not the equal of physical abuse and deprivation, much less genocide; vague intimations of unease are not the same as cancer. No one seems to count her blessings in recovery. I've heard no one say "Some people suffer more than I." For all the talk about sharing and caring, in recovery there's more evi-dence of self-pity than compassion. [Emphasis in original.][39]

Rosemond again casts the light of sanity on the insane and dan-gerous paranoia of Bradshaw's thesis by pointing out that each of us is flawed and when two imperfect people join together in an imperfect union and bring another imperfect being into creation, the resulting imperfections and collisions are in no way dysfunction, rather they are the very struggle of life and reality. "What America desperately needs," Rosemond says, "are people who will accept this reality rather than complain about it; who will reject the perversely attractive notion that pain and victimization are one and the same . . . ; who will com-mit themselves to the struggle of creating and sustaining a family, realizing that there is no struggle in life so tough and yet nothing else in life so worth the struggle."[40] Bradshaw's argument that as many as 96 percent of American families are dysfunctional in one way or another is shrinkage at its worst.

Not only does the codependency movement lack any scientific basis whatsoever, but the National Institute on Alcohol Abuse and Alcoholism recently sponsored a study that found no evidence to support the contention that people can develop "a personality disorder on the basis of their family membership."[41] Donald Goodwin, one of the leading alcoholism researchers, is even more forceful. Not only does he label the ACOA movement a hoax; he also states that children of alcoholics are "about like adult children of everybody else with a problem." Goodwin points out in no uncertain terms that the professional addiction therapists invented the concept of "adult children" simply to be able to "sell this concept to the public and [thus become] eligible for reimbursements from the insurance companies. In short . . . it was a way for therapists to tap into a new market and make money."[42] Difficult as it may be to believe, Bradshaw has grown men and women who attend his seminars sitting in a circle holding teddy bears, listening to a simulated maternal heartbeat, while Bradshaw urges them to imagine they're back in the womb or tiny infants. As Sykes notes, "Saint Paul may have put aside the thoughts of a child when he reached manhood; Bradshaw wants to reverse the process."[43] Bradshaw's latest book is titled *Creating Love: The Next Stage of Growth*[44] and it is little different from what has gone before. Despite Bradshaw's three degrees from the University of Toronto; his experience as a counselor, theologian, and management consultant; and his work as a student of Catholicism he, too, has his personal problems. It seems he wound up divorced after twenty years of marriage. This calls to mind Lynne Namka's statement, "make sure you choose a therapist who has fewer psychological problems than you do."[45]

Nevertheless, as noted earlier, when the effects of "self-help therapy" are compared with the effects of professionally administered therapy, one is just about as effective as the other. The most serious problem of all, however, is the fact that everyone who can read is led to believe that something is seriously wrong with his psyche and he is badly in need of a 100,000-mile mental checkup and overhaul.

VICTIMS OF MEDIA ABUSE

On any given day one can pick up the daily newspaper and after turning a few pages encounter ads inquiring "Are you depressed? Do you suffer from panic attacks?" and the like, followed by a list of "symptoms." These are blatant examples of "disease-mongering," i.e., efforts on the part of members of the psychotherapeutic establishment to convince you you're sick. As an example of exactly how this works, take the following quiz, answering each question honestly, total your score, and then interpret the results:

Survey of Anomalistic Experience Questionnaire

Circle either "yes" or "no" after each question.

At any time during your lifetime, have you ever on any occasion:

1. Seen something moving out the corner of your eye but have not been able to determine exactly what it was?   Yes   No

2. Read several paragraphs before suddenly becoming aware of the fact that you cannot remember anything you have been reading?   Yes   No

3. Started to fall asleep and then suddenly jerked awake because it felt like someone suddenly pulled the rug out from under you?   Yes   No

4. Felt at times in the late afternoon that you have no energy at all and that someone pulled your plug, draining you?   Yes   No

5. Felt so depressed on occasion that you just wanted to give up and end it all?   Yes   No

6. Awakened to the alarm clock in the morning and found it almost impossible to summon up the energy to get out of bed?   Yes   No

7. Had the feeling that your brain is numb and that it is impossible for you to think or remember anything?   Yes   No

8. Had trouble remembering your phone number,
   your address, bank account number, social security
   number, license plate number, etc., at least
   temporarily?　　　　　　　　　　　　　　Yes　No

9. Had sudden, unexplained, mysterious headaches?　Yes　No

10. Had the feeling that someone or something is out
    to get you and is causing your long run of
    bad luck?　　　　　　　　　　　　　　　Yes　No

11. Had the feeling that someone is standing
    behind you looking over your shoulder—
    but when you turn no one is there?　　　　Yes　No

12. Had the feeling you have forgotten something
    important but you cannot remember what it is?　Yes　No

13. Had the feeling that you are a robot, an automaton,
    or puppet and someone or something else is
    pulling your strings?　　　　　　　　　　Yes　No

14. Had a "missing time" experience, that is, you
    remember starting and finishing but nothing
    in between—a trip, for example?　　　　　Yes　No

15. Drank just one glass of beer or one small glass of
    wine but nevertheless found yourself looped
    and giddy?　　　　　　　　　　　　　　Yes　No

16. Believed that your fate is in the hands of
    supernatural forces or spirits that are controlling
    you and your behavior?　　　　　　　　　Yes　No

17. Seen or heard something so bizarre and
    incredible that no one on earth, no scientist
    or seer, could possibly explain it?　　　　Yes　No

18. Had the feeling that something horrible
    was going to happen and you could not
    explain why you felt this way?　　　　　Yes　No

19. Dreamed about something horrible happening
    and then at a later date saw exactly what you
    dreamed come true?　　　　　　　　　　Yes　No

20. Seen or heard things that no one else reported
   having seen or heard—even though they were
   there at the same time and place you were?   Yes   No

Scoring and Interpreting the Results

If you have answered yes to ten or more of these questions, you definitely need to see one of our highly trained and experienced staff psychologists. All of our personnel have had years of formal schooling and on-the-job service with thousands of individual people of all ages including inmates of prisons, psychiatric hospitals, clinics for the mentally ill, and homes for the deranged and mentally retarded. All of these highly qualified personnel will provide the badly needed counsel and advice your psychological condition requires. Each of these specialists will tell you that, even though you answered yes to all twenty items, there is not a damn thing wrong with you and that you are as normal and sane as grass and shoes. They will also inform you that each of these experiences is a common and ordinary psychological event experienced by just about every sane and normal human being who has ever lived. There is nothing unusual, supernatural, startling, or remarkable about any of these experiences that nearly every human being on earth has gone through as he lives his ordinary and routine life. These experiences are not only well known but well understood by every student of anomalistic psychology. Such feelings, experiences, and fears are truly universal and happen to everyone. Congratulations, not only are you normal but you are also a full-fledged, qualified member in good standing of the all-too-human race!

Psychological suggestion is, indeed, a powerful force that can be used quite effectively by both salesmen and propagandists to sell you a pig in a poke. Again, *caveat emptor.*

Although some ads are not disease-mongering and are instead aimed at securing research subjects for drug studies, the implications are that such behavioral problems are common and endemic in the general population. Again, the suggestion is clear that not only are panic attacks and manic depression common among the populace but that drugs can cure them. Moreover, as noted earlier, the psychotherapeutic professions have not only succeeded in convincing the public that most of us are "sick" but also that all of us are "victims." Little wonder that we have become a nation of malcontents and perpetual whiners.

In his amusing and insightful work *A Nation of Victims,* Charles J. Sykes wrote about "the Therapeutic Culture," a term accurately describing what has happened to us on a national scale.[46] It is now taken for granted that everyone of us is (1) sick; (2) maladjusted; (3) underdeveloped in that we have failed to reach our full potential; (4) incomplete or inadequate; (5) spiritually unfulfilled; or (6) suffering in some way or other that requires the services of a psychotherapist. Sykes notes that the American personality sees all of the eternal questions of human existence as psychological problems that require—no, demand—solutions that can only be furnished by the professional services of a psychotherapist. In fact, Jung specifically stated that only the psychiatrist is in possession of the knowledge and skills required to solve the problems of the human soul. As Thomas Szasz noted, every problem of human existence has been taken over by the medical profession and transformed into a medical problem that can only be solved by medical procedures, intervention, and drugs. As the population increased, so did the number of psychotherapists; and as the number of psychological helpers increased, so did the number of Americans who needed—and subsequently received—some form of psychotherapy. The result was that by the 1970s, approximately six million Americans were receiving some form of psychotherapy in clinics and hospitals, a million more from so-called lay therapists. In fact, as Zilbergeld catalogues, the United States had more professional therapists than librarians, fire fighters, or mail carriers—and twice as many psychotherapists as dentists or pharmacists. Martin Gross in 1978 called the nation "one giant psychiatric clinic" with, of course, the psychotherapists in charge passing out pills and advice for every aspect of contemporary life. In magazines, newspapers, books, and on radio and TV some psychotherapist or other was forever giving out wise, unquestionable instructions for eating, sleeping, working, thinking, having sex; fixing our society, behavior, attitudes, hopes and dreams; and telling us what to do, when to do it, how to do it, and why we should do it if we ever hoped to live a successful, meaningful, and happy life. One cannot help but wonder why so many individuals would be so willing to turn over the control of their lives to a group of strangers. Sykes's answer is because we have been brainwashed into believing (1) that we are all vaguely guilty of numerous undefined and unspecified sins; (2) that we are individually totally incompetent of deciding future courses of action for ourselves; and (3) science and the scientific medical specialists who can save our bodies from the terror of physical ailments like strokes, cancer, and heart disease can also save our mind and soul from the psychological horrors of anxiety, inadequacy, rejection, and loneliness. In Sykes's words:

> The professionalization of life—turning over larger and larger spheres of human existence to a new class of credentialed experts— seemed a perfectly reasonable response to the increasing complexity of the modern world as well as a recognition of the growing power of the scientific profession to make life more comprehensible and manageable. In particular, the rise of the therapeutic profession seemed to promise access to and understanding of the central preoccupation of the age, the self.[47]

Not only was this not in any way a reasonable response, it was a calamitous mistake and an error that, with a little more thought and a little less anxiety, would never have been made. To assume that either conversation or drugs—or a combination of both—could solve all the problems of human existence and make every life fulfilled and complete is the kind of magical and wishful thinking that has made one class of our citizenry, the therapeutic community, successful and wealthy; and another class, their clients, more miserable and unsettled than they were before they began placing their hopes on the promissory note that someone else could tell them what to think and how to live, and thereby make them happy.

Believe it or not, the vast majority of adults in this highly sensitive and suggestible nation were raised by decent, caring, well-intentioned, and moral parents. They also attended well-run, clean, good-intentioned, and effective schools, who—despite all of the criticism and claims—managed to do a good job of educating their charges and instilling in them the moral middle-class values. Though there are, of course, individual exceptions, in general, the vast majority of the population manage to avoid jail time, support their families, hold a job, and find some joy in daily existence. Most of us are also able to get along with each other without resorting to physical violence and most of us are also able to gain and maintain peace and cooperation with our employers, employees, friends, and family members. Because we are not always perfect at every moment, because there is conflict in every life at certain times, this in no way means that we are sick, victimized, dysfunctional, or in need of psychological repair. Thank God that this is so!

What we need least of all is the steady media drumbeat from TV and radio talk-shows, newspaper headlines, magazine articles, checkout counter newspapers, and pseudoscientific doctors and therapists, masculinists, feminists, and homosexuals waxing wise about abusers and victims and our national dysfunctionalism. As determined as all these sources are to create and maintain a culture of victimization, they *should not* succeed. If the majority of our citizens will look at themselves and their neighbors, and their basically decent communities, the propagandists *will not* succeed. Headlines are attention-getting only because of their rarity. If they were common and ordinary they would not be news. Airplane crashes are sensational because they are so rare. This—shocking as it may seem—is also true of murder, rape, and psychoses. This is *common sense,* a commodity that in this day of media sensationalism and excess seems to be in very short supply.

THE MEDICAL-PHARMACEUTICAL COMPLEX

Whenever one calls attention to a public problem these days, one is immediately branded as a conspiracy theorist or an alarmist. Nevertheless, within the health and mental health establishments there is a problem of which every taxpayer should be aware: the highly profitable relationships among the medical establishment, the pharmaceutical industry, and psychiatric hospitals.

In a recent book, Joe Sharkey, an investigative journalist, exposed "one of the costliest and most insidious medical scandals of recent times: the rapacious advance of the for-profit Mental Health Industry."[48] By the end of the 1980s it had managed to lay claim to about 25 percent of all the money spent by U.S. employers on employee health benefits. During the 1980s, the Recovery Era dictated broader insurance coverage for an ever-growing range of disorders, addictions, and behavioral problems. Investor-owned psychiatric hospitals expanded at a dizzying rate. Using "guerrilla marketing," co-opting the psychiatric professional by hiring clergymen, guidance counselors, and other trusted community figures as bounty hunters, these psychiatric hospitals sought to bring in paying customers for a plethora of "treatment programs." Most seemed to have one thing in common: patients miraculously improved the day their insurance expired. Beyond the horror stories, Sharkey examines the unholy alliance between modern "biopsychiatry" and the hospital, pharmaceutical, and "addiction" industries. It is an alliance that has succeeded in establishing as federal policy the astonishing notion that in any given six-month period more than 20 percent of Americans need professional psychiatric care—and should be covered for it with generous insurance benefits. As new health-care reforms provide for expanded mental-health coverages—in a formula that reflects the lobbying goals of the psychiatric industry—Sharkey blows away the public relations smoke-screen and shows what happens when modern marketing strategies are applied to psychiatric care.

Sharkey got interested in this problem when he discovered he was drinking too much. After trying Alcoholics Anonymous and discovering it was not for him, he looked next at an advertised treatment program at Fair Oaks Hospital in New Jersey. After Sharkey and his wife talked to one of the program personnel about the program and its costs they discovered it would cost a total of $30,000 with no guarantees of success. Moreover, the program director insisted that the entire Sharkey family had to be treated. The scam is called codependency. All members of the family are addicted or codependent on each other therefore *all* must be treated! The Sharkeys told them "No way!" and left. About ten days later they received a bill from Fair Oaks for $385, supposedly for "evaluation and diagnosis." Outraged, but not having the time to get a lawyer and sue, Sharkey sent it to his insurance carrier and they paid the bill. A few days later Sharkey read stories in the newspapers about ethical abuse in private mental hospitals in Texas, Florida, and Alabama and decided the story was worth looking into.

He quickly found that the number of private psychiatric hospitals jumped from 220 in 1984 to 444 in 1988. He also found that by 1990 the United States was spending more on inpatient psychiatric patients than on cancer. Between 1980 and 1987, he learned, the number of children between ten and nineteen years old in psychiatric hospitals increased 43 percent. In Illinois there was a fivefold increase in children admissions. He quickly discovered that in Texas psychiatrists were not only literally "kidnapping" young rebellious children but the hospitals were even paying bounties and bonuses to all the hospital personnel who brought "clients" in. Under the new psychiatric look they are no longer even called patients.

Sharkey also quickly discovered that psychiatric care is the fastest growing segment of health care costs, of which 85 percent now goes to inpatient treatment. Today the United States spends a total of $2,354 annually per citizen on health care, which is double that of each of twenty-four other industrialized nations including, among others, Britain, France, Sweden, and Japan. In looking at the increase in psychiatric care for children alone Sharkey was appalled by what he discovered. It seems that thousands of psychiatrists across the nation forged financial links with these four-hundred-some-odd psychiatric hospitals for profit during the 1960s with the understanding that their "diagnoses" would keep the patient census up. This national conspiracy continued into the 1970s, 1980s, and now into the 1990s. According to Dr. Ira Schwartz, an authority at the University of Michigan on youth policy, this mistreatment of children by these institutions and the "therapists" manning them is "the biggest child welfare scandal of the last fifty years." And, according to the psychiatrist Dr. Walter E. Afield, who has also looked into such practices, "the abuse boggles the mind."[49]

But how and why did such financial finagling and abuse come about?

There is absolutely no doubt that psychiatric profiteering is driven by the lavish liberalization of insurance coverage recently made available by the imperative known as the "Recovery Era." This is the belief that everyone is a victim, that none of us is responsible for his actions and behavior, and that most of us need to be under the care of a behavior expert, a psychiatrist.

In 1970 all health insurers were required by state and federal laws to cover thirty separate benefits. In 1994 this figure topped eight hundred, and psychiatric and substance abuse conditions accounted for over half of that number. The federal government has designated the 1990s as "the Decade of the Brain" and has, accordingly, funneled more research money into biopsychiatry, which is working overtime to establish the mental disorders and emotional disruptions as "physical diseases" that can be cured only by drugs and expensive medical intervention. The modern biopsychiatrists do not recognize the psychological origin of any mental or emotional disorder—they see them all as physical and medical and treatable with a drug. This includes your dislike of your mother-in-law, your unhappiness at failing to get promoted, and your grief over lost loved ones. Take Prozac or a neuroleptic and these will all go away! If this doesn't work then we'll give you several doses of electroshock and that will knock it all out of you! As Sharkey has accurately noted, modern Western concepts of treatment of the mentally disturbed emerged from the Middle Ages and in part reflected the established social order's alarm that people were beginning to think for themselves and undermine prevailing authority. Ever since, moralism, mysticism, pseudoscience, and politics have battled for the soul of psychiatry. Shortly after the beginning of our modern era psychiatrists were told that if they ever expected to amount to anything in the medical establishment they had to "go find people who need help." Moreover, they must become involved with education, social work, the churches, recreation, and the courts. They must integrate psychiatry into general society. Many of them took this as a holy mission and set out to do exactly that. They soon became the all-purpose experts (APEs). In 1946 there were only three thousand psychiatrists, in 1956 their number had risen to ten thousand, and in 1985 they numbered thirty-two thousand. As for their patient population, those they see in private office visits, the amount has shifted from 552,000 in 1955 to only 116,000 in 1984 because of the impact that the Comprehensive Care System and state mental hospitals made in the treatment of the mentally ill.[50] In the early 1960s there were six hundred Comprehensive Care Centers across the nation and they bore the brunt of care for the addicted and disturbed. Because of the difficulties and expenses of staffing and treating the severely disabled in the state hospitals, authorities conceived the brilliant idea that most of their charges could be deinstitutionalized since the narcoleptics were doing such a good job of keeping the dangerous and bizarre patients under tranquilized control. Staffing of the state hospitals became increasingly impossible because although the federally funded psychiatric training programs designed to meet the staffing needs of the state hospitals and care centers continued to grind out the psychiatrists, they all flocked to where the money was—in private practice in upper-middle class neighborhoods. Few, if any, wanted to practice at low-paying jobs where the truly sick and needy were found.

In 1966 Drs. M. Brewster Smith and Nicholas Hobbs reported that "most therapeutic talent trained at public expense has been invested not in treating hard core marginally psychotic people—but in treating the well-to-do worried well."[51] The results of deinstitutionalization succeeded in creating an entire subpopulation of people unable to take care of themselves now known as "street people" who quite literally have nowhere to go. In 1989 office visits to psychiatrists accounted for a mere 2.4 percent of the total 692 million office visits to M.D.s. In 1986, 49 percent of the admissions to private psychiatric hospitals, interestingly enough, were for emotional disorders, with depression leading the pack.[52] Yet institutionalization may not always be the best course of action. Mark Evans and his associates have determined that outpatient cognitive therapy is often much more effective.[53]

Modern organized psychiatry, says Peter Breggin, is a "mishmash of philosophy, psychology, religion, law enforcement and politics as well as social engineering and big business and occasionally science and medicine."[54] Moreover, if modern biopsychiatry has its way, psychiatry will give way to nothing but brain pathology. According to a recent article in the *American Journal of Psychiatry,* the new *Diagnostic and Statistical Manual IV* (DSM-IV) "will finally succeed in erasing the 'unfortunate' distinction that still exists in the lay world between mental disorder and physical disease."[55] God forbid! Nevertheless, because of psychiatric pressure, on January 1, 1990, California became the first state to officially declare that certain mental illnesses are actually biologically based brain diseases. Included are schizophrenia, schizo-affective disorders, bipolar and developmental disorders. The empirical research to support these claims is nonexistent. The medicalization of psychotherapy is in no way a step in the right direction. Instead, it is a move away from understanding and helping people solve the existential problems of human life and a step toward keeping them tranquilized and chemically dependent for the rest of their lives. For the first time in our country's history there is a threat to the nation's sanity and it's coming from the medical-pharmaceutical complex and their determination to make everyone a case file.

The summer 1994 edition of *Dendron,* an antipsychiatric anti-Therapeutic State newsletter, contained information about an eighty-year-old patient in a Chicago-area nursing home. Lucille Austwick, the patient in question, was told by her psychiatrist that her depression and her three-pound weight loss were endangering her life and that the only way he could save her would be to give her electroshock treatment. Not only did Lucille refuse but she said, "If they want to do that let them shock themselves." Her psychiatrist has gone to court to get a court order forcing her to take the treatment.[56] Have we now come to the point where no matter what the physician prescribes for us, we must comply and follow his demands? If I were the judge in Lucille's case I would rule that the psychiatrist receive the electroshock treatment since, obviously, he is the one who is psychotic. If one looks at any of the popular magazines lately, for example, *Time, Newsweek,* or *People,* one can't help but notice the full-page ads for all sorts of new medications aimed at making things better for all of us poor slobs. Many psychiatrists are now firmly convinced that the best thing they can do for us is to see to it that every man, woman, and child in the country is placed on a regimen of Prozac. Again, God forbid!

Dr. Philip Gold, chief of the neuroendocrinology branch of the National Institute of Mental Health, also considers this idea preposterous. Gold is adamantly opposed to the use of Prozac as "a psychic vitamin" to pep up a normal personality. In Gold's words, "People whose arousal systems are not perturbed do not respond to these agents. The idea that healthy people who take Prozac feel better is absolutely ridiculous."[57] Gold also is opposed to the idea set forth by some psychiatrists that drugs will someday solve all of life's problems.

He states, "To respond to the loss of a loved one or a cherished dream casually is grotesque. To 'feel better' means to feel one's feelings better, including sadness or anger, without getting stuck in them."[58]

SCIENCE VERSUS PSYCHOTHERAPY

A rather naive and silly therapeutic technique labeled Eye-Movement Desensitization and Reprocessing (EMDR) has recently entered the therapeutic armory and typifies the rapidly growing split between psychology as a science and psychotherapy as superstitious folklore. During a clinical EMDR session, clients who are victims of traumatic experiences and phobias are seated before the therapist and are told to visualize themselves during the trauma and think about the negative feelings it created for them (for example, helplessness or hopelessness). They are then asked what they would rather feel about themselves. Next, they are asked to think about their emotional reactions to the trauma and to notice their physical reactions to their emotions. All of these things are kept in mind while watching the therapist's finger move rapidly left and right about eighteen inches in front of their face. After about fifty finger-movement cycles clients take a deep breath and talk about the traumatic event. Francine Shapiro, the treatment's inventor and guru, claims that EMDR can do in five or six sessions what other treatment methods take four or five times longer to accomplish. In this day and age, of course, it's a godsend. Insurance companies love it. Shapiro has a nonresearch Ph.D. degree from the Professional School for Psychological Studies in San Diego, which no longer exists. Although several preliminary studies suggest the EMDR is no more effective than the same kind of treatment without the eye movement, Shapiro and other true believers argue later research will vindicate their faith.

One critic notes that "EMDR exposes a large and expanding rift separating the science of psychology and the practice of psychotherapy, an emerging class struggle between the research-literate and the practically trained. EMDR is a highly charged technique that splits the nation's increasingly troubled psychotherapeutic enterprise cleanly in two."[59] On one side are the research-trained psychologists who are schooled in methods of critical analysis and reserve judgment about new therapies until they have been submitted to controlled studies. On the other side are the clinically trained with no scientific background. They not only ignore and ridicule science but consider it irrelevant to their practice. The scientifically trained "find EMDR embarrassing—not because it doesn't work, but because there is no acceptable proof that it does. It exposes psychology to the potential for ridicule."[60]

Neil Jacobson, a University of Washington research psychologist, avers, "There are lots of claims but no data. People should not be allowed to make claims that go beyond what we know. The overselling of this procedure can be harmful. It's very easy to perform. That's part of its elegance. That's also part of what makes people nervous."[61]

Ironically, what is sparking most of the interest in EMDR has nothing to do with memory but more with the psychotherapist's fear of the impact of managed care on their survival. They have to appear successful in a hurry if they are going to be paid by the insurance companies. This is why many therapists have begun to apply EMDR to everything, not just post traumatic stress disorders (PTSD) and phobias. Now they are using it for panic attacks, attention deficit disorder, depression, addictions, and malaise of any sort. Anything that makes us confront our fears, face them, and emotionally defuse them by talking or writing about them will work to our benefit and finger waving has nothing to do with any therapeutic effects. Positive expectations and talking about the problem are also helpful for some people. The following quote perfectly describes what's wrong with EMDR:

> In performing EMDR, therapists keep from patients the knowledge that the hand waving is a decoy, that they have and always have had the ability to do the chasing down and memory editing of it, on their own.
>
> So the technique cultivates and reproduces powerlessness. It does this to therapists in selling them by testimonials. But mostly, it employs deception to keep clients powerless—and so it perpetuates the culture of victimhood. I feel ethically bruised just watching therapists apply a procedure that embodies the very thing—dependence, powerlessness—they are supposed to be treating.[62]

As we shall see in the pages ahead, the major problem with psychotherapy in general is that it is, much too often, counterproductive, destructive, and habit-forming.

NOTES

1. Jonas Robitscher, *The Powers of Psychiatry* (Boston: Houghton Mifflin, 1980); and David Hill, *The Politics of Schizophrenia: Psychiatric Oppression in the United States* (Lanham, Md.: University of Maryland Press, 1983).

2. Bernie Zilbergeld, *The Shrinking of America: Myths of Psychological Change* (Boston: Little, Brown & Co., 1983).

3. Stanton Peele, *Diseasing of America: Addiction Treatment Out of Control* (Lexington, Mass.: Lexington Books, 1989).

4. Richard Hughes and Robert Brewin, *The Tranquilizing of America: Pill Popping and the American Way of Life* (New York: Warner Books, 1980).

5. Daniel Goleman, "More Than 1 in 4 US Adults Suffers a Mental Disorder Each Year," *New York Times*, 17 March 1993, p. B1.

6. Darrel A. Regier et al., "The De Facto US Mental and Addictive Disorders Service System," *Archives of General Psychiatry* 50 (February 1993): 85–94.

7. Goleman, "More Than 1 in 4 US Adults," p. 1.

8. Regier et al., "The De Facto US Mental and Addictive Disorders Service System."

9. Ronald C. Kessler et al., "Lifetime and 12-Month Prevalence of DSM-III-R Psychiatric Disorders in the United States: Results from the National Comorbidity Survey," *Archives of General Psychiatry* 51 (January 1994): 8–19.

10. William E. Narrow, D. A. Regier, and D. S. Roe, "Use of Services by Persons with Mental and Addictive Disorders," *Archives of General Psychiatry* 50 (February 1993): 95–107

11. James I. Hudson and H. G. Pope, Jr., "Affective Spectrum Disorder: Does Antidepressant Response Identify a Family of Disorders with a Common Pathophysiology?" *American Journal of Psychiatry* 147, no. 5 (May 1990): 552–63.

12. Leslie Ansley, "What's Next?" *USA Weekend*, 1–3 October 1993, p. 18.

13. *Louisville Courier Journal*, 4 May 1994, p. A8.

14. John Griest, James Jefferson, and Isaac Marbs, *Anxiety and Its Treatment* (Washington, D.C.: American Psychiatric Press, 1986).

15. Edith Fiore, *The Unquiet Dead: A Psychologist Treats Spirit Possession* (New York: Ballantine, 1988), p. 123.

16. Edith Fiore, *Encounters* (New York: Doubleday, 1989), pp. 322–23.

17. Pfizer Company, double-page advertisement, *Time*, 21 March 1994.

18. Edward M. Hallowell and John J. Rotey, *Driven to Distraction* (New York: Pantheon Books, 1994).

19. Robert Sherrill, "Medicine and the Madness of the Market," *Nation* 260, no. 2 (January 9 and 16, 1995): 45–72.

20. See George F. Drinka, *The Birth of Neurosis: Myth, Malady, and the Victorians* (New York: Touchstone Books, 1984); Janet Gotkin and Paul Gotkin, *Too Much Anger, Too Many Tears: A Personal Triumph over Psychiatry* (New York: Quadrangle, 1992); and Peter Breggin, *Toxic Psychiatry* (New York: St. Martin's Press, 1991).

21. Zilbergeld, *The Shrinking of America*.

22. Ibid., p. 3.

23. Ibid., pp. 195–96.

24. Ibid., p. 202.

25. Ibid., p. 263.

26. Ibid., p. 221.

27. Jerome Frank, *Persuasion and Healing: A Comparative Study of Psychotherapy* (New York: Shocken Books, 1963), p. 102.

28. Zilbergeld, *The Shrinking of America*, p. 276.

29. Ibid., pp. 276–77.

30. Andrew Christensen and Neil S. Jacobson, "Who (Or What) Can Do Psychotherapy?" *Psychological Science* 5, no. 1 (January 1994): 10.

31. T. W. Campbell, "Psychotherapy and Malpractice Exposure," *American Journal of Psychology* 12, no. 1 (1994): 5–41.

32. Catherine Johnson, *When to Say Goodby to Your Therapist* (New York: Simon & Schuster, 1988).

33. Staff, "Psychiatric Disorders and Use of Mental Health Services," *Harvard Mental Health Newsletter* (Cambridge: Harvard University Press, 1993).

34. Ibid.

35. The books are *Bradshaw on: The Family* (Deerfield Beach, Fla.: Health Communications Inc., 1988); *Healing the Shame That Binds You* (Deerfield Beach, Fla.: Health Communications Inc., 1989); and *Homecoming: Reclaiming and Championing Your Inner Child* (New York: Bantam Books, 1992).

36. Bradshaw, *Homecoming*.

37. Ibid.

38. John Rosemond, "Helping Professionals [Are] Turning Us into a Nation of Whiners," *Lexington Herald Leader*, 19 September 1993, p. 3.

39. Wendy Kaminer, *I'm Dysfunctional, You're Dysfunctional* (New York: Vintage Books, 1992), p. 27.

40. Rosemond, "Helping Professionals [Are] Turning Us into a Nation of Whiners."

41. Stanley J. Katz and Aimee Liu, *The Codependency Conspiracy* (New York: Warner Books, 1991), p. 16.

42. Donald Goodwin, "A Psychiatrist Discusses Creative Writers and Alcohol," *Philadelphia Inquirer*, 2 January 1989, p. B1.

43. Charles J. Sykes, *A Nation of Victims: The Decay of the American Character* (New York: St. Martin's Press, 1992), p. 143.

44. John Bradshaw, *Creating Love: The Next Stage of Growth* (New York: Bantam Books, 1992), p. 32.

45. Lynne Namka, *The Doormat Syndrome* (Deerfield Beach, Fla.: Health Communications Inc., 1989), p. 152.

46. Sykes, *A Nation of Victims*, p. 37.

47. Ibid., p. 42.

48. Joe Sharkey, *Bedlam: Greed, Profiteering, and Fraud in a Mental Health System Gone Crazy* (New York: St. Martin's Press, 1994).

49. All are cited in Sharkey, *Bedlam: Greed, Profiteering, and Fraud*.

50. Ibid., p. 28.

51. M. Brewster Smith and Nicholas Hobbs, "Assessment of Professional Staffing Problems in Comprehensive Mental Health Centers (CMHC)," cited in *Nowhere to Go*, by E. Fuller Torrey (New York: Harper & Row, 1988), pp. 168–70.

52. Torrey, *Nowhere to Go*, and William E. Narrow et al., "Use of Services by Persons with Mental and Addictive Disorders," *Archives of General Psychiatry* 50 (February 1993): 95–107.

53. Mark D. Evans et al., "Differential Relapse Following Cognitive Therapy and Pharmacotherapy for Depression," *Archives of General Psychiatry* 49 (October 1992): 802–808.

54. Breggin, *Toxic Psychiatry*, Introduction.

55. Nancy C. Andreasen, "Changing Concepts of Schizophrenia and the Ahistorical Fallacy" (editorial on DSM-IV), *American Journal of Psychiatry* 151, no. 10 (October 1994): 1405–1407.

56. "Lucille Austwick Sparks National Campaign," *Dendron* no. 35 (Summer 1994): 1 and 3.

57. Cited in W. Gallagher, "How We Become What We Are," *Atlantic Monthly* 268, no. 9 (September 1994): 54.

58. Ibid., p. 55.

59. Hara E. Marano, "Wave of the Future," *Psychology Today* (July/ August 1994): 22.

60. Ibid., p. 23.

61. Ibid., p. 25.

62. Ibid.

2

The Short, Sorry History
of Psychotherapy

Mental healing and the religious spirit were inextricably mixed in their psychological origins. The healing arts have never lost their overtones of magic and supernaturality in the inner experience of the patient. For modern man, as for the preliterate, to heal is to assume the role of some great, extrahuman being, to partake of the larger spirit that religion has caught and structured into specific faiths.

Walter Bromberg[1]

According to Walter Bromberg,

Psychotherapy antedates psychiatry; the history of psychotherapy is the story of *doing* as opposed to *thinking* about doing. It developed around personal and social needs to do something for the distraught, the obsessed, the deluded. In answering urgent cries for help . . . psychotherapy became involved with religion, faith healing, occultism, self-help, and the euphoria of personality enlargement.[2]

Unfortunately all of these illogical, unscientific approaches to mental healing are still with us today. In fact, there is ample historical evidence to indicate that over the years the antiscientific forces have literally inundated and overwhelmed the few respectable scientific efforts that have been made to make psychotherapy a valid and reliable science based on experimental and empirical evidence.

The history of man's unsuccessful and sorry efforts to deal with his mental problems is well documented but, unfortunately, seldom read. Moreover, its message has never been received or acted upon. We have learned little from our misguided efforts in the name of healing and despite our vaunted scientific progress what few scientific contributions have been made to mental health have all been in neurology, that is, in *physical* health not *mental*. The assumption that *all* mental health is *all* physical health is a catastrophic mistake and a glaring failure to understand the basic nature of the human being.

Here, in summarizing and condensing this sordid story of stupidity, cruelty, and malpractice I have relied heavily on a number of standard histories of medicine, psychiatry, and psychology.[3] Students of the history of psychotherapy are urged to consult the original sources rather than to depend upon my summaries. Moreover, because of space limitations one cannot be comprehensive. Any serious errors and omissions as well as interpretations of the value and meaning of past practices are, of course, my own and not those of the other interpreters and historians.

Although the beginning of mental healing is buried in the mire of time and in the occult mud of magic and religion, many of the principles and practices then employed are still in use today. The oldest profession is that of the shaman, the medicine man—not the prostitute—and the shaman worked his magic through the use of amulets, charms, words, and ritual. Mesopotamian and Egyptian priests were, perhaps, the first psychotherapists in that they mixed sound advice and magic, which consisted of charms and incantations, in equal proportions for the drawing out of demons. Magical thinking was perhaps the first therapeutic principle and it is interesting to note that such belief is still a powerful force today, not only in nonliterate and primitive cultures, but also in the modern clinic where drugs, machines, and diplomas on the wall inspire the essential elements of belief and faith. Magical thinking is also very much alive and well in the public arena as well as in the clinic, and continues to be a part of the modern psychotherapist's arsenal. Without its presence he would have neither clients nor success. Like the shaman of old, the effectiveness of all modern psychotherapists depends as much upon the accepted norms and beliefs of his culture as it ever will upon his own personal skill as a healer.

It is fascinating to note that, as of old, the magic of words—a powerful weapon against demonic spirits—is equally as potent today. The modern psychotherapist has only two primary procedures: talk (advice) and pills (medicine), foregoing for the moment electroconvulsive shock therapy (ECT) and psychosurgery. While little historical evidence exists for the ancient use of electricity on the brain, ample evidence exists for primitive surgical procedures, including the bashing of holes in heads—purportedly to let out the demons. For example, skulls found in the ruins of ancient Peruvian cultures have holes drilled through them (trepanning) to allow the demons to escape.

Ancient cabalistic philosophy, which was based on a mystical interpretation of the Scriptures by medieval Jewish rabbis, believed the secret of the universe lay in the mysterious power of "the word." The symbol "Rx" atop the prescription blank is derived from a symbol of prayer to Jupiter. Many contemporary psychiatrists, and psychoanalysts in particular, hold similar convictions. The magic of words quickly evolved into the magic of charms, amulets, and talismans. In the medieval medicine of Paracelsus precious stones were assumed to have magical properties just as they are believed to have equal powers by the New Agers currently writing books about the healing powers of crystals.

A smidgen of rationality did begin to enter the healing practices of Aesculapian physicians during Roman times. They invented the practice of using dreams as the vehicle through which the patient could contact Aesculapius (the Roman god of healing) directly and have him beseech the gods to cure the ailment or prescribe a treatment. Ventriloquism was frequently employed by the attending priests to insure that the client's spirit succeeded in conversing with the god. Dream interpretation also began here. "Temple sleep" was used to diagnose the nature of illnesses and to forecast the future. Long preceding Sigmund Freud, Artemidoros of Daldianus used free association—his own, however—to interpret the meaning of dreams. Similar techniques were used at the site of the oracles.

Hippocrates, the father of medicine, opposed the use of amulets and charms and considered them vulgar. He believed all diseases came from natural sources—even epilepsy, which was thought of as a sacred disease. Although he believed that hysteria was due to the movement of the womb (the hysteron) through the body and prescribed a tight bandage round the abdomen as a cure for hysterical paroxysms (as well as the piping of warm vapors into the vagina), he was amazingly prescient in many of his notions about the behavioral disorders.

Mental problems were also noted by the Greek philosophers. Plato believed mental problems were partly physical, partly moral, and partly divine, arguing that incantations as well as medicines could effect cures. Even though Greek medicine declined, Alexandrian physicians made great advances in our knowledge of anatomy, physiology, pathology, and medicine. Although Rome was skeptical of Greek medicine and held its practitioners in contempt, physicians such as Asclepiades convinced such famous patients as Mark Anthony and Cicero of its virtues. Of all these medicine men, Celsus (25 B.C.E.–50 C.E.) was one who prescribed specifically for psychopathology, recommending the poisonous black hellebore for depression and white hellebore for mania. Yet like all shrinks, before and since, for delusional patients Celsus recommended the most stringent measures:

> If however, it is the mind that deceives the madman, he is best treated by certain tortures. When he says or does anything wrong, he is to be coerced by starvation, fetters and flogging. He is to be forced both to fix his attention and to learn something and to memorize it; for thus . . . little by little he will be forced by fear to consider what he is doing. . . . To be thoroughly frightened is beneficial in this illness and so, in general, is anything which thoroughly agitates the spirit.[4]

Despite the works of Celsus and Galen (a Greek physician who lived 130–200 C.E.), few medical men were interested in the mental disorders and it took the ascendancy of Christianity to give rise to a humane attitude toward the mentally disturbed. Unfortunately, even here, woven into the Christian doctrine, were the pagan notions of demons and demon possession. Aretaeus, a Greek physician of the second century C.E. nevertheless practiced "rational" medicine and urged humane treatment of the disturbed. Rational therapy placed an emphasis on bodily hygiene and in religious faith healing. Jesus, for example, cast out devils. The laying on of hands and the use of oil as a healing agent via purification is found throughout both the Old and New Testaments.[5]

During the Dark Ages all mental disorders were seen as the work of demons. Nervous disorders such as hysteria ceased to be diseases and became the work of black magic and witchcraft. The Church became the therapeutic agent and was responsible for driving Satan away from those possessed. Followers of St. Augustine practiced a humane form of treatment for the possessed and in the twelfth and thirteenth centuries within the monasteries and nunneries the mentally retarded and the disturbed were treated with both tenderness and concern.

Perhaps the very first hospital devoted to mental patients exclusively was the colony established in Gheel, Belgium, in the thirteenth century. Centered in a shrine, the colony at Gheel emphasized tender care, and providing food, rest, and spiritual calm for the disturbed. The emphasis was on providing help through physical and mental channels with no mention of demonology. In 1275, Bartholomew, a Franciscan friar, wrote a book dealing with mental illness and recommended diet, music, and sleep as the treatment of the mentally ill. Meanwhile, all around him witchcraft flourished and the demented and deluded were tortured and maimed.[6]

From this medieval healing stew—a mixture of demonology and alchemy—emerged in the sixteenth century the itinerant physician Paracelsus (1443–1541), who prescribed a number of medications for the mentally ill. He also dallied with astrology and magnetism, the forerunners of mesmerism, hypnosis, and suggestion. Paracelsus challenged the notion that "the healing touch" was the exclusive property of kings. The shifting of faith healing from kings to laymen, however, received its greatest emphasis, of course, during the Renaissance.

Witchcraft, demonology, and satanism became a cause during the medieval years. The nobility as well as the peasants and clergy believed in the magic and malevolence of the devil. His works were seen everywhere in disease, pestilence, and all human disorders. If they were not *his* doings directly, then they were due to his minions: incubi and succubi (demons thought to lie on sleeping women and men, respectively, with whom they sought sexual intercourse) and witches. To discover, apprehend, and convict witches and sorcerers an authoritative guide was needed. To meet this need, in 1484 two priests, Henry Kramer and James Sprenger, published the *Malleus Maleficarum* or *The Witches' Hammer.*[7] This book served as the inquisitor's Bible for over two centuries.

Divided into three parts, the *Malleus* defined how God allows devils to exist and to inhabit and possess man as well as to define acts of witchcraft and how to obtain confessions from the possessed through torture. Signs of demonic possession are spelled out and techniques for treatment—exorcisms—are stated in detail. Considerable space is devoted to cases of witchcraft by learned doctors who hoped to help others in their diagnoses. Feigning madness was but one of the signs as well as scars and blemishes, which were seen as the Devil's or witch's marks.

With the help of the *Malleus,* witch hunting became a medicolegal science. Medieval medical records explained how many mysterious illnesses were cured by the willingness of the demon to admit he was inhabiting and tormenting the body of the patient. Since the more physical ailments were left to the physicians, it is not surprising that the clergy would be left to deal with the spiritual or mental disorders. Those of unsound mind were obviously plagued by demons.

During the sixteenth and seventeenth centuries the birth of mathematics, astronomy, and the other sciences, along with the invention of the printing press, collectively, began to have an effect on belief in demons and witches. In the fifteenth century, for example, only about six items on neuropsychiatric medicine appeared; in the sixteenth approximately 250 items were noted; in the seventeenth 1,800 items appeared; and in the eighteenth century the number increased to three thousand items.[8] Even during the Renaissance, however, psychotherapy was a confused mixture of religion, folklore, and medical science. Although Robert Burton, author of *The Anatomy of Melancholy,* urged humane treatment of the deranged,[9] medical knowledge was in such a poor state that King Charles II was literally tortured to death by his bevy of physicians:

> In 1685 Charles II fell ill of kidney disease and began to experience convulsions. For the next five days a parade of doctors—as many as twelve during the day and six at night—tried out their ideas on his progressively deteriorating body.

First they began by bleeding him. . . . Then they cut off his hair, put blistering agents on his scalp, and applied plasters of pitch and pigeon dung to the bottoms of his feet. After this they blew the offensive-smelling herb hellebore up his nostrils so that he would sneeze and thereby release the humors from his brain. After that they poured antimony [a metallic element used in medical compounds] and sulfate of zinc down his throat so that he would throw up and cleanse his insides. To clean out his bowels, they administered purgatives. And to stop the convulsions, they gave him spirit of human skull.

All the while this was going on, they periodically administered juleps for spasms, a gargle for sore throat, liquids to quench his thirst, tonics for his heart, and beer and broth for food. Sedatives, laxatives, herbs like cowslip and mint, even bezoar (a concoction found chiefly in the alimentary organs of cud-chewing animals and believed to be an antidote for poison)—all were given to the royal patient. As further precaution he was not allowed to sleep or talk. Not only physicians but priests, ministers, and servants entered the royal chamber to be of assistance. Finally, on the fifth day, the doctors drew twelve more ounces of the king's blood and gave him more heart tonics. This seemed to do the trick. By noon Charles II was dead.

In summing up the monarch's royal treatment at the hands of his physicians, Thomas Babington Macaulay, the nineteenth-century English historian and statesman, declared that the doctors had tortured the king like an Indian at the stake.[10]

Fortunately, there were a few courageous, wiser heads who began to speak out against the old superstitions. One of these was Reginald Scot, who in 1584 earned the wrath of King James I by publishing *The Discoveries of Witchcraft.*[11] In this book Scot attacked the superstitions surrounding witchcraft and insisted on natural explanations for the alleged supernatural events. Instead of torture, Scot insisted the poor bedeviled needed food, kindness, and medical attention. He was particularly hard on the theory of incubi and succubi and their sexual molestations, arguing it was human behavior not demonic that accounted for pregnant nuns and such. Scot was not a medical man and was more interested in justice than in uncovering the psychological basis of witchcraft. He was not alone in his appeal to sanity; both

Paracelsus and Agrippa attacked the alleged disease of demonology. Johann Weyer also exposed the fallacies of demonology and studied cases of alleged demonic possession. He was one of the first to insist that patients be treated as individuals with emotional needs. As for incubi and succubi attacks, Weyer explained them as nightmares due to the combined effects of indigestion and imagination. One medical historian stated that Weyer was talking like a rational human being to the inmates of a gigantic insane asylum and undoubtedly with the same amount of success. Zilboorg calls Weyer "the first psychiatrist" and one who was able to solve, using psychiatric principles, cases the medieval world attributed to demons.[12]

Early in the eighteenth century the French encyclopedists*—as well as Voltaire and Rousseau—inveighed against demonology and mocked the clergy, insisting that belief in witchcraft was itself a form of madness. And, by the middle of the eighteenth century most medical authorities held that there were no demons and that melancholy, mania, or diseases were the true causes of human mental disturbance, not demonic possession.

In 1769, the British physician William Cullen stated in his book *First Lines of the Practice of Physick,* "we do not allow that there is any true demon mania. . . . In my opinion the species [of demon mania] . . . are melancholy or mania, feigned diseases or diseases falsely lived by spectators."[13] Robert Whytt, a contemporary of Cullen's, even went so far as to attribute incubi and succubi attacks to indigestion. In his words, "I shall just remark that a plethora, as well as other causes may so affect the nerves of the stomach as to give rise to the incubus."[14]

Both intellectualism and humanitarianism in the eighteenth century replaced the supernaturalism of the earlier years and Cullen was the first to state the "neurosis" theory of disease. He believed that disorders that did not depend on physical conditions such as infections or tumors were due to "nervous power." Cullen divided all diseases into

---

*The encyclopedists were primarily *philosophes* of the Enlightenment who wrote articles for inclusion in the first *Encyclopedia,* which was edited by Denis Diderot and Jean d'Alembert. The *Encyclopedia* helped spread the Enlightenment throughout Europe by setting forth the most advanced critical ideas in religion, government, and philosophy of the time. As well as being critical, the articles were distinctly secular and focused on humanity and its well-being rather than on divine law.

four classes: febrile diseases (fevers), nervous conditions (tics), wasting disease (weight loss), and local diseases (infections). Following up on the early work of students of the nerve tracts and nerve impulses, Cullen attributed some disorders to "motions in the animal economy," nerve impulses. These early notions, along with the work of the anatomists, eventually led to the science of neurology. Cullen, unfortunately, was unable to correlate his "neurosis" theory with a matching therapy and agreed with Hippocrates that the wandering uterus and ovaries rose to the brain and caused the convulsions that ended in hysteria. Cullen, nevertheless, clearly recognized the need for a psychology and a neurology in all clinical practice. At this time, also, an obscure French physician looking at nymphomania suggested that "one of the principal points to which a physician ought to attach himself is the study of the effects of the imagination . . . the mother of the greater part of the passions and of their excesses."[15] The intellectual atmosphere at this time was scientifically rather than theologically oriented and an antisupernatural climate of opinion prevailed among most clinicians in England, France, and Germany.

Oddly enough, it was the pseudoscience of Franz Gall's craniology and phrenology that led to the birth of neurology, psychiatry, and psychotherapy. Gall, also called "the First Quack," studied the differences in convolution between the brains of animals and human beings and reasoned, correctly, that the differences in mental capacity were in direct proportion to the quantity of convolutional gray matter. Gall was one of the first to show that the lack of gray matter in idiots accounted for their low mentality. His conviction that higher mental functioning was related to cortical convolutions and various concavities and convexities of the skull led him to phrenology, the science of temperament, character, and intellectual powers and an early type of constitutional psychiatry (which focused on the physical body). Hailed as a genius by many physicians, Gall—with his strongest supporter, Spurzheim—spread the word that one could tell one's fortune by his head shape. Gall and Spurzheim soon became controversial figures. Most of the French medical world took Gall and his phrenology seriously. Philippe Pinel, however, questioned Gall's location of the seat of insanity. Pinel wanted Gall to explain how exaggeration of the various faculties of the brain could cause insanity when, for example, the hypochondriac's disorder was in the nerves of the stomach. Following the Emperor Napoleon's dismissal of Gall's contentions as nonsense, from 1810 onward most French physicians lost interest in Gall's idea that our mental faculties lay under the bumps on our skulls and Spurzheim's supportive ideas that psychological faculties were distributed through various parts of the head and body.

The correlative fad of physiognomy, invented by the Swiss theologian Johann Casper Lavater in the late 1700s, argued that all human psychological traits are reflected in the face. Lavater also designed elaborate instruments for measuring the face and brow, for obtaining outlines of the head and face, and for relating facial features to personality types. Lavater's work *Fragments on Physiognomy* was published in 1775.[16]

During the latter part of the eighteenth century and the early part of the nineteenth a number of physiologists and anatomists zeroed in on the brain and nervous system and developed the nascent science of neurology. The work of Luigi Galvani, Charles Bell, François Magendie, and others vastly increased our knowledge of the brain and human behavior. In 1816 Johann Herbart argued for the existence of "mental processes" rather than "faculties" and Herbert Spencer posited the Darwinist notion that nervous and mental processes were adaptive via the mechanism of evolution. Out of the field of neurology which developed from 1850 to 1900 came many contributions to the early beginnings of clinical psychotherapy. Strokes were discriminated from *tabes dorsalis* (syphilitic loss of motor control), spinal muscular atrophy from neuritis (inflammation of the nerves), and multiple sclerosis from Parkinson's disease. Unfortunately, hundreds of other complaints remained unidentified and unclassified. Morbid fears, sexual impotence, neurasthenia, and the ever present "hysteria" were terms universally used to cover a lack of understanding. Although hysteria was largely confined to the female gender, Jean Charcot pointed to hysterical symptoms among men. Physicians working the Civil War battlefields also noted a number of psychiatric casualties among soldiers on the front lines. In 1869 Beard described a complex of symptoms consisting of

> dilated pupils, sick headache, pressure pain in the head, irritable eye
> (asthenopsis), noises in the ears; atonic voices, concentration inabil-

ity; irritability, hopelessness, morbid fear (authro-phobo-claustro-phobia, etc.); blushing, insomnia; tenderness of teeth; dyspepsia; sweating and dryness of skin; spinal hyperesthesia; palpitations; spasms; dysphagia; exhaustion; neuralgias; sexual disabilities; yawning; impotence, etc.[17]

Beard's treatment based on the idea of "nervous exhaustion" for this malady was, of course, purely medical and consisted of arsenic, caffeine, ergot (for congestion of the brain and spinal cord), blisters, phosphates, chloral (a sedative), belladonna, calomel (a laxative), and baths. Beard also added electrotherapy to this regimen since, from the days of Benjamin Franklin, electricity had been recommended for stimulant of the nerves and improvement of blood circulation. Leyden jars, and faradic and galvanic currents were widely used to treat hysterics and melancholiacs. Electricity—delivered to the head—was employed in English hospitals for the treatment of migraine, deafness, and other nerve diseases as early as 1767.[18] It is little wonder, therefore, that it is still used and recommended today. Treatment by electricity competed with baths (hydrotherapy) for neurasthenics and hysterics. Along with the inevitable "tonics," hydrotherapy and electricity were the major psychotherapeutic treatments at this time.

S. Weir Mitchell, perhaps the first American psychiatrist, also was a believer in and supporter of the idea of nervous exhaustion. In a remarkable little book titled *Wear and Tear, or Hints for the Overworked,* Mitchell reminded the public, in simple down-to-earth language, that brain fatigue and nervous exhaustion were preventable diseases susceptible to a hygienic regimen of rest and relaxation that eliminated stress.[19] In a second popular work, *Fat and Blood,* Mitchell answered all the therapeutic questions surrounding hysteria and neurasthenia with his widely celebrated "rest cure."[20] According to Mitchell, the sufferer must be restrained and rebuilt. Isolation is paramount, followed by rest and wholesome and nourishing food. Removal from the morbid surroundings in which the illness developed and flourished is the first step. The second is removal from contact with relatives and having only one nurse in attendance, preferably one emotionally indifferent to the family. This was one of the first clear recognitions of the role of the emotions in mental disorders and recognition as to how the hysteric feeds upon the attention and adulation received from others in the environment. Mitchell's rest cure became very popular both in the United States and abroad and found its way into the textbooks in 1880. The importance of suggestion and the psychosocial environment (i.e., the influence of people and surroundings) displaced the rest cure in psychotherapeutic thinking in the early 1900s.

ASYLUMS? OR TORTURE CHAMBERS?

No history of psychotherapy, no matter how brief, can afford to neglect the role and influence of those public institutions wherein society housed and houses its simpleminded, incompetent, and deranged. Although such as these were treated humanely in the medieval monasteries, this was not the case for the majority of the disturbed in the cities and towns of Europe from the fourteenth through the eighteenth centuries. To be considered mad was to be considered either inhuman or possessed. The mad were also considered totally insensitive to pain and changes in temperature and it was also generally believed they had to be confined and physically restrained.

Even today the majority of people think of a mental hospital as the place where we put crazy people or a bin where we keep the nuts. Like the majority of psychotherapists they conceive of the disturbed as being mentally ill or having a sickness of the brain. They think of disturbed people as not knowing anything or being unable to remember anything or use their minds. The mentally ill are objects of derision to be gawked at and made fun of and even talked about in their presence. Very few people understand that what the therapist really means when he uses the term "mental illness" has nothing whatsoever to do with the intellect or capacity to think. Rather, it concerns the patient's emotional life. The term "emotional hospital" should be substituted for "mental hospital" because the former is much more accurate. People who come for treatment are suffering from *emotional* disorders. Since the emotions are, of course, intimately connected with the physical body and since the mind and body closely interact, it is imperative that the needs of the entire person be attended to.

Typical of the medieval madhouses in the fourteenth century was

London's Bethlehem's Hospital, which began to admit the deranged in 1403. Generally known as "Bedlam," this institution quickly became the place where the dregs of London's population—lesser criminals, beggars, prostitutes, and the mentally retarded—were confined. These people were known as lunatics, since they were supposedly under the influence of the moon or "luna" and therefore were not responsible for their conduct. In Cuba even today natives in the interior will not go out on moonlit nights unless they carry an umbrella to protect themselves from the moon's beams. Who knows what strange malady the moon may impart?

Bedlam was a place for punishment rather than asylum. The hospital was operated for profit and every Sunday, for a shilling each, the cream of London society could visit the inmates and were allowed to gawk at, tease, and torment them. The conditions at Bedlam were abominable: the inmates were crowded together four or more to a small, narrow cell whose floor was covered by a dirty sack of straw. Vermin crawled everywhere. Hordes of rats ran across the floors at night feasting on the inmate's food and clothes and occasionally the flesh of the inmates themselves. Inmates who were deranged were naked, fettered and/or chained to the walls, and beaten by the brutal attendants several times a day. Under such horrendous conditions if any inmate had an ounce of sanity at the time of admission, it was soon erased and replaced by madness—delusions and hallucinations—the only avenues of escape from such a physical hell.

Conditions at Bedlam were typical of those at other asylums across Europe. There were, however, a few rare exceptions. The Spanish asylums at Valencia, Granada, Barcelona, and Zaragosa for example, treated their patients with kindness as did a few isolated institutions in Italy during the sixteenth century. No real change in the treatment of the poor and deranged, however, took place until Philippe Pinel started a therapeutic revolution during the second year of the French Revolution. Pinel, a quiet, retiring, and studious country doctor, while working in a private sanitarium in Paris, decided to apply to the insane the same principles of liberty, fraternity, and equality that marked the political revolution. Pinel enlisted the help of the Commissioner of Public Safety and Pierre Cabanis, physician to Vicomte

Mirabeau, and in 1793 drew up a plan to change the conditions in the lunatic asylum at Bicêtre. Following his appointment as chief physician, Pinel ordered the warden to unchain all the inmates, remove patients from dungeons, halt their beatings, clean away all refuse, and fumigate the cells. Improved food and drink was served and the nurses and attendants were ordered to treat all inmates with kindness and respect. Violence in any form was absolutely forbidden. The results were amazing. Inmates who hadn't talked or communicated in years became talkative and human again. Humane management and administration became the goal of Pinel's moral treatment plan. The new approach worked, and Pinel became famous and was shortly elected a member of the Institute of France and awarded a full professorship at the Salpetriere School of Medicine in 1803. Not only did Pinel inspire all of his students and other physicians who came to hear him, but as France's foremost alienist, Napoleon called upon him to investigate Franz Gall's claims. Pinel took Gall's techniques to the Bicêtre and tried to determine which types of skulls were predisposed to insanity. Pinel was unable to match Gall's charts with the skulls of the insane and, therefore, he had no choice but to denounce Gall's work as fraudulent. In spite of Pinel's efforts to make medicine as scientific as other branches of natural history, he soon ran into political difficulties. He was accused of being a royalist, lost his professorship and finished his life in obscurity. His insistence on humane treatment of the insane was, however, a beacon of sanity and hope in a vast wilderness of stupidity and horror.[21]

Another instance of human reason was shown in 1791 by the Englishman William Tuke, a York Quaker who, with his son Henry, began to investigate lunatic asylums in his area. Tuke was amazed and horrified by what he found. At St. Luke's Hospital, for example, he found that mental patients were coerced, beaten and bound, or neglected. When Tuke saw one young woman chained to a wall lying half nude on some loose, filthy straw, her body crusted with excreta, her hair matted, and a blank expression on her face, he was outraged and resolved to put an end to such conditions. With his Quaker friends Tuke founded the York Retreat, a rural farm in which kindness and a cessation of all prior medical treatments involving "bleeding, blisters

. . . evacuants, and such" were forbidden. Although Tuke was not a physician he had enough common sense to recognize that the current medical treatment of the insane more resembled torture than treatment. It was also obvious to any reasonable person that the "treatments" were totally ineffective and usually did more harm than good. The York Retreat soon became an ideal model for physicians from both Europe and America.[22]

With regard to early treatment of the deranged it is instructive to look at the way English physicians treated the manic attacks of King George III. Much of the time George was confined in a straitjacket. Parliament, unhappy with the king's doctors, called up a new batch of specialists in mental disorders. Drs. Munro, Baker, and Heberden recommended blistering the king's shaved scalp. Others advocated giving the King "the itch." Still others recommended that the king ingest the blood of an ass, to which the brains of a ram were added. Finally, Dr. Frances Willis, a clergyman turned psychiatrist, was called. Willis alternated leniency and firmness in dealing with the king during his delirium and strongly questioned the need for force in dealing with the deluded.[23]

As a result of the king's disorder, Parliament decided to look into the treatment of lunacy in the private asylums. What the committee discovered shocked all of England. One investigator reported that in the female section of Bedlam he saw ten naked females chained by one arm or leg to the wall. The chains allowed them merely to stand up or sit down. The male section looked like a dog kennel. Many of the men had iron rings around their necks fixed to a horizontal bar by a short chain. Other investigators reported that some of the keepers were so brutal and animallike that their "touch would taint putridity itself, and render it more abominable."[24] Another horror involved the case of a woman who asked to be released from her confinement. For her effrontery she was "flogged with a rope, tied to her bedpost for a week, not permitted to retire for the purposes of nature, and the stench in her room was abominable."[25] Such cruelties were found to be commonplace and even though members of Parliament were revolted, nothing was done because the "experts" in the treatment of the mentally disturbed argued that what they were doing was correct.

The wisest and best of these early "psychiatrists" in both England and colonial America taught that "stripes and blows about the body" were advisable for maniacs. Others agreed, insisting that "body pain may be exacted to purpose and without the least danger. Beating is often serviceable."[26] Physician John Battie also prescribed "blisters and caustics and rough catharticks" in disturbed patients, to cause pain and discomfort, and hence a reduction in excitement.[27] Today the same results are achieved with narcoleptics. As Walter Bromberg notes, "The therapeutic attitude of physicians and wardens [of colonial America] alternated between the sadism of punishing treatment and the guilt of having used it. Like despairing parents, physicians did not know whether to apply censure or gentleness to their erring children."[28] As is true today, each physician accused the other of ignorance. Both were correct.

Battie strongly recommended the use of "bleeding . . . and foetid anti-hystericks, opium, mineral waters, cold bathing, vomits."[29] Other treatments for raving maniacs were the scarifying and bleeding of the scalp. Blistering of the skin was done in order to defeat one of the basic causes of insanity: over-determination of blood to the head. The practice of having patients vomit frequently and severely was also believed to be highly efficacious in ridding the body of those elements that caused the madness.

Bleeding was considered the treatment of choice by no less a figure than Benjamin Rush, a signer of the Declaration of Independence, and one of America's first psychiatrists. Rush, a voluminous writer, in 1812 published the first American treatise on psychiatry, *Medical Inquiries and Observations upon Disease of the Mind.* Rush was convinced that "the cause of madness is seated primarily in the blood vessels of the brain."[30] Since "overcharging" the brain with blood is the cause of madness, relief can be obtained by ridding the body of blood to the point that fainting occurs. Bleeding was serious: on the average 600 to 1200 cubic centimeters of blood, a debilitating amount, was let during each treatment. Rush also recommended having the patient stand during treatment since this induced fainting more quickly and he advised keeping the patient in an erect posture for twenty-four hours at a time. Incredibly, Rush got his ideas from the techniques used for training

recalcitrant horses by enclosing them in stalls and then preventing
them from lying down or sleeping by driving sharp, pointed nails into
their bodies for two or three days and nights. Rush believed that if the
mad were kept awake in a standing position until the muscles were
fatigued, "the debility thus induced in those muscles would attract
morbid excitement from the brain, and thereby relieve the disease."[31]

Once the bleeding reduced the blood vessels "to a par of debility
of the nervous system," Rush then proceeded to stimulate the body
with diet, alcoholic drink, alkaline salts, tar infused in water and gar-
lic, and laudanum. A routine of baths, massage, exercise, and blistering and cupping (drawing blood to the skin's surface to ease congestion) then wound up the treatment.

Rush, along with other inventive and mechanically minded psychotherapists, also developed a machine he called the "gyrator" to be
used for "torpid madness" along with another mechanical device, the
"tranquilizing chair." The gyrator rotated the patient and, through
centrifugal motion, sent the blood to the head until nausea, vertigo,
and sweating occurred. As for the chair, it was a simple chair in which
the patient was strapped at the ankles, wrists, and across the abdomen
and chest with his head being confined in a wooden box. Rush developed the chair because the "mad shirt" or straitjacket did not allow for
bleeding. Pouring cold water on the patient was also recommended as
a method of calming.

Rush was not the only physician that believed "spinning" was a
cure for insanity. Dr. J. R. Cox of London obtained mental stimulation
and repose through the use of a "rotator," an ingenious device made up
of a large cage moved by a set of pulleys which rotated the patient until
he was nauseated and prostrate. Patients were subjected to repeated
spins lasting from four to six minutes several times a day. After each
treatment following nausea and often vomiting the patients usually fell
into a deep sleep and later were no longer maniacal. Another physician,
Christian Reil, invented a cage mounted on a moveable wheel. The
slightest movement on the part of the patient caused the wheel to spin
wildly and toss the patient from wall to wall. The patient *had* to stay
quiet and remain that way or suffer the consequences.

It is of some interest to note that Benjamin Rush also invented a number of mental disorders. One of his most curious was "anarchia." Rush described this disease as "The excess passion for liberty, inflamed by the successful issue of the wary."[32] This was one of the first diagnoses for behaviors that those in power found problematic. Anyone who was unhappy with the political structure of the time and actively worked for more freedom was considered mentally disordered and suffering from anarchia. In the middle of the nineteenth century another clever therapist—Dr. Samuel Cartwright—invented another peculiar disorder named "drapetomania." According to Cartwright, this mental disorder was specific to black slaves who had "an insane desire to run away from their owners." Blacks were also labeled with another form of insanity known as "dyasthesia Aethiopica"—an illness defined as "paying no attention to property." Such irrationalities raise the question of who is really the insane individual in such instances. The function of these diagnostic procedures was to provide support for a social order based on slavery, a practice that has continued into our own time.

Dr. J. R. Cox was one of the first to use music and the environment as therapeutic techniques. For torpid patients Cox's prescription was loud noises, screeches, and yells in rooms painted red and black or glaring white. To calm the maniac, the client was put into an airy, sunlit room painted green with redolent flowers and filled with soft harmonious music.

Fright was also a popular and highly recommended treatment procedure used by physicians of the early and mid-1800s. One of Pinel's patients who believed he had no head was cured after Pinel forcibly confronted him with the head of a man recently guillotined. Another physician treated a female opium addict by offering her a snuff box supposedly containing the drug. When she opened the box an artificial snake coiled in the box leapt into her face. Convulsed with terror she never used opium again—according to the psychiatrist. Francis Leuret, another French physician, preceded Pavlov and the behaviorists in the 1840s by forcibly suppressing the expression of any and all verbalizations of morbid or deluded notions. Every expression of the delusion was followed by a drenching with cold water. Leuret also matched his patients delusion for delusion. If the patient insisted he was unable to move his arms Leuret insisted he could not move any part of his body.

If the patient argued he was about to die Leuret argued that he was dead and in heaven. Leuret also replaced morbid thoughts with pleasant ones, often literally arguing his clients into sanity.[33]

Despite the occasional bursts of reason and sanity among the members of the medical profession, in the majority of cases, restraint was the treatment of choice in the public institutions. Both the deluded and the retarded were chained to the floor and left to wallow in their own excrement. If they were lucky they were taken into an open courtyard doused with cold water and washed with a broom. Deaths from disease or pneumonia, which were probably fairly common, were usually hidden and rarely reported. Investigators looking into the Lincoln Asylum in England in 1820, for example, found padded iron collars, heavy leather muffs and gags, leather belts with manacles, solid iron wrist locks (handcuffs), pointed iron leg locks or hobbles, and many of the respected Dr. Charlesworth's quarter boots— a device which kept the patient's feet at the end of the bed in an upright position securely locked to a foot board. Other clever and torturous devices such as steel cribs which restricted movement and the slightly larger Aubanel restraining bed which held its victim motionless and supine were in common use. Such treatment and confinement, as anyone with a modicum of intelligence would surmise, often led to rat bites, amputations from frostbite, and sores and infections galore.

Those sane enough and humane enough to object to such therapy and to argue against restraint as a mode of treatment were denounced and scourged as thoroughly demented. The general medical opinion of the day was that the insane belonged to another, lower order of beings and required stronger doses of drugs and force to calm and subdue them; that the removal of mechanical restraints would have to be replaced with manual restraint or some other form of coercion; and that the demented, left free and unattended, would quickly harm themselves and others. Despite the fact that many many unrestrained patients did improve and that humane treatment procedures proved to be effective, the subject was still intensely debated in the medical literature for almost fifty years. Treatment was considerably better in private hospitals than in the public institutions, primarily because patients with means received more consideration from the physician whose reward depended upon largess from a client who might not be generous to someone causing pain. In general, there was little or no uniformity to be found among the asylums in the so-called civilized world.

Leading the revolution against the cruel and inhumane treatment of the poor and incompetent in the middle of the nineteenth century was the indomitable Dorothea Dix, a woman no one in his right mind would dare to challenge. Dix took on the medical and political establishments and the public at large, and reduced them all to whimpering compliance with her determination to reform the American state asylums. Through her personal efforts and activities, Dorothea founded or enlarged thirty-two mental hospitals and brought about changes in the treatment of the poor and insane in eighteen penitentiaries, three hundred county jails and houses of correction, and five hundred almshouses. She also forced the enlargement of the medical staff of hundreds of institutions and badgered the legislatures of more than a dozen states to appropriate increased money for the state insane asylums. Between 1841 and 1848 Dix, almost single handedly, brought about a humane revolution in the treatment of the indigent and the disturbed. Most important of all, her influence fanned the spark of hope into a bright flame of optimism and a newly founded belief that, after all, something possibly could be done to help the hopelessly demented. The public's interest was aroused and hundreds of books, pamphlets, and journals concerned with mental problems also appeared. Many physicians began to specialize in the treatment of the deranged since it was now optimistically believed that insanity was not only treatable, but curable.[34]

In fact, the optimism reached such heights that many medical superintendents of asylums both here and abroad began to report an astounding number of cures and recoveries of those previously considered hopelessly insane. Cure rates in the 80, 90, and even 100 percent range were frequently reported. Inevitably, a return to insanity quickly followed as both remission rates and more accurate accounting procedures were developed.

In the 1850s those professionals concerned with the care and treatment of the disturbed began to see that insanity was a treatable condition and that treatment in hospitals should be clean, humane, and properly managed. Overcrowding must be kept to a minimum, as little restraint as possible should be used, the poor and the insane should be separated, and qualified physicians should be in charge of the hospitals. In the 1870s not only were the insane once again admitted into the family of humanity but many of the more perceptive physicians began to recognize that the trials and tribulations of life as well as many social, cultural, and environmental factors played a significant role in the causation of many mental disorders.

Little progress was made in the analysis and classification of patients, however, until near the end of the century when the German physician Emil Kraepelin adopted the life history idea and began to bring a semblance of order into the chaotic world of clinical nosology (classification of diseases). Kraepelin took each of the major mental maladies and described its history, its course, and its prognosis. His descriptions served as the basis for the new discipline of clinical psychiatry. Kraepelin's work not only led to improvements in psychiatric and neurological diagnosis but also, in time, to improvements in methods of treatment in the state asylums as well as a new emphasis upon clinical research and a scientific approach to the insane.

Adolf Meyer, a pathologist in the Eastern State Hospital in Illinois, was an outstanding leader in this regard. He insisted on the adoption of a truly scientific approach to the problem of the asylum and its inmates. Meyer set up a laboratory in the hospital morgue and carried out pathological studies on cases of neurosyphilis (syphilis of the central nervous system), senile dementia (loss of mental faculties due to age), the epilepsies, general paralysis, and actual mania. Even though little of use or promise was found, Meyer was astute enough to realize that the more helpful studies of the insane must begin while the patient is still alive. Through Meyer's work and leadership the medical aspect of patient care was integrated with the patient's personal history. Meyer, more than anyone else in the field of psychotherapy, succeeded in marrying neurology and psychology to create the new discipline of psychiatry.

Incredibly, the interest in animal magnetism and hypnosis led an eccentric American doctor named Elisha Perkins to conclude in 1796 that two pieces of metal—one iron, one copper—called tractors could draw pain from his patients' bodies. These ideas were so appealing that even George Washington bought one for his family's use. Physicians on the continent claimed miraculous cures with Perkins's tractors and even predicted the tractors would replace the physician and make medicine superfluous. When it was shown that the same miraculous cures could be produced using any type of substance (wood, paper, or anything else), and that the cures were due to suggestion alone, Perkins was out of business. In 1779 James Graham picked up the idea from Ben Franklin's experiments that electrical stimulation could cure disease and opened up a clinic using magnets and electrical devices to cure and rejuvenate the ill. Phrenology, when imported to the United States in the 1840s, also became very popular and resulted in hundreds of books. Mind readers, faith healers, mediums, and spiritualists all flourished; contact with dead spirits brought forth many specific suggestions and ideas for healing and curing the living of their many maladies. That all such things were utter nonsense and of no value whatsoever in no way deterred the hordes of believers.

In the 1880s many self-appointed healers arrived on the scene preaching spiritual healing. John A. Dowie, an Australian, claimed he was the reincarnation of the prophet Elijah and in 1888 traveled across the United States "healing" the sick with prayer and the laying on of hands. Another miscreant, Francis Schlatter, also claimed Jesus had granted him the ability to heal through touch. When he tried to carry on his scam through the U.S. Postal Service, he wound up in federal hands. Hundreds of healers arose and flourished briefly until the public caught on to their scams. Horace Fletcher, a food faddist, preached that uncooked cellulose in raw vegetables could save us all, especially when the stuff was properly chewed. Fletcher argued that only one-twentieth the ordinary amount of food was needed if it were chewed properly. Even the brilliant William James tried Fletcher's diet for three months before giving it up because, in his words, "It nearly killed me."[35]

Competing vigorously with such physical nonsense were a number of mental systems revolving primarily around religious or spiritualistic beliefs. The most famous of these systems was, of course, Mary Baker Eddy's Christian Science, which grew out of the mesmerist Dr.

Phineas Quimby's Science of Health. In Eddy's hands emphasis was placed on the belief that if the concept of matter could be dispensed with as an illusion of false materialism, disease would also vanish. All other types of medical treatment and psychotherapy were in error—particularly hypnosis—since it interfered with the communication of divine love. Between 1890 and 1910 the Church of Christian Science grew to be very powerful. Mind cure groups such as Eddy's usually clung tenaciously to spirituality as their primary therapeutic tool and through new thought and theosophy they managed to make room for new discoveries in neurology, psychology, and psychiatry and blended these into their spiritual practices.

Interest in theosophy* and other pseudoscientific and occultic health systems grew during the 1920s and 1930s. One researcher, for example, studying these psychotherapeutic eccentrics estimated that in the early 1940s from fifteen to twenty million Americans subscribed to and believed in these esoteric healers and their quackery.[36] Interest in spiritual and religious help was followed in the late 1940s and early 1950s by an explosion of books by popular helpers and healers designed to solve every human problem and disorder. Books with titles such as *You Must Relax*, *The Art of Real Happiness*, *Peace of Mind*, *How to Win Friends and Influence People*, *Be Glad You're Neurotic*, and *Outwitting Your Nerves* offered solutions to every human problem. What was a flood during the 1940s and 1950s has become, in our own time, a deluge of gargantuan proportions. Many of these self-help panaceas are, as we shall see, more harmful than helpful.

Despite the efforts of Pinel, Dix, and the other reformers, little progress was made in the treatment of those confined to public mental institutions in the late 1880s. While considerable progress was made in the area of physical hygiene and such diseases as tuberculosis, smallpox, and other bacterial disorders, the notion of taking steps to prevent mental disease was unheard of. Books on the evils of tobacco, alcohol, and overeating were common, but the idea of hygienic steps for the mind (controlling one's thinking to think only good things)

---

*Proponents of theosophy claimed the ability to establish a direct link with the divine principle through contemplation and revelation. Theosophists claimed these mystical insights could heal any ailment and were superior to empirical knowledge.

did not arise until 1863 when it was made the subject of a book by Dr. Isaac Ray titled *Mental Hygiene*.[37] Such ideas did not take hold, however, until 1908 when Clifford Beers published his book *A Mind That Found Itself*, exposing the existing evils in the care of the mentally ill.[38] William James wrote the introduction to the first edition and Adolf Meyer not only embraced the book but also suggested the name "mental hygiene" for the movement that Beers started. The book was based upon Beers's own personal experiences in Connecticut and New York hospitals where he was confined for seven years in straitjackets and padded cells, frequently mistreated by the doctors and staff.

Conditions, even in the better institutions, were deplorable. Consider the following quote, written by psychiatrist Walter Bromberg as he first began his career in 1928 at the Manhattan State Hospital on Ward's Island in New York:

The main structures of the Manhattan State Hospital, fronting the East River, were replicas of those designed by Kirkbride in the 1850s. Spacious high-ceilinged halls surrounded by wards and single rooms, a sitting room lined with wooden chairs, a nurses' station and office near the entrance, constituted the approved plan. The buildings that housed the "back wards," including the Inebriate Asylum, built in 1854, appeared more antiquated as one moved away from the Administration Building. Here patients of all varieties, cases of dementia praecox [the archaic term for schizophrenia], melancholias, manics, whiled away their years. The more disturbed were ordered to sit in straightback chairs while those more compliant pushed a heavy wooden block across the hall for the obvious purpose of polishing an overpolished floor. There was no communication between patients and little with the nursing staff; some argued with imaginary foes outside the windows; some sat in Rodinesque immobility; some giggled foolishly. During the nonwork hours, the halls looked like an old Hogarth print. Occasionally a cackling laugh issued from an upstairs window or a grunt from a restrained manic broke the empty hum.

In the morning, long lines of rag-tag patients filed from the halls under attendant-guards, en route to menial jobs in the laundry or on the grounds. The men, dressed in ill-fitting drab clothes, a cloth cap set at an idiotic angle, talked and gesticulated to themselves. The women patients, in clumsy shoes and dun-colored dresses, giggled or mumbled to the morning air. Occasionally one would depart from the file to emphasize a point to an imaginary persecutor or lunge at a vexing enemy. The scene was dreary, hopeless, eternal.[39]

While Clifford Beers's efforts, along with William James's philosophy of pragmatism and his psychology of everyday life, nourished the idea of prevention and mental hygiene in the psychiatric field, it was Adolf Meyer and his book *Principles of Psychobiology* which made the entire field of abnormal behavior less esoteric and mysterious.[40] As a neurologist, Meyer initially regarded insanity as a brain disease, but all of his laboratory studies in neuropathology—in the dissection of hundreds of brains in the search for lesions proved negative and led him to see the patient as a person with problems in unresolved emotional conflicts and a biological life history that must be understood if the problem of mental illness was ever to be understood. Meyers also gave impetus to studying the milieu in which mental illness occurred and stimulated the founding of the profession of psychiatric social work. The abolition of child labor and the development of child study associations and the child guidance movement also pushed the ideas of mental hygiene into the public limelight. Suggestions were even made that juvenile delinquency could be prevented along with crime since the prevention of crime lay in guiding children and removing the causes of emotional disorder at an early age. Psychotherapists of all persuasions began to see that social problems such as poverty, unemployment, illegitimacy, alcoholism, and drug use were at the root of the individual's problems and needed their attention if they were ever to have a major impact upon human mental disorders. It is important to mention here that the more perceptive psychologists and psychotherapists in the 1990s also clearly recognize that in the light of these overarching social disasters any and all efforts at the level of the individual person are futile.[41] The emotional disorders cannot be wholly eradicated if the patient must return to an environment which in large part caused the problem in the first place.

THE MEDICAL ANXIETY MAKERS

{T}he medical profession has contributed substantially to the institutional-ization of sexual anxiety. Hence sexual anxiety must be added to the not inconsiderable calendar of iatrogenic disorders.[42]

Intercourse during pregnancy was strictly forbidden by the eigh-teenth century physician because it led, so said "the authorities," to such dire results in the children as epilepsy, sexual precocity, and depravity. As for masturbation, in the secular literature up to the beginning of the eighteenth century it seemed to have excited no cen-sorious interest whatever. In general it was considered a useful form of relief and an antidote against the allurements of "dangerous women." The Church, of course, considered self-abuse a sin and it was a minister-turned-doctor that published the first book on the subject in 1710, an anonymous treatise titled *Onania, of the Heinous Sin of Self Pollution*. It was highly endorsed and widely recommended by Catholic physician Samuel August Tissot, who in 1758 published his own book, *Onanism: A Treatise on the Disorders Produced by Masturbation*. This is not only total nonsense but ignorant, arrogant, and irrespon-sible. Such crimes influenced even people as astute as Benjamin Rush, who in his, the first textbook on psychiatry to be published in the United States, stated that masturbation produced "seminal weakness, impotence, . . . consumption, dimness of sight, vertigo, epilepsy, . . . loss of memory, . . . and death."[43]

This medical nonsense spread across the entire Western world and led to the pernicious myth of "masturbational insanity." Poor, inno-cent masturbation was labeled as "an abominable sin," "a heinous crime," a "road to insanity." The medical men's preoccupation with the sinfulness of sex led to truly unbelievable idiocies including clitoridec-tomies (female circumcision), hysterectomies, circumcision, castration, and, while it maybe difficult for some readers to believe, to surgical removal of the penis since it was a "cure" for masturbation and one sure way to prevent the patient's insanity!

Concentration on sex diverted, for a time, the physician's attention from other organs of the body. Soon, however, the medical men dis-covered the anus which, being so close to the sex organs, obviously suggested itself as something which could be used to turn a profit. Sir Arbuthnot Lane, for example, was so afraid of constipation, which he believed led to the poisoning of the intestinal tract and autointoxication and then to tuberculosis and insanity, that surgical removal of the colon was Lane's procedure for "solving" the problem. This tragic period in the history of medical stupidity is brilliantly exposed by Alex Comfort in *The Anxiety Makers*:

> Yet when one reads the sexual and hygienic advice dispensed by physicians to the public over the ages one can only stand amazed that the authority of the doctor as counsellor has stood up so well. Generations have retailed to their patients a great flood of reproductive misinformation, most of it moralistic in intention as well as in content. Diseases and physical mischiefs have been invented and produced in the susceptible by medical intimidation.[44]

The flood of medical garbage reached its peak in the nineteenth century. Most physicians of the day regarded homosexuals not as sick but vicious, and the lash and dungeon were recommended treatments. If one was prone to excessive venery (indulgence in sexual encounters) the results were obvious to all: hunch back, red nose, baldness, constipation, and gout. Coitional postures other than "the missionary position" were considered harmful. Impotence was due to flaws in the system either in the seed or in the penis or due to bewitchment of excessive ardor. Cold feet are a hindrance to successful sex. Excessive sex shortens life, whitens hair, and produces baldness. Scabies, gonorrhea, and blindness all result from intemperance, as do bad breath, gooseflesh, and swollen gums. Worst of all was the panic over masturbation. Samuel Tissot proclaimed unequivocally that if you questioned a lunatic you always obtained a history of self-abuse. Moreover, deteriorated lunatics masturbate openly and persistently. Benjamin Rush agreed. Esquirol, the prestigious French medical authority, stated that masturbation "is recognized in all countries as a common cause of insanity." By 1838 Esquirol had added suicide, melancholia, and epilepsy to the list. German physicians soon included blindness, skin diseases, and other ills as well. Masturbational insanity reached England around 1829, and in 1839 Sir William Ellis, superintendent of

Hanwell Asylum, stated "by far the most frequent cause of fatuity is debility of the brain . . . in consequence of the pernicious habit of masturbation." In 1852, textbooks stated "the habit of solitary vice gives rise to hysteria, asthma, epilepsy, melancholia, mania, suicide, dementia, and general paralysis of the insane." This was the high point of the medical tide of stupidity. It wasn't, however, until 1953 that counselors and physicians began to openly advise that "masturbation is a normal and healthy act for a person of any age."[45] Mind boggling as these beliefs are, they were easily exceeded by the true horrors of the physicians' prescribed treatment procedures.

Since the prevailing medical opinion in the eighteenth and nineteenth centuries believed masturbation to be a harmful, as well as sinful, practice they attempted to cure it by any means possible. From 1850 to 1879 surgical measures were the popular treatment of choice. In fact, surgery, restraint, fright, and severe punishment constituted at least 50 percent of all procedures universally until 1904. During this period there was a widespread use of what Dr. R. A. Spitz termed "comic book sadism."[46] Bizarre therapies were commonplace and not restricted to medical eccentrics. During the 1880s sexually active children and adolescents were tied, chained, and infibulated in the same manner as mental patients, and were forced to wear many grotesque appliances. The poor innocents were encased in plaster of Paris, leather, or rubber. They were also beaten, and if none of the foregoing measures proved effective, they were then subjected to cauterization and denervation of the genitalia and even castration and clitoridectomy. Anything is better than insanity! God help the child of either sex who was unable or unwilling to keep his or her developing sexuality out of sight!

Antimasturbation devices and antimasturbation chastity girdles were sold widely. The few sane physicians who publicly protested this nonsense were shouted down and ignored. Dr. A. Eyer of St. John's Hospital in Ohio proudly published his cure in the 1894–1895 *International Medical Magazine:* "Clitoridectomy for the Cure of Certain Cases of Masturbation in Young Girls."[47] He first cauterized his subject's clitoris. This failing, the clitoris was then surgically buried with silver wire sutures, which the child tore and resumed the habit. Next

Eyer excised the entire organ, including the crura. Six weeks after the operation Eyer gleefully reported the child as saying: "You know there is nothing there now, so I could do nothing."[48] Cauterization of the spine and genitals, believe it or not, continued to appear in standard American textbooks up to 1905[49] and a Dr. Milton advocated blistering the penis with red mercury ointment making it too painful to touch to discourage the dreadful practice. Even after 1925, 10 percent of the recommended methods of dealing with masturbation appearing in American medical publications involved surgery.[50]

Since the insane were frequently seen masturbating openly, the great medical minds of the time put two and two together and concluded that self-abuse was the *cause*, not the result, of lunacy. Some did argue that if masturbation were associated with fear and insanity this was at least as much due to the guilt and repression it raised as to the practice itself. The frequency of autostimulation in all normal adults finally began to be realized, but the work of these anxiety-makers had its impact on the popular mindset well into the twentieth century and gave rise to the folklore that masturbation was the cause of pimples, that it would cause hair to grow in one's palms, it would stunt one's growth, sap one's physical strength, and so on.

Once the maddened surgeons were given a knife, no organ in the body was safe, particularly those body parts located in the general vicinity of the generative organs.

The large intestine is not, for most of us, either an organ usually associated with sex or an organ about which we habitually worry. Difficult as it may be to believe, the anxiety makers in the 1840s now began to attack the bowels and their irregularity as the prime source of all disease. Constipation rather than masturbation was now the enemy of humanity. If massage, purgatives, and enemas did not completely flush out the innards daily, then surgical enlargement of the anus or major surgery for inner cleanliness became the order of the day.[51]

Incredibly, William Arbuthnot Lane believed that the bowels were closely linked not only with disease but with longevity and the postponement of senility. Intestinal stasis must be eliminated and prevented because failure to keep the intestinal tract clean from stomach to anus is the direct cause of cancer, bad teeth, short life, and suicide.

Poisons in the small and large intestinal "kinks" cause all of the various diseases afflicting man. Lane's prescription for straightening out the internal "kinks" was to drink large quantities of mineral oil and liquid paraffin. As one observer noted, "Soon liquid paraffin was arriving in drums like beer at an inn. The fate of the ingested paraffin began to be appreciated when years later, Lane's patients and disciples began to die of natural causes, and mineral oil could be squeezed from their livers at post-mortem like water from so many sponges."[52]

If this procedure proved ineffective in curing various human ailments then total surgical removal of the colon was the only alternative; a heroic measure which Lane carried out with superb skill on hundreds of people suffering from rheumatic fever in children to thyroid disease in adults. Thankfully, most survived the operation. No one knows for sure exactly how many of these operations Lane performed, but his records indicate that the number ran well into four figures. Lane eventually became convinced that given the proper elimination of waste products, our cells were potentially immortal and death could be conquered.

After World War II there was a concerted movement on the part of the federal government and the Veteran's Administration to train psychotherapists in large numbers in order to deal with the mental problems of the war's psychiatric casualties. Of equal importance was the effect of the mental hygiene movement that gave rise to the concept of the "therapeutic team" and the recognition that the family doctor (general practitioners) as well as psychiatrists and psychologists all had an important role to play in helping restore the mentally disabled to a normal level of functioning.

A Boston psychiatrist, Abraham Meyerson, not only believed in the team approach but implemented the concept in the state hospitals of Massachusetts. Meyerson was also one of the first to push the idea that deterioration was not necessarily the fate of every schizophrenic. By surrounding the patient with a therapeutic setting, several helpers, and treating difficult cases through group therapy, significant progress with acute (brief and severe) and chronic (long lasting) cases was possible. This idea of a therapeutic community soon became the standard for all mental institutions and gave birth to the notion of therapy primarily as a re-educational process in which patients could learn from each other as well as from the therapeutic staff. Psychoanalytic and dynamic therapeutic approaches were also used until group therapy became technically identical with the old Freudian individual psychotherapy. Acting out, role playing, anxiety reduction, insight, and understanding all were effective and positive outcomes of the group process. Shortly thereafter there was another innovative move from analytic groups to action-oriented groups in the form of J. L. Moreno's psychodrama and the therapeutic values and emotional catharsis inherent in spontaneous and impromptu theater. People began to see a new self in their role interactions with others.[53]

The emphasis on groups gave rise to the idea of teaching people to look at themselves and their behavior from another's point of view and to gain insight into their own behavior while becoming more sensitive to the feelings of others. Such group work and training sessions became known as sensitivity training. This was the result of Kurt Lewin's work with the National Training Laboratory at Bethel, Maine, which was originally intended to develop effective ways to deal with complex interpersonal relations, and to teach human relation skills in industry.* Many therapists saw this approach as superior to the questionable theoretical assumptions of the Freudian approach. Expressing great dissatisfaction with both the Freudian approach and the psychology of John Watson, B. F. Skinner, and other behaviorists who denied the existence of "mind" or an "inner man," and based their theories on work with rats and other laboratory animals, psychologist Abraham Maslow created a "third force," known as humanistic psychology, a psychology concerned with the "total" human being. Maslow emphasized psychological health and optimal human functioning in what he called "self-actualization," i.e., reaching one's full potential. Stressing all of the positive human values rather than a "sickness and pathology" or a "mechanical and physiological" psychology, Maslow transformed the existential psychology of being into a therapeutic base which quickly developed into what was called the "human potential movement."

Allied with Maslow in this psychological revolution was the psy-

---

*Kurt Lewin, *A Dynamic Theory of Personality: Selected Papers* (New York: McGraw-Hill, 1935).

chologist Carl Rogers, a skilled counselor and therapist, who developed the nondirective (let the client make his own decisions) approach to helping people with their problems. Rogers saw the therapeutic situation itself as a growth experience and under his gentle, nonauthoritarian, nonmedical guidance, the client would change his self-defeating and harmful attitudes. Rogers believed every person has an internal drive toward health and development and if emotional blocks to this innate process are removed by focusing on the present rather than the past, healthy change will occur. This counseling approach is diametrically opposed to the medical approach of advising and medicating. Removing or reducing the destructive "force" in therapy was the ideal way to confront people's social and psychological problems. This approach was additionally advantageous in that it was relatively easy to learn, effective, and did not require years of specialized training or a vast store of medical knowledge. Any member of the therapeutic team could use it and help the patient.[54]

As a direct outgrowth of this movement and philosophy, a large number of new and unusual therapeutic approaches were developed. Many bordered on the nonsensical or absurd and most had little or no experimental or empirical support.

The development of Maslow's and Roger's human-centered therapeutic approach signals the end of the humanistic philosophy and humane and human-centered approaches to psychotherapy. While these ideas have had a significant impact on therapeutic thinking and training, especially among clinical psychologists and counselors, the effect on psychiatrists and other medically oriented therapists has been almost nonexistent. Instead, over the last few years we have seen the rise to power of biological psychiatry, the waning of psychological psychotherapy, the medicalization of mental illness, and the rise of the medically centered psychotherapeutic state.

Other than the drug revolution of the 1950s and the growth and development of the Community Mental Health Centers in the 1970s, there has been little of a psychotherapeutic positive and optimistic nature to applaud except the modern revolt against the biological medical model.

As theological models faded and naturalistic models were succeeding, the physician or healer came into his own and was given a unique kind of authority. Over the years the M.D.—unique among the professionals—was given three types of authority: expert, moral, and charismatic. Like Aesculapius, the Roman god of healing, the physician was seen as a possessor of expert power because he is supposed to know how the body and mind work in health and disease. Moreover, the M.D. also has moral authority based on the belief shared by the patient that the doctor's intent is to do good, alleviate suffering, and prolong life. The final authority is the M.D.'s charismatic authority. This authority entitles the M.D. to order others about and to control their behavior. Once again the M.D. is assuming the role of the priest and the shaman and is godlike. It is this priestly charisma that sets the M.D. apart from and above other mere human beings. If, however, the M.D. is perceived as not having any special attributes or godlike powers, half of his effectiveness is lost. To maintain his "specialness" he must act as if he is "a little tin god" or a priest with mysterious and occult powers. To impress the peasants he plasters his walls with impressive framed documents from prestigious schools of arcane knowledge; speaks in a mysterious Greco-Latin language, replete with technical terms and references; and performs many mysterious rituals to scare the diseases and disorders away. According to Siegler and Osmond, without his *necessary* charisma, "one cannot function as a doctor, and indeed cannot even be a successful medical impostor."[55]

What is tragic about all of this is that the typical psychiatrist is turned loose upon an unsuspecting public with more charisma than anything else. As was demonstrated in the earlier section on training, his knowledge base is slight, and in some highly critical areas, nonexistent. Studies have shown that his pills and instruments are ineffective and his cure rates are at, or below, chance level. Under such conditions, trying to maintain an aura of magic and attempting to observe the dictum "First do no harm" is difficult indeed.

While nonprofessionals and people in pain may well be willingly fooled by charisma, it is not as effective on more knowledgeable individuals. To many it is very evident that the "Emperor wears no clothes."

FREUDIAN FALLACIES AND JUNGIAN JUNK

Sigmund Freud—The most successful charlatan of our century.

Thomas Szasz

The Freudian Fallacy

So much has already been written about Freud and his contributions to psychology that it is difficult to add to what has already been said. Nevertheless, there are seldom-mentioned aspects of the man and his work that need to be aired despite the glare of adoration surrounding the great mental emancipator. Certainly one of the most enduring contributions of Freud's personality theory is the concept of the unconscious—the part of the mind that is hidden. Even though experimental evidence shows that his thinking on the subject is faulty, Freud believed, as we have seen, that all behavior, no matter how trivial, was usually motivated by unconscious processes.

Exactly how this works is supposedly illustrated by a conversation Freud had with a young man who, in expressing his pessimism about the state of the world, quoted a line from Virgil: "Let someone arise from my bones as an avenger." But the young man could not remember the Latin word for "someone" and asked Freud to supply it. He then challenged Freud to show how this trivial memory lapse could have been motivated by unconscious processes. Freud took the challenge and had the man concentrate on the word *aliquis* (someone) and report every association he had to the word with no censoring of any kind.

The man's associations to the word included fluidity, fluids, relics, and idiosyncratically, St. Januarius, whose blood was kept in a vial in a church in Naples. On a particular holy day, the blood liquifies. If this event is delayed for any reason, the people of Naples are aroused and wait for a miracle to happen. At this point the man blushed and said he had an association too intimate to express. When Freud reminded him that complete candor was required, the man alluded to information a woman might pass along. Freud then floored the man by correctly telling him he was worried that his girlfriend had missed her period and might be pregnant. Freud's clues, embedded in the association, were blood flowing on a particular day, a calendar saint, and the hope that the miracle of blood flow would take place.

Freud tried to explain the complex workings of the mind by dividing it into levels of consciousness. *Conscious* thought is concerned only with material of which we are momentarily aware. Mental work or knowledge that is available to our awareness, but that the person is not immediately thinking of, is part of the *preconscious*. We all know what a tiger looks like but until it is referred to and brought to awareness it is part of our preconscious. Most, or at least a large part, of our mental life is *unconscious*. People are normally unaware of material in or at the unconscious level of awareness—even though much of our behavior is influenced by it. The young man's inability to remember the word *aliquis* was influenced by those unconscious mental forces in which Freud believed. Much of the pathological behavior that Freud treated with psychoanalytical methods was behavior determined by unconscious thought. When things too unpleasant occur, they were repressed, Freud believed, that is, they were barred from conscious thought and shoved down into an unconscious level. Since so much relating to sex was disapproved or anxiety-arousing, it is no wonder, in Freud's view, repressed sex was such a driving force in human affairs. Freud's theory was not only strongly deterministic, but he also held that human behavior was under the control of strong instinctual pressures over which people have little or no control; in fact, he believed people are largely unaware of the reasons for their behavior. He also believed personality was formed in early childhood through interaction in the family, and through modification of the sexual instinct. The *id*, the primal, driving, instinctual force, is joined in childhood by the *ego,* the sense of self, and later by the *superego*, or conscience. This theory has had, over the years, a stupendous impact on our thinking about man's mental life. Yet, astoundingly, there is not one smidgen of scientific evidence to support any of it. Every experimental effort to validate any of its essential elements has ended in failure. Even more startling is the fact that none of the ideas expressed or elaborated upon by Freud— even his celebrated notion of the unconscious—were novel or new.

A number of writers have gone to great lengths to trace the concept of the unconscious mind from its beginnings in the distant past to Freud. Three of the most prominent efforts have been Lancelot L. Whyte's *The Unconscious before Freud*, Henri Ellenberger's monumental *The Discovery of the Unconscious*, and D. M. Klein's *The Unconscious: Invention or Discovery*.[56] As Whyte points out very emphatically, Freud did not discover the unconscious mind. His writing about it was the culmination of a cultural process that extended over centuries. Nietzsche expressed several of Freud's insights twenty or more years earlier.

The German Romantic movement had the greatest impact upon Freud and this thought. The fundamental principle was that in the unconscious mind lay the tie of the individual to the universal powers of nature. Thus, the wellsprings of human nature lie in the unconscious, and here the individual is linked with the universal. It can be the union of the individual soul with the divine, or a perfectly natural linkage of moments of human awareness with organic neurological processes within which they begin. From the eighteenth century on there was an increased interest not only in the normal aspects of mental life (sleep, dreams, etc.), but also in the unusual or pathological states (hypnosis, hallucinations, ecstasy, dissociation, epilepsy, etc.) and in the processes that underlie ordinary thought (imagination, judgment, selection, etc.). Although many of these things appear to fall into the realm of the irrational, this interpretation was an error. All sustained mental processes, including those of which we are aware, are primarily unconscious and are regulated by unconscious factors. Moreover, there is no reason to regard unconscious processes as basically irrational and in opposition to rational analysis. In fact, the little empirical research that is available suggests otherwise. Simply because we do not fully comprehend exactly how the mind is organized and functions does not mean that we should think of unconscious aspects as either irrational or pathological. Although Freud demonstrated that unconscious factors can sometimes lead to behavior contrary to reason, this is not sufficient cause to assume that every unconscious aspect is always irrational. Nevertheless, from 1750 to 1950 too many thinkers tended to regard the unconscious as the source of all the irrational forces in humanity and an ever-present threat to social and intellectual order.

Whether he intended it or not, Freud's emphasis on the pathological aspects of human behavior cast an unfortunate pall over most of our thinking about mental processes. What little understanding we do have about our mental life has come about primarily through speculative philosophy at first, then through clinical and laboratory studies, and only in the last few years through physiological and psychological studies of the brain and nervous system. It wasn't until the last decades of the nineteenth century that the first systematic efforts to base curative procedures on theories of the structure of unconscious mental processes were made. Despite the brilliance of the Freudian theories and ideas, cures for mental pathologies were not an immediate outcome. In Whyte's words, "Freud did not regard the benefits of psychoanalysis to the neurotic individual or even to the analyzed analyst as normally complete or permanent, and his own techniques have not yet led to important discoveries improving and extending them."[57] It seems clear now in the fifty years that have elapsed since Freud's death that he contributed few wholly satisfactory techniques for therapy. Although a number of important cumulative advances in the treatment of psychoses and neuroses have been made, they have not been based on any solid physiologically or psychologically experimentally established theory. Certainly not Freudian theory. The attempts and experimental efforts to determine the validity of certain Freudian ideas and hypotheses have been negative. Most of these efforts to empirically establish the truth or falsity of the Freudian dynamic took place shortly before and shortly after World War II and gave little support to Freud's major assumptions.

The early rumblings of discontent and disillusion with the Freudian edifice came to full fruition in the early 1980s. While reading Ernest Jones's biography of Freud, E. M. Thornton, a lay Fellow of the Royal Society of London, was struck by a passage quoted from one of Freud's letters written in the 1890s. Because it sounded like the imagery used by drug addicts, Thornton wondered if Freud was under the influence of some powerful drug when the passage was written. Her curiosity aroused, Thornton began an intensive inquiry into the rest of Freud's life and career. The resulting book, *The Freudian Fallacy*,[58] has been called in some circles "the Demolition of Sigmund Freud." Those who have managed to resist his canonization and elevation to secular sainthood have long found it difficult to understand his influence and prestige because his teachings and his theories are totally lacking in scientific support, and few, if any, have ever been cured of any psychosis or neurosis by psychoanalysis. Other forms of therapy are vastly more effective for nearly any class of mental disorder than any Freudian methodology or technique. Freud undoubtedly believed in the truth of his hypotheses when he pronounced them, but his scientific training should have prevented him from committing the sin of explaining one mystery with the substitution of another.

In subjecting the Freudian structure to the cold glare of logic and content analysis, only those who have been totally brainwashed would deny the truth of Thornton's findings. No doubt the publication of her book took a large amount of courage. No one has had a more profound effect on twentieth-century thought than Freud. His work has influenced all of the social sciences; he has, literally, changed the face of society. Psychoanalytic terms have become part of the language of everyday life, and many writers and thinkers have described Freud as a genius—one of the great thinkers of all time—and in a class with Newton, Einstein, Darwin, and Copernicus.

Yet Freud's central postulate—the unconscious mind—does not exist; it is a function with no scientific support whatsoever, and a contradiction in terms. More damaging yet, as Thornton has shown, Freud's theories were baseless and aberrational, and when he formulated them he was under the influence of cocaine, which specifically affected his brain. This latter fact is known by his own admission, as is his use of the drug during his medical practicing, from 1884 to 1887, and his resumed use of cocaine in the latter half of 1892—the year, incidentally, in which his revolutionary new theories emerged. In her book, Thornton shows, most convincingly, that Freud's theories were the direct outcome of his cocaine addiction. The addiction also accounts for Freud's delusions of persecution, memory lapses, suspicions, and denunciations of his disciples, as well as the incompatibilities and discrepancies in his work.

Although Freud's definitive biographer, Ernest Jones, discusses some of Freud's behavioral eccentricities, they are dismissed as the harmless peccadillos of a man of genius.[59] They are now seen for what they were: a dramatic picture of a tormented genius wrestling with the demons of his "unconscious mind" and following the classic course of the cocaine addict. Freud's rapid mood swings from elation to depression, episodes of clouded consciousness, periods of hyperactivity, paranoid mysterious heart symptoms, were not the "creative neurosis" that Jones described, but symptoms of the delusions peculiar to the later stages of cocaine addiction.

We must not, however, judge Freud's work on such grounds. It should stand or fall on its own merit. Many works of creative genius have come from those who have managed to probe the depths of human imagination, and Freud could have gained invaluable insight into his own mind from such consciousness expanders. Unfortunately, as Thornton points out, such drugs act not on the mind (which consists of learning, memories, etc.) but on the brain (the physical body, the "mechanics," so to speak) and affect most strongly the brain centers where sense data are interpreted and memories are stored. The false perceptions which deluded users interpret as emanations from the "deeper levels of the mind" and so vividly describe in the drug literature are actually "distortions arising from poisoned brain cells." It was, unfortunately, these drug-induced misperceptions that plagued Freud and produced his neurotic symptoms.

Brainwashed as we have been by the thousands of writers and intellectuals paying Freud tribute, it is still difficult for us to realize how, in just a few decades, psychoanalysis became such a dominating force in psychiatry. Thornton does, however, show how this came about. Freud hid his psychosis from his followers for a while (one by one his early disciples left him), and he selected his champions carefully, picking intellectuals with a philosophical rather than a scientific education, and those people who valued ideas for their own sake rather than for their factual value. These disciples were very good at propagating and publicizing his theories and ideas to a lay public and in dealing with criticism by calling it old-fashioned, rigid, or inhibited. The climate of the times was also in Freud's favor. Along with Darwin and rapid advances in medicine and biology, the ground was ready for, and receptive to, new ideas. Freud's theories were also helped along by exaggerated claims of innumerable cures obtained through psychoanalysis. G. Stanley Hall, in the American edition of Freud's early work, testified to "thousands of cures," which was, of course, impossible. In his practice Freud saw every patient for an hour each day, six days a week, and their analysis continued for years. Later in his career he devoted most of his time to training other analysts. Therefore, the total number of patients he analyzed in his entire career probably figured in tens rather than thousands. Moreover, few—if any at all—were or could have been "cured" by his treatment. Even his most famous patient, Anna O., was still ill at the end of her treatment. Analysts now concede psychoanalysis has little or no curative value. Practicing analyst Anthony Storr, in his 1968 essay, "The Concept of Cure," stated, "The evidence that psychoanalysis cures anybody of anything is so shaky as to be practically non-existent." When the American Psychoanalytic Association took a survey to test the efficacy of analysis, the results were so disappointing they were withheld from publication.[60]

Although Freud's theories, particularly those of the unconscious mind, are generally hailed as "discoveries" and accorded the status of established fact, more discerning critics see them primarily as inventions, and a number of medical historians have shown that most of Freud's thinking about unconscious mental processes can be traced back to the "Romantic" phase of German medicine, and specifically to Johann Friedrich Herbart (1776–1841) whose system is almost identical to that of Freud.[61] Ellenberger, in his history, *The Discovery of the Unconscious*, states, "There is hardly a single concept of Freud or Jung that had not been anticipated by the Philosophy of Nature and Romantic medicine."[62]

It is also interesting to note that Freud's fundamental hypotheses about repression and the unconscious mind grew out of Mesmerism and animal magnetism, which in the early nineteenth century were taken more seriously in Germany than anywhere else in Europe. Since strange aberrations of memory showed up in hypnotized people who recalled long forgotten events of childhood in the waking state, the concept of repression was born. And since hypnotized patients would occasionally be subjected to a flood or even a panorama of childhood memories so sharp it seemed they must have occurred the day before, it seemed there must be a reason for this. And there was. The neurologist Penfield found that when the temporal lobes of his patients' brains were physically stimulated, similar panoramic memories occurred. It is also well known that the temporal lobes are primarily affected in states of drowning and suffocation because their structure and peculiar blood supply makes them much more susceptible to anoxia (lack of oxygen), hypoglycemia (low blood sugar), and drugs than other parts of the brain. Of all parts of the brain, they also have the lowest seizure threshold and, consequently, the most rapid spread of an epileptic discharge.

Although the events recalled by Penfield's patients when stimulated by his electrodes involved more recent memories, they, too, were similarly unremarkable. One patient reported while the electrode was in place he saw a Seven-Up bottling company and a local bakery. Another patient when stimulated reported seeing a man and his dog walking along a road near his home. A third patient reported hearing a telephone conversation while another saw a man coming through a fence at a baseball game.

Under so-called hypnosis, the memories reported are evoked by similar mechanism, although it is not due to anoxia or electrodes. It is due to relaxation and suggestion and getting the individual into *a frame of mind that is conducive to recall*. In a series of experiments on hypnosis in which subjects' memories were tested while under hypnosis and while awake, during the awake and control condition the subjects had to do nothing but sit relaxed in an easy chair and try to recall as much as they could about their early childhood, beginning with the first thing they could remember up until the present. They were required to do so for an entire hour. What was most surprising was that, without exception, all of the 120 subjects participating in this exercise produced literally reams of material, and hundreds of memories of both significant and trivial events. Invariably, the comments of the subjects after the hour was over resembled "I hadn't thought of those things in years," or "I thought I had forgotten all about that cat I had in the first grade," and so on. Once these associational chains are started they quickly reveal a veritable ocean of experiential material. Once begun it becomes very difficult to stop. Most of the student subjects were perfectly ready to continue to recall much beyond the hour provided. Many had only progressed through the fifth or sixth grade before the hour was over.[63]

If you have any doubt as to the richness of human memory and the total number of events one can recall when one approaches one's past in a systematic and associative manner, try this exercise yourself. What you will discover is that each of us is another Proust, and every one of us is capable of writing another *Remembrance of Times Past*.* Since there is no real alteration of consciousness, none of these memories is of a repressed nature or even of a suppressed nature (intentionally buried in the mind), albeit some of them are definitely unpleasant, and even if they were not verbalized they *were remembered*. There is, in fact, no known mechanism by which memories can be repressed by the conscious mind or ego as Freud imagined. In Thornton's words, and she is quite correct, "Painful and distressing events are, as common sense tells us, those that most clearly *stand out* in our memory. We may 'put them out of our head,' i.e., turn our attention to something else, but they will return unbidden when some chance association recalls them to mind [emphasis in original]."[64] Moreover, the recovery of memories under any of the above conditions is essentially an involuntary process. Individual memories cannot be recalled at will. Occasionally, the memories recalled under hypnosis may have been of greater significance than the trivia mentioned. This probably occurred often enough to credit the process with the power of widening the field of consciousness to reveal *all* forgotten material. But for the most part, so-called hypnotic regressions are nothing more than suggestion and compliance along with the ingenuous use of the subject's imagination. Thornton is also correct in calling attention to the fact that any and all regressions to the first years of life, and even to birth, are especially suspect. At this stage of development the brain is still so immature that large tracts of nervous pathways and the brain mechanisms for establishing long-term memory are insufficiently developed. For this reason alone, Thornton points out, contrary to psychoanalytic theory, the first years of life are probably the *least* important for the development of future personality!

As for the topic of past-lives regression, despite the hysterical

---

*Marcel Proust, a French novelist, introduced exhaustive psychological analysis to fiction. In painful elaboration, his characters remember every detail and aspect of their lives.

claims of so-called psychotherapists and psychics, these productions are nothing more than the exercise of the subject's imagination and, if they are not outright frauds and hoaxes, they are excellent examples of cryptomnesia.* As for panoramic memories, it is particularly interesting to note that these are also common accompaniments of people undergoing near death experiences (NDEs) and, rather than having an otherworldly or unearthly basis, it should now be clear that most are the standard neurological accompaniment of temporal lobe anoxia.

Returning to Freud and his system, it is important to remember that his entire theoretical edifice was more or less a regurgitation of old theories he had read many years before. In one sense of the word, Freudian theory is, itself, a beautiful example of cryptomnesia. That all of these concepts and ideas flashed into his head as new and original concepts is, of course, not only completely compatible with his cocaine usage but is as excellent an example of cryptomnesia as can be found anywhere.

What is difficult to conceive is how anyone in his right mind could take so much of Freudian nonsense seriously. It is almost as bad as some of the other extremist views of the Freudian apostles who see the man watering his lawn with a garden hose as a closet masturbator. Following this same line of thought, the man who uses an automatic sprinkler is, in actuality, impregnating the universe!

Although Thornton has done a masterful job of poking holes in the Freudian curtain she is far from being the last to do so. Garth Wood, in his book, *The Myth of Neurosis*, compares psychoanalysis with a cure for cancer.[65] If one proposes a new treatment for cancer then it must be scientifically validated, shown to be at least as effective as other methods, prove that it will at least do no harm, insure that there is some scientific mechanism by which the cure works to diminish the cancer, and so on. If no one bothered to test the cure, to check its efficacy, to quantify its negative effects, to compare it with other treatments, and to determine whether it was the pill per se or merely the passage of time that brought about the cure, what then? Suppose the

*Cryptomnesia, or hidden memory, is a term used to describe the recurrence of forgotten information. The person experiencing cryptomnesia believes he is having an original idea, but in reality, the idea is something which was heard, read, or otherwise learned previously.

person proposing the cure then proceeded to hire a group of super-salesmen and flood the land with these dedicated peddlers

> possessed of an almost messianic belief in [the] pill's efficacy, wear-ing the cloak of science to cover their scientific poverty, peddling it to those whose judgment the disease had weakened in the despera-tion of their desire to be made whole. Live through the nightmare and experience a whole industry profiting from and preying on the gullible, the disappointed, the weak, as they sell shamelessly their snake oil equivalent, their "guaranteed" restorer of hair. Now, as you wake in a cold sweat to the reassuring familiarity of reality, consider Freudian psychoanalysis.[66]

Wood goes on to point out that it is well over eighty years since the psychoanalytic "pill" was invented, and yet, in 1985, Arnold Cooper, a past president of the American Psychoanalytic Association, was quoted in the *New York Times* as saying, "Psychoanalysis has been enormously successful clinically and vastly important culturally ... but the time has come to recast psychoanalytic assumptions *so that they can be tested scientifically* [emphasis added by Wood]." Yet in the same article, Adolf Grunbaum, a Freudian critic, stated, "Its scientific foun-dations are impoverished. To say that the theory is ill-founded does not mean it is false. I'm trying to lay bare the logical structure of the the-ory, and to show what must be done *if suitable evidence is to be found* [emphasis added by Wood]."[67] To these comments Wood adds,

> The situation is mind-boggling. The psychoanalysts are admitting openly that the theories on which psychoanalysis is based have never been validated by the scientific method, and this despite the con-stant assertions of Freud that it was above all else a scientific disci-pline. Of course, many of us have known all along that psycho-analysis was scientifically bankrupt, a mythical creation rather than the science it pretends to be. But how many patients, who have spent small (and frequently large) fortunes on the "treatment," know that it is not scientifically respectable? Do the analysts who take their money tell them? Do they know? Do they care? And if not, why not? ... Untested and unproved, it is dispensed by the unsci-entific for the consumption of the unhappy. [Emphasis in original.][68]

Wood also points out that although many have objected to the psychoanalytic claims, these objections have been studiously ignored. In 1953, Sir Karl Popper examined a number of theories that were having an impact on thinking. Included in the study were the theories of Einstein, Adler, Marx, and Freud. Popper felt that the theories of Adler, Marx, and Freud were in a different category than those of Einstein. What was most noteworthy about their theories was their enormous *explanatory* power. They explained everything that happened. Whatever happened always confirmed it. In Popper's words,

> A Marxist could not open a newspaper without finding on every page confirming evidence for his interpretation of history. . . . The Freudian analysts emphasized that their theories were constantly verified by their "clinical observations." . . . I could not think of any human behavior which could not be interpreted in terms of either theory. It was precisely this fact—that they always fitted, that they were always confirmed—which in the eyes of their admirers constituted the strongest arguments in favor of these theories. It began to dawn on me that this apparent strength was in fact their weakness.[69]

In other words, Popper was pointing out that it is easy to find confirmations of theories if all we look for is confirmations. To confirm the theory that all crows are black, we can rush about discovering large quantities of black crows. But even very large numbers of black crows are not sufficient to prove the theory. Just how many black crows do you need to convince yourself of the theory's truth? A million? A billion? It will depend on the person being convinced. If, however, just one white crow were to turn up, it would destroy the theory completely. The theory that says all crows are black forbids the existence of white crows, and as Popper knows, the more a theory forbids, the better it is. In sum, every genuine test of a theory is an attempt to falsify it, not to confirm it, and any theory that is not refutable by any conceivable event is nonscientific, or pseudoscientific. The irrefutability of both Marxism and Freudism is not a virtue; it is a vice. Nothing can prove psychoanalysis false. Everything confirms it and nothing denies it. Simply said, scientific inquiry doesn't matter to psychoanalysis; it is simply not relevant.

Both Sir Aubrey Lewis and Ernest Nagel agree with Popper. Lewis pointed to what he called "an unbridged gap" in psychoanalysis between what could be checked and observed experimentally, and the ambiguous concepts such as "instincts," "unconscious fantasies," and such, which purported to explain them.[70] Nagel noted that although it is permissible for a theory to be based on entities that cannot be directly observed, for example, protons and electrons, there must, however, be a demonstrable link between those entities and their observable effects in the world of the senses.[71] Psychoanalysis fails to provide this link.

Perhaps the one individual who has done the most to leave the psychoanalytic edifice in ruins, according to Wood, is Sir Peter Medawar. Medawar picked several samples of psychoanalytic writing from papers presented at the twenty-third International Psychoanalytic Congress held in Stockholm in 1963 and let the authors' own words damn them. Two samples should suffice. One analyst wrote about a patient who suffered from ulcerative colitis and who dreamed of snakes, and reported:

> The snake represented the powerful and dangerous (strangling), poisonous (impregnating) penis of his father and his own (in its anal-sadistic aspects). At the same time, it represented the destructive, devouring vagina. . . . The snake also represented the patient himself in both aspects as the male and female and served as a substitute for people of both sexes. On the oral and anal levels the snake represented the patient as a digesting (pregnant) gut with a devouring mouth and expelling anus.[72]

The second example is another analyst's explanation for the etiology of anti-Semitism:

> The Oedipus complex is acted out and experienced by the anti-Semite as a narcissistic injury, and he projects this injury upon the Jew who is made to play the role of the father. . . . His choice of the Jew is determined by the fact that the Jew is in the unique position of representing at the same time the all-powerful father and the father castrated.[73]

Medawar's comment on these and other examples was that he did not intend to poke fun at them, ridiculous though he believed them to be. Rather his purpose was to illustrate the olympian glibness of psychoanalytic thought. Although the contributors to the congress were concerned with very real and serious problems more difficult than those scientists face in the laboratory, there was never any hesitancy whatsoever, no admission of ignorance, or expression of any doubt about any pronouncement—none of the attitudes and expressions commonly found at similar gatherings of physiologists, biologists, or biochemists. In his words, "A lava-flow of *ad hoc* explanation pours over and around all difficulties, leaving only a few smoothly rounded prominences to mark where they might have lain."[74]

Wood is even more scathing in his denouncement of the analysts, and feels that Medawar let them off much too easily:

The effrontery of these brazen pseudoscientific poseurs takes away the breath. It is surely one of the most amazing phenomena of the twentieth century that such absurd and disgusting psychofilth is regarded as credible by so many. Sir Peter says that it is not his purpose to poke fun at them, but is not that what they deserve? If the scientific method is not sufficient to discredit them, then what is left in the armory of the commonsensible but the weapon of ridicule? Will laughter and scorn weaken the stranglehold of psychoanalysis on the culture of our age? We shall see.[75]

Unfortunately, what we have seen since Wood published his book is scarcely any diminution in the pronouncements of the credentialed but obtuse pseudoscientific psychoquacks. If anything, at the beginning of the 1990s we are currently witnessing a resurgence, if not a veritable renaissance, of psychotherapeutic garbage. While it is true that we have always had it amongst us, it has certainly seemed to have picked up speed in the last few years with the advent of the so-called New Age occultism and mysticism with its own peculiar brand of degreed but irresponsible and antiscientific zealots. Admittedly, it may be hard to top that very dandy fellow, Francis I. Regardie, M.D., of Los Angeles, who in the 1950s introduced his revolutionary new treatment called vomit therapy. Dr. Regardie, using a tongue depressor, cures his patients of whatever ailment they may have by having them regurgitate into a kidney pan. If the patient is puzzled at the request and resists the suggestion, the therapist provides a brief explanation and tells his client this is not the time for intellectual discussion. Regardie's procedure is to have the patient gag ten or twelve times. The gagging style itself provides an index to the client's level of inhibition. Some gag with finesse, others with delicacy, some without noise, whereas others will cough and spit. Still others will scoff and sneer. Those who gag without sound are the most difficult to deal with, as their character-armor is almost impenetrable and their personalities rigid. Others will retch with horrible completeness. This is a very literal application of the Freudian notion of catharsis.[76]

On the other hand we have Arthur Janov, the inventor of scream therapy, who believes devoutly that the search for meaning in life is, itself, most neurotic. The cure for everything is, of course, to scream your little head off and get rid of all that bottled up anger. On the other hand, Viktor Frankl's logotherapy rests on the assumption that man's search for the meaning of his existence and his failure to find it is the basis of his neurotic discontent.

Much of the foregoing information is neither well known nor understood by members of the helping professions. As a result, when these professionals encounter strange and unusual phenomena such as past lives, alien abductions, multiple personalities, or contact with the dead, they, too, yield to the transcendental temptation and invoke a religious or supernatural explanation.

As far as modern psychology is concerned Freud has been a total and unmitigated disaster. He has, in the long run, done considerably more harm than good and, as several critics have stated, psychoanalysis never was and never will be anything more than a fallacious pseudoscience. As many perceptive students of psychology have noted, Freud constitutes a problem rather than a solution.

Keith E. Stanovich rightly notes that Freud's notoriety has not only adversely affected the general public's conceptions about the field of psychology but has also contributed to many misconceptions and misunderstandings.[77] Freudian and psychoanalytic psychologists make up less than ten percent of the membership of the American Psychological Association. Moreover, Freud's theories and ideas have never been scientifically substantiated or confirmed. Freud not only was not a scientist but he never carried out a controlled experiment and believed that clinical case studies were all that was necessary to justify the truth of his speculations. Regarding his theories, none of the experimental work carried out to test the validity of his speculations has resulted in any positive results. For any theory to be considered scientific there must be an empirical link between the theory and behavior. Freud's theories seldom meet such a criterion. Case theories and personal introspection are not enough. The major problem with all the psychoanalytical theoretical speculation is that none of Freud's most salient claims are capable of or susceptible to *disconfirmation*. A theory that cannot be proven false is not only useless but, in the long run, harmful. Since psychoanalytical theory is immune to falsification it is in no way a scientific theory at all.

This is precisely the problem with Dr. Freud and his ideas. As for what *Time* has called "The Assault on Freud," it has been going on for quite a while.[78] Not only did Freud's ideas and concepts meet with considerable opposition at the time they were introduced, the opposition and their exposure to the light of truth has continued ever since. The initial experimental disillusionment with Freudian theory came in 1941 when the Rockefeller and Carnegie foundations endowed the Social Science Research Council, who hired Dr. Robert R. Sears of Harvard to investigate the Freudian theory of personality. After carefully studying 166 articles covering scientific attempts to verify Freudian claims, Sears concluded: "The experiments and observations examined in this report stand testimony that few investigators feel free to accept Freud's statements at face value. The reason lies in the . . . [fact that the] Freudian method makes psychoanalysis a bad science." Moreover, Sears noted, "perhaps a dozen other theories would provide as good as or better explanations" of the facts.[79]

What made the scientist's task even more difficult was that Freud never formalized his theories in such a way as to make them empirically testable. In the Freudian system vague speculations are made to appear as fact.

This was made clear in Andrew Salter's carefully thought out work, *The Case against Psychoanalysis*. In his preface to the 1963 edition Salter noted, "This book has been translated into more languages, and has been more reviled, than anything else I have ever written. Yet I do not take back a single word of it, for it is all true."[80]

The fact is Freud has failed, as he once feared he might. "You often estimate me too highly" he wrote to a friend at the turn of the century. "I am not really a man of science, not an observer, not an experimenter, and not a thinker. I am nothing but by temperament . . . an adventurer . . . with the curiosity, the boldness, and the tenacity that belongs to that type of being. Such people are apt to be treasured if they succeed, if they have really discovered something; otherwise they are thrown aside, and that is not altogether unjust."[81]

We now know that even the most favorable reports of psychoanalytic results show percentages of cures and near cures that are no different from results with other methods. The discouraging statistics gathered by the Fact-Finding Committee of the American Psychoanalytic Association led Weinstock, the chairman of the committee, to state "explicitly . . . that his Association made *no claims* of therapeutic usefulness for psychoanalytic methods [emphasis in original]."[82]

Most psychoanalysts now practice cryptoanalysis: they keep their sexual monomania and psychoanalytic terminology to themselves, thus concealing from the patient the fact that they are using obsolete methods. Or they speak learnedly of the newer Freudian discoveries, and use the same, old-fashioned methods. According to Andrew Salter,

> Someone has said (and I wish I could give due credit), all of psychoanalytic theory can be derived from three postulates:
>
> 1. Whatever it looks like—that isn't it.
> 2. If you can measure it—it's something else.
> 3. Whatever it is—it isn't nice.
>
> I think that summarizes it . . . [83]

Salter is again most eloquent when he said, "As for Freud's concepts of the human: Modern psychology has shown Freud's map of the mind to be as inaccurate and wildly forceful as the pre-Columbus maps

of the New World, and practical experience has shown psychoanalytical therapy to be insipid and unimpressive in its results."[84]

With regard to false memories, Salter wrote that Freud himself
was misled by them:

> Under the *pressure of the technical procedure* which I had used at that
> time, *the majority of my* patients reproduced from their childhood
> scenes in which they were sexually seduced by some grown-up per-
> son. With female patients the part of the seducer was almost always
> assigned to their father. I believed these stories, and consequently
> supposed that I had discovered the roots of the subsequent neurosis
> in the experiences of sexual seduction in childhood . . . When, how-
> ever, I was at last obliged to recognize that *these scenes of seduction had
> never taken place*, and that they were only phantasies [*sic*] which my
> patients had made up or *which I myself had perhaps forced upon them*, I
> was for sometime completely at a loss. . . . When I had pulled myself
> together, I was able to draw the right conclusions from my discov-
> ery: namely that the neurotic symptoms were not related directly to
> actual events but to phantasies [*sic*] embodying wishes and that as
> far as the neurosis was concerned psychical reality was of more
> importance than material reality. [Emphasis in original.][85]

Some of his patients' seduction experiences were, of course, veridical,
but Freud never knew which were which.

While the attacks on Freud have been thorough and convincing
and there is very little left of his system that is worthy of scientific
attention, he did leave an indelible mark on generations of therapists
who continue to use the Freudian psychodynamic approach. According to E. Fuller Torrey in his 1992 book, *Freudian Fraud*, the mark
Freud left was in no way either admirable or positive.[86] In Torrey's eyes
psychoanalysis has been a total and abject failure both as a successful
psychotherapeutic regimen and as a treatment of choice for any of the
most common neuroses or psychoses. This fact is better known, of
course, among the professional clinicians than it is among the general
population. Torrey is horrified over the fact that too many of the
nation's two hundred thousand professional therapists spend their
time doing counseling and psychotherapy based either directly or
indirectly on Freudian theory. In Torrey's words, "Talking to one's

therapist about your mother has become virtually a national pastime and continues to usurp an extraordinarily large share of professional resources that should be going to the seriously mentally ill."[87] According to Torrey, and he is correct, the true serious mental illnesses are the schizophrenias and depressions.

Most of Torrey's book is devoted to the negative impact that Freud's theories have had on American thought and culture. For years we all believed that childhood experiences—the earlier the more important—pretty much determined our adult personality. We now know otherwise. In fact, early childhood experiences are comparatively unimportant antecedents of our adult selves. Freud's manipulation of the nature-nurture or heredity versus environment controversy also confused our thinkers into believing that nurture was all and that nature (the environment in which one is raised) played an unimportant and insignificant role. This notion influenced literature, drama, pop culture, child-rearing, criminal justice, and the Democratic party itself. Most influenced was the entire counseling and psychotherapeutic industry, an industry that Freud essentially created. Freud was the idol worshiped by Emma Goldman, the socialist thinker; Walter Lippman; Karl Menninger; Margaret Mead; and John Bradshaw. In his efforts to be fair Torrey avers that some good did emerge: primarily the idea of psychotherapy, humanism, and our recognition of the unconscious. Nevertheless, Torrey insists that the adverse effects far outweigh the good. What Freud left us was narcissism, irresponsibility, and the denigration of women. These things and the perpetuation of the Freudian paradigm with its "unconscious baggage" constitute, on an overall basis, a kind of fraud.

For a time, anyone holding the notion that genes are important determiners of personality and behavior risked being labeled a neo-Nazi. These ideas were strongly embraced by socialists in the 1930s and by the liberals after World War II. Benjamin Spock, the child rearing guru of the 1940s and 1950s, followed Freud blindly and religiously and warned us of "the perils of the potty chair." William Healy, a British psychiatrist, recommended that a modified form of psychoanalysis be used to treat all criminal offenders. American penologists Bernard Glueck and William A. White bought and promoted these ideas, especially the notion that you cannot hold a person responsible for behavior that is largely determined by unconscious thought processes. Karl Menninger also made the implementation of Freudian theory to criminology his principal life's work and the majority of this nation's analysts promoted and supported the most liberal of social programs with regard to the treatment of criminals. None of this thinking or speculation has contributed anything positive to either criminal rehabilitation or a reduction in criminal violence.

Torrey, like others before him, sees Freudianism and psychoanalysis as a religion and its practitioners more in the roles of priests than physicians or scientists. There is little doubt that the entire Freudian edifice closely resembles the structure and function of a theological belief system. Dr. Josef Breuer, Freud's contemporary, recognized the similarity between psychoanalysis and religion long ago and once remarked, "Psychoanalysis in the hands of the physician is what confession is in the hands of the Catholic priest."[88]

Religion or not, the *Time* magazine reviewers conclude that Freud nevertheless

> still managed to create an intellectual edifice that *feels* closer to the experience of living, and therefore hurting, than any other system currently in play . . . Psychoanalysis and all its offshoots may in the final analysis turn out to be no more reliable than phrenology or mesmerism or any of the countless other pseudosciences that once offered unsubstantiated answers or false solace. Still, the reassurances provided by Freud that our inner lives are rich with drama and hidden meanings would be missed if it disappeared, leaving nothing in its place. [Emphasis in original.][89]

High drama, mythology, excitement, literature! This, of course, was Freud's intellectual appeal. Nice, but what we need now and have needed in the past, as Torrey concludes in the summary of his book, is much more: "the challenge of the 21st century is to place human behavior on a more solidly scientific foundation and to insure that all children have the maximum opportunity to develop the potential with which they have been born."[90] Perhaps the novelist Vladimir Nabokov has said best what has long needed to be said: "Our grandsons will no doubt regard today's psychoanalysts with the same amused contempt as we do astrology and phrenology."[91] Everything that has been said about Freud can be equally applied to Freud's chief rival, Carl Jung.

Jungian Junk

After his break with Freud in 1914, Carl Jung set out to develop his own system known as analytical psychology: a peculiar mixture of Western and Eastern religious mysticism, belief in the occult, and tidbits culled from medicine, psychiatry, psychology, the humanities, and the natural and social sciences. Scholars have called his "system" complex, esoteric, and obscure. Like most late nineteenth century German thinkers, Jung seemed compelled to "explain" everything in man's mental world. The result, of course, is that nothing is explained. This vast accumulation of seemingly profound insights, ideas, and concepts—like Freud's—rests upon an edifice of sand. Science, rationalism, and experimentation are all alien to Jungian thought. We are asked to accept Jungian precepts on faith alone, and the spiritual and mystical are given greater weight than any scientific or rationalistic formulations.

Jung saw the role of the psychotherapist and the doctor's primary task as one whose job is to "care for souls." And by soul, Jung meant the entire psychological person. As for the individual human psyche, Jung believed we all are made up of both a *personal unconscious* inaccessible to conscious reflection and connected to observable behavior and a *collective unconscious* which is a vast storehouse of genetically inherited knowledge. Not only is the collective unconscious a source of our psychic energy, it also shapes and structures every aspect of our conscious awareness. Moreover, it is the wellspring of human creativity and provides us with the source of direction in our lives. All of us also have a *transpersonal* nature which transcends our personal history and nature and connects us not only with the history of the human species but also with the divine nature of the universe. Jung believed that we are all ruled not by waking, conscious logic and reason but by powerful unconscious and transpersonal forces of which we are only dimly aware. We are also impelled to grow and evolve toward greater whole-

ness and unity in body, mind, and spirit. It is the therapist's job to
tend to this natural, instinctive growth. We can, with desire and
effort, attain complete self-realization.

As for our personality, each of us is made up of several unique but
interdependent structures: a *psyche* or total personality; an *ego*, the psyche's unifying force and center of consciousness; the *personal unconscious*
or all our forgotten experiences which often cluster into *complexes*; and
a number of universal mental structures or cognitive organizing principles called *archetypes* which can be discovered through the symbolic
interpretation of fantasies, myths, and dreams. Our active, basic archetypes form our psychological reality. Jung discovered these basic
archetypes via clinical work with his clients, introspection, and intensive study of literature, mythology, and comparative religions.

Some archetypes are more important in Jungian thought than others. The mask we wear in public, who we pretend to be to others, is
called the *persona*. Our unconscious, nurturing, feminine side is called
our *anima*, whereas the driving, aggressive side of ourselves is called
our *animus*. Both sexes contain both archetypes. Everyone is part male
and part female. The part of our personality we would rather not
accept or acknowledge, our dark side, is appropriately called the
shadow. The most important archetype of all is the *self* which, according to Jung, only emerges when we attain middle age and gain enough
experience to become unified and stable. Other lesser archetypes are
the hero, death, rebirth, and the wise old man.

Extroversion and introversion are the basic personality attitudes in
Jungian thought. An extrovert is oriented toward the external, social
world and the introvert focuses more upon the internal and subjective
aspects of existence. Jung also developed additional personality types
organized around four other personality dimensions: a thinking type—
people who were logical, objective, and rational; a feeling type—people who were centered around their affective and subjective experiences;
a sensation type—people who emphasized stimulation from the senses;
and an intuitive type—people who are primarily creative and imaginative. From this typology Jung developed a complex psychological system he believed applicable to our everyday behavior. Interestingly
enough, a popular and often-used personality test, the Myers-Briggs

Type Indicator, is loosely based on Jung's concepts. The test, a measure of personality type, which has been both overused and misused, leaves a lot to be desired in terms of psychometric validity and reliability.

Jung believed no one is psychologically healthy and that the course of normal human development warps and misshapes our personality and character. He regarded psychopathology as the expression of our unconscious effort to restore balance and to deal with the repressed forces in the unconscious. The greater the intensity of such forces the greater the degree of abnormality.

Like Freud, unfortunately, Jung's concepts are so enunciated that they defy any and all attempts at scientific corroboration and elaboration. Jung never recommended any specific set of psychotherapeutic techniques or procedures and recommended many different methods to help the unconscious to become conscious.[92] As a result, Jungian therapists use a varied set of humanistic and existential techniques to promote change. Dreams, as in Freud's view, are taken somewhat literally and their meaning draws on many unconscious archetypes and symbols. Jungian therapy typically lasts a year or more and the best clients are the upper-middle class, well-educated, middle-aged clients seeking greater wisdom and enlightenment. Growth—usually spiritual in nature—is the therapeutic goal.

Jung also saw the professional role of the psychiatrist as an overseer of the human soul and sincerely believed that only the psychiatrist-physician was properly trained to deal with any and all human soul problems.

John Kerr, a clinical psychologist, in *A Most Dangerous Method*, his study of the animosity between Freud and Jung based upon study of the men's diaries, letters, and journals; argues that the two men threatened each other with blackmail.[93] Freud believed that one of Jung's ex-patients had also been his mistress. Jung was certain that Freud was sexually involved with his (Freud's) sister-in-law, Minna Bernays. Both decided, reasonably, not to expose the other and went their separate ways. It is clear that neither of the two was anything approaching a saint. Most disturbing of all, however, were a number of charges made after World War II that Jung was, if not an outright Nazi collaborator, at least highly sympathetic to their cause.

It should also be mentioned that Jung turned away from Freud and natural science to form a new religion based on the idea of rebirth—a cult of personality centered on himself and passed down by priest-analysts. According to Richard Noll in his excellent 1994 book, *The Jung Cult: Origins of a Charismatic Movement*, Jung's antiscientific stance and his love of the occult also provided considerable aid and comfort to the Nazi philosophy.[94]

As for Freud, quite recently clinical psychologist Dr. Paul Scagnelli has published a book, *Deadly Dr. Freud,* in which he makes a strong case that at one time in 1914, after the Freud-Jung schism, Freud made plans to murder Jung, developed psychotic symptoms and murdered his elderly and rivalrous nephew, John Freud, as well as his eldest brother, Emmanuel, the father of John.[95] Scagnelli also argues Freud killed a number of his clients and friends with cocaine overdoses and committed a number of other professional misdeeds. Whether or not these sensational charges can or will ever be substantiated remains to be seen. Nevertheless, there is good reason to believe the human race is better off without either the house of Freud or the house of Jung.

THE REVOLT AGAINST THE PSYCHOTHERAPEUTIC STATE

While the appearance of the neuroleptic (mind-influencing) drugs in the 1950s has been widely hailed by the psychiatric establishment as the revolution of modern psychiatric treatment and clear proof that the major mental disorders are of biological origin (and thus, within the domain of medical treatment), these beliefs are easily challenged and clearly refuted on a number of grounds. While the barbiturates and phenothiazines (antipsychotics) did subdue excited patients, lessen resistance to psychotherapy, and replace incoherence with intelligible speech, there were some not-so-pleasant physical side-effects to spoil the rosy picture. Quickly, however, the march of drugs became so irresistible that in the 1970s spokesmen at National Institute of Mental Health (NIMH) concluded "drugs alone are the single, most powerful and economical treatment for schizophrenics and psychotherapy without drugs has provided no evidence for either its effectiveness or helpfulness." Exactly what the neuroleptics can and can't do will be discussed later. It is important here, however, to note that medication alone soon proved not to be the panacea it first seemed. No drug is without its side effects and, in many instances, the side effects are more debilitating than the disorder for which the drugs are originally prescribed. This problem will be discussed at length in later chapters.

Those who assume that dislike of their mother-in-law or their unhappiness with their job or boss can be cured by a pill are, themselves, badly in need of therapy. Yet this is the prevailing psychiatric opinion: every emotional nuance, and every human belief that runs against the behavioral status quo is due to a disease that can and must be cured by a medical doctor providing medical treatment. Moreover, only medical doctors should be given the power to commit individuals to a mental institution where they will be deprived of their liberty and freedom to decide what can and can't be done to their physical persons and, if they resist this oppression, then punished by confinement in locked and guarded wards and put into either physical or chemical straitjackets (or both) against their will. Currently, these are the powers given to psychiatry and this injustice—as well as other violations of human rights and freedoms—characterizes what has been known for some while now as "the psychotherapeutic state." Over the past twenty years the pharmaceutical industry and the health insurance companies have joined forces with the psychiatric establishment to form a conglomerate that has enormous social and financial power which, in turn, guarantees overwhelming political power. The result of this concentration of power has not been in the best interests of either the public at large or of any particular individual who is unfortunate enough to develop a mental health problem.

Over the last three decades enough injustices and abuses of these psychiatric powers have occurred to warrant a steady stream of outraged protestations. Because the threats made against the overwhelming power of the conglomerate have been so feeble and far-between, most have been derided and ignored. The justness of one's cause has never been a criterion by which decisions are made. One cannot, however, continue to ignore the legion of protests that has been made in the name of common sense, justice, and sound therapeutic practice.

One of the most effective protests appeared in 1980 when Dr. Jonas Robitscher, a psychiatrist and lawyer, in a long, impassioned, and definitive work titled *The Powers of Psychiatry*, addressed the issue of the psychiatrists' abuse of their authority and powers. Robitscher shows clearly not only exactly how psychiatrists exert their power (fifty-one ways to be precise) but also the many ways in which it is improperly exercised and abused. Robitscher notes that even when psychiatrists are aware of their authority and its potential for abuse and even when they act responsibly, harm can result.

According to Robitscher:

> Psychiatrists are not sued or held accountable for this indifferent-to-inadequate practice—standards of care are too imprecise and poor practice cannot, ordinarily, be proved to be negligent—but frequently they examine patients too superficially, commit them too quickly, impose intrusive therapy too readily, detain them in institutions for overlong periods, or overmedicate and polymedicate them. The doctor who has a choice of therapies but picks electroshock because the patient's Blue Cross coverage allows for only twenty-one days of in-hospital care, and electroshock can easily be accomplished in that period, will never be criticized for his therapy choice. Patients who need a personal kind of treatment get shunted into impersonal treatment. A patient who could get along well enough without medication is lulled into insensibility with Valium or treated to the point of tardive dyskinesia with Prolixin.[96]

Robitscher also notes that even when psychiatric practice is grossly improper, the patients who are victimized often don't recognize it as such—especially if they become drug-dependent cases. Since the patients don't know what to expect from therapy they don't even realize they've been abused. The psychiatrist also has an easy out with his statement that he was "exercising his clinical judgment." Psychiatric malpractice is hard to prove. Unfortunately, many extremely dubious practices have for so long been accepted as standard that patients have little basis for a malpractice suit even though unnecessary long-term confinements, breaches of confidentiality, and even sexual exploitation are much too common. When patients do allege that they have been exploited in treatment they are usually not believed. This is especially true in the field of sexual problems. William Masters of the Masters and Johnson team has said, "The sexually dysfunctional person is a pushover for seduction by an authority figure such as the psychotherapist. . . . The innumerable examples of patient seduction, both heterosexual and homosexual, are a disgrace to our profession."[97]

According to Robitscher, if psychiatry's house is to be cleaned it will be necessary to define the bounds of psychiatry and clearly label what constitutes overstepping them. All who are qualified as psychiatrists must understand the requirements of the profession and be willing to try to live within them. Psychiatrists would report on fellow psychiatrists, speaking up whenever there are any ethical violations of these rules. Finally, the profession would have to create effective disciplinary mechanisms so that erring psychiatrists would be deprived of the privilege of practicing. As Robitscher concludes, "As of today there is little indication that psychiatry is concerned enough with the proprieties of psychiatric practice to devote time and energy to such a housecleaning effort."[98]

Since the medical model is authoritarian, like their fellow physicians, psychiatrists do not see mental patients' rights as being as important as their therapeutic needs. In searching for a remedy for some of the profession's problems Robitscher suggests:

Part of the solution to the problem of abuse of psychiatric power is to have a better class of psychiatrists who practice psychiatry because of its potential to help patients achieve stability and independence, not because it may produce a higher standard of living or give the pleasure of exerting authority. But psychiatry is emphasizing symptomatic relief secured through medication, and it is becoming more biological, more anxious to identify with the rest of medicine, less interested in its psychological roots. We cannot expect the medically oriented psychiatrist to become interested in defining and limiting his authority. Until a new, less authoritarian breed of psychiatrists emerges, psychiatry will continue to exert too much power over too many people, gaining authority from its two antecedents, medicine and Freudian psychology, and providing care that either emphasizes the medical aspect of psychiatry or is a watered-down version of verbal therapy.[99]

Despite the enlightened views of Robitscher and many others, nothing of any consequence or significance in the direction of making psychiatry less authoritarian by the medically minded or drug-oriented has changed in the psychiatric profession as a whole since 1980. Despite a steady barrage of antiestablishment psychiatry and antipsychotherapy books and monographs over the past twenty years, little or no change in attitude or behavior has occurred. Despite the annotated and documented truth of this impressive literature, psychotherapists have refused to acknowledge its existence, and to read or heed it. Instead, they have inbred, institutionalized, and even sanctified the errors of their past.

NOTES

1. Walter Bromberg, *Man above Humanity: A History of Psychotherapy* (Philadelphia: J. B. Lippincott, 1954), p. 18.

2. Walter Bromberg, *From Shaman to Psychotherapist* (Chicago: Henry Regnery Co, 1975), pp. v–vi.

3. Ibid., also, Franz Alexander and S. Selesnick, *The History of Psychiatry* (New York: Harper & Row, 1969); Gerald Grob, *Mental Institutions in America* (New York: Free Press, 1973); Gregory Zilboorg and George Henry, *A History of Medical Psychology* (New York: W. W. Norton, 1953); George F. Drinka, *The Birth of Neurosis: Myth, Malady, and the Victorians* (New York: Touchstone Books, 1984); and Lowell S. Selling, *Men against Madness* (New York: New Home Library, 1940).

4. Fielding H. Garrison, *Introduction to the History of Medicine*, 3d ed. (Philadelphia: William Saunders, 1921), p. 96.

5. Ibid., p. 121.

6. Bromberg, *Man above Humanity*, pp. 40–41.

7. Henry Kramer and James Sprenger, *Malleus Maleficarum (The Witches' Hammer)* (1484); trans. Montague Summers (London: Rodker, 1928).

8. Heinrich Laehr, *The Literature of Psychiatry, Neurology and Psychology between 1459–1799* (Reimer, Berlin: Academy of Wissenshaften in Berlin, 1900), pp. 1459–1799.

9. Robert Burton, *The Anatomy of Melancholy* (1621), ed. Floyd Dell and Paul Jordan-Smith (New York: Tudor, 1927).

10. M. Hirsch Goldberg, *The Blunder Book* (New York: William Morrow & Co., 1984), p. 66.

11. Reginald Scot, *The Discoverie of Witchcraft* (1584) (Suffolk, N.Y.: John Rodker, 1930).

12. Gregory Zilboorg, *The Medical Man and the Witch during the Renaissance* (Baltimore: Johns Hopkins Press, 1935), pp. 84–87.

13. William Cullen, *First Lines of the Practice of Physick* (Edinburgh: Creech, 1769).

14. Robert Whytt, *Observations on the Nature, Causes and Cure of Those Disorders Commonly Called Nervous, Hypochondriac or Hysteric*, 3d ed., (Edinburgh: Balfour, 1767).

15. Cited in Cullen, *First Lines of the Practice of Physick.*

16. Johann C. Lavater, *Fragments on Physiognomy* (1775), cited in Bromberg, *Man above Humanity*, p. 120.

17. G. M. Beard, *A Practical Treatise on Nervous Exhaustion (Neurasthenia)* (New York: Wood, 1880).

18. Walter Bromberg, *From Shaman to Psychotherapist*, p. 156.

19. S. Weir Mitchell, *Wear and Tear, or Hints for the Overworked* (Philadelphia: J. B. Lippincott, 1871).

20. S. Weir Mitchell, *Fat and Blood: An Essay on the Treatment of Certain Forms of Neurasthenia and Hysteria* (Philadelphia: J. B. Lippincott, 1877).

21. Bromberg, *From Shaman to Psychotherapist*, pp. 82–85.

22. Ibid., p. 85.

23. Ibid., p. 86.

24. Ibid., p. 85.

25. Ibid.

26. John Battie, *Treatise on Madness* (London: Whitson and White, 1758), cited in Bromberg, *From Shaman to Psychotherapist.*

27. Ibid., pp. 79–80.

28. Ibid., p. 103.

29. Ibid., pp. 79–80.

30. Benjamin Rush, *Medical Inquiries and Observations upon Diseases of the Mind* (Philadelphia: Kimber and Richardson, 1812).

31. Ibid., p. 79.

32. Ibid., p. 81.

33. Francis Leuret, *Du Troitment Moral de la Foile* (Paris: Bailliere, 1840), cited in Bromberg, *From Shaman to Psychotherapist,* as are all the treatments described in this section.

34. Francis Tiffany, *Life of Dorothea Lynde Dix* (Boston: Houghton Mifflin, 1890).

35. Bromberg, *Man above Humanity.*

36. Lee R. Steiner, *Where Do People Take Their Troubles?* (New York: International University Press, 1945).

37. Isaac Ray, *Mental Hygiene* (Boston: Ticknor and Fields, 1863).

38. Clifford Beer, *A Mind That Found Itself*, 2d ed. (New York: Longman's, 1910).

39. Bromberg, *From Shaman to Psychotherapist*, p. 213.

40. Adolf Meyers, *Principles of Psychobiology* (Baltimore: Johns Hopkins Press, 1951).

41. George Albee, "The Futility of Psychotherapy," *Journal of Mind & Behavior* 11, nos. 3 and 4 (Summer/Autumn 1990): 369–84.

42. Alex Comfort, *The Anxiety Makers: Some Curious Preoccupations of the Medical Profession* (New York: Delta Books, 1969), p. 16.

43. Ibid., p. 76.

44. Ibid., p. 6.

45. All quotes in this paragraph are cited in Comfort, *The Anxiety Makers,* p. 77.

46. R. A. Spitz, "Masturbation and Authority," in *Yearbook of Psychoanalysis,* vol. 9 (Chicago: American Psychoanalytic Association, 1953), p. 113. Cited in Comfort, *The Anxiety Makers,* p. 95.

47. A. Eyer, "Clitoridectomy for the Cure of Certain Cases of Masturbation in Young Girls," *International Medical Magazine* 3 (1894-1895): 259–62. Cited in Comfort, *The Anxiety Makers,* p. 102.

48. Ibid.

49. Spitz, "Masturbation and Authority."

50. Comfort, *The Anxiety Makers,* p. 108.

51. Ibid., p. 118.

52. Ibid., pp. 125–29.

53. Bromberg, *Man above Humanity,* pp. 292–94.

54. Robert A. Baker, *An Introduction to Humanistic Psychology* (Lexington, Mass.: Ginn, 1980), pp. 1–48.

55. M. Siegler and H. Osmond, *Models of Madness, Models of Medicine* (New York: Macmillan, 1974).

56. Lancelot L. Whyte, *The Unconscious before Freud* (New York: Basic Books, 1960); Henri F. Ellenberger, *The Discovery of the Unconscious: The History and Evolution of Dynamic Psychiatry* (New York: Basic Books, 1970); and D. M. Klein, *The Unconscious: Invention or Discovery* (Santa Monica, Calif.: Goodyear, 1977).

57. Whyte, *The Unconscious before Freud,* p. 74.

58. E. M. Thornton, *The Freudian Fallacy* (New York: Dial Press, 1983).

59. Ernest Jones, *Life and Work of Sigmund Freud*, vol. 1 (New York: Basic Books, 1953).

60. Anthony Storr, "The Concept of Cure," in *Psycholanalysis Observed*, ed. C. Rycroft (London: Penguin, 1968).

61. See Klein, *The Unconscious*, for a discussion of Freud's discoveries as mere inventions; and Whyte, *The Unconscious before Freud*, and Ellenberger, *The Discovery of the Unconscious*, for the relationship between Freud's work and the German Romantic period in medicine.

62. Ellenberger, *The Discovery of the Unconscious*, p. 68.

63. Robert A. Baker, *They Call It Hypnosis* (Amherst, N.Y.: Prometheus Books, 1990).

64. Thornton, *The Freudian Fallacy*.

65. Garth Wood, *The Myth of Neurosis* (New York: Perennial Library, 1987), pp. 268–69, 274, 275.

66. Ibid., pp. 268–69.

67. Cited in Wood, *The Myth of Neurosis*, p. 269.

68. Ibid.

69. Karl R. Popper, *Conjectures and Refutations* (New York: Basic Books, 1962), p. 212. Cited in Wood, *The Myth of Neurosis*, p. 271.

70. Aubrey Lewis, "Philosophy and Psychiatry," *Philosophy* 24 (1949): 99–117. Cited in Wood, *The Myth of Neurosis*, p. 272.

71. Ernest Nagel, "Methodological Issues in Psychoanalytic Theory," in *Psychoanalysis, Scientific Method and Philosophy*, ed. Sydney Hook (New York: New York University Press, 1959). Cited in Wood, *The Myth of Neurosis*, pp. 272–73.

72. Peter B. Medawar, "Further Comments on Psychoanalysis," in *The Hope of Progress* (London: Metheum, 1972), p. 72. Cited in Wood, *The Myth of Neurosis*, p. 273.

73. Wood, *The Myth of Neurosis*, p. 274.

74. Medawar, "Further Comments on Psychoanalysis," p. 87. Cited in Wood, *The Myth of Neurosis*, p. 274.

75. Wood, *The Myth of Neurosis*, p. 275.

76. R. D. Rosen, *Psychobabble* (New York: Avon Books), pp. 165–66.

77. Keith E. Stanovich, *How to Think Straight about Psychology*, 3d ed. (New York: HarperCollins, 1992), pp. 2–3.

78. Paul Aray, "The Assault on Freud," *Time*, 29 November 1993, pp. 47–51.

79. Robert R. Sears, *Survey of Objective Studies of Psychoanalytic Concepts*, bulletin 51 (New York: Social Science Research Council, 1943), p. 52.

80. Andrew Salter, *The Case against Psychoanalysis* (New York: Citadel Press, 1952, rev. ed., 1963), p. v.

81. Jones, *Life and Work of Sigmund Freud*, p. 348.

82. Hans H. Eysenck, "Learning Theory and Behavior Therapy," in *Behavior Therapy and the Neuroses* (New York: Pergamon Press, 1960), p. 4.

83. Salter, *The Case against Psychoanalysis*, pp. v–vi.

84. Ibid., p. 1.

85. Ibid. pp. 2–3.

86. E. Fuller Torrey, *Freudian Fraud: The Malignant Effect of Freud's Theory on American Thought and Culture* (New York: HarperCollins, 1992).

87. Ibid., pp. 251–52.

88. Cited in Torrey, *Freudian Fraud*.

89. Aray, "The Assault on Freud," p. 51.

90. Torrey, *Freudian Fraud*, p. 257.

91. Cited in Torrey, *Freudian Fraud*, p. 259.

92. Y. Kaufman, "Analytical Psychotherapy," in *Current Psychotherapies*, 3d ed., ed. R. Corsini (Itasca, Ill.: F. E. Peacock, 1984), pp. 108–41.

93. John Kerr, *A Most Dangerous Method* (New York: A. A. Knopf, 1993).

94. Richard Noll, *The Jung Cult: Origins of a Charismatic Movement* (Princeton, N.J.: Princeton University Press, 1994).

95. Paul Scagnelli, *Deadly Dr. Freud* (Durham, N.C.: Pinewood, 1993).

96. Jonas Robitscher, *The Powers of Psychiatry* (Boston: Houghton Mifflin, 1980), p. 400.

97. William Masters, "Masters Blasts Innumerable Patient Rapes," *Medical Tribune*, 11 June 1975, p. 1.

98. Robitscher, *The Powers of Psychiatry*, p. 433.

99. Ibid., pp. 482–83.

3

Victims and Survivors:
The Hazards of Mental Therapy

If you're not careful about how you use it or spell it, the word "therapist" can quickly become "the rapist"

(Old clinical joke)

Over the years so many people have been victimized by evil and incompetent therapists there is now an entire literary genre devoted to such abuse and another literary genre made up of psychotherapists and other mental health professionals protesting such abuses of the therapists' powers. Sadly enough, protests and complaints against abuses of the psychotherapeutic state's powers have gone unheeded for years. In a recent anthology edited by Dale Peterson, *A Mad People's History of Madness*, a bibliography of writings by mad people and mental patients prior to 1982 lists over five hundred separate items.[1] Some of the most damning of the therapeutic cruelty and mistreatment recorded during the past fifty years are listed at the end of this book. Unfortunately, almost as many protests have been published by psychotherapists themselves who have not been able to tolerate the evil and the incompetence they witness daily. A list of such works published from the 1970s through the 1990s is also included at the end of this volume. So many professionals in the mental therapy field have become so disillusioned they have left the occupation entirely and no longer believe that mental therapy of any sort is desirable.

One of the most outspoken and forceful in this regard is psychiatrist-psychoanalyst Jeffrey M. Masson, who in 1988 wrote *Against Therapy*, a book which carefully details why he believes the very idea of psychotherapy of any kind is wrong. No matter how kindly or good intentioned people are, when they adopt the role of therapist they act to diminish the dignity, autonomy, and freedom of the person who comes for help.

Citing his own eight years of training, Masson says he could have learned it all in eight days of reading at home. The biggest of his disillusions, Masson says, is Freud's abandonment of the so-called seduction theory. Freud originally believed that women who told him about childhood sexual abuse were only imagining or fantasizing it and that the best judge of what really happened was the therapist. The idea that only an analyst could judge whether something was real or only a fantasy became standard doctrine and a foundation plank in psychoanalytic therapy. When Masson discovered that Freud later suppressed the seduction theory, he wrote a book about it: *The Assault on Truth: Freud's Suppression of the Seduction Theory*. Masson was damned by the psychoanalytic establishment as a result. His work was, however, welcomed by the feminist movement and this led Masson to write another book about the psychiatric establishment's mistreatment of women in the nineteenth century. The book, *A Dark Science: Women, Sexuality and Psychiatry in the Nineteenth Century*, specifies in detail the horrors inflicted on women in the name of mental health.

Against Therapy is the result of Masson's sixteen-year quest to understand the meaning of his professional career. What he has to say is worth listening to. First, he objects to the term "patient," which he considers to be condescending and haunted by false medical overtones. Carl Rogers's term "clients," Masson notes, only underlines the condescension. The issue, Masson believes, has to do with power and a pretension to knowledge:

> Had I studied medicine, or law, or philosophy, the kind of discoveries I have made would have been duplicated in those fields. I learned something, in the end, about the pretensions to knowledge. I learned something of the frailty of our ability to help another person who is in emotional distress, and especially about the pretensions to

this ability. I learned about power, and hierarchies, and dominance, the rationalizations for abuse, and the inability of many people to comprehend the suffering they cause others.[2]

When Masson expressed his unhappiness with psychotherapy and deplored those characteristics and needs of humans that led them to seek someone from whom guidance could be had, his friends asked what he would use to replace psychotherapy. Masson's answer is, "If something is evil, or dangerous, why replace it with anything? Isn't it enough merely to get rid of it? Why do psychiatrists torture people and call it electroshock therapy?"[3]

Masson's ideas about how people in emotional pain can live without psychotherapy are clear. Leaderless self-help groups which do not have a religious or authoritarian structure and in which no money is exchanged can be very helpful. As for recovery groups like Alcoholics Anonymous, their problem is that not all members share their spiritual or religious interests. According to Masson, "What we need are more kindly friends and fewer professionals."[4]

There can be no doubt as to where Masson stands with regard to psychotherapy: he's against it. Although many people *believe* they have been helped by psychotherapy, Masson questions whether they are *in fact* helped by therapy. Most would get better even if they did nothing. Nor is he impressed with statistical studies on the success of psychotherapy—their bias is all too evident. Nor should psychotherapy be replaced by psychiatry, "for psychiatry, in my opinion, has always been intrusive, destructive, and vicious. Generally, what is substituted for psychotherapy (behavior modification, or organic therapies, including medication) by authors, including Eysenck and Garth Wood . . . who criticize it, is worse."[5] Masson goes on to say that he is skeptical of anybody who profits from another person's suffering and that he definitely does not believe that drugs or other forms of psychiatry are better than "talk therapy":

On the contrary, I think they are less helpful and almost always harmful. I do not subscribe to the position that there are people who are "mentally ill" and require "real treatment," meaning psychiatric drugs . . . and then there are the rest of us, who merely need to be

talked to. I believe, on the contrary, that while there is no such medical entity as mental illness, there are innumerable kinds of suffering
and terrible emotional pain that many people, in fact most, undergo
at some time or various times in their lives. I am not denying the
magnitude of the problem, only the certainty of the solution.[6]

Masson makes clear he is not criticizing people who seek help.
Those in psychic pain and those who are suffering want relief and they
turn to psychotherapists, expecting them to possess the qualities of
compassion, understanding, integrity and infinite wisdom. Unfortunately, few—if any—have these characteristics. Moreover, these are not
the kind of traits that can be acquired in a "training program" or a
"workshop." And even if the therapist is a paragon of virtue, how would
a prospective client know this and how long would it take for the god-
like therapist to fully comprehend the life of the client—and all the
personality traits a life entails—so well that true help could be given?

The fact that some therapists are decent, warm, compassionate
human beings who sometimes help the people who come to them,
Masson says, does not counter the criticisms he is making. It only
means the helpers function in this manner in spite of being psychotherapists, not because of it.

Masson summarized his position by noting that the pretensions of
psychotherapy are in no way accidental. Instead, he says, "by its very
nature, psychotherapy must pretend to supply an objective, kindly,
and humane atmosphere to those who wish to express their deepest
feelings of pain and sorrow. The tragedy is that this legitimate need is
exploited, even if with the best of intentions, by experts who claim to
offer what has never been theirs to give."[7]

But what about those who do not possess the best of intentions?
When this condition prevails we do, indeed, have a horrendous state
of affairs. Although the number of cases in which psychotherapists
have been found to be abusing their clients is small, over the years
there have been enough to cause serious public concern and enough to
require continued client caution and institutional surveillance.

PSYCHIATRIC VILLAINS

In *Against Therapy*, Masson has supplied the case history of well known therapists John Rosen and Albert Honig, whose malfeasance and mistreatment of their patients almost defies belief. Highlights of Masson's indictments are included here, but his full treatment has to be seen in order for one to fully appreciate such cruel and callous behavior.

John Rosen

In 1983, Dr. John Rosen surrendered his medical license in Harrisburg, Pennsylvania, to avoid being tried by the State Board of Medical Education and Licensure of Pennsylvania, which accused him of sixty-seven violations of the Medical Practices Act and thirty-five violations of the Medical Board Rules. Rosen grossly abused his patients but claimed he was "helping them." He believed that all of his patients' psychoses arose from not having been loved in childhood, and his cures consisted of doing whatever he considered necessary—including violence—to shock the patient out of psychosis. Rosen believed he was omnipotent and that the end justified any means, therefore he threatened his patients with knives and clubs and then used insults, beatings, confinement, humiliation, and domination as a therapy he called "direct analysis." In the case of one of Rosen's patients, Sally Zinman, during one "treatment session," Rosen and an aide, an ex-Marine, without a word of warning "tore off all of [Sally's] clothes except her underpants" and then Rosen beat her "on the face and breasts (the aide held her down while Rosen beat her). She was then tied to her bed, still with no clothes on, and kept that way for twenty-four hours, under close guard."[8] She escaped a week later to her parents (who were living nearby), and then flew to Philadelphia (Rosen's treatment was taking place in Florida). At the airport she was met by Rosen's aides who took her, kicking and screaming, to his farm in Pennsylvania. There she was confined in a security room in Rosen's basement. When she escaped again and was returned by the police, despite the fact that there was no legal document ordering her return, Rosen then threw her across the room and ordered her watched around the clock. Eventually, Sally agreed to say the things Rosen ordered her to say, and behaved as he dictated, but she did this only to secure her release from him.

Sally remained an outpatient of Rosen's for the next two years. When she tried to end treatment, Rosen told her parents that Sally had gonorrhea and was going to give all her money away to poor blacks and that she would be dead in a year unless signed over to his custody. Sally's treatment, her "therapy," consisted of Rosen's suggesting various delusions to her, fondling her breasts and, once, her vagina. Rosen kept her brainwashed and terrorized. She was finally able to break from Rosen in 1973. Several years later, after Sally felt safe, she decided she would do something about her abuse and hired Virginia Snyder, a private investigator, to look into the matter.

Snyder quickly discovered Sally was not alone and that Rosen had been involved in the death of one of his patients in the security room and that he had kidnapped and abused many other patients as well. Rosen also assigned a patient, Claudia Ehrman, to two of his therapists, Jay Patete and Robin Samuels. Soon after, Claudia was found dead in her room at a facility run by Rosen. An autopsy revealed she died from lacerations on the liver caused by "blunt force injuries to the abdomen." Patient witnesses reported they saw Patete and Samuels hold Ehrman down and beat her in the abdomen, chest, and head a few hours before her death. Then in 1981, another patient, Janet Katkow, sued Rosen for malpractice and mistreatment. Rosen's treatment of her consisted first of forcing her to suck his penis, then later to lick his anus and eat his feces. He then forced her to become involved in three-way sex and engage in cunnilingus with another woman. Any refusal on Janet's part was followed by threats of "knocking her teeth out" or "beating the shit out of her."[9]

On other occasions at Rosen's insistence and under threat of physical violence, Janet was forced to have intercourse with another of Rosen's patients, a federal judge. After escaping from Rosen in 1974, Janet attempted suicide. When she was returned to Rosen's care against her will and lacking any legal commitment papers, Rosen told her she should kill herself. Luckily, she finally managed to escape and later file charges.

Another woman, Julia Blythe, was Rosen's patient from 1963 to

1979 and subjected to both homo- and heterosexual abuse—even though "she was never adjudicated incompetent, and was never committed to [Rosen's] care by virtue of any legal proceeding."[10] Three other women patients made similar accusations and two accusations concerned a fourteen-year-old boy and a ten-year-old boy.

Masson points out that while many psychiatrists will argue Rosen is not representative of the profession, one must wonder if there is something in the very nature of psychotherapy that leads to such abuses. "A prison warden, a slaveholder, and a psychotherapist have in common the desire to control" others for their own good. Yet, the analogy is faulty, some hold, because people in therapy are free to leave or quit.[11] But are they? Certainly not in the case of Rosen's patients or in cases where the patient may not be physically restrained but is instead, kept in a chemical straitjacket.[12]

Albert Honig

Another therapist in the Rosen camp was one Albert Honig, a doctor of osteopathy, and a former medical director of the Delaware Mental Health Foundation, "a unique therapeutic community." Honig also used emotional assaults, threats, and intimidation as brute physical force to keep patients in line as well and to cure them. Honig, who was over six feet tall and weighed more than two hundred pounds, sat on one teen in order to "get him to experience his anger."[13] Some of Honig's sadistic treatments were even photographed in training films he made. Mark, one of Honig's teenaged patients whom he physically and mentally abused, finally committed suicide while under Honig's care. Honig blamed the suicide on the boy's psychosis. Jeffrey Masson, who witnessed a film of some of Honig's therapy, said it was horrifying to watch and worse to have anyone call the bullying and humiliation of another human being therapy. But unfortunately, this is much too frequent.

One of Honig's patients, a man called Benjamin—a Ph.D. psychologist—was given therapy by being "dragged off, placed in a straitjacket, ankle restraints, and blindfold." His pants were "pulled down —in a room full of people—a group session—then he [was] shocked repeatedly with a cattle prod as he screamed in protest." This happened not just once but often—almost daily, in fact—during the months of Benjamin's therapy. "Honig brought about his great improvement . . . by forcing [people like Benjamin], under penalty of torture, to relate to people in a 'normal' way." Benjamin luckily had the mental fortitude to do what Honig asked. For those who were too young or too disturbed to be able to comply with Honig's treatment, his torture led to nothing but further degeneration.[14] Honig even told one patient who might have feared being a homosexual: "I think that every moment you're alive you have thoughts of sucking my dick." The patient became even more withdrawn, understandably, and had to be forced to visit Honig's office. Honig then hospitalized the patient against his will.

When in 1978 some concerned psychologists formed an ad hoc committee to end patient abuse, they zeroed in on the Delaware Valley Mental Health Foundation and supplied the district attorney's office with affidavits, case records, and witnesses to prove that patients were humiliated and abused worse than inmates of concentration camps. Therapists at Honig's "prison," according to the committee's statements, resorted to some incredibly inhumane practices involving sexual humiliation. For example, one therapist used "a stick to show the genitals of a female patient to a male patient in an 'anatomy' lesson given by one of the treating doctors." Another "coerced an unwilling male and female patient to share the same bed for sleeping . . . in an effort to force them to be sexually active." Another exposed "the genitals of a female patient by cutting off her dirty underclothes and displaying them to a predominantly male group of staff [members]." On another occasion a fifteen-year-old male patient was forced to masturbate into a condom and display it at a group session.[15]

Another almost unbelievable atrocity was committed by a Ph.D. male psychologist who "forced [a female patient] to eat the contents of several ashtrays. When she vomited, he then forced her to eat her own vomit. He did this supposedly to force her to say 'no' to him." Even though she did say no to him he wasn't satisfied. Several staff members watched this atrocity "without protest"—a common practice since no underling dared question a doctor's behavior.[16] After his behavior was reported by the Patient's Rights Committee to the executive director of the hospital, Sandy Mintz, the doctor who did this, was suspended for only one day and was defended by Dr. Honig. Verbal and physical abuse as described above was the dominant and preferred mode of therapy at Honig's concentration camp. However, the district attorney's investigation came to naught because the therapists were "using the devices (chains, cattle prods, exercisors, et al.) *in good faith in the sincere belief they would aid the treatment process*." And, as for the ashtray incident, although it represented an "inappropriate treatment" judgment was *"made in good faith by the therapist."*[17] Furthermore, the D.A.'s office defended Honig's practices on the grounds that treatment procedures at other hospitals—drug therapy, electroshock, and lobotomies—were even worse. Is this sufficient justification for cruelty, brutality and torture? Yet, the D.A.'s office wound up defending Honig's and the other therapists' behavior.[18]

SEXUAL ABUSES

Of all the abuses perpetuated by psychotherapists on their patients by far the most common is sexual abuse. Although it was frowned on in years past, later the issue of sexual contact with one's patients was the subject of great debate and surveys revealed that as many as one out of ten psychotherapists had sexual contact with patients. Since the early 1970s the American Medical Association, the American Psychiatric Association, and the American Psychological Association have all agreed that sexual activity with a patient is unethical. Therapists are, and should be, concerned about this issue. Even Hippocrates explicitly stated that a physician must not seduce his patients. Most state legislatures have passed laws prohibiting such practices. Yet a 1983 survey revealed that 15 percent of therapists have had sexual contact with a patient.[19] These, of course, were all the therapists willing to admit to it. The ones that should be surveyed, of course, are the patients. Unfortunately, only a very small number of victims ever complain to any authority. Further, only one-half to three-fourths of all such victims are aware that sex between therapists and patients is either unethical or illegal. If they are aware, only 1 to 4 percent of such victims ever press charges. Most of the time they are not believed.

If one understands the therapeutic relationship, the reasons for forbidding sexual activity are crystal clear: the process of therapy itself normally produces strong emotional feelings in the client for the therapist. The therapist is a helper, confident, friend, and parent, someone who cares and nurtures. Thus, it is in no way uncommon for clients to feel a deep and profound longing to be loved unconditionally by the therapist. They want to be hugged and nurtured in the way they never were by their parents. Such feelings can easily become sexual and sexual fantasies can arise out of such a close personal relationship. The emotions that normally arise as psychotherapy proceeds are called "transference." If such feelings arise in the therapist rather than the client they are called "countertransference."

Trained, competent, and caring therapists are intimately familiar with these emotions and if they are ethical as well they do not violate the trust their client has given them. If the therapist is both competent and ethical he knows that even if the client asks for a sexual relationship (verbally or otherwise) it is not sex the client is really craving, but simply care and validation. Peter Rutter, in his book *Sex in the Forbidden Zone*, states that client sexual fantasies are expressions of the need to be closely connected to someone else who can be trusted. In Rutter's words, the clients' desires for sex embody "what it means to be passionately and meaningfully involved with another person, irrespective of sexuality; with our own bodies and psyches; or with life itself." In their therapist the clients see "hope that their deepest wounds can be healed and that their true selves can be awakened, recognized, and brought out of hiding into the vitality of everyday life."[20] Who else would someone needing love, hope, and affection fix upon other than their therapist, a person who has been trusted with the most intimate details of his or her life, a person who obviously cares?

The competent and ethical therapist knows these emotions will arise and he should anticipate them and instruct his client that such feelings are normal and there is no harm in having them because he will not allow anything to happen; the client is perfectly safe to talk about her deepest feelings, shameful thoughts, or wishes. Once the client is reassured that such thoughts can be expressed with no harmful repercussions, a major step in successful therapy has been taken.

Unfortunately, when a particularly attractive client passionately insists on a sexual relationship, many clinicians yield to the temptation and take steps to hug and kiss her. This—even though no actual intercourse ever occurs—is a serious error. Experienced and ethical therapists are well aware that any and all such seductive game-playing is a violation of the patient-therapist trust. Clients who have been victims of such "passes" have often complained that all such erotic acts have been very damaging. As Markowitz so aptly notes,

> Sex with a client is not an affair with a stranger or a good friend: it is a deep betrayal of trust by someone who is invested by the therapeutic contract with the responsibility to protect the client from harm, to guide the client as wisely as possible through the pitfalls of powerful emotions, and to never use that relationship for the therapist's own benefit—almost the same job description as parenthood.[21]

It should be obvious that if there is such a thing as transference where the clients project onto the therapist feelings they have for their parents then sex with the therapist is incestuous.[22]

While it is true that in earlier years many therapists believed in or saw little harm in client-therapist sex and even advocated sex as a therapeutic procedure, this is not true today. Early in his development of psychoanalysis as a therapeutic procedure, Freud warned his students against taking sexual advantage of the trust and intimacy that was sure to develop. Unfortunately, many of Freud's disciples ignored his warning. Otto Rank slept with his famous client Anaïs Nin and Sandor Ferenczi frequently engaged in close physical contact with his patients. Wilhelm Reich advocated "genital excitation (of clients) during analysis" and he, at times, also "physically manipulated (clients) to appropriate therapeutic responses." It is also well known that two of Carl Jung's mistresses were former clients. Misbehavior of the famous, however, is no excuse for such behavior on the part of the lesser known or infamous.

Yet the practice of male therapists taking sexual advantage of female patients is so common that literally dozens of books dealing with such abuse have been recently published. Among the more notable have been Lucy Freeman's *Betrayal*, Ellen Plasil's *Therapist*, Evelyn Walker and Perry Deane Young's *A Killing Cure,* and more recently Barbara Noël and Kathryn Watterson's *You Must Be Dreaming.*[23]

Jules Masserman

In March 1966, Barbara Noël, a Chicago resident, went to Dr. Jules Masserman, a famous psychiatrist, because she was suffering from performance anxiety which was ruining her career as a professional singer. She was Masserman's patient for more than eighteen years. She had approximately two thousand or more sessions with Masserman and paid him over $100,000 without benefit of health insurance reimbursement. As a result of her therapy with him, Noël became addicted to the Amytal (a dangerous barbiturate) that Masserman administered to her by intravenous injections on at least two hundred occasions, ostensibly to lower her defenses and overcome her resistance to getting at the truth. On September 21, 1984, Noël awakened from her drug-induced sleep to find Masserman on top of her, having sexual intercourse with her unconscious body. Noël recalled other instances when she had awakened from the Amytal with bruises on her arms and pelvis, evidence which could indicate that she had been raped repeatedly by her therapist while under the influence of the drug. While under Masserman's medical care she also became addicted to alcohol, which has similar effects on the brain as Amytal.

From the outset Masserman behaved toward her in inappropriate and questionable ways, giving Noël gifts as well as poems and music he had written. After Noël's divorce, Masserman invited her to go sailing and flying with him and in the summer of 1982, with several other patients, she went to Paris with him, acting as his hostess and translator. His solicitations were not only clearly unethical, but when Masserman was president of the American Psychiatric Association he publicly condemned the behavior in which he himself engaged.

After leaving Masserman in September 1984 and seeing other therapists, Noël discovered five other of Masserman's patients had filed charges against him. Masserman categorically denies any wrong-doing and has never been charged with a criminal offense or lost a civil suit, although his insurance company has settled out of court with four of his accusers. Masserman also signed a consent order with the state of Illinois agreeing to give up his license to prescribe drugs or practice any form of psychotherapy or medicine. He has also been suspended from the American Psychiatric Association and the Illinois Psychiatry Society for violating the principles of medical ethics. Because of his prestige and status, however, Dr. Masserman continues to serve on the American Psychiatric Association Board of Trustees. In an afterward to Noël's story, Kathryn Watterson interviewed Masserman, who insisted Amytal was short acting (i.e., its effects last only thirty to sixty minutes) and not addictive. Every standard psychiatric textbook disagrees with the latter claim.[24]

Zane Parzen

Noël's story is in no way new or by any means uncommon. In San Diego in 1975, Evelyn Walker went to a psychiatrist, Dr. Zane Parzen, for headaches and depression. She placed her life in his hands and fell into a nightmare of drug addiction and sexual exploitation. After two-and-a-half years and more than twenty suicide attempts, she left Parzen's care. Parzen had not only physically and sexually abused her terribly, but nearly killed her in the process. Finally Walker hired famed San Francisco attorney Marvin Lewis, Sr., and through his brilliant presentation of her case won $4.6 million, the largest malpractice award ever levied against a psychiatrist. However, Parzen had managed to abuse numerous other female patients before he was stopped. Even after conviction, Parzen not only refused to admit doing anything wrong, but claimed he was only trying to help these poor women. Even when the hideous details of his mistreatment of patients was read into the record he grinned and smiled about it as if to ask what all the fuss was about. When Parzen himself was examined by fellow psychiatrists it became clear that Parzen was sicker than any patient he had ever had. He was both seriously depressed and paranoid. Unfortunately, Parzen did Walker serious and irreparable harm.*

In a 1986 study of psychiatrist-patient sexual contact, a survey of

---

*The entire sordid story is told in *A Killing Cure* by Evelyn Walker and Perry Deane Young (N. Y.: Henry Holt & Co., 1986).

1,057 male psychiatrists and 366 female psychiatrists revealed "that 7.1 percent of male and 3 percent of female respondents admitted to sexual contact with a patient during or after treatment."[25] Pope and Vetter, in a national survey of 1,320 clinical psychologists, found that 50 percent had treated patients who claimed to have had sexual relations with a previous therapist.[26] In another study of sexual exploitation by psychotherapists of all professional backgrounds, Pope and Bouhoutsos found that "70 percent of therapists reported treating at least one patient who had a sexual relationship with a previous therapist—96 percent of whom were male."[27] In 1987, Nanette Gartrell and her associates "reported that although nearly two-thirds of the 1,423 psychiatrists who responded to their survey reported treating patients who had been sexually involved with previous therapists—involvements they considered harmful in 87 percent of the cases—they reported sexual abuse in only 8 percent of those cases." Gartrell concluded: "Although the numbers of malpractice claims and complaints before ethics committees and licensing boards have increased in recent years, it is generally agreed that only a very small fraction of these cases ever come to public attention."[28]

As noted above, because of MDeism, the power and prestige of the offending physician, it is very difficult indeed to make charges of wrong-doing hold up in court. You are advised to work closely with your local prosecutor and wear a wire. This sting tactic is a very potent and successful tool for proving your case, even though after it is proved sometimes little is done to punish the offenders.

Not all the abuses committed are sexual in nature. Fraud is also a common offense. Jesilow, Pontell, and Geis's superb study of Medicaid fraud, *Prescription for Profit,* found psychiatrists were overrepresented in their sample of doctors who committed Medicaid fraud. Their most common offense was inflating the amount of time spent with patients, but there were also many cases of billings for fictitious patients and for therapy administered by someone other than the psychiatrist. Psychiatrists have also been caught dispensing drugs to patients and then charging the government for therapy time. Finally, they have also become involved sexually with patients or former patients and have billed the benefit program for their indiscretions and dalliances.[29]

Whenever this is done the sexual misconduct overshadows the

issue of fraud. According to Jesilow, Pontell, and Geis, all but one of the sex cases in their files involved psychiatrists. This is due to the intense intimacy that *has* to develop between physician and patient in the normal course of psychotherapy, but is not necessary in other medical specialties. Nevertheless, there is no excuse for the doctor taking advantage of both his patients and the taxpayers.

According to Jesilow, Pontell, and Geis, the extent of crimes physicians perpetrated against Medicaid is unknown, but estimates range from 10 to 25 percent of the total program cost which, in 1989, was $61 billion.[30] Some violations have truly been extraordinary. In Illinois, for example, one psychiatrist billed Medicaid for 4,800 hours during one year, which works out to almost twenty-four hours each workday of the year.[31] Another standard practice has been for doctors to bill for services to people who were dead at the time the alleged work was performed. Another trick is to overcharge. One psychiatrist charged Medicaid for sexual trysts with a patient, claiming he had submitted the bills for professional services so his wife, who kept his books, would not become suspicious.

The erosion of confidence, trust, and faith accompanying the exposure of physicians for malfeasance (such as the cases already discussed) surely weakens the social fabric. "It may be healthy for citizens to realize that doctors are not god-like, but it does not seem desirable to live in a society in which everyone distrusts everyone else."[32] Despite the widespread abuses of all types found throughout the medical community, "[o]nly very rarely . . . will a doctor complain about a colleague. Even when patients tell their current psychiatrist about previous episodes of sexual exploitation by other psychiatrists, silence is usually maintained."[33] Several motives for this are offered: first, psychiatrists assume that a mark against any psychiatrist besmirches them all; second, practitioners are all vulnerable to allegations of malpractice and therefore must stick together; third, psychiatrists have invested so much of themselves to become M.D.s, they owe allegiance and loyalty to all others who have survived the ordeal. The result of this nationwide situation is such that doctors now have to practice defensive medicine, ordering extra diagnostic tests, carrying out tangential procedures, and even refusing to treat some cases for fear of litigation.

Although only state medical boards can actually revoke a therapist's license, many of the boards have such a large backlog of complaints it will take them years to catch up. At present, even having your license revoked is not fatal. If you are unscrupulous you can still hang out a shingle and practice "psychotherapy." Currently, many major monthly magazines carry ads encouraging you and anyone else interested to become a psychotherapist by correspondence in only a few hours. All such "graduates" with a piece of paper stating they are psychotherapists or counselors who treat patients informally, strangely enough, cannot be touched by the professional groups and review boards.

Moreover, state statutes of limitations often tie would-be regulators' hands, as in the case of Mary Jo Jacobs, who was fifteen when she first began treatment with Dr. Mary Giffin, a respected Chicago psychiatrist. In 1988, twenty years later, Jacobs filed charges against Dr. Giffin stating that part of her treatment included oral sex and "touch" therapy. Although Giffin was expelled from the American Psychiatric Association and the Illinois Psychiatric Society, because the state's two-year statute of limitations had expired her license was not in danger and she is still practicing. As for losing her professional affiliations, Giffin smirks and says, "All that happens is that I don't have to pay my dues!"[34] As many therapists have noted, statutes of limitations shouldn't begin running until the victim understands that the responsibility for the relationship belongs to the therapist.

Other experts argue that subjecting sexual misconduct to criminal penalties will make therapists less willing to admit it and less likely to report colleagues who are guilty. Few therapists will blow the whistle on others because of the doctor-patient confidentiality rule. The American Psychiatric Association ethics committee at one time even seriously considered ignoring patient-doctor relations, but now see it as an evil. Nevertheless, the APA believes some—even many—offenders can be rehabilitated with one to five years of probationary supervision. Many others consider that any therapist who ever abused a patient should be out of business permanently. As mentioned before, all sexual contact between patient and therapist is harmful to the patient. California's guidelines, for example, like those of other states, specifically warn patients to be suspicious if any therapist tells sexual jokes, makes any improper physical contact, gives suggestive looks, stands or sits too close, schedules after-hours appointments, talks about his own marital or sexual problems, suggests waiving fees, or indicates in any way a sexual liaison is advisable. Any or all such approaches or suggestions should be firmly rejected and the proper authorities, ethical boards, and regulating agencies should be sought out. As noted before, the emotional ties formed during therapy often produce a transference-countertransference situation, and it may be difficult to diffuse a sexually charged atmosphere. However, almost without exception, patients who sleep with their therapists end up more emotionally disturbed and damaged than they were when treatment began.

The major reason why the problem is so serious is because patient-therapist sex *is* always destructive. Ninety percent or more of the victims are psychologically damaged by the experience[35] and it is the ultimate irony: someone already a victim bares body and soul and turns her most intimate self over to a stranger and ends up worse off than she was before. Early emotions aired and analyzed can be a powerful force for growth and healing. The relationship with the therapist often makes it possible for the client to come to terms with the various emotions that caused the suffering originally. It is the therapist's sworn duty to keep the therapy sessions a place of refuge—a place where the deepest feelings can be safely expressed. All responsible therapists know this and insure that the patient's trust is never violated.

Not all therapists are honorable however. Some are deliberately predatory and use the patient's vulnerability to convince her that sex is a perfectly legitimate treatment and that the only way she'll ever get well is to yield to the advances. In such a situation only the therapist wins. Emotions generated by the therapeutic intimacy are intense and when the therapist abuses them it is much akin to incest and its accompanying emotions. One survey disclosed that 11 percent of sexually exploited patients had been hospitalized as a result of their abuse and 1 percent committed suicide. Dr. Nina Folman, chair of the Massachusetts Committee on Professional Psychological Standards, who has treated over a hundred such victims, said, "I haven't seen anyone who hasn't had some suicidal thoughts."[36]

The Hippocratic Oath has unequivocally barred doctor-patient sex for 2,400 years, but the American Medical Association did not add its own ban until 1989. Fortunately nine states (Minnesota, Wisconsin, North Dakota, Colorado, California, Maine, Florida, Iowa, and Georgia) now see sex with clients in psychotherapy as a felony with penalties that can include lengthy prison sentences. Lesser penalties, of course, include revoking the physician's or psychologist's license. All the offenders have to do, however, is call themselves psychotherapists and go right on seeing patients. Most states require no license at all to practice psychotherapy.

As Carl Sherman noted in a 1993 *Psychology Today* article,

> While many offenders are inferior clinicians whose sexual misconduct fits into a pattern of general incompetence, a disturbing number are eminent experts at the top of their profession. This includes those who have every reason to know better. A researcher whose pioneering work helped document the extent and harm of sex in therapy was later sued for divorce and ousted from his psychiatric association for having an affair with a patient. And this past December [1992] the American Psychiatric Association expelled Charles Culver, MD for exploiting a patient through a personal relationship. He was a professor of Psychiatry and Ethics at Dartmouth Medical School—and the editor of a book on medical ethics.[37]

Many authorities recommend that the taboo against sex should be discussed at the outset of all psychotherapy. In California psychotherapists are required to give their clients a brochure discussing such taboos at the first session. Moreover, all clients in therapy should be warned that sexual misconduct is usually gradual and should be nipped in the bud. In a recent article in the *American Journal of Psychiatry*, psychiatrists Gutheil and Gabbard state, "Sexual misconduct usually begins with relatively minor boundary violations, which often show a crescendo pattern . . . A direct shift from talking to intercourse is quite rare; the 'slippery slope' is the characteristic scenario."[38] The first slips should be taken as warning signs:

- In a typical sequence, the relationship first changes from a last-name to first-name basis. "There may well be instances when using first names is appropriate, but therapists must carefully consider whether they are creating a false sense of intimacy that may subsequently backfire," Gutheil and Gabbard write.

- Next, conversation turns increasingly from the clinical to the personal. For therapists to talk unduly about themselves should warn of potentially dangerous departures from their proper role.

- Body contact often follows, beginning with friendly pats and progressing to hugs. Therapists should initiate nothing more intimate than a handshake, the authors advise, and gently discourage patients' attempts at closer contact.

- Trips outside the office are the most common next step.

- "Sessions during lunch are an extremely common form of boundary violation," the authors say. "This event appears to be a common way station along the path of increasing boundary crossings culminating in sexual misconduct."

- Patient and therapist may then get together for movies or other social events—a familiar dating pattern before they move on to bed.

- Along the way, gifts may be exchanged, debts waived (erasing the boundary that keeps therapy businesslike), and personal services rendered. Not all boundary violations lead to sexual misconduct, and some may be justified (for example, sending flowers to a patient who, after years of struggle with infertility, has given birth). But anything that blurs the distinction between therapy and rest of life, or between the role of "therapist" and "friend" deserves serious second thoughts.

- A therapist who talks excessively about himself or offers to drive you home is showing a dangerous tendency to fudge the hard line between life and therapy. An occasional pat or hug can be nurturing and therapeutic, but if any contact feels wrong to you, it *is* wrong. Don't hesitate to say no, seek another opinion or, if you feel in danger, walk out. In therapy, "let the buyer beware" translates into "trust your feelings."[39]

As to the frequency with which psychotherapists take advantage of their patients, accurate figures are, expectedly, hard to come by. Many therapists concerned about the problem argue that most therapists want to ignore it or cover it up in order to keep the insurance rates down. Recently, however, because in most cases it is male therapists and female patients, more women are willing to come forward. Because of the laws now making such sex a crime, fewer therapists are willing to admit indiscretions even in anonymous surveys. In the late 1970s as many as 12 percent of the therapists admitted such acts as compared to less than 1 percent in 1992.[40]

Even though it is true that some females throw themselves at the therapist, the patient's consent is still no justification for sex. The therapists' job is to protect their patients—even after the therapy is long over. Many therapists believe in the maxim "Once a patient, always a patient," and that the effects of transference can linger for years. In one national survey reported in *Newsweek*, 11 percent of patients who had sex with their therapists were hospitalized as a result; 14 percent attempted suicide and 1 percent succeeded.[41] Such sex, some experts claim, is more dangerous than drunken driving.

A problem of major proportions is that injured patients *rarely* sue their doctors. A three-year medical malpractice study released by Harvard University in 1990 refutes the claim that medical injuries are rare and that patients are litigation prone. A review of the medical records of more than thirty thousand patients in fifty-one hospitals found that only a fraction of injuries are ever acknowledged. Researchers estimated that 4 percent of 2.7 million patients in New York in 1990 were injured as a result of their medical care. In 1984, the study reported, more than thirteen thousand New Yorkers died as a result of medical injuries and more than half of these involved negligence. Nevertheless, the New York Office of Professional Medical Conduct disciplined only sixteen physicians. Far from being litigious, injured patients rarely sued. In fact, only one-eighth of those harmed in 1984 sued and only one in sixteen won his case.[42]

Most disturbing of all, however, is the behavior of psychiatrists in the Boston area:

> The roll call of psychiatrists disciplined in Massachusetts for sexual misconduct during that period (from 1985 to 1990) reads like a roster of Harvard faculty and alumni. Of the 13 psychiatrists in Greater Boston who lost or surrendered their licenses in the face of sexual abuse charges from 1989 through 1992, all but one had some Harvard affiliation. These were men presumed to have been above reproach by dint of personal reputation and associated with a great university; men whose profession, either through insufficient training or arrogant bent, put vulnerable patients at risk. . . . People at Harvard expressed dismay but they knew about these delinquencies all along well before the charges were made.[43]

FAMOUS THERAPEUTIC VICTIMS

Literary people, expectedly, have over the years spent lots of time and money in therapy of one sort or another. Writers are not only notorious for their fondness for alcohol, coffee, and nicotine, but many have indulged in other harder or stronger intoxicants and stimulants. When the inevitable overindulgence occurs, psychotherapy seems the only salvation.

When age and alcohol took their toll in the case of Ernest Hemingway and he became severely depressed, his therapist resorted to electroshock. After a few sessions of this, the subsequent amnesia got steadily worse as a result of the ECT treatment and pushed Hemingway over the line. Tearfully confessing that life was not worth living without his memory, Hemingway took a shotgun and blew out his brains. His therapist killed him just as surely as if he had held the gun and pulled the trigger.

Kate Millett, the brilliant novelist, was luckier than Hemingway. She survived, in spite of the misguided and totally insane attempts on the part of the psychiatric establishment to cure her depression, which wasn't "depression" at all, but profound and highly rational grief. In the brilliant and marvelous book *The Loony-Bin Trip*, Millett describes how she permitted her grief and anger to be converted into a disease.[44] Like Jonathan Swift and many others, she never lost her mind, only her freedom. Before she was totally destroyed, Millett—after spending thirteen years on lithium* and living with a hand tremor, diarrhea, the possibility of kidney damage, and all the drug's other side effects—in the summer of 1980 decided to ignore her psychiatrist and took herself off the drug. By doing so she saved both her life and her sanity. The full story of her refusal to be a "victim" is told in painful and graphic detail in her book. Millett was never "mentally ill" but because of faulty psychotherapy, she almost wound up dead.

The brilliant novelist William Styron was also lucky. After suffering from severe clinical depression which he described in great detail in his memoir *Darkness Visible*, he received many invitations to speak about the disorder.[45] Styron accepted some of the invitations because he wanted to assure other victims not to give up hope, not to yield to despair, and to stress that most sufferers do get well. Of most importance to Styron, however, was not the upbeat message but one much more important: a warning about the *misuse of medications, primarily tranquilizers*, in the treatment of depression by psychiatrists. "I wanted to point out that my own bleak experience had convinced me that virtually all the commonly prescribed minor tranquilizers (also known as the benzodiazepines) are of questionable value even for healthy people; for those suffering from depression they should be shunned like cyanide, and of them all the most indisputably monstrous is a tiny gray-green oval called *triazolam*, better known by the brand name *Halcion*. [Emphasis in original.]"[46]

Styron took Halcion as a remedy for the insomnia that often accompanies depression. The drug greatly exaggerated Styron's depression, intensified his suicidal feelings, and finally forced his hospitalization. After his book was published, Styron was deluged with mail from all over the country from people telling him about their own Halcion-induced horrors. One of my psychologist friends suffered

---

*A salt or powder form of a metallic element, lithium is used to treat depression, but can be very dangerous if it is not carefully monitored by the physician.

from insomnia and his family general practitioner, trying to help, put him on Halcion. My friend took the drug for only a few days and told me, "Never in my life have I encountered anything that created such horrible visions, weird fantasies, and incredible emotional disturbances." After one particularly horrible nightmarish night, he took the pills and flushed them down the drain. Styron also noted that his correspondents also mentioned other pills,

> notably Prozac, the anti-depressant which appears to be beneficial for many people. The spontaneous testimonials in favor of that medication convince me that, if my thick archive of correspondence is a revealing cross section, Eli Lilly's bonanza drug cannot be lightly dismissed. But Prozac, scarcely an all-purpose miracle medicine, is merely an improvement on an old formula. What is distressing is the fact that a significant number of people do have very bad reactions to Prozac, chiefly suicidal impulses (the letters to me reflect this), and it is Lilly's concerted efforts to minimize such sinister side-effects that remain even now indefensible. . . . But no one who wrote to me had anything but ghastly tales to tell about Halcion . . . made by the Upjohn Company.[47]

Styron sees Upjohn as the used-car salesman of the drug industry and a company that has ignored Halcion's injurious effects despite the fact that the drug has been implicated in numerous suicides and acts of violence, including several murders, one in Dallas County, Texas, which resulted in a jury deciding the drug was partly responsible for the killing.

A few years ago Styron was invited to lecture in Washington. He told the agent he was going to give a negative report on Halcion. The agent told him his fee was being paid by Eli Lilly, who didn't make Halcion. After his talk a press meeting, supervised by the acting director of the National Institute of Mental Health, was attended by twenty-five to thirty journalists. When Styron appeared to answer the questions the acting director hovered nearby. The first question was "Mr. Styron, that was quite a story about Halcion. Now what is your opinion concerning Prozac?" Styron said he had mixed feelings about it and although he had never used it himself he understood it helped some people, had no effect on others, and produced suicidal fantasies in still others. This caused the acting director to edge Styron away from the mike and tell the assembly that Prozac is virtually free of serious reactions and that no safer and more reliable treatment for depression has ever been found. Even though there were many other questions, Styron was not permitted to answer any more. One of the newsmen told Styron "Boy, the gov'ment sure did shut you up, didn't they?"[48] A fuller discussion of Prozac and other antidepressants is included in chapter 9.

Although it may not be as well known as it should be, George Gershwin's death was premature and could possibly have been prevented were it not for the misdiagnosis of his condition by his psychiatrist, the famous Gregory Zilboorg. Joan Peyser's biography, *The Memory of All That: The Life of George Gershwin*, describes Gershwin's death from a brain tumor that went undiagnosed until only days before his death.[49] Gershwin had symptoms as early as February 1934 when he unaccountably reported smelling burning garbage. Increasingly severe headaches, stomach problems, and erratic behavior began to plague him. Both Zilboorg and Gershwin's family shrugged these symptoms off. Zilboorg attributed them to a neurosis on the part of his genius patient and George's brother, Ira, agreed. Zilboorg was so enraptured with psychoanalytical ideas it never occurred to him anything could be organically wrong. Zilboorg saw the problem as psychological and the family accepted this because they, too, wanted to believe George's childlike behavior was due to his career difficulties. George died on July 11, 1937, after emergency surgery. He was only thirty-eight.

The late Hollywood star and leading man Gig Young was also a victim of a deranged therapist who assisted Young's demise—not so much by what he did as by what he failed to do. In the hands of a more reputable, better trained, and more orthodox therapist it is possible he could have confronted and overcome the demons that seemed to pursue him most of his up and down career. George Eells in his excellent biography, *Final Gig*, reports that Young was married five times, divorced four, an alcoholic and a depressive who finally exploded, murdered his bride, and then committed suicide.[50] Young first placed himself in the hands of Dr. Albert Duvall, a Westwood, California, psychiatrist who relied heavily on Wilhelm Reich's discredited theory of Orgone therapy.* Elaine, Gig's wife at the time, also saw Duvall and reported his treatment quickly became a sex farce with Duvall constantly trying to seduce her. Duvall finally transferred Gig to a Canadian psychologist, Dr. Al Hubbard, who at the time attempted to cure depression and anxiety through the use of LSD therapy. In 1966 Young checked into a hospital in Vancouver for a month where he received hallucinogenic therapy. Cary Grant also received the treatment. Neither of the two were ever helped by these brands of pseudotherapy.

The late poet Anne Sexton was not only sexually exploited by one of her therapists but was posthumously betrayed by another therapist's ethically dubious release of Sexton's confidential therapy tapes. This story is, however, considerably more complex than it appears on the surface. Anne Sexton, a confessional poet, lived on the edge of madness and despair most of her life. She had difficulty controlling her emotions and was sexually exploited in many unsatisfactory affairs, including one with one of her therapists who took advantage of her compulsive sexual behavior and acted out with her in therapy the repetition compulsion she was acting out in life. In 1974 Sexton committed suicide. In 1991 Diane Wood Middlebrook published *Anne Sexton: A Biography*. In this biography Middlebrook includes transcripts of tapes supplied to her by Sexton's psychiatrist, Dr. Martin Orne. Traditionally this is seen as a gross violation of medical ethics because there is a strong ethical presumption in favor of confidentiality.

In the past two decades there has been a sweeping change in a number of these ideas toward greater patient autonomy and less professional paternalism. At one time patients could not even see their own records—the physician argued he was protecting them from themselves. Now it is a matter of both law and ethics that patients not only have a right to all their records but they can also relieve their physician of the obligation to preserve confidentiality. According to Orne, Sexton did relieve him of this obligation. In 1964 when Orne ended eight years of psychotherapy with Sexton, they discussed the tapes and what should be done with them. Sexton told him to use

---

*For a discussion of Orgone therapy and its premises, please refer to chapter 11.

them in any way that he thought they would be helpful. He did; he
gave them to her biographer. At the time, in 1964, Orne didn't get a
signed statement from Sexton, whereas this would be mandatory
today. The tapes were, in fact, part of Sexton's therapy. Since she could-
n't remember what she said working with Orne, he had her take the
tapes home and listen to them before the next session, a therapy which
proved excellent. Orne released the tapes at the request of Sexton's
daughter, and only after he was assured that Middlebrook was a sober
and serious scholar and after Maxine Kinnin, Sexton's best friend, also
said Anne would have wanted this to be done.

What is questionable and censorable here are the facts of Sexton's
abuse. "When a patient is sexually exploited by her psychiatrist, when
she readily obtains prescriptions for drugs she is known to abuse, and
when she commits suicide after a psychiatrist [a woman who wouldn't
tolerate Sexton's demands and her testing of all the professional
boundaries] is unwilling to continue treatment, then issues of substantial public interest have been raised."[51] Under such circumstances,
according to Dr. Alan A. Stone of the Harvard Law School, psychiatrists have a responsibility not to cover up their mistakes or those of
their colleagues and surely not to cover them up by using the excuse
of "confidentiality."[52] Dr. Carola Eisenberg of the Harvard Medical
School, while understanding and forgiving Dr. Orne's actions, is still
uneasy about them. In her view, only the patients can speak for themselves and the Hippocratic Oath cannot be violated. Doctors who violate it—even if their action is within the law—act to the detriment of
all patients. No one can be certain whether Sexton would or would not
have approved of Orne's decision. It is precisely because she cannot
speak for herself that Eisenberg feels her silence on the matter should
have been respected.

Ewen Cameron

No chapter on the misbehavior of shrinks would be complete without
the relating the horrors of Dr. Ewen Cameron, one-time head of the
Allan Memorial Institute at McGill University in Montreal. While
working for the CIA in the 1950s, Cameron put his regular patients

into a drug-induced sleep for weeks or months at a time and subjected them to repeated electroshock therapy until their memories were destroyed and they didn't know who they were. He called these treatment procedures "psychic driving." Cameron's patients were also forced to listen repeatedly to recorded messages broadcast from under their pillows or wall speakers.

One schizophrenic patient spent eighty-six days in the sleep room and was subjected to 109 successive shock treatments. When this "cure" was terminated she could not read or write, had to be toilet trained, didn't remember her husband, her five children, or any part of the first twenty-six years of her life. Many other helpless victims were similarly treated.

Because of this unbelievable psychiatric abuse the U.S. Justice Department settled out of court and paid nine of Cameron's victims a total of $750,000. In 1992 the Canadian government (for whom he also worked) paid approximately eighty victims of Cameron's mistreatment about $80,000 each.[53]

Recently, Milton Rothman examined Cameron's work and concluded everything Cameron did was pseudoscience.[54] Cameron should have obtained consent from the patients on whom he experimented. He didn't. Between 1957 and 1961, fifty-three people, most of them women, were subjected—without their consent—to megadoses of LSD; sleep therapy induced by drugs for up to sixty-five consecutive days; and repeated, intense doses of electroshock. In addition, they were forced to listen endlessly to repeated recorded messages. In fact, one physician, Dr. Mary Morrow, approached Cameron for a fellowship in psychiatry. After a physical exam Cameron concluded Morrow appeared "nervous" and had her admitted as a patient instead. For eleven days Morrow underwent "depatterning" experiments that included electroshock treatment and barbiturates. She suffered brain anoxia and had to be hospitalized. Today she suffers from prosopagnosia; she cannot recognize people's faces. Cameron described her treatment in a psychiatric journal as an attempt to regress her to the level of a four-year-old child and then restructure the patient's memory. Cameron hoped to become as famous as Freud for his "new" treatment of schizophrenia.[55] Every patient who was not totally cooperative with Cameron was called paranoid. The CIA was interested in Cameron's work because of the amnesia he was causing in his patients. The CIA saw this as a way it could obliterate all memories of CIA operations by its former agents.

Rothman also noted, as have others, that Cameron knew nothing about the proper conduct of research and had no formal theory to support the experimental work he was doing. In his attempts to overcome the Chinese brainwashing attempts—his supposed goal—Cameron solved the problem by destroying the individuals, thereby making the cure worse than the disease.

Even though other psychiatrists knew Cameron was sick and deranged they refused to speak up after hearing about his truly insane work because of Cameron's power and prestige. Despite the fact that Cameron deliberately destroyed literally hundreds of lives, hardly any psychiatrist in history received more honors than Cameron. He was president of both the American Psychiatric Association and the World Psychiatric Association and after his death the *American Journal of Psychiatry* stated in an editorial:

> His world-wide success in his profession was, of course, due principally to his great knowledge and brilliance. But surely a great factor was also the softness—one is tempted to say loveliness—of his personality. Those who were privileged to know him, even briefly, will not soon forget the warmth and kindliness of this understanding man.[56]

Cameron's victims won't soon forget either.

SURVIVORS AND THEIR SUPPORTERS

Not all shrink victims were done in by their therapist. Some, like Kate Millett, managed to survive and escape and to get even with the incompetents who did them harm. Judi Chamberlin is one very admirable individual who has been an outstanding leader and a prime mover in the fight against psychiatric tyranny. In 1978 she published a landmark study, *On Our Own: Patient-Controlled Alternatives to the Mental Health System*. Chamberlin insists that the issue is and always has been the right of the patient to select or refuse treatment. This is always respected with regard to physical disorders, but is usually ignored when mental illness is the issue:

> Along with many other ex-patients, I don't share the psychiatric faith that the "cure" to "mental illness" is soon to be found. We believe that the kinds of behavior labeled "mental illness" have far more to do with the day-to-day conditions of people's lives than with disorders in their brain chemistry. We must work to change our own behavior when it distresses us, and work to help others who seek out help, but we must also work toward a future in which we are not systematically crippled by the imposition of beliefs in the inferiority of some people because of their color, their gender, or their expression of the pain we all sometimes feel. In short, we must work to eliminate the racism, sexism, and mentalism, which makes lesser people of us all.[57]

Chamberlain's alternative posed (and poses) a serious threat to standard psychological and psychiatric treatment and, as a result, has been generally ignored and opposed by the psychotherapeutic establishment. This is certainly understandable, because Chamberlin not only proposed alternative ways of treating people, but the alternate system has become so effective—in all of those places where it has been tried—it does pose a serious threat to the current and prevailing medical-pharmaceutical complex. Chamberlin was inspired to write *On Our Own* because of her own victimization as well as that of several friends.

Chamberlin herself spent about five months as a patient in six mental hospitals and the experience totally demoralized her. She was told she would have to be institutionalized for the rest of her life. She was locked up, denied contact with others, drugged, and brainwashed. Fortunately, she managed to escape and her rage and anger were turned in a positive direction: toward working to change commitment laws, to inform patients about their legal rights and increase Constitutional guarantees to patients, and to end the demeaning and harmful psychiatric system and replace it with true asylums where people can retreat to deal with the pain of existence. She envisioned a system of care in which such pain would not be labeled "illness" but would be seen as a natural consequence of a system that puts wealth, property, and power above the basic needs of human beings. Chamberlin also managed to set up many true alternatives to the present system, for example, voluntary, small, humane units that are responsive to their own communities and to their residents. She has clearly shown that patient-controlled services that do not have the hierarchial demoralizing structure of the traditional mental hospital not only can work but are infinitely more therapeutic than the professionally and money-dominated system we now have. More about this approach and other alternatives will be discussed in chapter 12.

Victims of psychotherapeutic tyranny come in all shapes, sizes, and manner of professions. Right after Phyllis Chesler received her Ph.D. in psychology in 1969 she founded the Association for Women in Psychology (AWP) and attempted to fight for women's rights in the mental health arena. She encountered a firestorm of opposition. At the American Psychological Association Convention in Miami in 1970 she asked the assembled APA members for $1 million in reparations for all the women who had never been helped by the mental health professions but who had, instead, been further abused by them: overly tranquilized, sexually seduced while in treatment, hospitalized against their will, given shock therapy, lobotomized and, above all, disliked as too aggressive, promiscuous, depressed, or incurable. The audience laughed at her. Many made jokes about her "penis envy" and others noted that "obviously she was crazy." Her book *Women and Madness* was published in October 1972 and, so far, has sold nearly two million copies.[58] Although published more than twenty years ago, the causes she promoted and the needs she delineated are for the most part, still unmet. One particular point needs reinforcing: "In the last twenty years, we have learned that psychotropic drugs [for example, thorazine]—all of which have negative side effects and should be very carefully prescribed and monitored—may be helpful in some cases, enabling verbal or other supportive therapies to take place. However medication by itself is never enough. Women who are depressed or anxious also need access to feminist information and support."[59] Such information and support, however, must never be used to convince women they are victims of sexual molestation, rape, incest, and abuse when they were not.

While many psychotherapists prefer to believe that those clinicians who take advantage of their position to sexually exploit their patients are just a few bad apples who managed to worm their way into the professional barrel, this is a very dangerous misconception. It is a problem facing every patient and every shrink in the psychotherapy business.

HEALERS: THE WALKING AND THE WOUNDED

There are good reasons why so many psychotherapists do take advantage of their position and wind up abusing their authority and the human beings in their care. The old assumption that the primary motive for anyone to take up the profession of psychotherapy is because the therapist himself is a little "off," and wants to understand himself better is much more fact than fiction. In Greek mythology Chiron was a centaur who taught medicine to Aesculapius and suffered an incurable wound at the hands of Hercules. As perhaps the oldest wounded healer, he typifies many of our modern psychotherapists who have had to confront their own inner demons and resolve their own buried conflicts before they have been able to move on to deal effectively with the problems of others.

In a classic and significant study of psychotherapists and their motives, *Children of Psychiatrists*, Thomas Maeder, a researcher, psychologist, and consultant in the biomedical field looked specifically at the problem of the wounded healer.[60] While it is a commonplace that psychiatrists are the craziest people in the asylums and that in many institutions the wrong people have the keys, there is a measure of truth in the observation that the helping professions—primarily psychotherapy and the ministry—do attract more than their share of the emotionally unstable. Maeder begins by stating, "Something is a bit odd about people who proclaim 'I want to help other people'—the underlying assumption being that they are in a position to help and that others will want to be helped by them."[61] What is attractive to many such individuals is the position of authority they have, the dependence of others on their wisdom and advice, or the hope that they will, vicariously, be helping themselves. Some people do, sincerely, believe they have something to offer and humbly accept the responsibilities. Others use the job and their role as an ego-enhancer as way of manipulating and controlling others. Many older and experienced psychotherapists readily admit, psychotherapists are those of us who are driven by our own emotional hunger. Many take perverse pleasure in heaping scorn and abuse upon members of other professional groups: "Psychiatrists are ignorant and pompous asses" psychologists say, while psychiatrists say that "all analysts are lunatics."

Although past statistical surveys have not been conclusive, nearly all indicate that psychiatrists and psychologists have problems with depression, drug and alcohol abuse, and suicide. Constantly associating with troubled, depressed, and unhappy people, the stress of transference and countertransference, and the inability to solve so many constant existential human problems finally takes its inevitable toll. While most therapists are not "crazy," Maeder does argue they do differ significantly in subtle ways from the general population. Many become therapists because they themselves were victims of childhood abuse and want to correct the injustice.[62] But there are many other motives.

Why, exactly, do people become psychotherapists? What little information exists is anecdotal. Various authors have given such reasons as to help and understand people, to gain professional status, and finally, to gain an identity—whatever this means. Other than the socially acceptable motives of benevolence, good-samaritanism, and community service, it is easy to see that a cure for one's own problems and a personal search for happiness is also involved. A study of the lives of twelve psychotherapists concluded they all came from dysfunctional families and as children they were forced into the role of holding the family together. This childhood role then became permanent for them. In a number of books aimed at helping the therapist resolve his transference problems and avoid critical therapeutic blunders, the resolution of the therapist's own family problems looms as a severe and ever-recurring personal problem in therapist's lives.[63] Other less-than-admirable motivations certainly include sublimated sexual curiosity, aggression, megalomania, and voyeurism.

Most important is the deep personal need to get rid of one's own psychological problems and overcome or rise above one's own emotional handicaps. If the therapist is lucky he can gain a clear victory over his handicaps and then, motivated by genuine care and concern, deal with others. If he is not so fortunate, he can then consciously or unconsciously use his profession as a way to avoid his personal hangups. He can use his power, his authority, his professional charisma to compensate for his flaws, rationalize his every weakness, and shift all blame onto others. In these cases the therapist is there not to help others but to help himself. The patient becomes "not an object of empathy and altruism but an unsuspecting victim who is taken into the therapist's realm of personal needs and subjective impressions and assigned a role there that he does not recognize and would not want. And in the course of this strange, unacknowledged process, the patient's own problems may be neglected."[64] Moreover, to protect himself, the therapist may become a cold, hardened, objective physician who does not allow his own emotions to intrude or to divert him from his mission of doing maximum good. The flaw in this is that this sort of therapist is not being selfless at all. Instead, because of such ostentatious self-denial, the therapist is giving in to a perverse gratification of his own deepest personal needs.

This kind of peculiar pathology seems particularly prevalent among pastoral counselors. In fact, the Church has unfortunately frequently served as a haven for the emotionally disturbed and in the case of pedophiles this has caused the Catholic Church in particular considerable embarrassment. The clergyman who is a repentant sinner and knows his own weakness is able to identify with others, understand them, and forgive and help them. The other type of minister—the rigid, unforgiving, damning preacher who is superior to all mortal men, the type who has no sympathy for any weakness and condemns their sins and transgressions—is totally unable to understand or help his parishioners because he cannot help or understand himself.

Other types of healers with problems are those who were denied a normal childhood and who grew up too soon without receiving the normal warmth, protection, and love that all children deserve. Those who were forced to become little adults usually grow up believing that hard work and responsibility are the only things that matter to others and that they are basically unworthy human beings. To attain self-satisfaction they must become selfless saviors of humanity and live only for their service. Such behavior is in no way motivated by altruism but by a desperate need to overcome the hollow person within. They love their God and their fellowperson but they forget to love themselves.

Dr. William Dewart, a clinical psychologist who has worked with many troubled clergymen over the years, observes that many ministers go into the church to compensate for feelings of inadequacy and to avoid domination by others. They believe they will only have to answer to God. Sadly enough, the poor soul entering the priesthood in the hope of getting around issues of authority and power "finds himself walking straight into one of the more authoritative political organizations in the world."[65] The psychotherapists in private practice have no such problems. Once the period of supervision is over, they are responsible to no one. What they do or don't do is strictly up to them. Unless the clients complain or unless the therapists confess, no one will ever know what takes place in the therapeutic sessions. This, of course, creates nearly all the "shrinkage" and all the psychotherapeutic problems and difficulties pointed to in this book. This lack of external accountability much too frequently leads to megalomania—an exaggerated belief in one's own self importance and grandiosity. In 1913, psychoanalyst Ernest Jones described such individuals in a paper titled "The God Complex." Jones's characterization of people with this complex also serves as an accurate job description for psychotherapy and for too many psychotherapists. According to Jones:

> The type in question is characterized by a desire for aloofness, inaccessibility, and mysteriousness, often also by a modesty and self-effacement They are happiest in their own home, in privacy and seclusion, and like to withdraw to a distance. They surround themselves and their opinions with a cloud of mystery, exert only an indirect influence on external affairs, never join in any common action, and are generally unsocial. They take great interest in psychology, particularly in the so-called objective methods of mind-study that are eclectic and which dispense with the necessity for intuition. Phantasies [sic] of power are common, especially the idea of possessing great wealth. They believe themselves to be omniscient, and tend to reject all new knowledge. . . . The subjects of language and

religion greatly interest them. . . . Constant, but less characteristic, attributes are the desire for appreciation, the wish to protect the weak, the belief in their own immortality, the fondness for creative schemes, e.g., for social reform, and above all, a pronounced castration complex.[66]

Jones said that people with God complexes were more likely than others to take up psychology and psychiatry as a profession. They tend to avoid psychoanalysis since this requires sensitivity, intuitions, and empathy.[67]

For any psychotherapist a high degree of self-assurance is necessary. Even though most therapists insist they're not in business to serve as role models and give advice, this is precisely what they do. In fact, their patients force them into this role by idolizing them. Many patients want to be like their therapist and even will adopt their therapist's tastes and mannerisms. Patients want advice and solutions from their therapists as well as love and affection in the transference situations. Just as they expected magic from their parents so, too, they want it from their therapist.

In Maeder's words, "The field of psychotherapy inevitably attracts people with God complexes and it is custom-designed to exacerbate the condition when it exists. Psychiatrists sometimes expect, and are often expected by others, to address questions that lie well outside the range of their expertise. They are expected to do so simply because they study human beings and, by erroneous implication, are therefore expected to understand all things human."[68] As noted earlier, they fall much too often into the role of All Purpose Experts (APEs). They frequently comment on law, politics, art, literature, philosophy, and ethics—areas in which their opinions are no better than anyone else's. Adulation from dependent clients is easily translated into delusions of self-importance. In one of his final essays, Carl Jung contributed to this delusion by stating "The psychiatrist is one of those who knows most about the conditions of the soul's welfare upon which so infinitely much depends on the social sum."[69] Earlier he had said:

When the patient assumes that his analyst is the fulfillment of his dreams, that he is not an ordinary doctor but a spiritual hero and a sort of savior, of course the analyst will say "What nonsense! This is just morbid. It is an hysterical exaggeration." Yet it tickles him; it is just too nice. And moreover he has the same archetypes in himself. So he begins to feel, "If there are saviors, well, perhaps it's just possible I am one," and he will fall for it, at first hesitantly and then it will become more and more plain to him that he really is a sort of extraordinary individual. Slowly he becomes fascinated and exclusive. He is terribly touchy, susceptible, and perhaps makes himself a nuisance in medical societies. He cannot talk with is colleagues any more . . . He becomes very disagreeable or withdrawn from human contacts, isolates himself, and then it becomes more and more clear to him that he is a very important chap really and of great spiritual significance, probably an equal of the Mahatmas in the Himalayas, and it is quite likely that he also belongs to the great brotherhood [of spiritual leaders and gurus]. And then he is lost to the profession. We have very unfortunate examples of this kind. I know quite a number of colleagues who have gone that way.[70]

Jung may be correct, but most of these types are not lost to the profession—they continue to practice. Sufferers from such narcissistic personality disorders often harbor

unrealistic notions of their abilities, power, wealth, intelligence, and appearance and feel entitled to things they haven't earned simply by virtue of their inherent greatness. This exalted view of themselves, however, lacking the comfortable and certain support of reality, is very fragile. Narcissists constantly need admiration and praise from others and can be incongruously devastated by relatively unimportant failures, which threaten the fragile tissue of their belief.[71]

Many of these people feel hollow inside and feel they are emotionally empty frauds. To counter these feelings they should cultivate genuine friendships and deal with people as equals. They need to learn how to be genuinely weak, fallible, human beings with real strengths weaknesses. This is truly difficult for most psychotherapists because, as a group, they tend to have very few friends. They will explain this away as being due to their long hours, busy schedule, and so on, when the real reason is that many therapists don't need friends, because they live vicariously through their patients.[72] The danger on the patient's side is that he begins to live in order to interest and please the therapist and becomes emotionally attached, clinging, in fact, and the therapist then can't bear to cure or release the client. It would be like losing a child. This, too, is why it is so difficult for therapists to retire; they need to be needed. There are many cases in which the patients continue in therapy because they feel sorry for the therapist. Whenever the therapist brings his own wounds into the therapeutic relationship the client is definitely at risk. Experienced clinicians know this and make it the center of just about every book that has ever been written about the problems and difficulties of doing psychotherapy.

THE PSYCHIATRIST–HOSPITAL CONNECTION

On the Oprah Winfrey show on January 5, 1994, parents and teenagers told stories of parents having their teenaged children institutionalized in mental hospitals (primarily for disobedience and rebellious behavior) and then regretting it deeply. Few, if any, of the children, were helped. All were medicated and none of the psychiatric medications did anything positive. Why? First of all, none of the teens was "sick," certainly not, in any way, "mentally ill." Obviously, none of them belonged in a "mental" hospital. They were psychiatric prisoners, deprived of their constitutional rights; victims of the medical-drug company establishment. Why, you might be inclined to ask, would any competent and responsible physician be willing to go along with the parents? The answer is simple: money. The hospitals, the doctors and the drug companies all profit.

Unfortunately this practice is in no way uncommon and has been going on for several years. The November 4, 1991 issue of *Newsweek* featured a story titled "Money Madness," which exposed the practices of many private psychiatric hospitals in which they were, literally, kidnapping patients in order to fill vacant beds.[73] Recently, in San Antonio, Texas, two security agents seized fourteen-year-old Jeremy Harrell from his grandparents and took him to Colonial Hills, one of seventy-three private psychiatric hospitals operated by a chain called Psychiatric Institute of America (PIA), to evaluate and treat him for drug abuse under the state of Texas's involuntary commitment law. (The guards were PIA employees.) The boy had never used drugs and the doctor who ordered Jeremy detained had never met him. Nevertheless, the hospital held Jeremy for five days and released him only after a state senator secured a court order. The doctor resigned and was stripped of his Texas license but the incident succeeded in bringing to light hundreds of similar incidents at PIA hospitals in Texas, Florida, Alabama, and New Jersey. State and federal investigators uncovered claims that hospitals were kidnapping patients, luring them with false claims, providing unnecessary treatments, and simply holding them against their will to tap their insurance benefits.

After insurance benefits soared in the 1980s, private psychiatric hospitals became big business. Then as employers felt the sting of rising health care costs, insurance plans began to limit psychiatric hospital stays to weeks rather than months. As stays became shorter the newer hospitals discovered they required more patients to fill the same number of beds. Thus the hospitals were trying to make money and survive while the employers were trying to save money, leading to all sorts of extremes.

Sadly enough, involuntary-commitment laws allow the psychiatric hospitals to detain people who *allegedly* pose a danger to themselves or others. But in many instances people have been locked up on the basis of hearsay. In another San Antonio Colonial Hills case, a carpenter was taken to the institution by force, locked up for several days, fed tranquilizers, and pressured to sign voluntary commitment papers. He was freed only after his lawyer got a court order. His insurance company paid roughly half of the hospital's $4,800 bill but is demanding a refund. The carpenter also sued the hospital since there was nothing wrong with him. In Florida, after a custody fight a mother committed her children (ages three, eight, and nine) to another PIA facility, claiming the father had sexually abused them. The hospital held the children for five weeks, running up a $10,000 bill. The hospital then returned the children to the parents' joint custody a mere twenty-four hours before the father's insurance benefits would have ceased. The judge in the divorce case ruled the mother's charges groundless but the hospital argued they believed the father was an abuser.

In another Florida case, a high school girl told her high school counselor she was depressed about her grandfather's death. The counselor recommended that the girl and her mother visit the hospital. When they arrived the counselor declared the girl suicidal and hospitalized her for fourteen days against her will. After nine days, with a lawyer's help, she managed to escape. Nevertheless, her family insurance plan was out $12,000. But just how common and widespread are these sorts of abuses? On November 28, 1992, the U.S. House of Representatives Select Committee on Children, Youth, and Families held a hearing (transcribed in *The Profits of Misery: How Inpatient Psychiatric Treatment Bills the System and Betrays Our Trust*) chaired by Representative Pat Schroeder (D–Colo.). They found that thousands of adolescent children and adults have been hospitalized for psychiatric treatment they didn't need; that hospitals hire bounty hunters to kidnap patients with mental health insurance; that patients are kept against their will until their insurance benefits run out; that psychiatrists are being pressured by the hospitals to alter their diagnoses to increase profits; that hospitals infiltrate schools by paying kickbacks to the school counselors who deliver students; that bonuses are paid to hospital employees, including psychiatrists, for keeping the hospital beds filled; and that military dependents are being targeted for their generous mental health benefits.

Schroeder says that a Department of Justice briefing showed, "Psychiatric hospitals and clinics are defrauding government programs and private insurers of hundreds of millions of dollars annually. Patients have been forcibly admitted into psychiatric treatment programs in situations where they posed no threat to the community or themselves. Often patients are subject to batteries of blood tests, X-rays, shock treatment, and other services not needed. FBI investigation have disclosed billings to the government in the hundreds of millions of dollars."[74]

While the PIA story is bad enough, an even worse story involves PIA's parent organization, National Medical Enterprises, Inc. (NME). According to the *Business Week* story, "Put the Head in the Bed and Keep It There," NME is Public Enemy Number 1 in the federal crackdown on health care fraud.[75] NME is a $4 billion operator of hospitals and psychiatric treatment centers headquartered in Santa Monica, California.

The case of twenty-one-year-old Banning R. Lyon furnishes a typical illustration of why the FBI and other federal agencies have targeted NME. When Lyon was fifteen, his parents divorced and he moved with his mother from Sonoma, California, to Dallas, Texas. Despondent over his parents' divorce, Lyon's high school counselor suggested he visit NME's Brookhaven Psychiatric Pavilion for a two-week evaluation. After only a few days in Brookhaven, he wanted out. Brookhaven insisted Lyon was suicidal and that he be kept, which he was, for 345 days. Until his insurance coverage expired Lyon was a Brookhaven resident. For seven of those eleven months, Lyon was also subjected to "chair therapy," a treatment that required him to sit in a chair facing a wall for up to twelve hours a day without talking, reading, or doing homework. His so-called therapy cost $41,400 in doctor bills, in addition to the hospital fees of $127,300, some of which were for care he never received. According to Lyon, "It was like dying and going to hell."[76] After his release, Lyon sued Brookhaven for fraud, inflicting emotional distress, and depriving him of his liberty. Remember—there was nothing wrong with Lyon and he in no way deserved to be confined in a mental institution. Such kidnappings are in no way unusual.

Lyon's case was only one of the government's investigations. The FBI and other agents raided eleven of NME's psychiatric facilities and grand juries in numerous cities probed allegations of false medical claims, conspiracy, kickbacks, and fraud against Medicare, Medicaid, and the Pentagon's insurance plan. This large-scale scam started as early as 1988 and lasted well into 1993 and involved the corporation's top executives, hospital administrators, and doctors at hospitals nationwide. Insurers also got after the organization. As a result of these suits and the settlements, NME's overall profit fell from $578 million in 1991 to $413 million in fiscal 1993. NME's psychiatric hospitals were largely to blame for this downturn and as a result NME's management structure was overhauled completely.

Unfortunately, in health care, whenever there is a clash between medical and business objectives, business always wins. Yet, according to Karen Morrissette, the Justice Department's deputy chief of fraud, medical rip-off artists who charge for unnecessary or nonexistent care account for as much as 15 percent of the nation's $900 billion health care bill.[77] This is why a crackdown on physician fraud and abuse is of major importance in any health care reform package. Although health care scams have gone on for years, they have mostly been ignored because psychiatric claims have made up such a small percentage of the overall insurance claims. Doctors are reluctant to tell on each other, but the Justice Department has decided this shall not continue. When they looked into NME's operations they found that the doctors and hospitals had to collaborate to cheat Medicare, the patients, and the insurance companies. The cheating was done by maintaining a high hospital patient head count. Only cooperative physicians were able to decide on admissions and when it came to discharges, "the insurance expiration date decided most of them," according to one of NME's former controllers who was, of course, dismissed. In cases where doctors insisted on letting patients go before their insurance expired, the doctor was forced to meet with top management who explained the situation, and, of course, the patient was retained. Also, Friday discharges were eliminated to keep the head count high over the weekend. Special entertainment was given to keep patients from leaving and persuasive techniques were used on patients who wanted to leave before their insurance expired.[78] Hospitals also encouraged their doctors to diagnose only ailments covered by the insurers. For example, biofeedback and art therapy, usually not covered by insurers, was billed as group therapy! Dual diagnoses, such as both chemical dependency and depression were also charted since this provided a better chance of capturing benefits. Doctors who refused to cooperate were fired. Those who did prospered. One ethical psychiatrist, in a letter to the chief executive officer of NME's hospital group, stated, "The way this hospital operates is not only against the principles of most basic medical education but I believe many current procedures are unethical and possibly illegal."[79] One of his specific complaints was an edict that nurses should ignore doctors' orders for discharging patients.

Some of the psychiatric hospitals rewarded their most cooperative doctors by giving them two patient referrals for every patient they brought in. One of the most successful of these psychiatrists, Nishendu Vasavada, medical director of NME's Twin Lakes facility from 1988 to

1991, treated more than twenty-five hospital patients at a time. He received $15,000 a month for a ten-hour week, 50 percent of his salary as a year-end bonus, and about $20,000 a month to cover rent, staff, and billing services for his private practice. Unfortunately he had little time to see his patients,

> Instead Vasavada hired therapists to check on them daily and notify him of any problems. Vasavada often met only briefly with his patients, yet he charged them his $125 fee for a daily visit. Hospital employees called these brief encounters "wave therapy"—a practice in which busy doctors merely wave hello and goodbye to patients, according to the investigator's deposition. A government investigator says *wave therapy* is common at psychiatric facilities. Vasavada, who has not been accused of wrongdoing, declines to discuss his compensation. But he says he never compromised medical care. Vasavada argues that psychiatrists routinely work with teams of therapists and nurses to treat patients and therefore do not spend as much personal time with patients.[80]

Yet the well-being of patients is what has the federal prosecutors worried. This kind of fraud, they argue, is not purely a financial nor a victimless crime. Banning Lyon, for example, says "It's difficult for me to trust people now. Especially doctors."

Evidence that Lyon's lack of trust is well justified is amply furnished by Walter Bogdanich's book, *The Great White Lie*.[81] Interestingly enough, before the book was released the American Hospital Association sent a memo to all of its members, 6,000-plus hospitals, stating Bogdanich's book "is a well-researched and compellingly written compilation of true stories that show hospitals at their very worst. Murdered patients, drug-pushing doctors, incompetent technicians, venal CEOs, self-dealing boards . . . they're all here, and it's not a pretty picture." The association sent the memo in an effort to prepare the hospital CEOs and their publicity people for all of the questions they would likely be asked because of the book's expected publicity.

According to Bogdanich, *The Great White Lie* is the myth that all hospitals and all doctors are equally good and competent and equally deserving of the public's complete and unquestioning trust. By no means. The medical community well knows who is good and bad but chooses not to share this information with the public. The result is that hospital care for most Americans is a crapshoot. The AHA memo, in fact, confirms Bogdanich's claim that hospitals want to hide information. According to the AHA memo, "Let the public know that your hospital welcomes public scrutiny of its performance but remind questioners that most quality related information *is not yet available in a format that is useful to consumers* [emphasis added]." Examples of some of the things they don't want you to know are the following:

- In many hospitals shortages of hospital pharmacists results in dangerously long work hours and a lack of quality control. This leads to patient deaths because of medication mistakes.
- Failure to oversee incompetent M.D.s who were performing questionable or unnecessary procedures.
- Hospitals that refused, dumped, or scared off sick patients.
- Employing poorly trained nurses who compromised patient care.
- Failure of the federal authorities to "catch" a hospital with a 90 percent error rate in their billing.

As for the problem of dangerous hospitals, Bogdanich notes that in recent surveys by the hospitals' national accreditation organization and the Joint Commission on Accreditation of Health Care Organizations (JCAHO):

- 1,700 hospitals failed to meet important insurance standards;
- Fifty-one percent of hospitals did not have adequate monitoring to determine if unnecessary surgery was being done and, even when the surgery was necessary, whether the operation was done safely;
- Fifty percent did not adequately monitor the care of patients in intensive care and coronary care units;
- Fifty-six percent did not adequately monitor and evaluate the quality of care given by the medical staff;
- Forty percent had deficiencies concerning safety standards.[82]

Although more than one-third (approximately 1,700) of the 5,208 hospitals surveyed between 1986 and 1988 failed one or more of the standards listed above, only a handful (fewer than one hundred) lost their accreditation. While the accrediting commission permitted the public to know who flunked, they would not reveal the details of specific failures. A new category of hospitals was also created: a hospital not bad enough to lose accreditation but one with enough problems merited a conditional accreditation. To learn the names of these is in no way easy and, once again, you will not be told about their specific problems. The commission also will not tell you if your hospital is one of the 1,700 with serious problems. One of the presidents of the accrediting body told the *American Medical News* that public dissemination of hospital-specific data is premature and that the media and public are not equipped to use it responsibly.[83]

According to Dr. Sidney M. Wolfe, a physician and director of the Public Citizen Health Research Group, a recent Harvard study of New York hospitalizations showed that their findings, when projected nationally, indicate that in a single year eighty thousand patients died in U.S. hospitals as a result of negligent care.[84] The AHA urges their members not to be defensive about Bogdanich's book and to point out to reporters that they should "Place the approximately thirty serious incidents in the book in the context of the more than thirty million admissions to hospitals annually." Rest assured, the serious incidents in Bogdanich's book are many more than a mere thirty. As for seriousness, ask any one of the eighty thousand deceased patients just how "serious" their demise is.

NOTES

1. Dale Peterson, *A Mad People's History of Madness* (Pittsburgh: University of Pittsburgh Press, 1982).

2. Jeffrey Masson, *Against Therapy* (New York: Atheneum, 1988), p. xiv.

3. Ibid., pp. xiv–xv.

4. Ibid., p. xv.

5. Ibid., p. 1.

6. Ibid., pp. 1–2.

7. Ibid., p. 9.

8. Ibid., p. 136.

9. Ibid., p. 144.

10. Ibid., p. 145.

11. Ibid., p. 147.

12. Ibid., pp. 124–51.

13. Ibid., p. 157.

14. Ibid., p. 158 (note).

15. Ibid., p. 160.

16. Ibid., p. 161.

17. Ibid., p. 162.

18. Ibid., pp. 153–59.

19. Jacqueline Bouhoutsos, "Sexual Intimacy between Psychotherapists and Clients," in *Women and Mental Health Policy*, Leonore Walker, ed. (Beverly Hills, Calif.: Sage, 1984), pp. 207–28.

20. Peter Rutter, *Sex in the Forbidden Zone* (New York: Ballantine, 1989), p. 21.

21. Laura M. Markowitz, "Crossing the Line," *Family Therapy Networker* (November/December 1992): 30–31.

22. Glen O. Gabbard, *Sexual Exploitation in Professional Relationships* (Washington, D.C.: American Psychiatric Press, 1989).

23. Lucy Freeman and Julie Roy, *Betrayal* (New York: Stein & Day, 1976); Ellen Plasil, *Therapist: The Shocking Autobiography of a Woman Sexually Exploited by Her Therapist* (New York: St. Martin's Press, 1985); Evelyn Walker and Perry D. Young, *A Killing Cure* (New York: Henry Holt & Co., 1986); and Barbara Noël and Kathryn Watterson, *You Must Be Dreaming* (New York: Poseidon Press, 1992).

24. All information presented here on Dr. Jules Masserman can be found in Noël and Watterson, *You Must Be Dreaming*.

25. Nanette Gartrell, Silvia Olarte, and Judith Herman, "Psychiatrist-Patient Sexual Contact: Results of a National Survey," *American Journal of Psychiatry* 143, no. 9 (1986), p. 227.

26. Kenneth Pope and Valerie Vetter, "Prior Therapist-Patient Sexual Involvement among Patients Seen by Psychologists," *Psychotherapy* 28, no. 3 (Fall 1991): 429–38.

27. Kenneth Pope and Jacqueline Bouhoutsos, *Sexual Intimacy between Therapists and Patients* (New York: Praeger, 1986).

28. Nanette Gartrell et al., "Reporting Practices of Psychiatrists Who Knew of Sexual Misconduct by Colleagues," *American Journal of Orthopsychiatry* 52, no. 2 (April 1987), p. 247.

29. Paul Jesilow, Henry N. Pontell, and Gilbert Geis, *Prescription for Profit: How Doctors Defraud Medicaid* (Berkeley, Calif.: University of California Press, 1993), pp. 132–33.

30. Ibid., pp. 132 and 133.

31. Pawel Horoszowski, *Economic Special Opportunities: Conduct and Crime* (Lexington, Mass.: Lexington Books, 1978), p. 151.

32. Eliot Freidson, *Professional Dominance: The Social Structure of Medical Care* (New York: Atherton, 1970), p. 68.

33. Alan Stone, "The Legal Implications of Sexual Activity between Psychiatrist and Patient," *American Journal of Psychiatry* 133 (1976): 1138–41.

34. Melinda Beck, Karen Springer, and Donna Foote, "Sex and Psychotherapy," *Newsweek*, 13 April 1992, pp. 53–58.

35. Rutter, *Sex in the Forbidden Zone.*

36. Carl Sherman, "Behind Closed Doors: Therapist-Client Sex," *Psychology Today* (May/June 1993): 66.

37. Ibid., p. 70.

38. Thomas G. Gutheil and Glen O. Gabbard, "The Concept of Boundaries in Clinical Practice: Theoretical and Risk Management Dimensions," *American Journal of Psychiatry* 150, no. 2 (1993): 188–96.

39. Ibid., p. 195.

40. Gartrell et al., "Reporting Practices of Psychiatrists."

41. Beck, Springer, and Foote, "Sex and Psychotherapy," p. 55.

42. Eileen McNamara, *Breakdown: Sex, Suicide and the Harvard Psychiatrist* (New York: Pocket Books, 1994).

43. Ibid., p. 200.

44. Kate Millett, *The Loony-Bin Trip* (New York: Simon & Schuster, 1990).

45. William Styron, *Darkness Visible* (New York: Random House, 1990).

46. Ibid., p. 28.

47. William Styron, "Halcion Nights," *Ace Magazine* 5, no. 1 (February 1993): 10.

48. Ibid. Those interested in Prozac's (Fluoxetine's) side effects should consult Martin H. Teicher et al., "Emergence of Intense Suicidal Preoccupation during Fluoxetine Treatment," *American Journal of Psychiatry* 147, no. 2 (February 1990): 207–10. Also see "Letters to the Editor" columns in that journal, 1990–1994, inclusive.

49. Joan Peyser, *The Memory of All That: The Life of George Gershwin* (New York: Simon & Schuster, 1993).

50. George Eells, *Final Gig* (New York: Harcourt Brace Jovanovich, 1990).

51. Diane W. Middlebrook, *Anne Sexton: A Biography* (Boston: Houghton Mifflin, 1991).

52. Alan A. Stone and Carola Eisenberg, "Confidentiality in Psychotherapy," *New England Journal of Medicine* 325, no. 20 (November 14, 1991): 1450–51.

53. Milton Rothman, "The Tale of a Respected Pseudoscientist," *Skeptical Briefs* 3, no. 1 (March 1993): 5.

54. Ibid.

55. D. Ewen Cameron, "The Depatterning Treatment of Schizophrenia," *Comprehensive Psychiatry* 3 (1962): 65–76.

56. Editorial, *American Journal of Psychiatry* 124 (1967): 261.

57. Judi Chamberlin, *On Our Own: Patient-Controlled Alternatives to the Mental Health System* (New York: Hawthorne Books, 1978), p. xvi.

58. Phyllis Chesler, *Women and Madness* (New York: Doubleday, 1972).

59. Phyllis Chesler, "Twenty Years since *Women and Madness*: Toward a Feminist Institute of Mental Health & Healing," *Journal of Mind & Behavior* 11, nos. 3 and 4 (Summer/Autumn 1990): 320.

60. Thomas Maeder, *Children of Psychiatrists* (New York: Harper & Row, 1989).

61. Ibid.

62. Daniel Goleman, "Psychotherapists Seen as Victims of Abuse," *New York Times*, 9 September 1992, p. 8.

63. Thomas Maeder, "Wounded Healers," *Atlantic Monthly* 263, no. 1 (January 1989): 37–47.

64. Ibid., p. 46.

65. Ibid., pp. 41–42.

66. Ernest Jones, "The God Complex," cited in Maeder, "Wounded Healers," p. 43.

67. Ibid., p. 43.

68. Ibid., p. 44.

69. Carl Jung, "God, the Devil, and the Human Soul," *Atlantic Monthly* 200, no. 5 (November 1957): pp. 57–63.

70. Ibid., pp. 60–61.

71. Ibid., p. 45.

72. Maeder, "Wounded Healers," p. 46.

73. "Money Madness," *Newsweek*, 4 November 1991, pp. 50–52.

74. Cited in Louise Armstrong, *And They Call It Help: The Psychiatric Policing of America's Children* (Reading, Mass.: Addison-Wesley, 1993), p. 265.

75. Catherine Yang and Eric Schine, "Put the Head in the Bed, and Keep It There," *Business Week*, 18 October 1993, pp. 68–70.

76. Ibid., p. 68.

77. Ibid.

78. Ibid., p. 69.

79. Ibid.

80. Ibid., p. 70.

81. Walter Bogdanich, *The Great White Lie: How America's Hospitals Betray Our Trust and Endanger Our Lives* (New York: Simon & Schuster, 1992), pp. 25 and 26.

82. Both lists are from Bogdanich, *The Great White Lie*, pp. 25–26.

83. Jesilow, Pontell, and Geis, *Prescription for Profit*, p. 199.

84. Ibid.

4

The Schizophrenia Scandal

The symbol that most specifically characterizes psychiatrists as members of a distinct group of doctors is the concept of schizophrenia; and the ritual that does so most clearly is their diagnosing this disease in persons who do not want to be their patients. . . . Schizophrenia has become the Christ on the cross that psychiatrists worship, in whose name they march in the battle to reconquer reason from unreason, sanity from insanity; reverence toward it has become the mark of psychiatric orthodoxy, and irreverence toward it the mark of psychiatric heresy.[1]

In 1980 Theodore Sarbin, one of America's most distinguished psychologists, and an authority on role theory, along with his colleague psychologist James Mancuso, solved the mystery of schizophrenia—a solution that psychiatry and the medical profession have refused to acknowledge because it does not fit into its biomedical philosophy and framework. As a result, they still insist that schizophrenia is a brain disease due to faulty genes, or faulty biochemical, neurological, or anatomical forces in the brain. This is a disease that nearly a century of intensive research has not only failed to find but within the biomedical framework has yet to find any biological or psychological marker that can differentiate diagnosed schizophrenics from normal human beings without creating unacceptable proportions of false positives and negatives.

What Sarbin and Mancuso independently, along with Jay Haley and others discovered is that schizophrenia as a "disease" is a *social construction*, a construction generated to deal with people whose behavior is not acceptable to others who are, socially, more powerful.[2]

While there is little doubt that some individuals, on occasion, behave in ways that others would call crazy or psychotic, this in no way proves or establishes as a fact that this behavior is due to a brain disease. This was the unwarranted assumption made by nineteenth- and early twentieth-century physicians who attributed all unusual behavior to disease processes. Because of their psychological ignorance, they could not tell the difference between patients with organic brain disorders from people using unusual behavioral stratagems to solve their identity and existential crises, and their problems of living. In fact, because so many people diagnosed as schizophrenic failed to fit the prototypic description (i.e., they did not suffer from hallucinations or lack of affect), Eugen Bleuler himself suggested that the plural "the schizophrenias" be used. The kinds of behavior that diagnosed "schizophrenics" showed proved to be so varied and the patients' actions were so specific to their individual life histories that Sarbin stated, "The notion of a common cause for such an assortment of human actions can be entertained only if . . . we reduce the interesting array of polymorphous [various or varied] actions to a small number of categories, for example, delusions, flattened affect, and hallucinations, and, further, if we arbitrarily redefine the categories as 'symptoms' of a still-to-be-discovered disease entity."[3]

Because of his skepticism about the disease concept of schizophrenia, in the early 1960s Sarbin followed two strategies: the first was to determine what sort of behavior was regarded as a "symptom" of schizophrenia by so-called mental health experts; the second was to determine from the published experimental literature what, if anything, could be used to support the schizophrenia hypothesis. To carry out the first strategy Sarbin asked fifteen experienced therapists to name the single most significant item of behavior used to diagnose schizophrenia. All but three listed hallucinations and many added that hallucinations indicated an underlying thought disorder. Sarbin's results were in line with an earlier 1965 survey of 346 English psychiatrists by Willis and Bannister. Their survey confirmed that thought disorder was considered to be the most important characteristic of schizophrenia.[4] Therefore for the next few years Sarbin studied "hallucinations" in the laboratory, in the clinic, and in the library, publishing a number of papers on the topic.[5] Following the history of the concept from the sixteenth century to the present, Sarbin discovered that conduct described as hallucinatory was always based on the self-report of imaginings.

According to Sarbin, the word "hallucination" belongs, in behavioral terms, to a family of words that includes day-dreaming, imagining, fantasy, fictions, inventions, and fabrications. Hallucinations or false perceptions are, then, the mental health establishment would have us believe, much more common. Moreover, perfectly sane and normal people have these on occasion and are never threatened with involuntary confinement or a diagnosis of schizophrenia.[6]

The imaginings that are constructed by so-called normals—imaginary companions in childhood, adult dreams of glory, imaginary interactions with celebrity figures, religious encounters, playful or romantic fantasies—all are the same sort of topics covered by psychiatric patients. Normals also claim their imaginings are "real." In a 1966 experiment by Juhasz and Sarbin, volunteer college students were induced to imagine they were tasting salt solutions and were so sure they were, they were willing to testify in court. Actually they were tasting only distilled water.[7]

It is now both well known and widely acknowledged that people have experiences in which they assign an equal degree of credibility to their imagining as to veridical perceptions. When religious figures and theologians say that God spoke to them and told them to spread His word, few church members and believers consider such reports hallucinations. Oddly enough, the same report coming from a street person or a drunk would quickly lead to a diagnosis of schizophrenia from a psychiatrist. In Sarbin's words, "Social status considerations may insidiously insert themselves into the clinician's diagnostic matrix. The frequency of schizophrenia diagnoses among persons who are poor and black supports the claim that social structural features of the diagnostic setting supply a readiness for professionals to employ pejorative interpretations of atypical conduct."[8] Sarbin also adds that if the person's identity has not been degraded earlier, then the imagining may be considered as creative, mystical, or transcendent experiences.

In fact, in the therapeutic setting even the most ordinary statements of hopes, fears, desires, and imaginings can be misinterpreted by the therapist as clear indicators of pathology. This is most clearly shown by Seth Farber in his book, *Madness, Heresy and the Rumor of Angels*.[9]

As Farber observes, the mental health expert's approach to people whose behavior is different is to assume automatically that the behavior is psychopathological. Then they assume the behavioral symptoms are due to a defective psychophysiological system contained in the body. If the individual is unhappy, for example, this is seen as brain damage or something wrong in the neuronal pathways and all situational and environmental influences are ignored. To illustrate exactly how this works Farber tells "Ellen's" story from her own point of view and then from the mental health expert's perspective. The expert, first of all, reduces all people to "patients" who are sick and in need of diagnosis. Ellen is an intelligent, eloquent, and creative twenty-eight-year-old woman who resumed her college career in education. She had a happy, untroubled childhood, but when she was around twelve she became lonely, alienated, isolated, and withdrawn. In her teens she became more contemplative, sensitive, and philosophical. Old for her age, she wrote poetry and philosophy. In her late teens she attended an experimental college where she felt more at home but still different from her schoolmates. When she began to have "peak experiences" in the Maslowian sense (i.e., to feel one with the universe) and to see visions and hear heavenly voices, she left the experimental college and went home. She had minor problems with her family, had trouble eating, and was anxious a lot of the time. She finally went to see a social worker who kept after her to go to a mental hospital and get some rest. Finally she agreed to see a psychiatrist.

The psychiatrist told her she was about to have a nervous breakdown and his diagnosis was as follows:

EXPERT: As a defense against the pressures of the world and parental deprivation at an early age she had a defective self and became preoccupied with her inner thoughts and she regressed to a primitive level of ideation.

TRUTH: No, she was very creative, philosophical, and wrote poetry. Her first ten years were very happy.

EXPERT: She repressed traumatic childhood experiences and over-idealized her memories of childhood. Superficial sense of happiness a reaction-formation against underlying sense of emptiness.

TRUTH: She loved children, animals, people, and was a happy, integrated girl—at peace and innocent.

EXPERT: In early teens showed the beginning of a schizophrenic deterioration; inadequate self-esteem prevented her from establishing satisfactory "object relations" to meet demands of adolescence.

TRUTH: Ellen was a sensitive, philosophical person alienated from her more superficial, less reflective peers. The inference that she has a weak ego is unwarranted. Unhappiness is not an indication of psychopathology.

EXPERT: Due to her weak ego she couldn't get along with her peers. She rationalizes this by assuming an attitude of superiority. She seeks compensation for poor interpersonal life by retreating into a dream world.

TRUTH: Ellen *was* superior to her peers in every sense of the word. Her intellectual retreat from shallowness, competitiveness, and the hypocrisy of the world around her is normal, natural, and in no way pathological.

EXPERT: Due to impaired psyche patient is unable to adjust to environment. Her characterological defenses have broken down and she is unable to distinguish between fantasy and reality—schizophrenic breakdown is imminent —prognosis is poor.

TRUTH: Expert can see only pathology. His naivete and lack of understanding of peak experiences blinds him to her inner psychological state.

EXPERT: Pathology is in full bloom—the patient is plagued by auditory hallucinations, magical thinking, religious delusions. She must be placed under psychiatric care immediately and placed on a strict regimen of medication.

She will need to remain on medication for the rest of her life.

TRUTH: The expert totally misunderstands Ellen, her psychology, and her experiences. There is no magical thinking, only creative thinking of a religious-mystical nature that the expert with his limited mentality fails to understand. Ellen did not actually hear voices. Instead, they were feelings of uniqueness and consolation.

Unfortunately for Ellen, the "expert" hospitalized her, gave her Thorazine and Navane which caused her to lose her vision and ability to read. This heavy sedation caused her to sleep for three days straight. Upon awakening she was given more drugs which left her numb, catatonic, apathetic. When taken off Thorazine and given Navane and Lithium, her vision cleared but she was constipated, had dry mouth, and gained eighty pounds. All her normal body rhythms were interrupted. In her words, "I felt like a dead person in a body that lived." Such drug effects are typical. Ellen later said in order to get out of her hospital prison, "I played a game to get by. It wasn't even a game, it was survival." True, in the mental health system only total compliance is accepted and in Farber's words, "Any criticism of the mental health system is viewed as a sign of serious psychopathology."[10] In Thomas Szasz's very wise words, "In short, psychiatrists are the manufacturers of medical stigma, and mental hospitals are their factories for mass-producing this product. . . . Being considered or labeled mentally disordered—abnormal, crazy, mad, psychotic, sick, it matters not what— is the most profoundly discrediting classification that can be imposed on a person today."[11]

Ellen was lucky. Because of her superior intelligence she managed to survive, keep her sanity, and escape. Others, unfortunately, are not so lucky and, "[i]n the name of mental health, billions of individuals have had their dreams destroyed in these ostensibly therapeutic institutions."[12]

Sarbin notes that whether a particular belief is identified as delusional has nothing to do with the truth. Beliefs held by previous generations of scientists and later proved to be erroneous are not normally considered delusional. The process of constructing images and beliefs is the same for so-called schizophrenics and so-called normals. People using the terms *hallucinations* and *delusions* never seem to be interested in determining what these things *mean* in the lives of the person having them. Whenever such things are investigated in depth it is usually discovered that the patient's hallucinations and delusions, as the patient's way of making sense of their world, play a very significant role and function in the patient's adaptation and worldview and eventual recovery.[13]

Sarbin's second strategy, to determine if published research supported the schizophrenia hypothesis, resulted in his discovery that most of the theories of schizophrenia in the early 1970s were supported on the basis of only one or two experiments. When these experiments were replicated the results did not support the theories. The rise and fall of early schizophrenia theories—none of which exists today—led Sarbin to conclude the theories, both somatic (physical) and psychological, all have a half-life of about five years.

Following up this early work, Sarbin and Mancuso reviewed every research article on schizophrenia published in the *Journal of Abnormal Psychology* for the twenty-year period beginning in 1959, as well as an extensive review of selected articles from psychiatric journals. A total of 374 reports of experiments dealing with schizophrenia were reviewed. All the reporters were looking for "a reliable diagnostic marker, psychological or somatic, that would replace the subjective (and fallible) diagnosis." The discovery of such a marker certainly would establish the long sought-for validity for the postulated entity "schizophrenia."[14]

Nearly all of the studies compared the *average* responses of "schizophrenics" on experimental tasks with the *average* responses of persons not so diagnosed. Hundreds of experimental tasks were specifically designed to show that schizophrenics were cognitively or linguistically deficient, perceptually inefficient, affectively dysfunctional, and psychophysiologically impaired. It was assumed schizophrenics would perform poorly.

After analyzing the 374 studies on several dimensions, Sarbin and Mancuso concluded the criteria for selecting subjects for the studies were faulty and unreliable. To bring their research up-to-date, Sarbin and Mancuso performed the same analysis on the *Journal of Abnormal Psychology* reports for the ten-year period 1979–1988. These experiments followed the same pattern discerned in the earlier analysis.

Although about 80 percent of the studies reported the schizophrenics performed poorly when compared with the controls, high variability in performance was the rule and the reported mean differences were small. There was a considerable overlap of the distributions of the experimental and control groups. While many theorists took these small mean differences to support the credibility of the schizophrenia hypothesis, this degree of credibility dissolved when it was shown that a large number of the experimental subjects were on neuroleptic medication and there were large differences also present in both socioeconomic status and education. Mean differences in performance could well be related to cognitive skills, a correlate of education and socioeconomic status. Moreover only docile patients were recruited. Any of the many hidden variables would account for the small mean differences observed.

Sarbin and Mancuso have stated, "One conclusion is paramount: the 30 years of psychological research covered in our analyses has produced no marker that would establish the validity of the schizophrenia disorder."[15] After studying Sarbin and Mancuso's results some theorists argued that psychological variables are too crude to identify the disease process and that biochemical, neurological, and anatomical studies would probably reveal the ultimate marker for schizophrenia. Yet those studies using somatic-dependent variables have proved to be no different and variation is, again, the rule. Arguments such as (1) size of the hemisphere brain ventricles; (2) disarray of neurons in the hippocampus; (3) encephalitis; (4) focal infections; (5) hemodialysis to rid patients of pressured schizotoxins; (6) excessive dopamine; (7) faulty genes; and (8) what have you have all been propounded as the cause of schizophrenia. Again, high degree of variability marks all of these measurements and no conclusive indicator or marker has been found to date.

These facts have, in no way, however, discouraged or chastened the biomedical believers. Typical of the biomedical point of view is Dr. Irvin

Gottesman's *Schizophrenia Genesis: The Origin of Madness.*[16] His comprehensive review of schizophrenia covers early accounts of the disorder.*

SCHIZOPHRENIA GENESIS:
THE ORIGINS OF MADNESS

As physicians, psychiatrists are supposedly bound by the Hippocratic Oath which stipulates "first do no harm!" However it is nearly impossible to practice psychiatry without doing considerable harm. How, for example, can a psychiatrist validate his identity as a medical doctor without labeling others as mentally sick—that is to say, without dehumanizing others and thoroughly destroying their identities?[17]

Typical of the medical point of view is Gottesman's comprehensive review of schizophrenia which covers early accounts of the disorder, historical views of insanity, and misguided clues to its causes, as well as how we now go about diagnosing the disorder and separating it from other psychoses. He provides some personal accounts from the mouths of its victims, and also an excellent summary of the epidemiology and demographics of the disorder as well. Of most interest here is the finding that the disease is practically nonexistent in primitive cultures and seems definitely to be a disorder of highly civilized populations. Gottesman also provides succinct summaries of the evidence for and against the argument that schizophrenia is inherited, and the evidence from twin studies bearing on the argument. Particularly insightful are his chapters on the role of psychological contagion and psychosocial and environmental stressors in the disorder. His discussions of how our knowledge about schizophrenia influences our society and our views on genetic counseling, marriage, immigration, sterilization, and future research are also excellent.

Where his survey is badly deficient (to the point of perplexity) is his summary dismissal of the work of anyone who disagrees with the classical, clinical-medical, academic point of view. In Gottesman's view:

---

*Interestingly enough, insanities involving "thought disorders" were not identified until the eighteenth and nineteenth centuries. Such cases were exceedingly rare in the seventeenth century.

... schizophrenia is a mental illness, a psychosis, a form of insanity, and not simply—as Ronald Laing, Thomas Szasz, or Herbert Marcuse and others have argued—the manifestation of a deviant or alternative lifestyle or evidence that society itself is sick. Individuals *can be* diagnosed as schizophrenic even if they are *currently in remission* and have few or no symptoms at the present time. [Emphasis added.][18]

With regard to the average psychiatrist's skill in diagnosis, it certainly is true individuals *can* be and *are* frequently diagnosed as schizophrenic when they are saner and more in touch with reality than the M.D. doing the diagnosing. To Gottesman's credit, however, he is alert to the problem and says, "If on the other hand, everyone who is mentally disturbed is labeled schizophrenic, clinicians are 'crying wolf' and doing more harm than good to patients by exposing them to inappropriate treatments."[19]

But the most serious and glaring omission of all is Gottesman's abject failure to consider the work of any researcher or theorist who goes against the medical-clinical grain. No mention is made of Sarbin and Mancuso and the work of Jay Haley and Bateson are summarily dismissed as "ideas difficult to test" and the clinical research and findings of workers like Courtenay A. Harding, who has shown that even the most profoundly disabled schizophrenics make good recoveries, are ignored.[20]

Gottesman also subscribes to Bleuler's clinical definition that a schizophrenic has the following characteristics:

1. An ordinary person would consider the patient's train of thought incomprehensible, confused, and misunderstandable.

2. The patient lacks emotional empathy.

3. The patient is in a state of stupor or excitement which lasts for several days.

4. The patient experiences hallucinations and illusions (i.e., false perceptions) for several days.

5. The patient experiences delusions (i.e., false beliefs).

6. The patient neglects everyday, ordinary obligations and behaves aggressively for no reason.

7. Friends and family report the patient is no longer herself and her behavior is bizarre.

8. There are intermittent depressions.

A summarization of Gottesman's findings provides us with the following conclusions:

> With regard to the inheritance of schizophrenia, though familiarity is necessary to prove the genetic argument, it is certainly not sufficient. The vast majority of schizophrenics will have neither parent who is overtly schizophrenic—some 89 percent—and will have neither parents nor siblings who are affected. Further, a sizable majority—about 63 percent—will have clean pedigrees, i.e., negative family histories. The role played by *possible shared experiences within the family* is still, according to Gottesman, unclear. Conclusion: Genes *alone* are neither sufficient or adequate . . . to account for the disorder. Significant environmental contributions seem to be: insults to the brain, demoralizing or threatening physical environments, emotionally intrusive experiences, emotionally demanding experiences, affective and emotional understimulation, i.e., institutionalization and disruptions to attention and information processing. Biological markers of schizophrenia such as the density of dopamine receptors in the brain are quantitative traits not qualitative Mendelian ones. . . . We have no direct way to measure the hypothetical liability to developing schizophrenia. Liability remains elusive but we assure it exists so that we can consider models for development and transmission. Although it is easy to convince reasonable people about the validity of inferring liability in the relatives of schizophrenics, even reasonable people became skeptical about inferring liability in the families of schizophrenics who have no affected relatives, and such schizophrenics constitute the vast majority of cases.[21]

Gottesman, like other defenders of the medical status quo, pins his hopes on neurological and biomedical research. Since the 1990s are the "decade of the brain," certainly hard science will soon solve the problem of just where in the brain the specific schizophrenic virus, transmitter, receptor, lesion, neuronal pathway, chromosome, or what-have-you can be found! All the neurosciences are on the brink of, about to discover, a "new promising drug without side effects" that will solve the biological mystery of schizophrenia once and for all! Such blindness and ignorance prevent the supporters of the medical point of view from seeing what should be perfectly clear to them. Schizophrenia as disease does not exist.

In summary, as Cohen and Cohen sadly report,

> [A]fter decades of intensive biological research, no one has yet marked a single biological abnormality of any sort identified with schizophrenics and only schizophrenics, no matter how broadly or narrowly diagnosed, grouped, or categorized. Since there is no diagnostic test which can confirm a diagnostician's impression that an individual so designated is, in fact, schizophrenic—or that a "normal" person is not, in fact, schizophrenic—we still have not established that schizophrenia is a disease, what sort of disease it is, or what causes it.[22]

When the results of studies carried out by Lipton and Simon were published, it was found that because physical examinations are not mandatory and therefore are often not performed, organic disorders were frequently unnoticed. Lipton and Simon estimated that in the New York State hospital system alone 7,318 patients were misdiagnosed as schizophrenic.[23] This means that all of these patients were receiving medications inappropriate to their needs. If such misdiagnosis existed in other branches of medicine the public would rise in fury.

One of the saddest aspects of this failure to recognize schizophrenia for what it is is the current practice of drugging patients into insensible stupors based on the faulty assumption of the effect of excessive dopamine in the brain. When first introduced into hospitals in the 1950s the phenothiazines were called "major tranquilizers." Now they are called neuroleptics or antipsychotics. Since these drugs appeared to inhibit the action of dopamine at certain receptor sites and thus were believed to suppress "crazy" behavior, the M.D.s concluded high dopamine levels in the central nervous system produced psychotic behavior. If the drugs only suppress psychotic behavior, then the role of dopamine in schizophrenia is strengthened. Yet as Sarbin and Mancuso observed, the drugs chemically suppress a wide variety of neural connections; they suppress *all kinds of behavior* not just "crazy" behavior.[24]

In his 1983 book, *Psychiatric Drugs: Hazards to the Brain*, Peter

Breggin agrees and shows that the major tranquilizers directly impede and damage major parts and functions of the human brain. The associated psychologic effects of this damage are a general reduction in brain functioning, apathy, lethargy, emotional flatness, etc. These are exactly the effects that the therapists want and what they regard as "signs of improvement." Breggin argues that the drugs disable the brain and when we listen to the reports from patients who have taken these drugs there can be no doubt that he is correct on all counts.[25] Bleuler himself, in 1978, commenting on the passive inactivity of the schizophrenic stated, "years ago he was shackled, strapped to his bed, or isolated. Today the entire pressure of social therapy and pharmacotherapy with psychotropic drugs and neuroleptics works out toward the same end. For this reason it may be said that the adynamia of the schizophrenic can be interpreted as a partially successful therapeutic effort."[26]

Hundreds of studies nevertheless insist that drugs reduce the length of hospital stay, make the patients amenable to treatment, prevent relapses, and allow patients to leave the hospital. Nevertheless, in our time, it seems all treatments are effective, especially drug treatments! When they were first introduced etherization, insulin coma, lobotomy, and electroshock were all hailed as panaceas. Breggin cites an interesting passage, a description of the maximum benefit one could expect from the phenothiazines taken from Noyes and Kolb's 1958 edition of *Modern Clinical Psychiatry*:

> If the patient responds well to the drug, he develops an attitude of *indifference* both to his surroundings and to his symptoms. He shows *decreased interest* in a response to his hallucinatory experience and a *less assertive* expression of his delusional ideas. Even though not somnolent, the patient may be quietly in bed, *unoccupied* and *staring ahead*. He may answer questions readily . . . but will offer *little or no spontaneous conversation*, however, questioning shows that he is fully aware of his circumstances.[27]

All of the above emphases are Breggin's and support his contention that the drugs serve as "brain disablers." In fact their effects, according to Cohen and Cohen, closely resemble the rare disease epidemic or lethargic encephalitis whose symptoms progress from somnolence to all types of muscular disorders, e.g., dyskinesia, hyperkinesia, and Parkinsonism. Unfortunately, irreversible secondary neurological syndromes are a common aftereffect of continued phenothiazine usage. In fact, the prevalence of drug-induced dyskinesias is now considered a major iatrogenic disaster.[28] Current estimates of the prevalence of tardive dyskinesia (TD)—the most serious and often irreversible drug complication—in populations undergoing long-term drug treatment are at least 10–25 percent while individual studies demonstrate a prevalence in certain populations of more than 50 percent.[29] In the late 1980s and early 1990s the TD problem is getting worse—not better.[30]

TARDIVE DYSKINESIA: A CURE WORSE THAN SCHIZOPHRENIA

The world's foremost opponent to the use of neuroleptic medications has been Dr. Peter R. Breggin, who, for well over a decade, has protested mightily against their use. Amassing a prodigious amount of information, Breggin has convincingly shown that the neuroleptics cause serious damage to the highest centers of the brain, producing chronic mental dysfunction, tardive dementia, and tardive psychosis. The most serious of the drug-induced disorders is a chronic neurological disorder known as tardive dyskinesia and is characterized by jerky, abnormal movements of the voluntary muscles. Most cases are permanent and there is no known treatment. TD closely mimics Parkinson's disease, Huntington's chorea, and lethargic encephalitis. Drug damage to the higher brain centers, considered the mental equivalent of TD, also occurs. The use of neuroleptics to treat schizophrenia is almost universal in psychiatry and most psychiatrists use them as the first line of treatment. This is done despite the fact that various researchers have shown that the neuroleptics have no specific ameliorative effect on any mental disorder and that they are nonspecific brain-disabling agents that perform a chemical lobotomy *partly* through the disruption of dopamine neurotransmission in the limbic and frontal lobe pathways.[31] The drugs do not cure anything. Instead, they flatten the emotions, produce disinterest and apathy, and enforce docility. Rather than helping schizophrenics, in a controlled study Mosher and Burti demonstrated that nearly all patients having their first schizophrenic episode can be treated *more successfully without neuroleptics* than with them.[32] TD can show up after a few weeks or months on medication, but usually occurs after six months to two years of medication. If the condition is detected early and medication is stopped, an estimated 20 to 50 percent of the patients can improve or recover. Because many cases go unreported or are covered up, it is difficult to determine the total number of TD cases in the nation today. Breggin estimates that the amount exceeds one million. The problem is so serious that both the American Psychiatric Association and the Food and Drug Administration have issued warnings about neuroleptic use. In Breggin's words, "It is no exaggeration to call tardive dyskinesia a widespread epidemic and possibly the worst medically-induced catastrophe in history."[33]

While TD is bad enough, the neuroleptics have also been indicted in cerebral atrophy, actual *shrinkage of brain tissue*. Studies involving computerized axial tomography (CAT scans) of schizophrenics treated with neuroleptics found enlarged lateral ventricles and sulci indicating shrinkage or atrophy of the brain. The ventricles tend to expand in proportion to tissue shrinkage within the confines of the skull. Also, sulci deepen or enlarge when the cortex shrinks. In CAT studies of drug-treated schizophrenics enlargement of the lateral ventricles is the most common finding.

While some studies have also found cerebral atrophy in untreated patients, mounting radiologic evidence from PET, MRI, and CT scans has shown chronic brain dysfunction and brain atrophy in neuroleptic-treated schizophrenic patients. The total number of relevant CT scan studies is estimated to be over ninety, and most of these show damage.[34] Autopsies have also shown that the neuroleptics can also damage the basal ganglia and the caudate nucleus.

Since the dopamine neurons play a major role in the functioning of the cerebral cortex and are critical in an individual's mental life, and since both human and animal studies confirm the neuroleptics suppress the dopamine neurotransmitter systems, we should not be surprised at a limbic and cortical equivalent of TD—disturbances capable of causing persistent cognitive deficits, tardive dementia, and brain atrophy in neuroleptic-treated patients.

Although some researchers have argued that schizophrenia, rather than the neuroleptics, is the cause of the brain atrophy Breggin has convincingly shown such arguments are badly flawed.[35] Most convincing is the failure to find any evidence of cerebral atrophy in postmortem examinations of schizophrenics prior to the introduction of neuroleptics. Also, most organic brain disorders involving atrophy are not reversible, few clear up spontaneously, and their characteristics— short term memory problems, progressive neurological losses, and the gradual deterioration of intellectual functions—are not found in schizophrenics. Breggin also notes that Clozapine, even though it seems less damaging than the other neuroleptics, still suppresses the AIO dopaminergic neurons and may be equal to or worse than other neuroleptics in its long term effects on the brain.

Breggin insists that the dangers of neuroleptics should be spelled out in both the *Physician's Desk Reference Manual* and in all drug company advertisements. The general public should also be warned about these drugs and informed consent obtained from patients and their families before neuroleptics are used. Methods for better treatment of those damaged by neuroleptics should be the focus of future research and every effort should be made to reduce and curtail neuroleptic usage. Finally, non-pharmacologic treatment procedures using psychological techniques and self-help groups should become standard and universal practices for all of the behavioral disorders. It is also imperative that the patient's right to refuse treatment—a right well established and respected in general medicine—should be more thoroughly extended to psychiatry. A voluntary psychiatry, based on informed consent, should be both mandatory and universal.[36]

What is particularly ironic here is that evidence from controlled, random-assignment studies clearly shows that given the proper social environment most newly identified schizophrenics can be treated successfully without the neuroleptics. According to Karon, such social environments can be successfully adapted for use with veteran and chronic cases as well.[37] But the neuroleptics quickly calm very excited individuals without inducing sleep, and patients do become more compliant and manageable. Sadly enough, long-term outcome in schizophrenia is not one whit better today than it was before the introduction of neuroleptics, when two-thirds of "schizophrenics" recovered without any drugs at all.[38] Karon concludes that "unfortunately, political and economic factors and a concentration on short-term cost-effectiveness, rather than scientific findings, currently seem to dictate the type of treatment."[39] Let's face it: drugs are easy to administer, and ably staffed social environments are expensive to erect and maintain. As Szasz has stressed, psychiatry's only visible sign of their power and ability to heal is the drug and their power to prescribe it. Even if the drug prescribed causes severe or irreversible damage, what is the psychiatrist to do? He is neither educated nor trained to apply psychosocial healing techniques and aside from the use of neuroleptics and hospitalization there is nothing else he can do, which is anathema to the typical M.D. psychiatrist. With the drug companies denying any and all side effects, and the patients and their families expecting that the doctor will "do something" and would "never do harm," the pressures to use drugs are enormous. When Breggin, during a television interview, argued against the use of neuroleptics and expanded on their dangers, the National Alliance for the Mentally Ill (NAMI), assisted by the American Psychiatric Association, tried to have Breggin's medical license revoked. The charges were, fortunately, dismissed. The NAMI, of course, considers schizophrenia to be a brain disease, removing all blame and responsibility from the patient's family. Unfortunately, as long as the psychosocial alternatives to the drug treatment of schizophrenics are not widely known and recognized by the medical establishment, drug usage seems inevitable—especially when the drug companies are so aggressively pushing their multibillion dollar profitable products.

According to the DSM-III-R and DSM-IV, the psychiatrists' Bible, the characteristic symptoms of schizophrenia include disturbances in the content of thought such as delusions or false beliefs; disturbances in the form of thought such as loose associations or incoherence; disturbances in feeling or affect such as apathy or emotional flattening, or at its most extreme: catatonic behavior. No single individual ever shows all of these disturbances. One of the most important defining features of insanity is that it is always interpersonal and as one sharp observer noted, "It always takes two to make a psychotic:

an observer and an actor." Moreover, if we separate psychotic individuals from their ordinary problems of living and from their individual sociopsychological development in particular family environments it then becomes possible to ignore the contributions of these factors to the victims' unusual behavior and attribute it neuroanatomical or biochemical disturbances. Contemporary psychiatrists think they know and understand biochemcial disturbances and they have a DSM label for them, so they can then consistently ignore the psychological and developmental aspects.

Nevertheless if we ever hope to understand what schizophrenia is and what it is not, we must forget all the biomedical nonsense and look at the real causes of the problem as a surprisingly large number of researchers have done in the past. What is truly infuriating and scandalous is the modern psychotherapeutic state's refusal to accept or even acknowledge the very existence of this substantial body of work. We will now summarize the most significant opposition to the biomedical model, work that has for much too long been dismissed or ignored.

In 1972 the distinguished anthropologist Stanley Diamond, after reading a National Institute of Mental Health report estimating that sixty million Americans were probably ambulatory schizophrenics, was also shocked to find the work of Harry Stack Sullivan, who years earlier stressed the important role of the social environment in schizophrenic disorders, had been ignored by current psychiatry. Diamond was also appalled by psychiatry's failure to place the problem of schizophrenia in its proper social context. In a marvelous essay, "Schizophrenia and Civilization," published in his 1981 book, *In Search of the Primitive: A Critique of Civilization*, Diamond stressed that the term "schizophrenia" had become a synonym for mental illness in our society. Moreover, Diamond also noted that the mental health establishment is committed to the belief that schizophrenia is a brain disease and that further large appropriations of money will, eventually, uncover the cause and cure. This, Diamond noted, "is tragically wrong." According to Diamond this assumption is not "merely a scientific idea, but is deeply related to the fact that the tragic contradictions of life have little or no standing in our society. We seek to cure people of everything; we tinker with the machine. All the ills that the flesh and spirit of man are heir to are reduced to abstractions. We are dedicated to the proposition that pain can be eliminated."[40]

In Diamond's view, schizophrenia expresses the failure and breakdown of the culture in which we live. Since our culture does not provide an adequate ground for the development of the self, pathological behavior is the result. Schizophrenia is a mental construct, an object of research. A bureaucracy is based on this research construct, which has a real stake in the very disease it is supposed to heal. The average physician is under great pressure to become a pill-pusher for the pharmaceutical industry, a pressure increased by the expectations and demands of the patient. It is, therefore, hardly surprising that the average M.D. knows or cares little about preventive medicine. He is restricted by his society, its structure, and the "reactionary character" of the American Medical Association (i.e., the reluctance to take preventive steps, and instead waiting until a disease appears to act). And, Diamond stresses, the mental health establishment is, itself, a pathological symptom of the society that created it. It is, sadly, part of a fragmented social process within which the alienated study the alienated.

After decades of research no one in NIMH or the medical establishment has any idea as to either the cause or the cure of schizophrenia—despite the fact that a whole research industry has arisen in pursuit of this hypothetical disease. When faced with someone who is mentally ill, the reflex response on the part of psychiatry is to commit them to a custodial institution, a mental hospital, and as Diamond incisively notes, "In the ordinary course of events there is simply no place for such persons in a class-structured, urban society, cross-sected by a highly technical subdivision of labor. Nor can the shrunken nuclear family or its quasi-kin network accommodate people who make extraordinary demands upon their day-to-day resources."[41]

Commitment is therefore socially expedient. And if a shortage of funds demands that the mentally ill be released, they have nowhere to go and wind up on the streets, where they become the homeless. Thus far our mental hospitals have not been turned into therapeutic communities of reciprocating, autonomous, working, and loving persons. They have, instead, become drug wards for those in chemical straitjackets. Though the drugs do permit the release of patients into society at large and the outpatient clinics keep such patients tranquilized and malleable, in no way are the patients' problems being attacked and ameliorated. As a result "the society generates more breakdowns than its institutions can handle, more 'inadequacy' than it can absorb."[42] Thus, as Diamond observes, although we seem to be controlling mental illness, our social pathology deepens and the dependence on drugs or their equivalent is a growing and general characteristic of our civilized society.

Using the analogy of a South Vietnamese alien who was suffering from culture shock but was misdiagnosed as a paranoid schizophrenic by a team of psychiatrists, Diamond shows how easy it is to mistake certain internal mental processes as *ipso facto* pathology:

> Predictable symptoms in the schizophrenic reaction constitute an effort at adaptation to a series of experiences that are perceived as discontinuous and absurd, contrary to expectations and destructive of hope; the future disappears. On the esthetic level, these discontinuous experiences destroy the sense of life as a drama of meanings, as a tragedy that can be endured. This is equivalent to a failure of socialization. . . . The experience of culture shock is, then, a schizophrenic or, if you will, a schizoid reaction . . . the schizophrenic reaction among ourselves is a type of homegrown experience of culture shock.[43]

Diamond also correctly indicts the family as the major contributor to the schizophrenic's psychopathology. The individual's reaction to the social imperatives inherent in the structure and function of the family makes all of us some of the time and some of us most of the time feel like "visiting Vietnamese drifting through a world full of strangers, a world without landmarks, in which we endlessly reify ourselves and others. In other words, schizophrenia as we know it, gives every indication of being a protest against and a response to the problem of learning how to be human in contemporary society."[44]

Diamond next looks at a NIMH study of a schizophrenic and his family in which, during the course of study, some of the psychiatrists found family members were as disturbed as—if not more so—than the patient being observed. As seen through the eyes of a cultural anthropologist, the schizophrenic reaction "is no more and no less than the ultimate pathology of modern society; that pathology may be seen in its actuality as a society-wide dynamic manifested in varying degrees and combinations in all individuals according to their temperaments, their talents, and their precise circumstances."[45]

Many psychiatrists now claim that schizophrenia is statistically predictable in its distribution at a rate of one per one hundred throughout the civilized world and that it is increasing in frequency. Other psychiatrists argue schizophrenia is a universal phenomena found throughout the human family. Diamond strongly disagrees and cites George Devereaux's 1939 observation, "Schizophrenia seems to be rare or absent among primitives. This is a point on which all students of comparative society and anthropology agree."[46] In authentically primitive societies schizophrenia as a diagnostic category is irrelevant. There are a number of reasons for this:

1. The rights to food, clothing, and shelter are completely customary; each person learns as an organic part of the socialization process the requisite variety of skills. *Functionlessness* is not a problem in primitive society.

2. Rituals at strategic points in the bioculturally defined lifecycle permit the person to change roles while maintaining, and expanding, identity. His ordinary humanity is celebrated in an extraordinary way. The lifecycle is a normal curve; it does not collapse in the middle, leaving the aged without wisdom, work, or honor, their only alternative being the dissimulation of youth.

3. Rituals and ceremonies permit the expression of ambivalent emotions and the acting out of complex fantasies in a socially prescribed fashion. It is customary for individuals or groups of people to "go crazy" for self-limiting periods of time without being extirpated from the culture.

4. The ramifying network of kinship associations sets the developing person firmly in a matrix of reciprocal rights, obligations, and expectations. *Social alienation* as we experience it in civilization is unknown.[47]

Leopold Bellak, another psychiatrist who has spent a lifetime researching schizophrenia, has also called attention to the inadequacy of research and research methodology in dealing with the problem: "Tragicomical is the number of continuing attempts to still find a single diagnostic biological factor (disregarding the social and psychological aspect). With a little encouragement, it may not be difficult to find as many as 100 different claims for a single cause of schizophrenia, despite all the evidence for heterogeneity."[48] Bellak also recognizes that magic claims for depression as well as schizophrenia are also prevalent. At the height of the spurious claim of the diagnostic character of the dexamethasone suppression test,* Bellak said he heard one faculty member at a grand rounds lecture say that anybody who doesn't use it diagnostically risks a malpractice suit.

Although hallucinations and delusions, the primary symptoms given for schizophrenia, also occur in primitive societies, there are no mental hospitals or asylums in primitive societies or any institutional equivalents. Diamond sees this as proof that the schizophrenic process in primitive societies is well provided for and socially contained and thus never becomes a clinical entity. This happens only in societies that do not provide creative channels for its expression and exiles its alienated to specialized institutions or drugs them into insensibility. In Diamond's view, primitive cultures fully realize that the major function of all culture is to make men human and, at the same time, to keep them sane. The civilization we know is failing to do this. Schizophrenia then, according to Diamond, "is no less and no more than the subjective aspect of the socioeconomic dynamic of alienation."[49] There is no question that Diamond is correct.

HOW TO BECOME A SCHIZOPHRENIC

Of all the books written about schizophrenia, its genesis, cause, developmental course, misconceptions, misdiagnoses, and mistreatments as well as its cures, none is more comprehensive, accurate, thorough, and clearer in style and statement than John Modrow's classic *How to*

---

*According to some M.D.s, some blood sugar elements (dexamethasone) are suppressed in schizophrenics but not in normal people.

Become a Schizophrenic. Modrow, who is a recovered schizophrenic and is, perhaps, the unrecognized and unappreciated world's foremost authority on this disorder, has performed a truly invaluable service and has made the major contribution to our understanding of the causes and cures of this pseudodisease.

Modrow's paternal great-grandmother died in an institution for the insane in Washington state and, as a result, Modrow's mother, fearful of the genetic hypothesis combined with both her parents' attitudes and beliefs (which were helped along by ignorant psychiatrists who reinforced the notion that schizophrenia is a genetically transmitted disease) led to branding John a potential schizophrenic. Tainted by this label, all of his behavior became suspect and, finally, after a long series of unfortunate events, John also wound up in an institution. His mistreatment and misadventures with the biological psychiatric establishment led him to devote ten years of research and study to the preparation of his book.

In Part I, "A Recipe for Madness," Modrow shows precisely what social and psychological ingredients are necessary to produce a schizophrenic. Contrary to current psychiatric opinion, a considerable amount is known about the etiology of schizophrenia. Using the insights of well-known psychiatric researchers Harry Stack Sullivan, Theodore Lidz, Gregory Bateson, and many others, Modrow has developed a comprehensive theory that clearly and simply explains the experiences of all those who have been diagnosed as schizophrenic.

In Part II, "The Making of a Schizophrenic," Modrow reviews the first sixteen years of his life up until his schizophrenic breakdown in 1960 and his subsequent recovery in early 1961. Along with Scott and Ashworth, Modrow sees schizophrenia not as an illness but as the culmination of a series of progressively worsening personality disorders spanning three or four generations.[50]

In Part III, "The Medical Model Reexamined," Modrow brilliantly refutes "the various pseudoscientific slanders which have been perpetrated against schizophrenics by members of the psychiatric profession."[51] As Modrow notes, the majority of current psychiatrists consider schizophrenics as biologically inferior people who suffer from either brain defects, biochemical defects, genetic deficits, or any combination of the three. Despite the numerous devastating criticisms of this idea, it is still maintained. Modrow also notes that some of the world's greatest psychiatrists—Carl Jung, Hary Stack Sullivan, and R. D. Laing—had schizophrenic episodes similar to his own. Perhaps the most devastating proof that schizophrenia cannot be a disease is the work of Courtenay Harding of the University of Vermont and others, who have shown that on a long-term basis even the most profoundly disabled schizophrenics, generally, make good recoveries.[52] If schizophrenia is a disease due to faulty genes, or to brain or metabolic diseases and is therefore, incurable, then such cures cannot be explained. In this regard, according to Modrow, it is the psychiatrists—not the schizophrenics—who are divorced from reality.

Biological psychiatry's argument that psychiatrists are *legitimate* medical practitioners treating a *real* illness and they, thus, are fully entitled to a doctor's high status and high pay is also destroyed in Part III. Modrow demonstrates that the medical model benefits everyone *except* those for whom it was, ostensibly, designed to help: the schizophrenics themselves.

How to Build a Schizophrenic

Schizophrenics, according to Modrow, do not exist; what we have instead are "human beings who have undergone terrifying, heart-breaking, and damaging experiences, usually over a long period of time, and as a consequence are emotionally disturbed—often to the point of incapacitation."[53] As far back as 1906, Adolf Meyer, the founder of modern American psychiatry, argued schizophrenia is not a disease but is instead due to a breakdown of habits of feeling and thinking.[54]

Modrow points out that studies done on the families of schizophrenics have shown that the disorder cannot be localized in a single individual but is merely a part of a larger pattern of disturbed family relationships. Looking at a number of specific family examples, Modrow shows clearly that schizophrenia is a learned response to disturbed family relationships and communication failures. Most interesting has been the discovery that all of the families of the schizophrenics were more neurotic and more disturbed than the schizophrenic himself.

Gregory Bateson and others have shown precisely how parents produce schizophrenia in their children by placing them in a no-win predicament called a double bind.[55]

In a double bind situation, for example, the mother acts like a loving mother but as soon as the child responds to her she immediately withdraws and expresses hostility toward the child. In the mother's view the child's very existence arouses her anxiety and hostility. Yet she keeps making loving overtures toward the child, then rejecting him when he responds. Such a situation continued over a span of years is certainly enough to drive anyone over the edge. Scott and Ashworth add to this by showing that such personality disorders as the mother evinced above may well span three or four generations and project a fear of going insane from generation to generation. When the parents project their own fear onto the patient and treat him as if he were already insane or nearing the condition, a self-fulfilling prophecy is created in which the parents' fear produces anxiety at first and then a psychotic panic. Scott and Ashworth suggest that schizophrenia is transmitted through the *belief* that madness is inherited rather than by heredity itself.

Theodore Lidz, who early in his career studied patients whose mental problems were organic, i.e., caused by brain lesions, toxic poisoning, and metabolic disorders, soon concluded that schizophrenics were a different breed entirely. They did not suffer disorientation, memory loss, and intellectual degeneration that marked the brain-damaged. In Lidz's studies of the families of schizophrenics over a period of years he found all of them to be schizophrenic—either one or both parents were so egocentric they were unable to separate their own needs and feelings from those of their child. Moreover in those families Lidz calls schismatic, those that are marked by open marital discord and competition for the child's loyalty, the child is caught in a bind in that trying to please one parent causes rebuff and rejection by the other. In the second type of family, which Lidz calls skewed, one parent—usually but not always the mother—seeks completion through her child and is incapable of viewing him as anything other than an extension of herself. Sadly enough, the children who become schizophrenic are the ones closest to their parents emotionally and if they have any defects it is in their love for these defective parents, for whom they have sacrificed their individuality and ultimately their sanity.[56]

As a result of living in these defective families schizophrenics distort reality in accordance with their parents' needs rather than their own. This makes such children particularly susceptible to a schizophrenic breakdown.

The work of Harry Stack Sullivan has made what are perhaps the most valuable contributions to our understanding of the disorder by showing the importance of the loss of ego defenses and the similarity between the schizophrenic's thinking and the thinking of normal people. Sullivan has shown schizophrenia occurs when the individual's security operations upon which he depends to maintain his self-esteem fail totally. When this happens the individual suffers from an intense state of panic and, in this state, has a terrifying vision of himself as a person of no value or worth.[57] Such panic states—which are the most appalling and devastating experiences any person can undergo—are totally disorganizing. These panic states can be induced in a number of different ways. One of the most common is being subjected to very severe and often cruel disparagement by people who are deemed significant and on whose good opinion the individual is largely dependent for his self-esteem. This sort of treatment usually has a long history. A second type of panic begins with the psychological immaturity of the victim and the stunting of his growth by his subservience to and distortion of reality in accordance with his parents' needs. His inability to function as an adult can trigger emotional crises and then schizophrenic episodes when he encounters job promotions, leaving home for the first time, marriage, or parenthood. A third cause of panic is the intrusion into the person's awareness of abhorrent cravings, feelings, or thoughts. Examples of such may be homosexual, incestuous, or homicidal impulses or thoughts. These can cause an intense panicky revulsion and the fear that one must, indeed, be subhuman to have them. Such experiences alone will not bring on schizophrenic attacks unless the individual's ego defenses also have broken down.

Once the panic state has happened five things then occur as a result: (1) a splitting or dissociation of the personality; (2) a drastic narrowing of interests; (3) insomnia; (4) the return of the repressed or split-off portion of the personality which invades and takes over the ego; and (5) the formation of an explicit delusional system.

According to Modrow, "Far from being a disease, schizophrenia is actually a very purposeful and meaningful attempt by the individual to cope with a catastrophic loss of self-esteem."[58] When defensive measures of the individual's ego fail he then distorts reality in order to regain the feeling of worth.

One of the personality splits that comes from the panic state, as described by W. R. D. Fairbairn, is the result of a parent's intolerably cruel behavior. In order to feel emotionally secure, the child will idealize the parent and delude himself by believing his parent's cruelty is really his own fault so all he needs to do is change, "be good," and then he will be loved.[59] A second aspect of the splitting, described by H. Guntrip, is the situation following an especially traumatic panic-producing event in which the individual emotionally withdraws from external reality into a safe inner world. This leaves the conscious ego dazed and lost, drained of emotion, interest, and energy. In this state, everything seems unreal and the individual also feels numb and absorbed in a narrow circle of repetitive ideas to the exclusion of everything else.[60]

Because the future seems hopeless, the individual retreats further from the world of reality into the inner world and memories of a happier past. Here we may find the individual reading, thinking, and identifying with a heroic or historical person or expanding on exotic religious ideas. These things take his mind off panic-producing thoughts. If he is thinking about Buddhism, Jesus, or Kennedy the repulsive sexual and homicidal thoughts are kept at bay.

Such thoughts also ward off the feelings of deadness and depersonalization—feelings of estrangement from others and even himself. In fact, these obsessive thoughts bolster his faltering sense of identity and, at the same time, protect him against anxiety and panic. As a result the thoughts become highly addictive and the individual is literally unable to stop thinking. And as long as he is thinking he is unable to sleep. This cascade of unending thought will continue twenty-four hours a day—day in and day out. According to Modrow, "prolonged sleep deprivation has been the pattern in every schizophrenic I have ever talked to and is mentioned in the autobiographies of various schizophrenics." This was certainly true in his own case. "I myself was virtually unable to get any sleep in the 6 or 7 weeks immediately prior to the onset of my psychosis."[61] The reasons for this are also well known. When a panic episode occurs, catecholamines (adrenaline, noradrenaline, and dopamine) are produced in superabundance, causing a hyperaroused state which leads to prolonged wakefulness. It alone is sufficient to produce illusions, visual hallucinations, and other psychotic symptoms. Once the boundaries between sleep and waking are lost, the individual's field of attention is further narrowed, the retreat into the inner world is enhanced, and his usual reality-orientation fades. It becomes increasingly difficult to separate fact from fiction, dreams from realities, and always in the background are Fairbairn's "internal persecutors" (imagined accusers which arise from feelings of guilt). As the individual's reality-orientation fades, the persecutors come to seem more real and are harder to keep out of his field of awareness. When this happens again the individual panics, narrows his focus of attention even further to keep the persecutors from awareness, and the vicious circle continues. The ego retreats further and further into the world of unreality.

In Modrow's words, "As individuals . . . proceed into a panic state, terror floods their entire being as they view themselves as loathsome, inhuman creatures whom nobody could possibly respect. In this profoundly demoralized and despairing state, these individuals desperately clutch at any idea or notion which would provide them with a feeling of dignity or self-respect."[62] Sullivan concurs.

SCHIZOPHRENIC ETIOLOGY

Part II, the longest section of Modrow's work, describes in detail his own family history, his mother's beliefs in genetic determinism, his father's dislike of children, his many and varied guilt trips, his religious confusion, and brainwashing, seven weeks of prolonged sleep deprivation, his delusion that he was John the Baptist, his hallucinations, and finally his full recovery. One of the most poignant statements in the book points out that being labeled a schizophrenic causes a hundred times as much suffering as the illness itself: "Since recovering my sanity in 1961, I have spent decades struggling to gain some measure of self-understanding and self-esteem. In this regard, I never fully recovered from what psychiatry and my parents did to me until I finally realized I had never been ill in the first place."[63]

Modrow also shows the total inadequacy of the medical model to deal with the origin and nature of his so-called symptoms. He shows clearly that his hallucinations were due to purely psychological rather than medical causes and are fully understood in terms of the events that preceded them: the personality splitting, prolonged sleep deprivation, his drastically narrowed focus of awareness, and his religious obsession. In addition, with regard to hallucinations Modrow cites Silvano Ariti's discovery that auditory hallucinations occur in three stages: (1) the individual projects his own feelings of self-disparagement on to the external world—he even feels hostility in the air; (2) believing others are talking about him, he then puts himself in what Ariti calls the listening attitude; (3) finally, he hallucinates; he hears voices because he *expects* to hear them.[64] Although it is commonly believed that hallucinations are predominantly auditory, visual hallucinations are also very common.

With regard to hallucinations per se, normal people can also hallucinate without being judged psychotic. Johnson, in studying normal people who lost their mates, found that 50 percent of the women and 66 percent of the men hallucinated.[65] Bentall and Slade and Young et al. surveyed normal college students and found that between 13 to 15 percent of them have had occasional auditory hallucinations.[66] Mott, Small, and Anderson have shown that 35 percent of the relatives of psychiatric patients hallucinated, 34 percent of nonpsychotic medically ill patients have hallucinated, and 58 percent of unselected medical students also reported having hallucinated.[67] Since normal people hallucinate under stress, Modrow correctly notes that his hallucinations were an expression of his humanity, not a symptom of a disease.

The fact that Modrow's religious beliefs were false does not necessarily mean he was suffering from a brain disease or that he could not think logically and realistically. He was, certainly, capable of both. The mere fact that schizophrenic delusions are often illogical or bizarre is not proof that schizophrenics cannot think rationally. It is also important to remember that delusions—false beliefs—in the general population are also very common:

> For instance, in our culture the most ordinary people have the most extraordinary delusions of grandeur: they believe that after they die they will become demigods, and live forever in a beautiful mansion in the sky. There are also large and growing numbers of people, many of them well-educated and sophisticated, who believe their lives are controlled by the stars, and who are incapable of making decisions without first consulting an astrologer [one such person was President of the United States]. Moreover, with the advent of the so-called New Age movement many delusions and superstitions once confined to schizophrenics, borderline schizophrenics and other marginal people, are now becoming almost the norm. There are millions of people who firmly believe that little green men from outer space are going to land *en masse* on this planet and usher in a New Age—just as tens of millions of other people firmly believe that Jesus Christ is going to return and usher in a thousand-year Reich. There are also hundreds of apparently normal and well-adjusted people who sincerely believe they have been kidnapped by alien creatures and taken aboard UFOs where they had undergone complicated and often painful medical examinations. The ability of ordinary people to delude themselves is virtually limitless.
>
> Delusions are so common that their absence rather than their presence should be taken as an indication of abnormality.[68]

Modrow's delusions were derived from his Protestant fundamentalism and they were not, in any way, caused by a disease. Modrow next correctly observes that one cannot question the status of schizophrenia as a *real disease* without thereby calling into question the legitimacy of psychiatry as a medical specialty. In the psychiatric view schizophrenics are biologically inferior persons made of intrinsically inferior material—poor brains, bad chemistry, or defective genes.

In examining this view Modrow comes into his own as a satirist. For example, in response to the statement "The natural history of the disease [schizophrenia] is one of deterioration," Modrow notes, "the deterioration Dr. Joseph Coyle speaks of has not occurred in us schizophrenics but in psychiatry itself."[69] Modrow argues "that the assumption that schizophrenia is a brain disease is 'a giant step backward' " resulting from three trends: ideological, economic, and political.

When Szasz rightly claimed that schizophrenia was a fake disease and psychiatry fraudulent medicine, psychiatry panicked and repudiated its entire psychological heritage and conducted a massive propaganda campaign to convince the public the "illnesses" they treat are every bit as real as diabetes or cancer.

The economic need to categorize schizophrenia as a disease was due to psychiatry being threatened by competition from hundreds of other nonmedical psychotherapies—encounter group therapies, Scientology, and such, as well as clinical psychology, clinical social work, etc. all taking clients away. It became necessary to convince the general public that all mental disorders are of a biological nature and can only be properly treated by medical men.

Finally, as the political climate of the country became more conservative, both political and psychiatric reactionaries discovered they both believed in biological determinism. If biological determinism is correct, the poor are poor because they are inherently stupid and inferior. Inequality of the sexes, the races, and the social classes are biologically determined. Money devoted to social programs or to helping schizophrenics is a total waste! Similarly, "until medical science discovers a cure for schizophrenia sometime in the future in perhaps five, ten, or a thousand years from now people afflicted with this disease are totally beyond help."[70] Thus all social rehabilitation programs are a waste of time and money.

To justify this point of view and to salve psychiatry's collective conscience (and the medical model), schizophrenia was attacked on a wide variety of fronts: as a brain defect; a biochemical defect; and a genetic defect. Modrow looks at each of these arguments in turn and demolishes them all with a broad battery of facts that neither psychiatry nor its flimsy medical arguments can ever hope to counter or defend.

Schizophrenia as a Brain Defect

At one time E. Fuller Torrey, a very competent and outspoken psychiatrist, believed that schizophrenia was caused by the herpes simplex virus and he tried to show that enlarged ventricles in the brains of schizophrenics prove brain atrophy has occurred,[71] despite the fact a dozen or more brain scan studies show no difference at all between the ventricular size of schizophrenics and that of normal controls.[72] Moreover, many people have enlarged ventricles but still no psychiatric problems. Torrey's claim that some schizophrenics have ventricular enlargement and this proves schizophrenia is a brain disease is totally false. The same is true of the claim that lack of oxygen at birth causes hippocampal damage and thus schizophrenia. One patient had the entire hippocampus removed and did not become schizophrenic. Arguments about the hypofrontal pattern, that is, diminished metabolism in the frontal lobes, as a cause have also been demolished by the facts. Finally, the argument that schizophrenics have smaller brains and crania than normal people is not only ridiculous but, again, betrayed by anatomical measurements.

Schizophrenia as a Biochemical Defect

For over a hundred years psychiatric researchers have been trying to develop a biochemical diagnostic test for schizophrenia and for a hundred years they have failed. Most psychiatrists still have hope that a biochemical marker will soon be found, based, most will tell you, because such a marker—the dexamethasone suppression test (DST)—for diagnosing depression has recently been found. Unfortunately, and sadly, it was also recently discovered that stress and anxiety rather than depression are more strongly related to nonsuppression of dexamethasone and the DST. In a word, the DST as a means of diagnosing depression is worthless and psychiatrists have no basis at all for believing any such procedure for diagnosing schizophrenia will fare any better. All biochemical changes that do occur with the disorder are the results of the *effect* of the disorder—not the *cause* of the disorder.

Literally hundreds of biochemical theories have been proposed, tested, and found wanting. Among these have been (1) the taraxein hypothesis—a hypothetical blood substance no one but Dr. Robert G. Heath could find; (2) the ceruloplasm hypothesis—a copper-protein which proved to be due to lack of vitamin C in the diet of the experimental group of patients; (3) the adrenaline-adreno chrome hypothesis, the notion that some process in schizophrenics transformed adrenaline into a hallucinogenic agent similar to mescaline, evidence of which couldn't be found anywhere, however; (4) the peculiar odor hypothesis, that the sweat of schizophrenics has a strange odor and when this smelly substance, trans-3-methyl-2 hexanoic acid (TMHA), was found in schizophrenics the discoverers' prestige soared. It just as quickly collapsed when TMHA was also found in the sweat of normal people; (5) the serotonin hypothesis—since LSD blocks the effects of serotonin, a chemical found in the brain, then, obviously too much or too little serotonin is the cause. No differences in serotonin metabolism in schizophrenics and normals has been found; (6) the endorphin hypothesis—an excess amount of endorphins causes schizophrenia. However, schizophrenia causes considerable anguish and if there is an excess of endorphins in the bloodstream all it means is that the brain is trying to *reduce* the pain; it is certainly not *causing* it. If endorphins cause schizophrenia, why don't morphine and heroin also cause it? (7) The dopamine hypothesis (unlike others this theory has not been abandoned)—according to this theory schizophrenia is the result of overactive dopamine neurotransmission. Since the neuroleptic drugs block the dopamine neurosystems in the midbrain, limbic system, frontal lobes, and cortex and make the schizophrenic patients more docile and easier to manage, then such drugs are specific antischizophrenic agents. Many psychiatrists argue such drugs, rather than being true antischizophrenic agents, are nothing more than pharmaceutical lobotomies or chemical straitjackets. Modrow carefully reviews the evidence for and against the dopamine hypothesis and concludes that the neuroleptic drugs have no antischizophrenic properties but instead are brain disabling agents. Their alleged effectiveness is the main support for the dopamine hypothesis and the fact that such drugs modify or suppress schizophrenic symptoms is beside the point—many brain disabling agents do this, including ethyl alcohol! As Modrow states,

"In the long run, schizophrenics are better off not taking neuroleptic drugs. . . . Neuroleptic drugs do not correct biochemical imbalances. They *cause* them. These drugs cause irreversible brain diseases, psychosis, and even death!"[73]

Modrow also argues that Hans Selye's general adaptation syndrome beautifully explains the biochemistry of schizophrenia. It explains the increased dopamine turnover seen in the more disturbed, the "alarm" reaction, resistance, the stage of exhaustion, and all other results of the dopamine research. Yet, despite the general acceptance of Selye's theory, why has psychiatry ignored it? The answer, Modrow explains, is simply that if it were accepted, the medical supporters would have to admit that schizophrenia doesn't represent a brain abnormality but rather how a normal brain reacts to certain types of stress. Viewing schizophrenics as emotionally and/or mentally disturbed, but not ill in the medical sense, would require that ideas about hyperactive dopamine neurotransmission be completely abandoned. The idea that drugs which block dopamine have a specific antischizophrenic effect would also have to be abandoned. This would, in turn, deprive psychiatry of the pseudomedical rationale for prescribing and administering neuroleptic drugs. Psychiatry would then have to face the grim fact that for thirty-eight years it has been inflicting irreversible brain damage on hundreds of thousands of people *for no medically justifiable reason whatsoever*!

Schizophrenia as a Genetic Defect

In November 1988 the respected British science magazine *Nature* published two articles about the discovery of a schizophrenia-causing gene. The gene, located on the long arm of the fifth chromosome, according to Dr. Robin Sherrington and associates in London, caused a susceptibility to the disease.[74] The second article, by Dr. James L. Kennedy and coworkers from Yale, Stanford, and the Karolinska Institute of Stockholm, stated they were unable to find the gene reported by Sherrington and associates.[75] All of the so-called studies which supposedly prove schizophrenia has a genetic cause instead prove just the opposite: that schizophrenia has a psychogenic (a psychological, nonphysical) cause. For example, if one identical twin is schizophrenic the probability of the other twin being schizophrenic is about 46 percent. If one fraternal twin is schizophrenic, the probability of the other twin being affected is only 14 percent.[76] If the disease is caused by a genetic defect, however, then it is implied that the concordance for identical twins should be 100 percent not 46 percent. Even those favoring a genetic explanation are forced to admit the twin studies offer at best weak and inconclusive evidence.

All things considered, it would be marvelous indeed if a schizophrenia-causing gene or genes could be discovered. It would make the treatment of schizophrenia simple and easy, wouldn't it? No. Even if such a gene were discovered it still would not prove schizophrenia is a disease. For, as Modrow shows us, "the concept of disease refers neither to social undesirability nor to heritability, but to cellular pathology: histopathological lesions and pathophysiological processes."[77] In other words, disease has nothing to do with what is socially acceptable or if something can be inherited. The concept of disease has to do with cell abnormalities; with injuries and wounds to or improper functioning of organs and tissues. Even if the genetic marker is ever found and—rest assured it will not be—this by itself will and would not ever prove schizophrenia is a disease.

What is most discouraging about Modrow's short essay on the faulty reasoning underlying the genetic assumptions about schizophrenia is that the scientific public seems to be totally incapable of profiting from experience, i.e, those who should read Modrow's book will not.

Another equally enlightening book about human genetics and biological determinism, *Not in Our Genes*, by R. C. Lewontin, S. P. R. Rose and L. C. Kamin—two biologists and a psychologist—also examined the genetics of schizophrenia and reached conclusions identical to Modrow's regarding family studies, twin studies, and adoption studies. According to these authors not only is madness a matter of labeling, it is not even a property of the individual. It is, instead, merely a social definition wished by society on a proportion of its population. During the heyday of Communism dissent was easily suppressed by diagnosing all dissidents as psychotic, drugging them, and locking them away. Is the same thing happening in America today?

In the June 1993 *Scientific American*, John Horgan summed up the current state of human genetic research. It is, unfortunately, in very sorry shape. Horgan has performed a tremendously useful service by summarizing exactly what is known about behavioral genetics. The results may well come as a shock to those who have long believed that nearly every bit of human behavior is determined by our genetic heritage. After studying various family, adoption, and twin studies which try to link behavior to genetics Horgan emphasizes it is now crystal clear that several genes—each of which may exert only a tiny influence—*acting in concert with environmental influences*—are responsible for behavior.[78] It is highly unlikely that any gene bearing a one-to-one correspondence with a given behavior—especially mental disorders—can ever be found because the diagnosis of mental illness itself is so quixotic, subjective, and biased. Evan S. Balaban, a Harvard biologist, notes, "It is very rare to find genes that have a specific effect. For evolutionary reasons, this just doesn't happen very often."[79] Moreover, Balaban thinks that this sort of research is dangerous in that it could lead us back into the old quagmire of eugenics and genetic cleansing of the human race.

As Horgan says "no good can come of bad science" and it should be obvious to everyone that behavioral traits are not only extraordinarily difficult to define but, more obvious is the fact that practically every claim made for a genetic basis to specific behaviors can also be explained as the result of environmental effects. The mere fact that so very many of the earlier research studies in this field have had to be retracted should give anyone pause. Harvard geneticist Jonathan Beckwith is right when he states, "This has been a high enterprise, and for the most part the work has been done shoddily. Even careful people get sucked into misinterpreting data."[80]

British psychiatrist R. D. Laing, in the 1960s and early 1970s, agreed in principle with Modrow that schizophrenia is essentially a family disorder, not a product of a sick individual but of the interactions of the members of a sick family. Within this family one child will be singled out as the family "whipping boy." This child is always at fault and never able to live up to parental demands or expectations. If, at the same time, this child is browbeaten into believing that he is basically evil, diseased, flawed, and damned if he does/damned if he doesn't, then the child is placed in Gregory Bateson's double bind. Whatever he does is wrong. Under such circumstances the retreat into a world of fantasy is the only escape—the only logical response to the intolerable pressures of existence. Schizophrenia is, therefore, not a disease but a rational, adaptive response of the individual to the insanity of human existence. Psychiatric treatment by hospitalization or by drugs is in no way therapeutic or a blessed liberation from oppression. It is, instead, more brutality and mistreatment by a hostile world.

There are, of course, socioeconomic reasons for this state of affairs. In their excellent book, *Exploding the Gene Myth*, Ruth Hubbard, a Harvard biologist and her associate Elijah Wald ask the question: Is human behavior genetic? Their answer is a loud and resounding *no*.[81] One who listens to the propagandists would swear that it is. Doctors, health insurance companies, schools, and the criminal justice system believe so. Hubbard and Wald are particularly critical of the multibillion dollar project, "The Human Genome Initiative," which aims to map every gene on the DNA of a prototypical human. Hubbard and Wald most effectively succeed in deflating the grandiose and science-fictiony promises of therapeutic benefits that are supposed to emerge from the project. They point instead to the real threats to human privacy and civil liberties already resulting from the unregulated increase in genetic predictions made by these neoeugenic elitists.

Enthusiasm of scientists and the media about new genetic information and technologies needs to be tempered with realism. Hubbard and Wald also insist that all citizens—not just hot-shot scientists—should participate in making decisions about how to regulate information, protect privacy, and avoid discrimination in the future. Their plea is for a society that emphasizes safe, healthy living for everybody, not just a search for ideal or improved genes.

If one looks at the headlines today, it is easy to find genetic explanations for everything from cancer to alcoholism to criminality to homosexuality. As noted earlier, such explanations are always exaggerated or unfounded and they completely ignore the complex interactions of genes with the environment at every level. For example, high heritability (the degree to which a trait stems from genetic factors) should never be equated with inevitability, since the environment can still drastically affect the expression of a gene. For example, the genetic disease phenylketonuria, which causes profound mental retardation, has a heritability of 100 percent. Yet, eliminating the amino acid phenylalanine from the diet of the affected person prevents the retardation from occurring.

Like the ridiculous eugenic theories of seventy-five years ago (for example, that races should never mix, each must remain "pure"), the new genetic determinism is serving a conservative social agenda. The neoconservatives can hardly wait to blame all ill health and misfortune—particularly schizophrenia—on the victims rather than on a sick society and horrible social and environmental conditions.

Modrow, in the final two chapters of his book, completely demolishes biological psychiatry's view of schizophrenia. First, if schizophrenia were a degenerative brain disease then none could recover or emerge from the psychosis stronger and better integrated than before. Yet studies by C. M. Harding, M. Bleuler, and several others all report a rate of recovery and improvement in schizophrenics of more than 50 percent and many of these patients were profoundly disabled, long-term cases.[82] Such recoveries offer the strongest possible evidence that schizophrenia is a reversible, functional disorder. A number of other successful non-pharmacological treatment procedures are presented in Breggin, Karon and Vandenbos, and Mosher and Burti, among others.[83]

Second, the situational nature of schizophrenic symptomatology, the fact that a person can be schizophrenic in one social situation and normal in another, also proves schizophrenia is not an organic disease. One female patient in a catatonic stupor in the hospital, upon being told she had to serve as bridesmaid at her sister's wedding, left the hospital, served normally and without incident at the wedding and then returned to the hospital and resumed her catatonic stupor.

Modrow also cites other case history evidence that clearly indicates even when obviously psychotic, many schizophrenics show amazing intellectual skills and abilities—not the loss of cognitive skills one would show with organic psychoses. Most of the time schizophrenics leave the impression they are sane and reasonable people. The exception to this occurs when one gets into a discussion with them about their delusional beliefs. Moreover, most schizophrenics show exceptional empathic abilities and it is, of course, these exact abilities that render them vulnerable to the schizophrenic disorder.

The fact that so many schizophrenics are intellectually brilliant and far superior to the psychiatrists that attend them is hilariously depicted in Jay Haley's essay "The Art of Being Schizophrenic."[84] To be a good and effective schizophrenic, Haley says, one must have the right sort of family—particularly the mother and proper siblings. The schizoid must also be the scapegoat, the representative failure in the family, and the focus of his parents' lives. He must also hold the family together by offering himself as a problem and he must master manipulativeness. He must conceal his emotions and continuously remind the family that they have driven him mad. But only in the mental hospital, Haley insists, can schizophrenia achieve its full flowering. There, the schizophrenic can single-handedly drive his doctor mad too!

In Modrow's final chapter he takes on the psychiatric profession and exposes to full public view most of psychiatry's pretensions, inadequacies, flaws, and incompetencies. There can be no doubt that Modrow is a justifiably angry man. According to him, if psychiatry were to abandon the medical model, "[p]sychiatrists could no more retain their identities as legitimate medical practitioners while admitting that schizophrenia and other mental disorders are not real diseases than the clergy could retain their identities as representatives of God while adopting atheism as their official creed."[85] Psychiatrists cannot afford to admit—or even consider the fact—that schizophrenia is not a physical disease. This is a fact that, literally, could put them out of business, therapeutic competition being what it is today.

Psychiatrists' training is the same as that of general practitioners. What little specialized training they do have is in using the DSM so the proper drug can be prescribed. They are in no way trained to deal with emotional problems. Psychiatrists do not have the required social and psychological training because they firmly believe such causes don't exist. Since all mental disorders are emotional disorders, one would suppose the ability to understand and empathize with the patient would be fundamental. It is not. Medical schools teach students to regard the patient as merely a physiological machine because if one becomes emotionally involved judgment could be disrupted. This may be true in surgery but not in psychiatry, where the ability to empathize is mandatory.

As a result, shrinkage is so common that the harm can be categorized into physical harm, psychological harm, and social harm. Physical harm is easily accomplished by prescribing the neuroleptics, by electroshock therapy, by insulin coma therapy, and, incredibly, by psychosurgery. Much of the actual shrinkage of the brain tissue, ventricular enlargement, is due to the drugs and electroshock. Other less well known atrocities used on schizophrenic patients include (1) refrigeration or hypothermia therapy, immersing the patient in freezing water for seventy-two hours (many patients have died as a result); (2) anoxia therapy, gradually reducing the oxygen in breathing masks until the patient convulses, similar to insulin coma and metrazol shock therapy; (3) starvation therapy, depriving the patients of food for thirty days, the assumption being that starvation causes helpful biochemical changes; and incredibly, (4) sodium cyanide poisoning therapy, using cyanide in the treatment of catatonics. According to Dr. Warren S. McCulloch, a series of more than sixty patients were "decerebrated" ten times with sodium cyanide. This means that the good doctor poisoned them until all cerebral functions were obliterated. The situation resembles what the young lieutenant in Vietnam told his superior: "You see, sir, we had to destroy the village in order to save it!"

As for psychological harm, the psychiatrist with his good intentions but total ineptness tells the schizophrenic—whose sense of self and self-esteem is so badly damaged he has to resort to delusions and hallucinations to feel he is of any value or worth—that he is diseased and has a sick mind. Then, to make matters worse, they tell him his problems are due to a biological defect treatable by drugs but essentially incurable. As Modrow notes, "if any person is deprived of all hope of his or her ever developing into a person of any value or worth, that person will inevitably undergo a psychological decline characteristic of schizophrenia."[86] The lack of self-insight is viewed as a sign of psychosis. If psychiatrists keep insisting all mental disorders are biological they make it impossible for their clients to ever attain any *psy-*

chological insight or *emotional understanding* of their problems. Usually psychiatrists do the opposite: they teach their patients to misunderstand themselves, to see themselves as physically diseased!

As for social harm, Modrow states unequivocally, "Aside from their authority to prescribe drugs, the only skill most psychiatrists possess its their ability to paste dehumanizing labels on their patients."[87] Unfortunately these labels never wear off and they do immeasurable social harm since employers and the general public see anyone with the label "schizophrenic" as inferior, biologically defective, and a liability—definitely not someone you'd want to hire or associate with. Despite the oath "first do no harm," Modrow argues, "it is nearly impossible to practice psychiatry without doing considerable harm. How, for example, can a psychiatrist validate his identity as a medical doctor without labeling others as mentally sick—that is to say, without dehumanizing others and thoroughly destroying their identities?"[88]

There is also an economic force at work. Most psychiatrists do not have either the time or the desire to delve into their patients' life history and personal problems. With the medical model the job is simple, "All they need to do is write a prescription for Haldol or Thorazine, toss it at the patient, and say, 'Take your pills, sickie.' . . . The medical model is also a great benefit and source of comfort to the schizophrenic's parents for it absolves them of all responsibility for causing their child's mental breakdown. What a relief . . . their son or daughter's problems stem solely from a physical disease—an illness for which no one is responsible."[89] Bye-bye guilt!

Finally, within the last decade a number of researchers have argued that schizophrenia is not one but several different diseases. There is—despite this wishful thinking—not one shred of evidence to support this claim. Modrow also argues that the ordinary madness-sanity dichotomy is itself a mere artificial convention attempting to cover up the fundamental unity of the mind. Trying to understand schizophrenia—a function that is purely a psychological disorder—and its causes from a strictly medical or biological perspective is always doomed to failure. In Modrow's words, "[I]t's like trying to understand Judaism by analyzing blood or urine samples taken from Jews."[90] Modrow is brilliantly correct on all counts!

*   *   *

Before ending this chapter it is important to cite the work of Bertram Karon, who recently surveyed the entire field of psychotherapy versus medication for treating schizophrenia. Karon concludes that although it is believed in psychiatric circles that schizophrenic patients must be treated with medication, this conclusion

> is based on poorly designed studies, the most serious flaw of which is the absence of psychotherapists experienced in the treatment of schizophrenic patients by psychotherapy. Labeling therapists without such experience and training as "experienced" does not substitute for *relevant* training and experience. . . . [Several studies] indicate that appropriate and careful use of psychosocial treatment is more effective in the long run than medication as currently used. . . . The optimal treatment for a schizophrenic is psychotherapy, from a competent therapist, without medication, if the patient, the therapist, and the setting can tolerate it.[91]

Karon also, in agreement with Modrow and Breggin, ironically notes, "Unfortunately, political and economic factors and a concentration on short-term cost-effectiveness rather than the scientific findings, currently seem to dictate the type of treatment. The data seem to clearly indicate the value of psychosocial treatments, including individual psychotherapy, as opposed to medication."[92] Too bad for all those victims of the biopsychiatrists' drugs.

In a recent fascinating and thoughtful article "Schizophrenia and the Brain: Conditions for a Neuropsychology of Madness," R. Walter Heinrichs makes the point that if schizophrenia *is* a brain disease that manifests itself in behavior, the behavioral consequences must be understandable in terms of functional properties of affected brain areas or systems, i.e., schizophrenia must make neuropsychological sense.[93] Heinrichs makes the fact that it doesn't very clear, stressing that schizophrenia is a heterogeneous illness and there is little consistent evidence linking schizophrenia to any particular brain abnormality, and the abnormalities that have been found do not produce the behavioral deficits seen in schizophrenia. The question of whether schizophrenia is one disease or many points up the inadequacy of current diagnostic procedures based on the DSM-III-R and the DSM-IV. What researchers are calling schizophrenia may well be a number of illnesses other than the one assumed. What Modrow experienced and what he calls schizophrenia may well be a totally different disorder from the one treated by the average neuroleptic-dispensing biological psychiatrist.

To put the icing on the cake, a recent article in the *American Journal of Psychiatry* by James D. Hegarty et al., "One Hundred Years of Schizophrenia: A Metaanalysis of the Outcome Literature," concludes:

> Overall less than half of patients diagnosed with schizophrenia have shown substantial clinical improvement after follow-up averaging nearly 6 years. Despite considerable gains in improvement rates after mid-century, there has been a decline since the 1970s. These historical changes [i.e., the improvements early in the century] probably reflect improved treatment, shifts in diagnostic criteria, and selection bias related to changes in health care.[94]

A comment to Hegarty's article by Dr. Nancy C. Andreasen, the editor of the *American Journal of Psychiatry*, points out that "information is not knowledge" and that a decline in improvement rates is nothing to be proud of.[95] What is even more baffling is the unwillingness of psychiatry to push both research and practice into psychological, behavioral, and psychosocial treatment procedures for the treatment of schizophrenics. In light of the fact that these are the only procedures that seem to work and offer any promise at all, psychiatry's refusal to abandon its futile medications borders on the irresponsible and the bizarre.

NOTES

1. Thomas Szasz, *Schizophrenia: The Sacred Symbol of Psychiatry* (New York: Basic Books, 1976), p. xiv.

2. Theodore Sarbin and James C. Mancuso, *Schizophrenia: Medical Diagnosis or Moral Verdict?* (Elmsford, N.Y.: Pergamon Press, 1980); and also Jay Haley, "The Family of the Schizophrenic: A Model System," *Journal of Nervous & Mental Disease* 129 (1959): 357–74.

3. T. R. Sarbin, "Toward the Obsolescence of the Schizophrenia Hypothesis," *Journal of Mind & Behavior* 11, nos. 3 and 4 (Summer/Autumn 1990): 261.

4. J. H. Willis and D. Bannister, "The Diagnosis and Treatment of Schizophrenia: A Questionnaire Study of Psychiatric Opinion," *British Journal of Psychiatry* 111 (1965): 1165–71.

5. See T. R. Sarbin, "The Concept of Hallucination," *Journal of Personality* 35 (1967): 359–80; and "Imagining as Muted Role Taking: A Historicolinguistic Analysis," in *The Function and Nature of Imagery*, ed. P. Sheehan (New York: Academic Press, 1972), pp. 333–54. Relevant studies by T. R. Sarbin and J. B. Juhasz include the following: "The Historical Background of the Concept of Hallucination," *Journal of the History of the Behavioral Sciences* 3 (1967): 339–58; "Toward a Theory of Imagination," *Journal of Personality* 38 (1970): 52–76; "The Social Psychology of Hallucination," in *Hallucination: Theory and Research*, eds. R. Siegel and L. West (New York: Wiley, 1975), pp. 241–56; "The Social Psychology of Hallucinations," *Journal of Mental Imagery* 2 (1978): 117–44; and "The Concept of Mental Illness: A Historical Perspective," in *Culture and Psychopathology*, ed. I. Al-Issa (Baltimore: University Park Press, 1982), pp. 77–110.

6. See Ghazi Asad, *Hallucinations in Clinical Psychiatry* (New York: Brunner-Mazel, 1990); Edmund Parish, "The International Census of Waking Hallucinations," in *Hallucinations and Illusions: A Study of the Fallacies of Perception* (London: Walter Scott, 1897), pp. 18–27; and Ian Stevenson, "Do We Need a New Word to Supplement 'Hallucination'?" *American Journal of Psychiatry* 140 (1983): 1609–11.

7. J. B. Juhasz and T. R. Sarbin, "On the False Alarm Metaphor in Psychophysics," *Psychological Record* (1966): 323–27.

8. Sarbin, "Toward the Obsolescence of the Schizophrenia Hypothesis."

9. Seth Farber, *Madness, Heresy, and the Rumor of Angels* (Chicago: Open Court, 1993).

10. Ibid., p. 23.

11. Szasz, *Schizophrenia*, p. 22.

12. Farber, *Madness, Heresy, and the Rumor of Angels*, p. 24.

13. L. S. Benjamin, "Is Chronicity a Function of the Relationship between the Person and Auditory Hallucination?" *Schizophrenia Bulletin* 15 (1989): 291–310.

14. Sarbin and Mancuso, *Schizophrenia*.

15. Ibid., p. 4.

16. Irvin Gottesman, *Schizophrenia Genesis: The Origin of Madness* (New York: W. H. Freeman & Co., 1991).

17. John Modrow, *How to Be a Schizophrenic: The Case against Biological Psychiatry* (Everett, Wash.: Apollyon Press, 1992), p. 227.

18. Gottesman, *Schizophrenia Genesis*, p. 36.

19. Ibid., p. 36.

20. Courtenay M. Harding, "Long Term Functioning of Subjects Rediagnosed as Meeting the DSM III Criteria for Schizophrenia," (doctoral diss., University of Vermont, Burlington, Vt., 1984); and C. M. Harding et al., "The Vermont Longitudinal Study of Persons with Severe Mental Illness. II. Long Term Outcome of Subjects Who Retrospectively Met the DSM III Criteria for Schizophrenia," *American Journal of Psychiatry* 144 (1987): 727–35.

21. Gottesman, *Schizophrenia Genesis*, p. 233.

22. D. Cohen and H. Cohen, "Biological Theories, Drug Treatments, and Schizophrenia: A Critical Assessment," *Journal of Mind & Behavior* 7, no. 11 (1986): 13.

23. A. A. Lipton and F. S. Simon, "Psychiatric Diagnosis in a State Hospital: Manhattan State Revisited," *Hospital & Community Psychiatry* 36 (1985): 368–73.

24. Sarbin and Mancuso, *Schizophrenia*.

25. Peter Breggin, *Psychiatric Drugs: Hazards to the Brain* (New York: Springer, 1983).

26. M. Bleuler, *The Schizophrenic Disorders: Long Term Patient and Family Studies* (New Haven, Conn.: Yale University Press, 1978), pp. 217–18.

27. Cited in Breggin, *Psychiatric Drugs*, p. 17.

28. P. S. Applebaum, K. Schaffner, and A. Messel, "Responsibility and Compensation for Tardive Dyskinesia," *American Journal of Psychiatry* 142 (1985): 806–10.

29. Cohen and Cohen, "Biological Theories," p. 22.

30. Peter R. Breggin, *Toxic Psychiatry* (New York: St. Martin's Press, 1992).

31. Breggin, *Psychiatric Drugs*; Cohen and Cohen, "Biological Theories"; and L. R. Mosher and L. Burti, *Community and Mental Health: Principles and Practice* (New York: W. W. Norton & Co., 1989).

32. Mosher and Burti, *Community Mental Health*.

33. Breggin, *Psychiatric Drugs*, p. 183.

34. J. R. Kelso, Jr., et al., "Quantitative Neuroanatomy in Schizophrenia: A Controlled Magnetic Resonance Imaging Study," *Archives of General Psychiatry* 45 (1988): 533–41.

35. Peter R. Breggin, "Brain Damage, Dementia, and Neuroleptics," *Journal of Mind & Behavior* 11, nos. 3 and 4 (Summer/Autumn 1990): 425–64.

36. Ibid., p. 462.

37. B. P. Karon, "Psychotherapy versus Medication for Schizophrenia: Empirical Comparisons," in *The Limits of Biological Treatment for Psychological Distress*, eds. S. Fisher and R. P. Greenberg (Hillsdale, N.J.: Lawrence Erlbaum Associates, 1989), pp. 105–47.

38. J. Haley, "The Effect of Long-Term Outcome Studies on the Therapy of Schizophrenia," *Journal of Marital & Family Therapy* 15 (1989): 127–32.

39. Karon, "Psychotherapy versus Medication."

40. Stanley Diamond, "Schizophrenia and Civilization," in *In Search of the Primitive: A Critique of Civilization* (New Brunswick, N.J.: Transaction Publications, 1981), p. 228.

41. Ibid., p. 230.

42. Ibid., p. 234.

43. Ibid., p. 238.

44. Ibid., p. 239.

45. Ibid., p. 253.

46. Ibid., p. 254.

47. Ibid., pp. 253–54.

48. Leopold Bellak, "The Schizophrenic Syndrome and Attention Deficit Disorder," *American Psychologist* 49, no. 1 (January 1994): 26.

49. Diamond, "Schizophrenia and Civilization."

50. R. D. Scott and P. L. Ashworth, " 'Closure' at the First Schizophrenic Breakdown: A Family Study," *British Journal of Medical Psychology* 40 (1967): 109–45.

51. Modrow, *How to Be a Schizophrenic*, p. 4.

52. Harding, "Long Term Functioning of Subjects," and Harding et al., "The Vermont Longitudinal Study."

53. Modrow, *How to Be a Schizophrenic*.

54. Ibid., pp. 10–17.

55. Gregory Bateson et al., "Toward a Theory of Schizophrenia," in *Steps to an Ecology of Mind* (New York: Ballantine Books, 1956), pp. 201–27.

56. Theodore Lidz, *The Origin and Treatment of Schizophrenic Disorders* (New York: Basic Books, 1973).

57. Harry S. Sullivan, *Schizophrenia as a Human Process* (New York: W. W. Norton, 1962).

58. Modrow, *How to Be a Schizophrenic*, p. 25.

59. W. R. D. Fairbairn, *An Objects-Relations Theory of the Personality* (New York: Basic Books, 1952).

60. H. Guntrip, *Schizoid Phenomena Object-Relations and the Self* (New York: International Universities Press, 1968), p. 64.

61. Modrow, *How to Be a Schizophrenic*, p. 244. Examples of autobiographical accounts include A. Boisen, *Out of the Depths* (New York: Harper & Row, 1960); D. P. Schreber, *Memoirs of My Nervous Illness* (London: William Dawson & Sons, 1955); and Mark Vonnegut, *The Eden Express* (New York: Bantam Books, 1975).

62. Mo'drow, *How to Be a Schizophrenic*, p. 24.

63. Ibid., p. 148.

64. Silvano Ariti, *Interpretation of Schizophrenia*, 2d ed., (New York: Basic Books, 1974).

65. F. H. Johnson, *The Anatomy of Hallucinations* (Chicago: Nelson-Hall Co., 1978).

66. R. P. Bentall and P. D. Slade, "Reliability of a Scale Measuring Disposition toward Hallucination: A Brief Report," *Personality & Individual Differences* 6 (1985): 527–29; and H. F. Young et al., "Disposition toward Hallucination, Gender, and EPQ Scores: A Brief Report," *Personality & Individual Differences* 7 (1986): 247–49.

67. R. H. Mott, I. Small, and J. M. Anderson, "Comparative Study of Hallucinations," *Archives of General Psychiatry* 12 (1965): 595–601.

68. Modrow, *How to Be a Schizophrenic*, pp. 155–56.

69. Ibid., p. 161.

70. Ibid., p. 164.

71. E. Fuller Torrey and M. R. Peterson, "The Viral Hypothesis of Schizophrenia," *Schizophrenia Bulletin* 2 (1976): 136–46.

72. F. Benes et al., "Normal Ventricles in Young Schizophrenics," *British Journal of Psychiatry* 141 (1982): 90–93.

73. Modrow, *How to Be a Schizophrenic*, p. 195.

74. R. Sherrington et al., "Localization of a Susceptibility Locus for Schizophrenia on Chromosome 5," *Nature* 336 (1988): 164–67.

75. John Horgan, "Eugenics Revisited," *Scientific American* 271 (June 1993): 122–31.

76. I. I. Gottesman and J. Shields, *Schizophrenia: The Epigenetic Puzzle* (New York: Cambridge University Press, 1982).

77. Modrow, *How to Be Schizophrenic*.

78. Horgan, "Eugenics Revisited."

79. Cited in Horgan, "Eugenics Revisited," p. 127.

80. Ibid., p. 124.

81. Ruth Hubbard and Elijah Wald, *Exploring the Gene Myth: How Genetic Information Is Produced and Manipulated* (Boston: Beacon Press, 1993).

82. See Courtenay M. Harding, "Long Term Functioning of Subjects";

C. M. Harding et al., "The Vermont Longitudinal Study"; M. Bleuler, *The Schizophrenic Disorders*; L. Ciompi, "Catamnestic Long-Term Study of the Course of Life and Aging of Schizophrenics," *Schizophrenia Bulletin* 6 (1980): 606–18; and L. Ciompi, "The Natural History of Schizophrenia in the Long Term," *British Journal of Psychiatry* 136 (1980): 413–20 among many other studies with similar conclusions.

83. See B. Karon and G. Vandenbos, *The Psychotherapy of Schizophrenia: The Treatment of Choice* (New York: Jason Aronson, 1981); Mosher and Burti, *Community Mental Health*; E. Walkenstein, *Beyond the Couch* (New York: Crown, 1972); and Judi Chamberlin, *On Our Own: Patient-Controlled Alternatives to the Mental Health System* (New York: Hawthorne, 1978) as just a few of the many published studies which support this finding.

84. Jay Haley, "The Art of Being Schizophrenic," *Voices* 1, no. 1 (Fall 1965): 139–47.

85. Modrow, *How to Be a Schizophrenic*, p. 223.

86. Ibid., p. 226.

87. Ibid., p. 227.

88. Ibid.

89. Ibid., p. 228.

90. Ibid., p. 238.

91. Karon, "Psychotherapy Versus Medication," p. 146.

92. Ibid., p. 147.

93. R. Walter Heinrichs, "Schizophrenia and the Brain: Conditions for a Neuropsychology of Madness," *American Psychologist* 48 (1993): 221–33.

94. James D. Hegarty et al., "One Hundred Years of Schizophrenia: A Metaanalysis of the Outcome Literature," *American Journal of Psychiatry* 151, no. 10 (1994): 1409.

95. Nancy C. Andreasen, "Changing Concepts of Schizophrenia and the Ahistorical Fallacy," *American Journal of Psychiatry* 151, no. 10. (1994): 1405–1407.

5

Iatrogenesis: False Memories, Satanic Ritual Abuse, and Alien Abductions

It is a true saying. Hell is paved with good intentions.

John Wesley[1]

One of the real tragedies of modern medical practice is the unintentional creation of a new, or, in many cases, more serious and disabling disorder by the therapist's misguided efforts to heal. Such disorders created by the physician or therapist are called *iatrogenic* from the Greek *iatros* meaning "healer." Sadly enough the prevalence and extent of such disorders is much greater than is generally thought, especially in the area of psychiatric and psychological disorders.

Hell, according to John Wesley and others, is beautifully paved with good intentions. Over the last few years, during the late 1980s and early 1990s, a number of naive psychotherapists have constructed three major superhighways across Hades' infernal landscape. Number one, and the most heavily travelled, was constructed and is constantly being improved by therapists who are falsely convincing their clients they are victims of childhood sexual molestation. The second major Stygian interstate has been built by counselors convincing both themselves and their clients of the existence of satanic ritual abuse. The third and final expressway, although not quite as long and wide but certainly more scenic and varied, is being built by therapists and pseudotherapists persuading people they are victims of "alien abduc-

249

tions." The engineering processes and procedures used to accomplish these iatrogenic feats of construction are, however, identical.

The needed materials are: a person with a problem of some sort seeking an answer; a therapist, counselor, or guru; social compliance on the part of the person with the problem; a number of suggestions from the therapist; and finally, a total relaxation of the reins of the client's imagination. This combination results in what is usually referred to as "hypnosis" or "trance," terms which are both inaccurate and misleading.*

Creating an iatrogenic condition is easily undertaken. The "hypnotic ritual" is unnecessary in most instances, as the majority of people can be persuaded to relax, close their eyes, and take slow, deep breaths. Nearly everyone possesses some degree of intelligence, imagination, and memory; and although some individuals are more suggestive than others, all of us, without exception, are prone to suggestion. When these factors are combined with a therapist's stimulation of memory (which is virtually indistinguishable from imagination), what emerges ninety-nine times out of a hundred is a mixture of both fact and fiction. Our memories are never 100 percent accurate, and the farther away in time we are from the event we are trying to recall, the less accurate our account will be. When a therapist suggests to patients who are in this relaxed, susceptible state that they were abused as children (possibly by Satanists), or that they have been abducted by aliens, the ideas become "memory," and an iatrogenic disorder is born.

FALSE MEMORIES OF CHILDHOOD SEXUAL ABUSE

In a recent article titled "Making Monsters," Richard Ofshe and Ethan Watters described precisely how the therapist and his unwitting client conspire to create confabulated stories of childhood sexual abuse and molestation.[2] Ofshe and Watters chose the title, "Making Monsters," because an increasingly large number of psychotherapists have been promoting "recovered memory therapy." This peculiar form of therapy

---

*For a thorough discussion of why these terms are inaccurate or misleading, see Robert A. Baker, *They Call It Hypnosis* (Amherst, N.Y.: Prometheus Books, 1990).

leads the clients to see their parents as monsters who sexually abused them during their childhood and causes the parents to see their children as monsters out to destroy lives and reputations. In little over a decade recovered memory therapy has managed not only to destroy the lives of hundreds of clients and their families but has become such a cruel and vicious practice that a network of international organizations—the False Memory Syndrome Foundation—has been formed to fight against and correct the harm this therapy has done. There are over five thousand families and their members who protest they have been falsely accused. Many of them have already proved that they are innocent in court, after taking legal action against the obsessed and incompetent therapists. Incredibly, such protests on the part of outraged parents are seen by the psychotherapists as a backlash against women and children and proof that the widespread sexual abuse and the rights of women and children are continuing to be ignored.

It is difficult to know exactly when the child abuse iatrogenic therapy movement began, but there can be no doubt that the Ellen Bass and Laura Davis's book, *The Courage to Heal*, played a significant role in the current epidemic of sex abuse survivors. According to the Bass and Davis scenario (1) every adult female who has a problem in living, no matter what the problem may be (depression, headaches, low self-esteem, interpersonal difficulties, or phobias), obviously suffered sexual abuse as a child; (2) this abuse has been repressed and deliberately forgotten by shoving it down into the unconscious part of the mind; (3) this repression is the reason why the victim now suffers; (4) the only way such problems can be cured is by going to an "abuse therapist" who will hypnotize the victim, take her back to the time of abuse and the abuser and the memories of both; (5) until these hidden memories are recalled and brought to the surface no cure is possible; (6) the victim who has difficulty remembering the abusive events is in "denial," the unconscious mind is protecting itself and fighting to keep the horrible memories hidden; (7) once the therapist uncovers the hidden memories of the abuse and abusers recovery is automatic; (8) once the abuser is known the victim is urged to attain redress via confrontation and legal means.[3]

Whether or not any of these eight statements bears resemblance to the psychological truth is of little matter. The therapist is on a holy mission: to save the long-suffering, abused female survivors and right the horrendous crime of child sexual abuse! Believe every story of childhood abuse uncovered by the crusading psychotherapist! Such stories *must* be true or the therapist couldn't possibly have found them could they?

The work of Bass and Davis is among literally hundreds of books, pamphlets, and other literature now available. All are intended to persuade the unwary reader that all male adults and many female adults are lechers, rapists, and pedophiles—or worse.

There is little doubt that many children have been abused in the past and are currently being abused. Such facts do not justify the total incompetence and widespread malpractice perpetrated by hundreds of crusading and zealous therapists who are now convinced that each and every human psychological ailment is due to childhood sexual abuse. In fact, the entire therapy is shockingly based on a total lack of understanding of (1) the nature of human memory; (2) how the human mind works; (3) the nature of suggestion; (4) what hypnosis is and is not; (5) the nature of repression; and (6) the nature and etiology of human psychopathology. Truly, in this instance a little learning is indeed a dangerous thing. False memory therapy is based upon a number of mistaken ideas, misinformation, and lack of proper training in the use of suggestive techniques and procedures.

This is especially true if the unwary therapists offer abuse checklists which are so general that no one reading the list is exempt. Patients go to therapists because they believe the therapist knows how and is able to them. They also believe the therapist has the answer to their problem. If the therapist is warm, sympathetic, self-assured, and persuasive, it is easy for the client to believe that the therapist is all-knowing. If the therapist answers the client's complaints with an authoritative diagnosis of child abuse, it is most difficult, indeed, for the client to resist. When the client says she (usually) has no early memories of abuse and the therapist confidentially assures her this is not only both typical and common but that such memories can be triggered and recovered fully via relaxation, guided imagery, and hypnosis, it is almost impossible for the client to resist.

Magnifying the problem is the fact that we don't remember very much about our early childhood. Little, if anything, earlier than our third or fourth year is ever recalled—early childhood amnesia is a universal phenomenon because of lack of maturation of the central memory system. Of further significance is that a continuous record of past memories does not usually show up until sometime after our fifth year. Instead of telling the client about these psychological facts the therapist informs her that the reason for failure to recall is due to repression. Bass and Davis have stated,

> If you don't remember your abuse, you are not alone. Many women don't have memories, and some never get any memories. This doesn't mean they weren't abused.
>
> If you don't have any memory of it, it can be hard to believe the abuse really happened. You may feel insecure about trusting your intuition and want "proof" of your abuse. This is a very natural desire, but it is not always one that can be met.[4]

Bass and Davis go on to argue that the clients' failure to remember specific instances of abuse *proves* they were in fact, abused. Therapists reading and believing this nonsense and repeating it to their clients are laying another dozen miles of asphalt in hell. Distraught people, anxious and depressed, told by their therapist that they are victims of childhood sexual abuse who have repressed all memory of this abuse and are in denial because their own minds are protecting them, and who are assaulted by a media barrage of other such instances of abuse, would be superhuman if they did not begin to believe they too are victims!

Memories are, unfortunately, so unreliable and so influenced by suggestion it is impossible to determine what the truth is by memory alone. Bass and Davis and their ilk apparently do not understand this nor are they aware that all of their assumptions about repression are not only wrong, but *badly wrong*. As Kihlstrom recently stated,

> Memories are personal, and nobody can say to someone else that they don't have a particular memory. And, for that matter, nobody can say to someone else that they do have a particular memory, but they

just can't remember it. But that doesn't mean that there is no right or wrong in memory. The crucible for memory is the truth about what happened, the fact of the matter. Incest and other forms of abuse and trauma occur all too frequently in our society, and the survivors of these experiences deserve our respect and support. But uncorroborated memories of these sorts of things have no special status. They should be taken seriously, and they should be investigated, but they should not be accepted uncritically by either the patient who remembers them or the therapist who receives the report. . . .

Unfortunately, the vagaries of memory are such as to make it impossible to get at the truth by remembering alone. Many people, including many . . . counselors and social workers don't seem to understand this. In many cases, therapeutic work with patients is based on a view of memory processes that is simply, but wildly, incongruent with established principles.[5]

Memories: True or False?

In her 1992 book, *Trauma and Recovery,* Dr. Judith L. Herman, a psychiatrist at Harvard Medical School, admits that certainty is not possible in most cases of alleged childhood sexual abuse. She nevertheless insists that airing all these charges of molestation is a healthy antidote to decades of legal and psychiatric neglect suffered by the abused victims. Until recently, she argues, perpetrators of child sexual abuse committed virtually "perfect crimes" since the children rarely reported it and when they did they weren't believed.

The trauma of child abuse causes a number of symptoms but the most frequent is a mental reaction known as dissociation. A child exposed to continued abuse and sexual assault will, typically, (1) imagine the abuse is happening to someone else; or (2) the child will detach itself from the pain by deadening its body; or (3) may (according to many theorists) invent an alternate personality to whom all these horrible things are happening in order to protect the "real" self; or (4) as most psychotherapists claim, the knowledge of the trauma will undergo repression, the memories will be hidden or placed in the unconscious mind where they are then entirely forgotten.[6]

Dr. Herman prefers the term "delayed recall" to repression or dissociation and argues that many abuse victims have partial amnesia and that most of these memories of abuse that turn up years later are accurate. She cites a number of studies in support. One, carried out by Linda M. Williams of the University of New Hampshire, found that thirty-eight of a hundred adult women did not remember childhood sexual abuse that was documented in their hospital records seventeen years earlier.[7] Dr. Lenore Terr agrees that amnesia of abuse is not uncommon, and in her book, *Too Scared to Cry,* she argues that children who suffer repeated and brutal sexual assaults may forget not only the specific assaults but many other events in their childhood as well. Terr is very sensitive to the possibility of false memories and observes that while memories of sexual abuse are sometimes fabricated via the suggestions or persuasions of others, those children who have blocked out prolonged abuse do have some symptoms, for example, indifference to pain, lack of empathy, and an avoidance of emotional intimacy. Terr does not deny that some children fabricate tales of abuse. In her words, ". . . I think that a very small number of bearers of false tales will still come forward with the sensational accusations—with the powerful way of getting rid of someone or of collecting money for somebody. They did it at Salem. And they did it at the fictional school of Lillian Hellman's play *The Children's Hour* and they'll do it again."[8] She also understands why these accusations are made:

> Children make false accusations, not only for their own sakes but for the sakes of others. Most often they have been pushed. But sometimes it is spontaneous. Some of these young accusers come to believe their stories . . . One child I know of had been asked by a social worker 25 times on tape whether her daddy had asked her to suck his "pee pee." Twenty-five times the child said, "No." But when the question was asked for the 26th time, the child said "Yes." She gave no further details. A judge stopped all parental visitation for the next year on the basis of that 26th answer.[9]

Dr. Herman, however, insists that therapists rarely have enough power or influence over their patients to impose or implant false memories of abuse. She admits that even though hypnosis and other suggestive techniques may heighten the tendency to create memories in order to please the therapist, in the more than two hundred trauma cases she witnessed only one client base a claim of being sexually abused solely on hypnotic revelations.

Psychologists who have empirically and experimentally studied the concept and process of so-called repression, have not found any evidence to support the views of clinicians like Herman and Terr. This is the conclusion of David Holmes in "The Evidence for Repression: An Examination of Sixty Years of Research," the most comprehensive survey yet of the experimental evidence for repression. Holmes states, "One cannot prove the null hypothesis, and therefore we cannot conclude that repression does not exist, but after sixty years of research has failed to reveal evidence for repression, it seems reasonable to question whether continued expenditure of effort on this topic is justified. Regardless of how fascinating the repression hypothesis is, the time may have come to move on."[10]

If repression of extremely traumatic experiences is common, how does one explain the findings obtained with children who witness parental murder? In one study, not a single child aged five to ten who had witnessed the murder of a parent had repressed the memory. To the contrary, they had difficulty not thinking about it.[11] Studies have shown that for most traumatic events, including sexual abuse, *not forgetting* is the critical clinical problem and therapy must provide procedures to deal with painful memories that won't go away.

While memory ordinarily is an active and constructive process, the terror that comes with trauma promotes such things as somatic (bodily) sensations, behavioral enactments, nightmares, and flashbacks. Clinicians and researchers dealing with traumatized patients have repeatedly observed that the sensory experiences and visual images related to the trauma do not fade over time and appear to be less subject to distortion than ordinary experiences.

Anthony Greenwald in his review of unconscious cognition and implicit (covert or hidden) and explicit (overt or clearly recalled) memories shows that the old psychoanalytic assumption of repression and the notion that the cognitive system unconsciously constructs and uses a representation of the exact nature of an ego threat in order to manage an effective defense, is simply unnecessary.[12] A simpler account of repression uses empirically established phenomena of implicit memory as the basis for understanding apparent instances of recovery of repressed memories. The implicit-becomes-explicit memory account is far simpler in its theoretical interpretation than the psychoanalytic account which requires a sophisticated cognizant (and near omniscient) unconscious agency. Note also, Greenwald says, that the implicit memory account can also explain false memories as well as the paramnesias* and déjà vu. Greenwald gives as an example the first-time viewer who is not surprised by the plot turns of a movie he is watching and who might mistakenly conclude he has seen it before.

In reviewing what takes place between therapists trained in the Bass and Davis tradition and their clients, it is obvious that the therapist, convinced of early incest or rape, manages over the course of the therapeutic sessions to also convince the clients of sexual abuse. This seems especially clear in the case of Betty Petersen and her story as revealed in her book, *Dancing with Daddy,* and in the sad case of Paul Ingram, which is described in separate, detailed accounts by Lawrence Wright and Richard J. Ofshe.

In the Petersen case, Betsy supposedly repressed memories of sexual abuse by her father until she was forty-five years old. After entering therapy for problems she was having with her children she told the therapist she thought her father did something to her when she was three years old but she didn't really know whether it happened or was a dream. The therapist assured her it did indeed happen. Betsy had to work very hard to retrieve memories of incest and states in her book, "I had no memory of what my father had done to me, so I tried to reconstruct it. I put all my skill as a reporter, novelist, [and] scholar to work making that reconstruction as accurate and visible as possible. I used the memories I had to get to the memories I didn't have."[13]

In the second case, Paul Ingram's daughters accused him of rape and child abuse. Ingram at first denied everything, but after a psychologist worked on him during endless hours of interrogation Ingram's memories of abusing his daughters began to appear. This psychologist also was able to convince Ingram's son that his obvious hypnopompic or waking dreams were real and that he too had participated in the abuse carried out by his father.[14]

---

*A distortion of memory in which fact and fantasy are confused.

The therapists, of course, deliberately dig for memories because they believe they exist and must be rooted out if the client is to get well. Moreover, therapists must break through denial, the client's protective defense which enabled them to tolerate the abuse when it happened. Elizabeth Loftus notes that while memory blocks are protective in many ways they also cut survivors off from a major part of their past history and leave them without an explanation for poor self-image, lack of esteem, and other mental difficulties.[15] Another reason therapists suggest ideas such as repression is because of the therapists' "confirmatory bias." All of us, including therapists, look for evidence that confirms hunches rather than looking for things that deny them. It is difficult for us to abandon long held and cherished beliefs.

Loftus notes that the therapists ask questions that elicit behaviors and experiences they believe are characteristic of victims of childhood abuse. In other words, the therapists invariably find what they are looking for. Therapists are providing their clients with illusory memories rather than unlocking memories that are authentic.

False memories are easily created, and have been over and over by Loftus and other therapists who expose clients to misinformation and suggestion. A large body of research has shown that new post-event information can easily be incorporated into memory and it can change an individual's recollection. Loftus, as much as any other memory authority, has helped us to understand how we can be tricked and how suggestions from popular literature and media events as well as therapy sessions can affect our autobiographical recall. Although some clinicians have argued that all such misinformation leading to false memories is trivial, traumatic memories can never be changed because they leave indelible impressions in our minds. Terr, for example, says, "traumatic events create lasting visual images . . . burned in visual impressions."[16] Yet, as Loftus shows, memory is very malleable, even with life's most traumatic experiences. She gives a number of impressive examples to prove that genuinely traumatic events are not preserved in memory in pristine form. Among the many interesting cases in which the traumatic event was actually experienced but the memory of it radically changed involves the 1986 explosion of the space shuttle *Challenger*.

Harsch and Neisser asked people to recall how they heard the news of the explosion. The subjects were questioned on the morning after the explosion, and again nearly three years later. While most described their memories as vivid, no one's later recollection entirely corresponded to the original response and over a third were wildly inaccurate. One subject, for example, originally said she was discussing business on the phone when her best friend interrupted to tell her. Later she "remembered" hearing the news in class and thinking it was a joke until she walked into a TV lounge and saw it was true.[17] Clearly even the remembered details of real traumatic events change over time.

Of even greater interest is the fact that people commonly remember events that never happened. An amusing example is found in a recent biography of former President Ronald Reagan. Reagan, it seems, often remembered cinematic scenes and mistook them for real events. During one of his campaigns he told the story about a bomber hit by antiaircraft fire. According to Reagan a wounded gunner was trapped and couldn't get out of the airplane. His commander, seeing the gunner's plight, told him "Never mind, son, we'll ride it down together." For this heroic act the commander was posthumously awarded the Congressional Medal of Honor. Unfortunately, no such award was ever made. Instead Reagan was confusing reality with the 1944 movie *A Wing and a Prayer* in which the pilot tells his radioman "We'll take this ride together." When the White House was confronted a spokesman said, "Well, if you tell the same story oftentimes its true." Many people were convinced that on occasion Reagan could not distinguish films from facts.

This is an excellent example of *confabulation*, a universal phenomenon. Confabulation is a tendency of ordinary, sane individuals to confuse fact with fiction and to report fantasied events as actual occurrences. It occurs in just about every situation in which a person attempts to remember very specific details from the past. We remember things not the way they really were but the way we wished them to be. Our memories are both creative and recreative, and we can and do easily forget. We blur, shape, erase, and change details of the events in our past. Many people walk around with their heads full of false memories. Moreover, the unreliability of eye-witness testimony is well documented. When all of this is further complicated and compounded by the impact of suggestions provided by the hypnotist-therapist, as well as the social demand characteristics of the typical hypnotic situation, it is little wonder that the resulting recall bears slight resemblance to the truth.

Confabulation shows up without fail in nearly every context in which hypnosis and other suggestive techniques, such as guided imagery,* are employed. In a well-publicized Arizona murder case in 1980, the wife of the victim, who was a witness to the crime, was hypnotized and asked to give details about what happened. During hypnosis the hypnotist suggested that the murderer's car was driving away so that she could see the rear license plate. He then asked the wife, "What was its number?" Even though the wife later reported she wanted to open her eyes and inform the hypnotist that she had not seen the car drive away, when he continued to suggest to her how clearly the departing car could be seen, it appeared on her mental television screen and the license plate came into sharp focus. Then, she heard herself describe the car, describe the license plate as green and white, and read off the letters and numbers. Immediately after she was released from the hypnosis situation the wife informed the hypnotist that the information she had provided had to be mistaken. The police soon corroborated her statement when they found that the colors and number arrangements she reported did not fit those of any state in the union.[18]

There have also been a number of clinical and experimental demonstrations of the creation of pseudomemories that have subsequently come to be believed as veridical. Baker and Boas successfully treated a case of dental phobia by suggesting to the patient that a prior unpleasant dental experience was actually very pleasant. The pseudomemory was effective in permitting major dental surgery some months later without emotional upset.[19] Another researcher, E. R. Hilgard, implanted a false memory of a bank robbery that never occurred. His subject found the experience so vivid that he was able to select from a series of photographs a picture of the man he thought committed the robbery. In another instance Hilgard deliberately assigned to the one individual concurrent life experiences of two different people, and then

---

*A technique of therapy in which the therapist suggests imaginary scenes and scenarios to a relaxed client.

regressed the individual at separate times to points in each "life." The subject subsequently gave very accurate accounts of both experiences, so that anyone believing in reincarnation would conclude that the man really had lived two different lives.[20]

In a number of experiments designed to measure eye-witness reliability, Elizabeth Loftus found that details supplied by others invariably contaminated eye-witness memories. People's hair changed color, stop signs became yield signs, yellow convertibles turned to red sedans, the left side of the street became the right side, and so forth. The results of these studies led her to conclude, "It may well be that the legal notion of an independent recollection is a psychological impossibility." As for hypnosis, she believes,

> There's no way even the most sophisticated hypnotist can tell the difference between a memory that is real and one that's created. If you've got a person who is hypnotized and highly suggestible and false information is implanted in his mind, it may get imbedded even more strongly. One psychologist tried to use a polygraph to distinguish between real and phony memory but it didn't work. Once someone has constructed a memory, he comes to believe it himself.[21]

In my own work on hypnosis and memory the power of suggestion to evoke false memories was also clearly and dramatically evident. Sixty volunteers observed a complex display made up of eight nonsense syllables and pictures of a number of common objects, for example, a television set, clock, typewriter, and book, and were instructed to memorize the nonsense syllables in the center of the display. They were given two minutes to accomplish this. Nothing was said about the common objects. Following a forty-minute delay, the students were questioned about the nonsense syllables and the other objects on the display. They were also asked to state their confidence in the accuracy of their answers. Some were questioned under hypnosis and others while they were wide awake. The students' suggestibility was studied by asking them to report on the common objects. They were also asked specific questions about objects that were not included in the display. The subjects' attention had not been directed at the objects specifically (only at the syllables), and they were often unsure about what they saw and didn't see. When they were asked questions such as "What color was the sports car?" and "Where on the display was it located?" they immediately assumed there must have been a sports car present. A lawn mower and calendar were similarly suggested.

Although thirty-five subjects in the hypnoidal condition reported the color of the suggested automobile, thirty-four wide awake subjects also reported the color.* Similarly, although twenty-six subjects in the hypnoidal state reported the suggested lawn mower's color and position, twenty-seven who were awake reported its color and position. For the nonexistent calendar, twenty-four hypnotized subjects reported the month and date, and twenty-three wide awake subjects reported them.

As for suggestibility per se under all conditions, fifty out of the sixty volunteers reported seeing something that wasn't there with a confidence level of at least a two (a little unsure) or greater; forty-five reported seeing something that wasn't there with a confidence level of three (sure) or greater; twenty-five reported something that wasn't there with a confidence level of four (very sure) or greater; and eight reported something not there with a confidence level of five (absolute certainty). Interestingly, five of these eight who reported they were certain of the object's existence were wide awake. When they were allowed to see the display again, they were shocked to discover their error.[22]

These matters are further complicated by so-called hypnotic regression, taking the subject back to an earlier time in his existence, and "inadvertent cueing," having the hypnotist, as if unintentionally, reveal to the person being regressed exactly what response is wanted. How this complicates the situation is most clearly seen in an experimental study of hypnotic age regression carried out by R. M. True. True found that 92 percent of his subjects who had been regressed to the day of their tenth birthday could accurately recall the day of the week on which it fell. He found the same thing for 84 percent for his subjects for their fourth birthday.[23] Other investigators, however, were not able to duplicate True's findings. When Martin Orne questioned True about his experiment he discovered that the editors of *Science,* in

---

*Many subjects were questioned more than once (i.e., while hypnotized and while wide awake). Therefore, the number of responses does not always correspond to the number of subjects.

which True's report had appeared, had altered the procedure section without True's knowledge or consent. Orne discovered that True had inadvertently cued his subjects by asking them: "Is it Monday? Is it Tuesday? Is it Wednesday?" etc., and he verified their responses by using a perpetual desk calendar that was in full view of all of his subjects. Further evidence of the prevalence and importance of such cueing came from a study by O'Connell, Shor, and Orne, in which they found that in an actual group of four-year-olds, not a single one knew the day of the week.[24]

The hypnotic reincarnation or past-life regression literature is replete with examples of such inadvertent cueing. Wilson, for example, has shown that hypnotically elicited reports of being reincarnated vary as a direct function of the hypnotist's belief about reincarnation.[25]

Every clinician and forensic hypnotist using regression techniques should be alert to the possibility that much of the material pulled from the patient's past—particularly tales of abuse, sexual molestation, and such—may well be products of the patient's imagination or responses to inadvertent cues supplied by the hypnotist. Suspect in this regard are a number of the hypnotic procedures advocated by Martin Reiser in his thirty-two-hour training course and in his textbook, *Handbook of Investigative Hypnosis*.[26] Three procedures which may serve to increase the amount of confabulation are (1) the technique of "affectless recall," in which the subject is asked to relive the events of the crime but not the emotions involved; (2) the practice of using metaphors derived from television production, such as asking the subject to "zoom in on" or to "watch in slow motion" the film of the crime stored in the subconscious; and (3) encouraging subjects to assume a separate identity and to refer to themselves as observers of the crime rather than as victims or participants. The first of these could well be a major source of distortion for recalling affect-laden material; the second is an invitation to confabulate if the images asked for were never stored in the first place; and, the third is, particularly for highly hypnotizable subjects, in Campbell Perry's words, "a free ticket to fantasy island."[27]

Loftus and her associates have also noted that children's memories are easily manipulated. In one study the subjects saw a short film about a girl playing at a neighbor's pond even though she had been warned not to go there. In the film the neighbor reprimands her from four feet away. He never touches her or even raises his hands as if to do so. When the girl goes home and a policeman shows up she tells the policeman that the neighbor hit her. The experimental subjects are later questioned about the film and when they were asked, "Did the man hit the girl?" the adults correctly remembered the man did not. Nearly 30 percent of the children age four to seven, however, erroneously said that the man hit the girl. Of forty-one false claims, thirty-nine children said it happened at the pond, one said it happened at the girl's house, and one said he didn't remember exactly where the girl was when the man hit her.[28]

People often believe that they experienced an event even in the absence of specific hypnotic suggestions. In 1989 Pynoos and Nader looked at memories of a violent sniper attack. In February 1984 a sniper fired repeated rounds of ammunition at children on their playground from a second-story window across the street from an elementary school. Scores of children were pinned down by the gunfire, many were injured, and one child and a passerby were killed. When 10 percent of the student body, approximately 113 children, were interviewed six to sixteen weeks later and asked to recall the experience and answer some specific questions, even nonwitnesses—those on vacation, those on the way home, those who missed school the day of the attack—had memories and recalled the attack. One girl said she was at the school gate near the sniper when the attack began. She was actually half a block away. A boy on vacation said he was on his way to school when he saw someone lying on the ground, heard shots, and turned back. The truth was a police barricade kept everyone from approaching the block around the school.[29]

Dr. Maggie Bruck of McGill University and Dr. Stephen Ceci of Cornell have shown clearly and unequivocally that planting false memories in small children is incredibly easy. The way the child is approached and the manner in which the child is questioned determines the truth or falsity of the information obtained. Certain approaches will increase the likelihood of obtaining false reports and unreliable information from young children. Persistent questioning can easily lead the child to describe events that never happened. Also, therapists and social workers, particularly those who specialize in sex-abuse cases, have a pre-conceived notion of what has happened and by asking the child leading questions actually suggest these things to the child, who then readily reports it back as if it were true. According to Bruck and Ceci, "We find nothing in a child's memory is impervious to being tainted by an adult's repeated suggestions."[30] Asking the same questions repeatedly over several weeks—as is routinely done in sex-abuse cases when children are typically questioned by case workers, social workers, parents, police, and lawyers before they testify in court—is almost guaranteed to produce a false account: "The more often you ask young children to think about something, the easier it becomes for them to make something up that they think is a memory."[31] Moreover, the accounts of their false memories are usually very credible. When Ceci showed videotapes of the children telling both true and false memories to professional groups of child abuse experts, including social workers, lawyers, psychologists and psychiatrists, the experts were able to discriminate the truthful reports from the fantasies only one-third of the time.

The children aren't intentionally lying but they are simply unable to recall and explain what actually happened. The child's basic uncertainty makes it very easy for adults with their conventions, biases, and preconceptions to dominate the child and win his agreement to anything they say. These results contradict previous studies of children's suggestibility which concluded they could be influenced about minor details but not the major facts regarding events that happened. "The bottom line is that even very young children can give accurate accounts if the interviewers haven't usurped their memory through repeated suggestive or leading questions. Interviewers ought to safeguard against this by testing at least one alternative plausible hypothesis about what happened."[32]

Sexually abused children are often reluctant to admit the abuse and it is difficult to question children without leading them and giving them suggestions. When case workers encounter children whom they have very good reasons to suspect of being abused, emotional outrage at such injustice often blinds them to what they are doing. They well know that merely asking a four-year-old to tell them if any bad things have ever happened to them is rarely productive.

No matter how difficult it is to obtain the truth in such instances, it is a most grievous error indeed to "believe the children" and destroy the lives of families and even send many innocent people to prison. What adds insult to injury is when the accused fight back to defend themselves, they and their supporters are regarded as criminals, antifemale, antichild, vicious pedophiles, or worse. Ofshe and Watters have eloquently summarized our current dilemma:

> Recovered memory therapy seems to have been produced by a series of mistakes. Most obviously, practitioners manage to ignore research showing that their principle techniques, social influence and hypnosis, cause false or grossly inaccurate memories. They refuse to acknowledge that three generations of researchers have tried and failed to confirm the existence of the repression phenomenon, in even its most conservative form. They ignore the fact that no evidence has been found to suggest that the human mind is capable of hiding from itself the kind of traumatic events elicited from clients in recovered memory therapy. . . . In short, these therapists are out of touch with modern research on the subjects on which the miracle cure depends. . . . [T]he therapists are like the physicians who once bled patients in order to cure them. But unlike those physicians, who were limited by the primitive state of medical knowledge of their time, the promoters of repressed memory therapy ignore reliable research, misuse their authority and techniques, and damage the lives of their clients and their clients' families.[33]

There is no doubt whatsoever that repressed memory therapy is shrinkage in its worst possible form. Such therapy does not and never has ever cured anyone. It does not provide any lasting relief, does not cure unhappiness of any sort. Instead, life's problems get worse rather than better after the individuals become convinced they were mistreated in childhood. The result is usually isolation from family and friends. Whatever was the cause of the original problem remains, of course, untouched and untended. Worst of all, the stress of the recovered memory therapy may aggravate the original problem or even precipitate new ones.

Repression?

Some therapists, unfortunately, continue to believe in the Freudian concept of repression despite the fact that hard experimental research has shown it does not exist. Some clinical findings do agree with the repression theory: people forget things and later recall what they have forgotten; people remember pleasant experiences more often than unpleasant ones; and sudden trauma may cause people to forget some of the events surrounding the trauma. These facts, however, in no way support the Freudian repression concept that we forget the horrible and that we are totally unable to recall such events because the mind deliberately buries them in our unconscious. Nor is there any empirical evidence that such forgotten terrors strive to enter our conscious minds and, unless they are brought to the surface, they can poison our lives and trigger all sorts of behavioral disorders. Sixty years of experimental research has failed to produce any evidence to support the folklore of repression.[34] In fact, experimental research has shown our memory mechanisms are fairly straightforward and rather simple. What seems important to us at any given time and what affects us emotionally is what we remember. What is not important to us or is of little emotional impact is forgotten. Unless we attend to something, unless it makes an impression on us, we cannot and do not remember it. While we do remember pleasant rather than unpleasant things, it is not because we can't remember the unpleasant but simply because the pleasant makes us feel good and gets our attention while the unpleasant is usually ignored. Of course, if the unpleasant is emotionally arousing then we do recall it as well. We also remember things that are important to us better than those we consider of no consequence or in which we have little or no interest. If an experience is important as well as unpleasant, for example, if someone pulls a gun on you and threatens your life, you definitely *will* remember it and will have no difficulty at all in doing so. Many studies of both children and adults exposed to torture, imprisonment, and natural disasters show they have no difficulty in recalling these terrors. While it is true that we may go for years without recalling a particular horrendous experience, if the occasion arises, however, we can recall it with no difficulty whatsoever.

As noted earlier, several years ago an experimental study designed to determine the effects of hypnosis on memory showed that students who were asked to sit quietly in an easy chair and recall as much of their early childhood as they could had no difficulty doing so.[35]

Concerning the effect of hypnosis on memory, hypnosis per se does not improve our ability to remember either primary or incidental memories. As noted earlier, false memories were shown to be easily implanted and they could not be discriminated from true ones. While it's often assumed that hypnosis can stimulate recall, most hypnotic attempts at recall are either misinterpreted or total failures. It is now well established that shock, trauma, and anxiety at the time of highly emotional events can suppress many details that will not be recalled until the initial anxiety and emotion has dissipated. It is not "hypnosis" that improves recall but merely the passage of time and the dissipation of the anxiety and fear.[36] This sort of traumatic and post-traumatic amnesia is well documented by the common experience of people involved in auto accidents who have no memory of the accident or of the brief period preceding or following. Experiences of extreme pain or emotional trauma also cause forgetfulness, as can as head injuries or physical assaults on the brain such as electroshock therapy or intoxication. These sorts of events are never repressed however, and it is clear the failure of recall is due to physical injury to the brain's memory mechanisms, not because of repression. In some cases, failure to remember is simply due to our failure to pay attention to the original stimulus event. To remember anything you first must attend to it. If you are extremely fearful or anxious it is difficult to concentrate or to attend closely to anything.

Finally, Pope and Hudson recently examined all published studies claiming repression of memories of childhood sexual abuse and found only four. When these four studies were reviewed to determine if the investigators included confirming evidence that abuse had occurred, and if their subjects had developed amnesia regarding abuse, none of the four studies provided clear confirmation of either trauma or adequate documentation of the alleged amnesia.[37] Although surprised by their findings (in view of the hundreds of clinical claims as well as belief in the universality of repression) Pope and Hudson state even the *clinical* evidence does not permit us to conclude that people can repress memories of childhood sexual abuse. In fact, the most common clinical experience is the difficulty of those who are victims of real sexual abuse to forget rather than to recall.

Recognizing that memory is reconstructive, not reproductive (memories are not "stored" as on a videotape and reproduced or replayed on command), Yapko in 1992 surveyed over 860 psychotherapists across the United States regarding the roles of suggestion in psychotherapy. The results showed that not only were most psychotherapists misinformed about hypnosis and its uses but a significant number erroneously believe that memories obtained through hypnosis are more likely to be accurate than those simply recalled. They also erroneously believe that hypnosis can be used to recover accurate memories even from as far back as birth:

> Unfortunately, many psychotherapists believe in past lives, the retrievability and accuracy of infantile memories, and the infallibility of hypnosis as a tool for recovering accurate memories. Many continue to maintain the rigid but unfounded belief that accurate memories of all experiences *must* be in there somewhere in one form or another and that all one needs is the right "key" to "unlock" them. False memories that are detailed and dramatic may be accepted as true simply because of the psychotherapist's preexisting beliefs. . . . I am deeply concerned that psychotherapy patients will be led to believe destructive ideas that are untrue, recall memories of terrible events that never actually happened, jump to conclusions that are not warranted, and destroy the lives of innocent people—and even their own lives—in the process all in the name of 'psychotherapy.'[38]

The sad fact is that all of Yapko's fears have already come to pass and that many ignorant and naive therapists have done and are currently doing more harm than good.

SATANIC RITUAL ABUSE

If the shrinks are creating havoc with repressed memory therapy, is it possible that they could, via client manipulation, actually implant a false memory for sexual abuse? Not ethically, of course, but it was done unintentionally in the case of Paul Ingram which was referred to earlier. This case, described in detail by Lawrence Wright in "Remembering Satan" in two successive issues of the *New Yorker* magazine, is horrifying not because of what Ingram did but because of what was done to Ingram. Ingram, who is from Olympia, Washington, was arrested for child abuse in 1988. At the time he was Chief Civil Deputy of the Sheriff's Department and chairman of the local Republican party. Accused of rape and sexual abuse by his adult daughters, Ingram at first denied everything but after lengthy interrogation and therapeutic pressure by a psychologist (which included accusations of denial and fire-and-brimstone religious threats), Ingram came to admit not only abusing his daughters but that he was also a member of a satanic cult. When the prosecution called in Richard Ofshe as an expert witness, Ofshe decided to test Ingram's credibility by making up a totally false story in which Ingram was supposed to have had his son and one of the daughters have sex in front of him. Ingram at first could not remember any of this but after praying for a day and concentrating on it, he began not only to believe it but wrote a three-page detailed statement confessing to the scene Ofshe had invented. This experiment demonstrated convincingly Ingram's extreme suggestibility. After Ofshe's investigation it became clear that no crime of any sort had been committed, no cult had ever existed, and Ingram's confessions were coerced—internalized false confessions. The two psychologists originally called in to work with Ingram had diagnosed him as suffering from a dissociative disorder similar to multiple personality disorder. They both believed satanic cult activity was rife in the community and that Ingram's crimes were due to his having been programmed by the (nonexistent) satanic cult. So much for the inept "shrinks."

Unfortunately, this is not the first time that highly suggestible and vulnerable individuals have been made to believe they were guilty of a crime of which they had no memory and which the objective evidence proves they could not have committed.

While it is difficult to determine precisely when the current rash of satanic ritual abuse accusations actually began, we do know that, like Bass and Davis's book, a book, entitled *Michelle Remembers,* set off a veritable wave of accusations and claims. The case began in 1976 when twenty-seven-year-old Michelle Smith suffered a miscarriage, and called her former psychiatrist, Dr. Lawrence Pazder, to help her cope with her feelings of emotional loss. Since Dr. Pazder had treated her earlier for some phobias and other problems, he was shocked when in Michelle's first session she entered the office in a trancelike state and proceeded to scream at the top of her voice for the first half hour. After calming down, Michelle began to recall long-lost childhood memories of torture and ritual abuse by members of a satanic cult that included her parents. She also recalled being forced to participate in ritual murders, drink blood, and sacrifice animals. She remembered a ceremony called the Feast of the Beast at which Satan himself appeared. Finally, Michelle was saved at five years of age by a heavenly figure called *Ma Mere*. The precise details of Michelle's ordeal are provided in *Michelle Remembers,* the book she wrote with Pazder. Unfortunately, there is nothing whatsoever in the way of facts to corroborate the authenticity of her story or her memories.

Why would these memories be hidden all these years if they were true? Once one understands the mind's natural tendency to reconstruct, reorganize, and confabulate, we can be quite confident that Michelle's memories are a blend of both fact and fiction. What is interesting is that these sorts of memories of murder, rape, torture, abuse, and such are really quite common among people who have had very ordinary, prosaic, and protected childhoods.

In many instances such memories, rather than pointing to mistreatment or parental abuse, instead reflect the rage, frustration, resentment, and powerlessness of children in a world dominated by larger and much more powerful adults. Rather than being *real* memories of *real* events in the lives of those who report them, they are, for the most part, inventions and fabrications, cryptomnesic (hidden) memories of horrors and hurts experienced vicariously. In other words, the "memories" are actually scenes from television or movies which the "abused" child does not recall ever seeing.

In the rare instances in which children were subjected to any of these aforementioned indignities, the most natural response is to protect themselves from the horror. To avoid being paralyzed by their painful recollections, they doctor their memories, making them less traumatic than the reality. Often the horror may take on a bizarre and different aspect or form, and children rewrite their abuse at the hands of parents they love in the form of torture by Satanists, or abduction by aliens. In this fashion they protect themselves from the terrible pain of the truth—punishment at the hands of those they love.

Cryptomnesia is one of the human mind's most common and universal protective mechanisms. The term itself we owe to the Swiss psychologist Theodore Flournoy and his investigations of Mlle. Helene Smith, fully recounted in his book *From India to the Planet Mars*. While the phenomenon of "hidden memories" was well known to the "Mesmerists" and "animal magnetists" much earlier as a product of the "hypnotic trance," it had not been carefully researched or identified as a purely *psychological* phenomenon. The fact that a person can, especially in the hypnotic regression state, remember and report facts that the normal waking self had forgotten completely was, in a sense, Flournoy's discovery. He termed the process by which these memories were forgotten "cryptomnesia," from the Greek words for "hidden" and "memory." Flournoy also emphasized that cryptic memory was much more extensive than anyone had realized before.

It is now well established that "hypnosis" is, after all, nothing more than highly imaginative role playing—the sort of thing in which anyone with sufficient motivation can engage.[39] Whereas most people have assumed that hypnosis is a prerequisite condition for any and all psychological regressions, it may come as a surprise to find that not only is hypnosis not necessary, but that which we have called hypnosis is nothing more than the use of suggestion to arouse the imagination of the patient. That this can be done with only a few well chosen words, or that the client can do it to him- or herself without the need of external assistance lends further support to the wonders of belief, suggestion, and the power of the human imagination. The recent discovery by the UFOlogist community that many victims of alien abductions did not have to be hypnotized in order to remember their abductions is considered proof that the abductions were real. Unfortunately for them, it only substantiates the power of the human imagination.

Once this imagination is aroused incredible events can transpire.

With the help of the media, child sexual abuse has now become the most popular and widespread crime in the nation. Accompanying many of these sex abuse charges during the past decade has been the added accusation that a large proportion of these cases of abuse are due to the children being forced to commit sexual atrocities in the rituals of satanic cults. This notion of child sexual abuse carried out by satanic cults has become a national obsession within the last few years and is currently being compared, with good reason, to a modern witchhunt in the vein of the infamous Salem trials.

In the March/April 1990 issue of *The Humanist,* investigative journalist and editor David Alexander spoke with Dr. J. Gordon Melton, Director of the Institute for the Study of American Religion at Santa Barbara. Melton predicted we would be in for a wave of Satanism in the years ahead. He also predicted the satanic panic would be kept alive by an unlikely coalition of religious fundamentalists and psychotherapists. He could not possibly have been more prescient. Since the late 1980s Satanism and anti-Satanist hysteria has become a growth industry and large numbers of Christian fundamentalists, political extremists, incompetent psychotherapists, and mentally disturbed individuals have become self-appointed experts on satanic cults, satanic ritual abuse, and devil-worship. Worst of all, these pseudoexperts are holding seminars, workshops, and training sessions designed to convince anyone who will listen—particularly naive and impressionable psychotherapists—that America's children are in mortal danger. These people believe that there is a vast, underground organized satanic conspiracy stretching across the United States from coast to coast and that this ungodly group is ritually sacrificing tens of thousands of innocent children every year. Moreover, thousands of other children are being horribly abused by Satanists—including by their own parents and guardians—day in and day out. Included in the abuse is the sacrificing of animals, the murder of babies, the eating of human flesh, ritual sexual perversions, and other unspeakable obscenities.

Media personnel, police agencies, social workers as well as psychotherapists and mental health experts have been duped an propagandized by the Satan-mongers into believing these sensational and irrational tales. They, in turn, have helped to spread what Jeffrey S. Victor has called "Satanic Panic" from one end of the nation to the other. In David Alexander's words, "Exploiting the irrational fear of the superstitious, the credibility of the well-intentioned, and the media's insatiable appetite for ratings through sensationalism, a few fanatical individuals and their organizations have built an industry of fear by spreading nonsense as scholarship."[40] It is hard to believe that anyone in his right mind could take this utter nonsense seriously. Incredibly, many members of the healing profession do, including psychotherapists who should know better. One of the reasons they don't is that they too fall prey to the "cult influence" and to the victims who feed off gullible therapists.

If we look closely at victims such as Michelle Smith, author of *Michelle Remembers*, for example, we find a very strange person indeed. Michelle claims she had an alcoholic father who abandoned the family and an alcoholic mother who died when she was fourteen. After Michelle had a miscarriage, she sought therapy and recalled abuse at the hand of Satanists. She also remembered a visit from Satan himself and lots of satanic rituals, murders, cannibalism, etc. The problem is that Michelle's memories are not consistent with Satanism and devil worship. Since the Satanists in Michelle's cult cut off the middle fingers of their left hands they ought to be easy to locate and identify, yet no effort to do so was ever made. Moreover, none of the claims made by Smith were ever corroborated. Dr. Pazder became enamored of Michelle, and she later divorced her husband and married the therapist.[41] Stability is not a word in Michelle's vocabulary.

Nor can much be said for Lauren Stratford, another who claims she was abused as a child by her parents' Satan-worshiping group and then when she was older bred babies for ritual sacrifice to Satan.[42] In her book, *Satan's Underground*, Lauren describes how she also saw Satan in person and witnessed him perform a miraculous healing. She reported other paranormal events and was a big hit on the TV talk show circuit although she was a little confused about her children. On Sally Jesse Raphael's show Lauren could remember sacrificing only one baby but on Oprah Winfrey's show she suddenly remembered two more that got the satanic axe. Apparently, her memory comes and goes.

Another cake-taker is Jennifer Peters (a pseudonym), who has run the gamut of satanic ritual abuse and managed to have inflicted upon

her poor person every indignity ever dreamed of by Satan's most dev-
ilish minions. Jennifer, too, recovered all her memories via the ministrations of her therapist, Linda, who in short order, discovered Jennifer
had been sexually abused by her father. For a period of eighteen
months Jennifer went to work on all her early memories and, with
Linda's assistance,

> [t]hree scenes flashed through me in a millisecond; a group of peo-
> ple in black robes, chanting; me at a gravesite, clutching my father's
> hand as an ancient corpse was brought out of the earth; me standing
> in a dim room as a pair of large hands, holding a bloodied infant,
> moved across my field of vision. I sat bolt upright and told Linda, "I
> am losing my mind." It took me the better part of an hour to make
> myself tell her what I'd seen.
>
> Three sessions later the images were still with me. I had sub-
> jected myself—and Linda—to every possible rationalization I could
> conjure up. "I am psychotic. I was psychotic as a child. These are
> images from childhood nightmares. They are scenes from movies I
> somehow saw when I was small. Or they are metaphors, images that
> stand for how angry I really am down inside."[43]

Linda, Jennifer's therapist, said it was possible they were dreams of
media images from childhood, they were symbolic images for feelings,
or they were real memories. Linda explored this last possibility and was
wildly successful. For the next six months Jennifer had between three
and ten memories a week dating back to when she was four years old.
She remembered being taken to "devil parties" by her father, watching
ritual torture and then the sacrifice of animals and humans and being
forced to help cannibalize the corpses; being tortured with electric
shock; being kept in cages for long periods; being raped with all sorts
of objects, including hot pokers, burning sticks, arm and leg bones of
dug-up corpses; being forced to have sex with animals and dozens of
people at a time. By the time she was five, she had to torture and kill
animals, was given to Satan in a ritual marriage, was forced to have
intercourse with a little boy that the Satanists then killed, had to "give
birth" to a disemboweled infant's corpse while being called the "mother
of evil" and told her womb was full of death, was forced to choose

among a group of other children as to which ones would live and which ones she would have to kill. During this period she was threatened with death constantly, forced to take drugs, deprived of both food and sleep, and brainwashed to believe she would eventually grow horns. Also, she was fed human eyeballs and tongues and was told these would remain in her body watching her and telling the cult if she did anything they told her not to do. She described many more similarly degrading scenes.

According to Jennifer, she recovered all these memories by reliving each of them over and over again, writhing on the floor, crying, screaming, choking, beating her hands and face, and weeping and wailing while the hospital nursing staff offered solace and comfort. Oddly enough, in spite of all this horrible physical abuse, doctors and nurses could not find any physical signs of mistreatment.

Jennifer was candid enough to state flat out that she had to learn to fend for herself because Linda told her her case was too complicated for someone with only a master's degree to handle. Jennifer then went in search of a Ph.D. and "interviewed a horde of them," before settling on one that she trusted. In her words, "I had to take care of myself and stop seeing people who were unwilling or unable to become allies for me." One can't help but wonder if the reason she lost so many allies was simply that it soon became obvious that all these tales were the grossest of fictions and that Jennifer was one of the world's most dedicated prevaricators. Jennifer admits that even she is puzzled that all during her childhood "nobody noticed—my teachers, my parents' friends, even my mother. . . . I wonder why nobody did anything to help me."[44] Could it be, Jennifer, nobody did because it never happened? Jennifer's tale is typical of literally hundreds of others which follow the same pattern.

Difficult as it may be to believe, none of the horror stories told in these fictions bears even a remote resemblance to the truth. When investigators took the time and trouble to check into these myths they found the same familiar and fictitious pattern emerging. All of them take the form of recollections elicited during months of intensive psychotherapy in which the subject "recalls" things that happened to her in early childhood. Michelle's case was at least "original." Passantino and associates, who analyzed Lauren Stratford's book and memoirs and reconstructed her life history after interviewing family and friends concluded the entire book was one wild and elaborate fantasy so far from the truth she lied even about her family structure.[45] Her claims of abuse changed with the weather and the physical scars she attributed to satanic abuse were almost certainly self-inflicted. Her stories about the children she bred for sacrifice proved to be ridiculous because there was no evidence of any sort that she had ever been pregnant. Even more stunning was the fact that no one ever bothered to check out any of Stratford's claims. In 1990 the publisher of *Satan's Underground* withdrew it, but some distributors continue to circulate it.

Jenkins and Maier-Katkin summarize their analysis of these alleged occult survivors in the following manner:

> These survivor tales require us to believe that the sophisticated satanic rituals of 1890s Paris . . . were commonplace in remote rural or suburban communities during the Eisenhower era. The regularity of blood sacrifices implies that the cults were so powerful as to have no fear of legal intervention. They could abduct and kill with impunity in a time of far lower homicide rates, when missing persons were likely to attract more law enforcement concern than today. Further, no individual from such a cult ever betrayed its secrets or ever revealed its existence to a local church or newspaper. No religious revival ever forced a defection or an investigation, and no local politician sought celebrity by exposing such heinous crimes.
>
> This calls less for a suspension of disbelief than a complete rewriting of the history of the United States and Canada. . . . The only contemporary parallel to such a picture comes from popular Gothic fiction by authors such as Robert Black or H. P. Lovecraft, whose protagonists so often stumbled across diabolical secrets shared by remote communities. As a portrait of the reality of rural or suburban America in mid-century, the survivors' reminiscences are monstrously improbable.[46]

While there can be no doubt whatsoever as to the role played by misguided religious fundamentalists, we are less willing to blame the psychotherapy industry for their significant contributions to the current satanic panic. Mincing no words, David Alexander lays part of the blame for Satan-mongering right on Geraldo Rivera's doorstep for his

October 25, 1988 NBC-TV special, "Devil Worship: Exposing Satan's Underground." Incredibly, this program was watched by more people than any other television documentary in history. Unfortunately, it was made up mostly of misinformation, and it substituted hype and sensationalistic exaggeration for the simple sober truth. According to one sociologist, it also triggered a small panic in upper New York state.

Equally pernicious—if not more so—is the role played by the psychotherapeutic community who naively validated the claims of a number of disturbed and hysterical individuals whose overwrought imaginations caused them to believe they were subjected to ritual torture at the hands of satanic cults or else believed their children were being abused while in day care by satanic cultists.

Sherrill Mulhern, an anthropologist, published what is perhaps the most authoritative study of exactly how the therapeutic community allowed itself to be duped by these pseudovictims. Mulhern's essay looks at why so many educated professionals came to believe these satanic fabrications despite the fact that no federal, state, or local law enforcement agencies—despite intensive investigation—were ever able to come up with any supportive or substantiating evidence of the existence of these cults. Mulhern convincingly shows that the key factor in their acceptance of such "survivor" stories was what Irving Janis has called "group think"—a group situation in which the need to maintain cooperative interaction among members creates social pressure to conform.[47] Such pressures, in turn, suppress critical analysis of, skepticism of, and dispute about prevailing beliefs. Maintaining friendly relations inhibits all expressions of deviance. Anyone disagreeing is subtly rebuked for disloyalty and one's perception of reality is altered. People will change their perceptions and beliefs to fit the group norm. Critical thinking and reality testing are suppressed by pressures to "think alike." This sort of group think is neither unusual nor rare and is very common in religious or semireligious organizations.[48]

Again, as in the case with false memories, none of the therapists is willing to acknowledge that the therapeutic disclosure process itself has anything to do with the horrible allegations and claims the victims so readily create. Therapy—the iatrogenetist insists—is disinterested and value free and the courageous therapist is only doing his noble duty to help these piteous victims. The result of this is that,

[s]hielded by the mental health perspective of belief, therapists and their patients continue to spread the satanic cult rumor. Together they speak out authoritatively in public forums, describing the behaviors and practices of a network of cults that no one but the alleged victims has ever seen. Medical professionals are part of a cultural elite, presumed to speak with scientific authority that is rarely questioned. However, in this case they are using that authority to accredit the belief that thousands of apparently normal people switch into satanic alter-personalities and meet on a regular basis to commit wholesale slaughter right under our noses.[49]

Mulhern also reviews the clinical evidence showing how easily hypnosis leads to confabulation, hypnotic hypermnesia (i.e., false memories), and fallacious reporting. Moreover, because of Freud's abandonment of his initial "seduction theory" of hysteria modern clinicians are now much more willing to see such claims not as fantasies but as the gospel truth. The clinicians cited four types of evidence that convinced them the victims' claims were real: (1) the violence and emotionality displayed in the abreaction (acting out) of the recovered memories; (2) the abundance of vivid detail in reporting the memories and the logical consistency in describing the abuse; (3) manifestation of body memories, for example, spontaneous bleeding, muscular contractions, appearance of marks on the skin prior to and during the recall; and (4) their conviction that patients who had never met were saying exactly the same thing. Although the first three items seem convincing, in no way do they constitute evidence. For example, while stigmatics can bleed, this does not prove their memories are historically correct.

After one reads Mulhern's account there can be little doubt that 99 percent or more of the survivor accounts of satanic ritual abuse (SRA) are iatrogenic and that the attending therapist in the hypnotic process is "demanding" the production of satanic abuse fantasies. They are also responsible for the intensity of the violence and emotionality of the abreaction, the vivid detail and logical consistency. They "demand" these. As for the narrative consistency, they are also as responsible for it as the clients themselves.

Therapists look for molestation anywhere and everywhere they turn and they seem very skilled at finding it—even though it has probably never existed. If the clients have ever heard of SRA, their information derives from traditional, rural folklore about black magic, witches, and devil worship; from newspaper articles reporting satanic cult rumor stories; from popular culture entertainment like horror movies and tabloid newspapers; and from speeches and books of self-proclaimed survivors. This accounts for the similarities between the stories of clients who don't know one another and who may even live in different countries.

Over the last decade numerous investigators have tried to restore a sense of reason and sanity to this barrage from the therapeutic community. As a result of this hysteria, hundreds of dollars and thousands of hours have been wasted in police and therapeutic seminars designed to deal with satanic crimes. Despite all of the rumors and panic, fewer than a hundred credible reports of SRA were filed nationally between 1985 and 1990 when the rumor and panic were at their maximum. None of the people accused were members of any satanic church or identified devil-worshiping cult and only a fraction of those accused were ever convicted.[50] Of the few who were convicted, most were associated with day care centers and involved a single pedophile or pornographer. Most of the allegations of SRA are frivolous and are filed in connection with custody disputes. In such cases many children are coached, threatened, or chose to lie because of their own desire to get even. The simple naivete of "believe the children" merely confuses and complicates an already complex and muddled imbroglio. After the so-called experts—the social workers, lawyers, police, detectives, and other mental health personnel—have worked the victims over, questioning them repeatedly, putting in and taking words out of the children's mouths, it is a miracle indeed if the children know their names. If any therapy is to ever take place it is usually made even more difficult by this insane legal circus.

In spite of all the claims made about occult groups and cults that worship Satan, the only one of any size or stature is the Church of Satan, founded in the mid-1960s by Anton Szander LaVey, a former circus animal trainer. LaVey wrote *The Satanic Bible*, which rejects the Christian versions of both God and Satan and the book is anything but "satanic." In fact, *The Satanic Bible* urges the believer to reject all anti-social behavior including criminal acts against children, drug abuse, harming animals, and all such un-Christian acts—exactly the opposite of what the religious fundamentalists, who have never read the book and base their accusations solely on the title, maintain.[51]

Despite the facts that reports occasionally show up in the media detailing widespread satanic activity, that law enforcement authorities seem obsessed with Satanism, and that many members of the psychotherapeutic community see SRA and Satanists behind every bush, it can be confidently stated:

1. There is no organized satanic conspiracy afoot in the United States today;
2. Few—if any—children are being abused and sacrificed by Satanists in the nation today;
3. According to FBI statistics, what Satanists exist in the nation today are few in number, loosely organized, expressly forbid murder, child abuse, the mistreatment of animals, and they are all protected by the U.S. Constitution;
4. The cult conspiracy theory that has been prevalent in the past is due to beliefs fueled by conservative Christian fundamentalists and the social mechanisms of rumor—panics, subversive mythology, and urban legend;
5. If satanic ritual abuse exists, it exists only on a very small scale and the ritual trappings are used as a means to silence the victims;
6. Any and all criminal acts attributed to the Satanists are the acts of a few isolated individuals—such self-styled Satanists make up their own rituals and use their "satanic connection" to justify their antisocial acts;
7. The violent behavior—including murder—shown by some isolated individuals calling themselves Satanists is a *symptom* not a *cause* of their violence, i.e., they perform violent acts first, and claim affiliation with Satanism afterward, using Satanism as a convenient (but inaccurate) excuse;
8. Religious fanaticism, opportunism, and self-promotion has led

a small number of individuals to continue to foster and foment the satanic scare.

Robert Hicks, in his masterful study of how the legal system has handled Satanist and anti-Satanist claims, has emphasized that the more experienced and better trained the satanic investigators were the more skeptical they were of any satanic connections. In the preface to his book Hicks points out that:

> Few members of the law-enforcement community have taken the time to combat publicly the overstatements, generalizations clearly false and absurd "facts," and excursions into illogic relating to the impact of Satanism and the occult or crime. Those who do are soon confronted with an organized crusade to protect teens and small children from the alleged satanic threat. To fight this perceived menace, people have banded together to influence the legislative process in Virginia, Idaho, Texas, Illinois, and other states to enact laws or modify criminal codes. Skeptics have not responded in kind.[52]

Hicks and his book have drawn the fulminations of one of the most rabid of hysterical anti-Satanists, Carl Raschke, a professor of religion at the University of Denver. Raschke, author of an incredible piece of twisted propaganda called *Painted Black* and an ardent anti-Satanist, is a true believer in every tale, legend, rumor, and report of SRA, satanic cults, or Satanism. Raschke, for example, after reading *The Satanism Scare*, a work declaiming SRA, found it to be "politically correct propagandizing among aging academics left over from the 1960s" and that "the book is a rather laborious, 300-page-plus, blinking and bleeping parade of sophistic reasoning, non-sequitur, spurious appeal to authority and systematic disfigurement and denial of sheaves of actual evidence about Satanism and occult-related crime."[53] Raschke also believes that 75 percent of women who tell stories of sexual abuse in childhood are able to confirm the facts behind the memory.

Kenneth Lanning, however, the FBI's specialist in child sex abuse, has continually insisted that the material evidence for SRA is nonexistent.[54] In a survey of more than eleven thousand psychiatric and police workers across the country, researchers found more than twelve thousand accusations of group cult sexual abuse based on satanic ritual, but not a single one that investigators were able to substantiate.[55] Over the last decade, as we have seen, accusations of cult molestation and SRA have been made and many people have been led to believe there is a nationwide network of satanic cults preying on the young. The survey, the first national authoritative investigation, clearly shows this to be false: "After scouring the country, we found no evidence for large-scale cults that sexually abuse children."[56] The survey included 6,910 psychiatrists, psychologists, and clinical social workers, and 4,655 district attorneys, police departments, and social service agencies. It was designed to obtain firm evidence if any existed. The only thing the survey did find, according to Gail Goodman, who conducted it, was a few cases of "lone perpetrators or couples who say they are involved with Satan or use the claim to intimidate victims. . . . If there is anyone out there with solid evidence of satanic cult abuse of children, we would like to know about it."[57] A few years ago the Kentucky Association of Science Educators and Skeptics carried out a statewide search for Satanists and satanic cults. The only things uncovered were a few rumors and fears hurriedly discussed by the police and local authorities. Previous, smaller studies carried out by Michigan State Police, the Virginia Crime Commission, the Attorney General's Office in Utah, and by the British government had similar findings. The diehard believers, however, will not be convinced. To them it only proves how adept the Satanists are at eluding detection.

Saddest of all was Dr. Goodman's conclusion that

> [o]ur research leads us to believe that there are many more children being abused in the name of God than in the name of Satan. Ironically, while the public concerns itself with passing laws to punish satanic child abuse, laws already exist that protect parents whose particular variants of belief in God deny their children life-saving medical care. The freedom to choose religions and practice them will, and should, always be protected by our Constitution, but the freedom to abuse children in the course of those practices ought to be curtailed.[58]

ALIEN ABDUCTIONS: "FOLIE A DEUX: ABDUCTEE AND THERAPIST"

Of all the iatrogenic disorders, perhaps the most absurd, deviational, and preposterous is the rapidly proliferating belief among some pseudotherapists that the skies of the planet Earth are being invaded by alien life forms in Unidentified Flying Objects (UFOs). These life forms are, via mysterious and unearthly means, kidnapping, examining, and returning to their beds thousands—if not millions—of ordinary citizens. In fact, these alleged abductions are noteworthy for the fact that no one of political power, national prestige, or distinction is ever selected for abduction. Such people are avoided by the aliens like the plague. This fact alone should arouse all sorts of questions about the nature of any extraterrestrial and its motivations as well as its intelligence. Are aliens so ignorant and uninterested in human affairs they are unaware of human social structures? Are they so unintelligent they are totally unable to profit from experience and learn? For nearly fifty years now reports of alien abductions have poured in and, with regard to most of them, the alien behavior is pretty much the same from abduction to abduction. The first abduction to attract major public attention was the notorious case of Betty and Barney Hill. On September 19, 1961, while returning from a Canadian vacation where they visited Betty's sister, the Hills claimed they were abducted.

During the visit there had been considerable discussion about UFOs and extraterrestrials since Betty's sister was intrigued by them. As they neared home in Portsmouth, New Hampshire, Betty saw a strange light in the sky which seemed to be following their car. Puzzled, Barney left the main road and tried for a better look. Both decided the light was a UFO, became anxious and drove home on the back roads to evade the spaceship. The trip took them two hours longer than expected and this made them wonder what had happened to the time. After reaching home, Betty called her sister and told her about the light and their experience. Betty's sister warned about the possibility of their being exposed to harmful radiation and suggested something unusual may have happened. Betty became more and more anxious about UFOs, began to believe the missing time indicated they must have been abducted and, after reading Major Donald Keyhoe's books about flying saucers from outer space,[59] began to have nightmarish dreams and to believe she and Barney suffered from radiation effects. Most of her fears were heightened by her discussions with friends and neighbors and a local UFO investigator. Gradually, she became convinced she must have been abducted and the two missing hours made her more and more convinced. In September 1963 Barney developed severe anxiety attacks and entered psychotherapy. Before long, since Betty also was developing somatic complaints, the therapist referred them both to a Boston psychiatrist, Dr. Benjamin Simon, for hypnotherapy. When he examined the couple Simon was able to elicit many details from Betty although Barney recalled very little of what supposedly took place. Barney believed in his "abduction" only after he had listened to his wife's stories many times and had become influenced by his wife's strong convictions.

Betty gave an account of meeting humanoid creatures with a big head, large "wraparound" eyes, no nose, a mere slit for a mouth. Also reported was a medical examination including close attention to the sex organs, and a long needle inserted into the navel. Before leaving the spacecraft Betty was shown a screen with a map on it showing, supposedly, the star system from which the aliens originated. When Betty later drew this map from memory, some astronomers believed it was a sketch of the Zeta Reticali star system, although others said it would fit numerous configurations of stars.

Dr. Simon concluded the abduction never happened and was a subconscious fantasy due to Betty's reading and the marital tensions between the mixed race couple—Betty was white and Barney black. Barney died in 1969 of a cerebral hemorrhage. As of this writing (1995), Betty is still alive and still interested in UFOs claiming that she has seen thousands since her abduction, and that she still is able to communicate with them telepathically.

This case was made famous by John Fuller in his book *The Interrupted Journey*,[60] and was also the subject of a two-hour television film as well as numerous magazine articles, essays, book chapters, and movies.

The above details have served as the model for nearly all subsequent tales of abduction, including the light in the sky; missing time;

floating up into the spaceship; a medical exam by big headed, slant-eyed, small humanoids; telepathic communication; and memory retrieval under hypnosis by a hypnotherapist. With only a few minor variations, this typical case history dominated all the occasional reports of alien abduction for the next decade.

In Pontalillo's words,

> It is not at all surprising then that every abduction reported since this massively reported case has adopted virtually identical thematic patterns of medical exams and needle motifs. Any material differences from case to case are usually in the form of additional detail concerning a specific event or, less frequently, minor additions to the basic theme. As we approach the end of the third decade since Hill's revelations, the broad outlines of the abduction phenomenon have changed little indeed.[61]

In January 1976 another most unusual event occurred. Although it was not reported until a year later, three Kentucky women detailed one of the first "mass" (more than two) alien abduction accounts. On the night of January 6, 1976, Mrs. Elaine Thomas, age forty-nine; Mrs. Louise Smith, age forty-four; and Mrs. Mona Stafford, age thirty-six; went to a restaurant near Stanford, Kentucky to celebrate Mrs. Stafford's birthday. They left the restaurant around 11:00 P.M. to drive home, and at approximately 11:30 P.M. they saw coming toward them what looked like an airplane on fire. As it got closer it hovered over their car. It was oval, very large, and as big as a football field. Bluish-white light came out of its bottom—the car was pulled backward and they felt it being taken aboard the UFO. The car was then filled with a hazy fog and they lost consciousness.

They awoke in Hustonville, eight miles from the UFO site, sitting in Mrs. Smith's car with pounding headaches and in a daze. They drove home to Liberty, Kentucky, too stunned to talk, one hour and twenty-five minutes late, with no memory of anything between the sight of the blush-white light and their presence in Hustonville.

After reading everything they could find about UFOs and even contacting Betty Hill and discussing her abduction with her, the three women contacted UFO researchers in Cincinnati who arranged to have them undergo regressive hypnosis by Dr. Leo Sprinkle. Under hypnosis they told the typical abduction story including meeting the "little, gray" aliens. Although they also took a lie detector test, the polygrapher said the results were inconclusive due to the fact the women's memories had been contaminated by the hypnotic regression.

It is important to note that the women did not go public with their abduction story until January 1977—a year later. During this year they hashed and rehashed their story among themselves and two of the alleged abductees also had additional encounters with the aliens in their homes. Eighteen months after the alleged abduction, Dr. Otto Billig, a Vanderbilt University psychiatrist, interviewed Mrs. Smith and Mrs. Stafford at great length. Both women felt their experience had a deeply religious meaning and that they had been chosen for the delivery of an earth-saving message. Unlike Dr. Sprinkle, Billig, a more experienced and better trained psychologist, realized from the outset that one of the three women had undergone a hypnagogic dream* which was such an unusual and traumatic experience for her and her friends they had to interpret it any way they could—which at the time, in their psychological setting, made sense only in quasireligious terms involving UFOs and aliens. According to Billig the women were sincere in their beliefs. Not only were the events and the experiences preceding the abduction unusual but,

> If we can judge from similar experiences, one may conclude they may have become tired from the activities of a long day and as the drive wore on, their original enthusiasms probably died down.
>
> Their drive home at night on a lonely road with little traffic could have lulled them into a state of drowsiness. The driver mentioned that she became drowsy and attempted to fight off sleep. Whether she actually feel asleep or not, her level of consciousness may have become dulled; she may have turned her attention to herself and to her own thoughts, thoughts possibly preoccupied with fantasies as she drove "well-nigh automatically," needing to pay little attention to the road. She may have found herself in a state of "highway hypnosis." Such cases are not uncommon and may occur not only at night, but at any time of day during monotonous drives.[62]

---

*A hallucinatory dream which occurs as one is falling asleep.

Based on the information gained from his interview, Billig was able to reconstruct the abduction scene and the women's frightening experience. First, one of the women spotted a bright red object in the night sky and reported it to the others. Her companions looked and saw the object but due to extreme drowsiness did not regard it as threatening until one or more of them slipped into the hypnagogic state which borders sleep and waking. The instant this happened the red object became a ball of light approaching the car, swelling in size and appearing extremely large. Mrs. Smith admitted she had fallen asleep and awoke only intermittently feeling she was in a spaceship.

> She recalled under hypnosis, months later, that she saw strange crea-tures and complex machinery. She attributes the onset of her drowsi-ness and that of the others, as well as their lack of control, to the blinding light emanating from the spacecraft. Regardless of the cause, whether externally induced or not, the women's unmanage-able drowsiness indicated their level of consciousness was severely reduced. Attempting to function under such conditions intensified in each the feelings of discomfort and stress. Such feelings often fal-sify the accuracy of one's judgment or one's memory, and anyone may have difficulties in recalling the sequence of impressions before falling asleep. It is highly questionable that the abductees could establish the precise succession of events under such circumstances. It was only later, as they recalled the events of the evening, that they found strange new meanings that they had not realized previously.[63]

Of most importance was the fact that none of the three women agreed on exactly what had happened and on the exact sequence of the events. In fact Billig and other interviewers discovered that some of the events that supposedly happened on the night of the alleged abduction did not occur until months later. In the time between the abduction and when the women reported it, the three discussed and debated the event and finally consolidated their various impressions and interpretations and integrated them into an entirely new complex of experiences and into a coherent, agreed-upon story.

The description that Louise Smith, the leader of the three, gave independently of her encounter was remarkably similar to symptoms experienced during the hypnagogic state described in the psychiatric literature as early as 1936. People in this state see approaching balls of light that increase in size and change color; they are also overwhelmed by feelings of helplessness and loss of control and feelings of floating up into the air (going into the spaceship) or moving through solid walls. Mrs. Smith also felt she was smothering as pressure on her chest became heavier and she also felt the surrounding temperatures had increased and the heat had become unbearable.

All of these experiences are typical of the hypnagogic and hypno-pompic hallucinations accompanying sleep-paralysis. Typically, individuals having these experiences as they begin to fall asleep see lights and/or round objects that swell to gigantic size. At times, these objects rush toward the individual, threatening to crush him. A heavy feeling may press on his body and, at other times, feeling of floating or weightlessness may happen. This hypnagogic state is a fairly common, but not well known, sleep disorder occurring between sleeping and waking. It is, in fact, a "waking dream" and the sleeper is, literally, half asleep and half awake and is subject to a number of hallucinatory experiences whose content is determined—like dreams and night-mares—by the sleeper's internal fears, anxieties, beliefs, recent books read, movies seen, and so forth. As with all hallucinations, perceptual discrimination becomes reduced and distorted which makes it difficult to judge the size and distance of objects or the reality of their existence. Most disturbing is the fact that they seem so real, since the mixture of "real" experiences from the immediate environment and the "unreal or hallucinatory material from the dreaming brain are inextricably intertwined."

Objects may also change in size and appearance, and may or may not be under the partial control of the environment, since most of the experience follows the dictates of the viewer's inner needs, fears, and apprehensions. Feelings of distaste may develop and the individual may experience physical pain. The mouth, lips, and tongue as well as the face and skin and hands may feel hot and dry. Stigmata of various types may also occur, including localized erythema (abnormal redness of the skin). Vague, difficult to define, and unpleasant feelings may be present, and vague feelings of sexual arousal and stimulation may also occur. The latter, however, are much more common in cases of hypno-pompic hallucinations, which will be discussed shortly. Most often after awakening from the hypnagogic state the victim tends to remember the experience with unusually deceptive vividness, convincing him more strongly as to its reality.

Billig also noted that the hypnotic session with Dr. Sprinkle only served to reinforce the women's conviction that they had indeed "been abducted by aliens." Had Billig seen the women first it is likely we would never have heard their story at all.

Because this is one of the alien abduction proponents' strongest cases; it involves multiple abductions, as well as honest and credible individuals with no possible motives for fabrication; it offers some of the strongest evidence for the "reality" of the abduction experience. A team of British researchers were interested in the case and since both Mrs. Smith and Mrs. Stafford still lived in the Liberty, Kentucky, area, I reopened the case in the summer of 1994 and obtained a lengthy interview with Mrs. Smith. Mrs. Stafford declined to participate. The researchers' belief was that an understanding of what really happened in this case would be helpful in understanding all other claims of alien abductions.

Mrs. Smith today is a very bright, alert, level-headed individual who remembers clearly the events surrounding her alleged abduction and its aftermath in 1976 and 1977. She was not only quite articulate about all of the interest surrounding her report but she also had a small photographic album commemorating her interviews with the Mutual UFO Network (MUFON) team and Dr. Sprinkle's hypnosis session. Most interesting was Mrs. Smith's reply to my question about the hypnotic interview, "Had you ever heard of people being abducted before you were hypnotized?" Her answer was an emphatic "No." To the questions: "Were you interested in UFOs and had you seen any strange lights in the sky prior to your talks with the MUFON people and the hypnosis?" and "Did you ever consider the possibility that you might have been abducted before the talks with Betty Hill and the hypnotic interview?" her answers were again "No." Mrs. Smith freely admitted that both she and Mrs. Stafford were on friendly terms with the Hills and that conversations with Betty and their hypnotic regressions had convinced them they had been abducted. The three women were indeed victims, not of extraterrestrial aliens, but of overzealous UFOl-ogists who put pictures of aliens, spaceships, operating tables, and such into their memory banks.

While there were significant differences in the reports of exactly what happened on the highway at the time of the UFO encounter, the accounts of the three following regressive hypnosis are remarkably alike. Such confabulations mirror the scenario in the head of the hyp-notist, not memories in the heads of the three women.

While it was difficult to reconstruct exactly what transpired after the women left the restaurant because of conflicting accounts from various reports and interviews,[64] my interview with Mrs. Smith clari-fied these problems. What follows:

Louise Smith was driving with both Mona Stafford and Elaine Thomas in the front seat beside her. Leaving the restaurant at a late hour—well past their respective bedtimes—and driving home on a lonely road with little traffic, Mona and Elaine fell asleep, leaving Louise very drowsy and fighting to stay awake. When Louise, now entering a hypnagogic state, came to a stone wall with a cattle gate, she left the highway and came to a halt, staring down the country lane ahead of her. She now had the hypnagogic hallucinatory experience of seeing a bright, on-rushing light, feeling engulfed and swallowed up by whatever was behind it. The light also seemed to enlarge and change color as it rushed toward her. This hallucinatory experience is called "The Ishakower Effect"—named after the Viennese psychiatrist Oskar Ishakower who discovered this unusual reaction many people experience as they are falling asleep.[65] It is also accompanied by sleep paralysis and other hypnagogic hallucinations. Mrs. Smith next reported a feeling of helplessness, loss of control, floating, and also a feeling that she was in danger of smothering as the pressure on her chest became heavier.

All of her symptoms were typical of the hypnagogic states as reported in Andreas Mavromatis's book *Hypnagogia*[66] and the psychi-atric literature, yet, Mrs. Smith did not associate any of them with UFOs and a UFO abduction until the ideas were suggested to her by her neighbors, her contact with the MUFON personnel, and her sub-sequent hypnosis by Dr. Sprinkle.

Her impressions of losing control of her car, of it being pulled backwards, of the speedometer reading eighty-five miles per hour, and the other images previously mentioned were all hallucinations and confirm the fact that she was having a hypnagogic experience. Her statements also served to fill in the memory gaps of the other two sleeping women and led them to confabulate memories of being examined, having eyeballs removed, and so forth, as a direct result of Mrs. Smith's suggestions. As for the reports of Mrs. Stafford and Mrs. Thomas, it appears they were asleep during the missing time interval and took their cues as to what "really happened" from the leadership of Mrs. Smith. In fact, Mrs. Stafford referred to Mrs. Smith throughout Dr. Billig's interview as "Ma" and "Mom."

Both Billig and I discovered that from the outset the hypnosis sessions were designed to verify "what really happened," that is, to verify the abductions. Several months elapsed between the alleged abductions and the hypnosis sessions, but during this interval the three women were constantly preoccupied with their experience and discussed it among themselves continuously. They were, of course, ridiculed by their fellow citizens, some of whom referred to them as "astro-nuts." Since they received little encouragement and support from their community, in January and February 1977, the three turned to the UFO organizations for confirmation and verification. Mrs. Smith went so far as to write to Betty Hill and, subsequently, spend considerable time on the phone with her. All their UFO contacts proved to be very supportive and helped convince the three of the "reality" of their abduction. Struggling for months to fill their memory gaps, kindly Dr. Sprinkle provided welcome relief from their puzzlement. Everyone in the UFO community had already prejudged the abductions to be a fact which, interestingly enough was allegedly confirmed by a polygraph test. Also, the only things sought in the hypnosis sessions were (1) details of the spaceship; (2) descriptions of the aliens; (3) details of the physical examinations and surgical operations; and (4) the motives of the aliens. Nothing remotely suggesting that the data obtained was faulty—that it was fantasy, confabulation, or that it reflected stories and information previously acquired from the MUFON representatives, Betty Hill, and other UFO believers—was ever considered. Like Betty Hill, the Kentucky women might have dismissed their experience as merely a dream rather than factual event had not UFO-believing friends insisted their alien contacts were real and something much more than fantasies or dreams.

Louise, Mona, and Elaine, who had led rather quiet and anonymous lives before their abduction, now found attentive and supportive audiences everywhere they turned. While some ridicule did come their way, on most occasions socially important people and media representatives sought them out and took seriously everything they said. Louise's life became much more satisfying and rewarding as a result of her experience and her self-esteem increased significantly. Mona Stafford's life was also enhanced and, after being visited by an "angel" a few days after the abduction, Mona grew increasingly more spiritual and dedicated her life to helping others. Elaine also became more religious and more concerned with social issues.

The important lesson here, as in most situations in which regressive hypnosis is employed, is that the hypnosis procedures and questions rather than being designed to determine the truth are instead designed to reinforce and confirm the hypnotist's preconceptions, convictions, and embedded biases. It is not hypnosis, per se, that is at fault, but the way in which the hypnotist misuses his tool.

The significant point here is that the particular abduction experience is only one of an increasingly large number of false and misleading memories implanted with almost surgical precision by unwitting and unknowing psychiatrists, psychologists, and legions of amateur hypnotherapists, who in their zeal to "help people" have totally forgotten not to do harm. Whether these well meaning busy-bodies are totally naive about the ease with which the thought-content and memories of so-called hypnotized clients can be manipulated and controlled, or whether they, in their zeal to find what they are looking for, simply don't give a damn is the critical question.

As for the alien abduction syndrome it is significant that, with few rare exceptions, all of those individuals claiming abduction arrived at this conclusion, like Louise Smith, after having been subjected to regressive hypnosis of zealous UFO believers. Even in the case of Betty and Barney Hill in the late 1950s, psychiatrist Dr. Benjamin Simon used regressive hypnosis. Despite Simon's warning that hypnosis is not necessarily a magical road to the truth and that the Hills' recall was most likely a fantasy, these cautions were ignored in the rush to entertain and titillate the public. While much is made of a few cases in which an abduction was claimed without the benefit of regressive hypnosis, extensive investigation into such cases revealed they were elaborately staged hoaxes.[67] It is also significant that all those writing about and believing in alien abductions are very familiar with each other's works. This is true of nearly all of the abductees as well, most of whom report they never knew that they too had been abducted until they read about the abduction experiences of others.

*   *   *

What is tragic in this health area is general lack of training and clinical experience in the use (as well as abuse and misuse) of hypnosislike therapeutic techniques and procedures. As a result of their failure to understand what they are doing, the hypnotherapists have succeeded in laying mile after mile of macadam in hell. These road crews sincerely believe that they are protecting thousands of innocent children, punishing hundreds of evil child rapists and molesters, fighting hordes of satanic demons, and saving thousands of lives. They see themselves as helping all of those poor unfortunate souls who cannot find treatment, solace, or understanding from those cruel and unfeeling psychotherapists who refuse to accept and acknowledge that the fact they have been abducted and molested, not only by evil fellow human beings and Satanists but by alien monsters from beyond, as well. It is high time the public realizes that all of these sensational human disasters have been dumped upon the American scene by a credulous group of well-meaning but naive and misguided zealots: mental health professionals who should know better. Acting in the name of "therapy" and aided and abetted by an enthusiastic and uncritical media, these foolish alarmists have seriously and irreparably harmed hundreds of innocent people and have raised the anxiety level of an already beleaguered and overstressed populace. Acting in the name of the healing arts they have failed to attend to the primary—the fundamental—

principle of all healers: First, do no harm! Not only have they done harm, they have also, in the process, managed to discredit science, medicine, psychology, psychiatry, and the art of social service as well.

NOTES

1. John Wesley, *The Journal of John Wesley* (London: Epworth, 1938).

2. Richard J. Ofshe and Ethan Watters, "Making Monsters," *Society* (March/April 1993): 4–16.

3. Ellen Bass and Laura Davis, *The Courage to Heal: A Guide for Woman Survivors of Child Sexual Abuse* (New York: Harper & Row, 1988), pp. 78–82.

4. Ibid., p. 90.

5. John Kihlstrom, "Recovery of Memory in Laboratory and Clinic," (Paper presented at Rocky Mountain/Western Psychology Association Meeting, Phoenix, Ariz., April 1993).

6. Judith I. Herman, "Child Abuse," in *Trauma and Recovery* (New York: Basic Books, 1992).

7. L. M. Williams, "Adult Memories of Childhood Abuse: Preliminary Findings from a Longitudinal Study." *APSAC Advisor* 5, no. 3 (1992): 19–21.

8. Leonore Terr, *Too Scared to Cry: Psychic Trauma in Childhood* (New York: Basic Books, 1990), p. 176.

9. Ibid., p. 177.

10. David Holmes, "The Evidence for Repression: An Examination of Sixty Years of Research," in *Repression and Dissociation*, ed. Jerome Singer (Chicago: University of Chicago Press, 1990), pp. 98–99.

11. C. P. Malmquist, "Children Who Witness Parental Murder: Post-Traumatic Aspects," *Journal of the American Academy of Child Psychiatry* 25 (1986): 320–25.

12. Anthony G. Greenwald, "New Look 3: Unconscious Cognitions Reclaimed," *American Psychologist* 47, no. 6 (1992): 766–79.

13. Betty Petersen, *Dancing with Daddy: A Childhood Lost and a Life Regained* (New York: Bantam Books, 1991), p. 66.

14. Detailed accounts of the case include Lawrence Wright, "Remembering Satan, Parts I and II," *New Yorker*, 17 and 24 May 1993, in book form as *Remembering Satan* (New York: Knopf, 1994); and also Richard J. Ofshe, "Inadvertent Hypnosis during Interrogation: False Confession Due to Dissociative State, Misidentified Multiple Personality, and the Satanic Cult Hypothesis," *International Journal of Clinical & Experimental Hypnosis* 15, no. 3 (1992): 125–56.

15. Elizabeth F. Loftus, "The Reality of Repressed Memories," *American Psychologist* 48 (1993): 518–37.

16. Terr, *Too Scared to Cry*, p. 103.

17. R. S. Harsch and Ulrich Neisser, "Substantial and Irreversible Errors in Flashbulb Memories of the *Challenger* Explosion." (Paper presented at Psychonomics Society Annual Meeting, November 1989).

18. Robert A. Baker, *They Call It Hypnosis* (Amherst, N.Y.: Prometheus, 1990), p. 194.

19. S. R. Baker and D. Boas, "Partial Reformulation of a Traumatic Memory of a Dental Phobia," *International Journal of Clinical & Experimental Hypnosis* 31 (1983): 14–18.

20. E. R. Hilgard, "Hypnosis Gives Rise to Fantasy and Is Not a Truth Serum," *Skeptical Inquirer* 5, no. 3 (Spring 1981): 25.

21. Elizabeth F. Loftus, *Eyewitness Testimony* (Cambridge: Harvard University Press, 1979).

22. R. A. Baker, B. Haynes, and B. Patrick, "Hypnosis, Memory, and Incidental Memory," *American Journal of Clinical Hypnosis* 25, no. 4 (1983): 253–62.

23. R. M. True, "Experimental Control in Hypnotic Age Regression States," *Science* 110 (1949): 583–84.

24. D. N. O'Connell, R. E. Shor, and M. T. Orue, "Hypnotic Age Regression: An Empirical and Methodological Analysis," *Journal of Abnormal Psychology Monographs* 76, no. 3 (1970): 1–32.

25. Jan Wilson, *Mind Out of Time* (London: Gollancz, 1981).

26. Martin Reiser, *Handbook of Investigative Hypnosis* (Los Angeles: Lehi, 1980).

27. C. L. Perry et al., "Hypnotic Age Regression Techniques: Applied Uses and Abuses," in *Hypnosis and Memory*, ed. H. M. Penatti (New York: Guilford Press, 1988), pp. 78–97.

28. Elizabeth F. Loftus, T. G. Miller, and H. J. Burrus, "Semantic Integration of Verbal Information into Visual Memory," *Journal of Experimental Psychology of Human Learning & Memory* 4 (1978): 19–31.

29. R. S. Pynoos and K. Nader, "Children's Memory and Proximity to Violence," *Journal of the American Academy of Child & Adolescent Psychiatry* 28 (1989): 236–41.

30. Maggie Bruck and Stephen Ceci, *The Child Witness*, Society for Research in Child Development, Social Policy Report (Chicago: University of Chicago Press, 1993).

31. Ibid., p. 27.

32. Ibid., p. 30.

33. Ofshe and Watters, "Making Monsters," pp. 11–12.

34. Holmes, "Evidence for Repression."

35. Baker, Haynes, and Patrick, "Hypnosis, Memory, and Incidental Memory."

36. Baker, *They Call It Hypnosis.*

37. H. G. Pope and J. I. Hudson, "Can Memories of Childhood Sexual Abuse Be Repressed?" Unpublished paper.

38. Michael D. Yapko, "Suggestibility and Repressed Memories of Abuse: A Survey of Psychotherapeutic Beliefs," *American Journal of Clinical Hypnosis* 36, no. 3 (1994): 169.

39. Baker, *They Call It Hypnosis.*

40. David Alexander, "Giving the Devil More Than His Due," *The Humanist* (March/April 1990): 5.

41. Michelle Smith and Lawrence Pazder, *Michelle Remembers* (New York: Pocket Books, 1989).

42. Lauren Stratford, *Satan's Underground: The Extraordinary Story of the Woman's Escape* (Eugene, Ore.: Harvest House, 1988).

43. Jennifer Peters, "This Long Ascent into the Light," *Matrix* (January 1990): 6 and 7.

44. Ibid., p. 7.

45. Gretchen and Bob Passantino with John Trott, "Satan's Sideshow," *Cornerstone* 18, no. 90 (January 1989): 23–38.

46. Philip Jenkins and David Maier-Kotkin, "Occult Survivors: The Making of a Myth," in *The Satanism Scare*, eds. J. T. Richardson, Joel Best, and D. G. Bromley (Hawthorne, N.Y.: De Gruyter, 1991), pp. 135–36.

47. Irving Janis, *Victims of Group Think* (Boston: Houghton Mifflin, 1972).

48. Sherrill Mulhern. "Satanism and Psychotherapy: A Rumor in Search of an Inquisition," in Richardson, Best, and Bromley, eds., *The Satanism Scare*, pp. 145–72.

49. Ibid., p. 146.

50. Alexander, "Giving the Devil More Than His Due."

51. Anton Szandor LaVey, *The Satanic Bible* (New York: Avon Books, 1969).

52. Robert D. Hicks, *The Pursuit of Satan* (Amherst, N.Y.: Prometheus Books, 1991), p. 10.

53. Carl Raschke, *Painted Black* (New York: Harper & Row, 1990).

54. Kenneth Lanning is cited in Debbie Nathan's "Satanism and Child

Molestation: Constructing the Ritual Abuse Scare," in Richardson, Best, and Bromley, eds., *The Satanism Scare*.

55. Gail Goodman et al., "Abstract of Final Report to National Council on Child Abuse (NCCAN)," (Davis, Calif.: Department of Psychology, University of California, 1995); cited here from partial reprint in "Report from New York Times News Source," *Louisville Courier Journal*, 31 October 1994, p. A7.

56. Ibid.

57. Ibid.

58. Ibid.

59. Donald Keyhoe, *Flying Saucers are Real* (New York: Fawcett, 1950); and *The Flying Saucer Conspiracy* (New York: Henry Holt, 1955).

60. John Fuller, *The Interrupted Journey* (New York: Dial Press, 1966).

61. J. Pontalillo, *Demons, Doctors, and Aliens: An Exploration into the Relationships among Witch Trial Evidence, Sexual-Medical Tradition, and Alien Abductions*, Occasional paper #2 (Arlington, Va.: International Fortean Organization, 1993), p. 12.

62. Otto Billig, *Flying Saucers: Magic in the Skies* (Cambridge, Mass.: Schenkman, 1982), p. 24.

63. Ibid., p. 26.

64. See L. H. Stringfield, *Situation Red: The UFO Siege* (New York: Doubleday, 1977); J. Gansberg and A. L. Gansberg, *Direct Encounters: The Personal History of UFO Abductees* (New York: Walker & Co., 1980); and Billig, *Flying Saucers*.

65. Oskar Ishakower, "A Contribution to the Psychology of Phenomena Associated with Falling Asleep," *International Journal of Psychoanalysis* 19 (1938): 331–45.

66. Andreas Mavromatis, *Hypnogogia* (London: Routledge, Kegan & Paul, 1987).

67. See Philip J. Klass, *UFOs Explained* (New York: Vintage Books, 1974); and *UFO Abductions: A Dangerous Game* (Amherst, N.Y.: Prometheus Books, 1989).

6

The Inattentive Child: One of the Saddest Manipulations

In the world of the psychiatric power brokers, the weaker and more defenseless the charges, the easier they are to manipulate. With regard to children, one of the saddest manipulations of all is the very popular but scientifically unfounded condition from which millions of American school children are presumed to be suffering: Attention Deficit Disorder (ADD) or hyperactivity.

The issues here are those of social power and social control. These conflicts are so evident and so pervasive it does not require either education or psychological training to recognize them. A clear example of this is Ida Fogle's passionate essay titled "The Business of Fixing People."[1] Fogle, with little in the way of education and training, in 1991 took a job typing "psychoeducational evaluations" on the computer in a psychologist's office. Fogle was only part-time office help and the people with whom she interacted were all M.A.s and Ph.D.s.

The evaluations she typed usually concerned test results of children and young adults, most of whom were brought in due to problems with school. Almost without exception the diagnosis was Attention Deficit Disorder or Attention Deficit Hyperactivity Disorder (ADHD). Fogle worked in the office for months before seeing an evaluation that didn't mention ADD or ADHD. The symptoms indicating the disorder included "child squirmed in seat" or "fidgeted with hands." "Of course they did," Fogle notes, "Imagine you're a child being taken to a strange doctor where you'll have to sit at a table for three hours taking tests to figure out what's wrong with your brain. Wouldn't you squirm and fidget?" A large percentage of these young people ended up on Ritalin—a stimulant drug. "I personally found this alarming," Fogle notes, "but the parents were ridiculed and chided if they questioned the sanity of putting the kids on drugs. Sadly, few parents did question it."[2] Fogle states she never saw any references to the youths' habits, how much junk food they ate, television watching, or anything else relevant to their past which could have an effect on present behavior. "No one makes money when you turn off the TV or refuse to buy junk food. But if you take your child to a psychiatrist who provides therapy and also refers you to a physician who writes a prescription for Ritalin which is then filled by a pharmacist, just look at the people who profit."[3]

What really broke her heart, Fogle says, were the kids who were brought in to be "fixed" because they were nonconformists. The reports she typed often made reference to "inappropriate dress." Inappropriate dress as a psychological problem should center on something extreme— dress which shows such impaired judgment that it would pose actual physical danger to the wearer, e.g., like a skirt and high heel shoes in an ice storm. But that's not what the shrinks meant. They were referring to anything not "mainstream." Teenagers would come in whose main "problem" was a punk haircut or an interest in skateboarding. Skateboarding gets a lot of bad press because it is something the kids do autonomously, away from the guidance of an authority figure.

One teenager was referred because he dropped out of high school. He nevertheless earned his G.E.D. (general equivalency dipolma), was working at a steady job, and supporting himself. Yet, because he was from a good family who brought him up to respect money and power, he was "ruining everything" by hanging out with lower-class types and working at low-paying jobs. Fogle says he made more than she did, but after all, she's poor white trash and didn't deserve better. Because the kid rejected his family's values he was obviously sick and had a medical problem curable by drugs!

Another boy wanted to enroll in a vocational educational program in carpentry, but the school counselor kept trying to talk him out of it and into a print shop because, in the counselor's words "it would make him more employable." Nobody was willing to give him a chance at what he wanted to do. If you dare to go against the standardized test scores, God help you—no one else will!

Fogle went to the clinic expecting to find kind, sympathetic, understanding therapists but, instead, found people who were from upper-middle to upper-class backgrounds who had no understanding of people unlike themselves. An overwhelming class-consciousness pervaded everything they did. In fact, a failure to worship money was viewed as a "mental problem." Fogle repeatedly heard remarks like "Well, what can you expect? Her mom's only a waitress," or "Her father must not be very bright either, he's only a truck driver." To the therapists there were only two categories: the wealthy and therefore the important and deserving (the desirable clientele), and the second class, the unwealthy, the unimportant, and the undeserving.

Although, on occasion, a child of a working class family with exceptional insurance might slip in, mostly, only the moneyed elite who were able to pay what was necessary to fix whatever was wrong showed up. Fogle said, "They'd bring their family members in to the behavior-repair-shop just like they'd take a coat to have it altered. I saw many young people who were struggling against everything to find and hold their own identity, to come to some sort of consciousness and I always cheered for the kids to win. Much of these kids' behaviors seemed to me like healthy reactions to a sick society. I often felt that their problems were caused by the school, their parents or other authority. But it was always the children who were tinkered with."[4]

One of the world's foremost authorities on child behavior and ADD and ADHD is in 100 percent agreement with Fogle. In a classic paper, "Attention Deficit Disorder: The Emperor's Clothes, Animal 'Pharm,' and Other Fiction," Dr. Diane McGuinness exposes everything that is currently amiss with the pseudodisorder known as ADD or hyperactivity and the material included in the DSM.[5]

McGuinness, first of all, reports that two decades of empirical research have not provided any support for the validity of ADD or ADHD as noted in the *Diagnostic and Statistical Manual,* and she is mystified as to why such a diagnosis continues to exist. She is also puzzled by the fact that approximately one-third of all elementary school boys are now being treated as an *abnormal* population because they are fidgety, inattentive, and unamenable to adult control. The most common treatment for this "disorder" is to put them on Ritalin (methylphenidate) which, in the short term, gives the impression the child is better able to pay attention and thus process information more efficiently.

Diagnosis, rather than therapy, has become the central issue in ADD research. The DSM-III contained sixty-five pages on childhood and adolescent disorders which, according to Hinshaw, included "many unreliable classifications that have received little or no empirical support."[6] Because drug use requires a diagnosis, and a diagnosis implies a disease, now normal children's behavior and their behavioral problems are classified as medical problems, justifying the use of medication. Many drugs merely reduce the symptoms of the disease and there is no doubt that Ritalin does slow down the overactive, energetic, and disruptive kids. The parents, seduced by media hype, find that the drugs are inexpensive and a quick way of treatment. Moreover, the drugs take the onus off the parents and ascribe the child's behavior to causes beyond their control. It becomes a miraculous substitute for the learning of self-discipline and self-control. The problems causing the symptoms of disruptive and inattentive behavior in the first place, such as serious learning problems, or family and emotional problems are often not dealt with at all. Drugs do not help children read or do math, teach the child how to control his behavior, teach sensitivity to others, nor do they stop Dad's drinking. They do not provide improvement in attentional control, as is widely claimed. While children *appear* more attentive, objective studies have shown the learning process is not affected. As McGuinness reports,

> Methodically rigorous research indicates that ADD and hyperactivity as 'syndromes' simply do not exist. We have invented a disease, given it medical sanction, and now must disown it. The major question is how we go about destroying the monster we have created. It is not easy to do this and still save face, another reason why physicians and many researchers with years of funding and an academic reputation to protect are so reluctant to believe the data.[7]

Moreover, an entire series of studies has shown that aggression is associated with socioeconomic status, family hostility, and delinquency, whereas hyperactivity is related to academic achievement problems.[8] Family variables—especially alcoholism—were also found to be highly related to childhood aggression[9] and another study showed that children with conduct disorders and hyperactivity usually came from deviant families.[10] McGee, Williams, and Silva found that poor control of attention is strongly related to academic problems, lower intelligence, plus speech difficulties and poor motor coordination.[11] All such studies show that the medical-disease model is inappropriate when applied to childhood behavior problems. The implication is that the child has the disorder, rather than the family, the teacher, or the school system. Drugs are being given to the wrong people! As McGuinness notes, "the child's behavior is often a reaction to learning or family problems, and not the cause of the problems. The direction of causality is inferred from the unlikely possibility of the child's behavior playing a causal role in the parent's alcoholism, or being solely responsible for a hostile family environment. And it is far more likely that low IQ and/or poor academic skills produce fidgety, inattentive symptoms, than the reverse."[12]

In her 1985 review of the literature on hyperactivity and ADD McGuinness estimated that between 10 and 15 percent of the total population of children had been classified as ADD or hyperactive. Only four years later this total had risen to 33.5 percent—a problem of overinclusion and "medical innumeracy"* without historical precedent. The lack of any valid diagnosis for ADD, McGuinness adds, coupled with the arbitrary nature of current diagnostic practices has led to a bandwagon phenomenon that can only be described as a national disaster.[13]

Looking at all of the empirical research that has been done on ADD children in laboratory settings it is very clear that when ADD children are matched for initial ability with a control group, their performance is essentially identical and the differences that do show up reflect the ADDs' unwillingness to persist in tasks they simply don't like. Moreover, ADD children perform just like other children on all tasks where they are in control of the situation (tasks which they

---

*Flagrant misuse of statistics.

choose to perform), but they fail to do well in tasks controlled or required by someone else. On these latter tasks they show frustration accompanied by a distortion of the sense of time. Their dislike of adult control and their desire to exert self-control seems to be the core of the problem. This, rather than an inability to maintain attention, is the real problem. The data clearly show that if ADD children have problems maintaining attention to a task, such a deficit cannot be demonstrated in controlled laboratory conditions.[14]

Nowadays, unfortunately, children are treated with drugs instead of being treated on an individual basis with techniques of behavior modification, individual and family therapy, or through special education as they were for decades. Medication is now the answer, since hyperactivity is reduced immediately and attention is, reputedly, focused. Although physicians generally warn parents about the drug's side effects, these often go unmonitored and unobserved. At present there are few—if any—follow-up studies on the long-term effects of these drugs. The major questions however are: Do the drugs work? Do they really make the child learn more efficiently? Do they make the child happier and better able to cope? Are drugs and behavioral techniques more effective than behavioral techniques alone? In general, studies of the impact of drugs on school performance show that academic skills do not improve merely by taking drugs. If ADD children are put on a drug that enhances attention they should be superior to other children of their age and ability. This, however, is not the result. Thorley could find no evidence that stimulant medication had any impact whatsoever on school performance.[15] Moreover, Barkley and Cunningham reviewed a number of studies on the impact of drugs on academic performance and found no improvement.[16] In a meta-analysis* study of the efficacy of drug treatment, Kavale did find something was making children stick longer with a task they may not prefer.[17] What caused this is debatable, yet there was no evidence, despite several decades of longitudinal research and meta-analysis, that improvement over time with stimulant medication has occurred. Another series of studies by O'Leary and his colleagues showed that when the

---

*A common statistical analysis technique in which individual research studies rather than single patients make up the database that is analyzed.

appropriate behavioral modification approach was used, children on stimulant drugs could stop medication entirely while their academic skills and general behavior continue to improve.[18] The research also showed that the learning difficulties produced the attentional problems—not the reverse—a point stressed in 1985 by McGuinness.

As for the children's opinions about the drug treatment, most said it made them feel worthless and lowered their self-esteem. In 1976, Whalen and Henker reported that children came to view the drugs as a crutch and felt unable to control their own behavior without them. They also believed their normal off-drug behavior was not their fault.[19]

McGuinness sorrowfully concludes that drug therapy has not and will not do anything to promote any academic, social, or emotional well-being for the child. Moreover, because of the initial impact of the stimulants on behavior, the medical practitioners are not going to be dislodged. She notes that all of her objections to the drugging of children have been raised before and were cavalierly dismissed. There is no evidence to support the use of drugs with children, yet their use continues and is, in fact, increasing as the biopsychiatrists gain more and more power and influence. In McGuinness's words:

> People who employ drugs, especially to modify behavior, must convince the scientific and lay communities that these drugs have no harmful effects either physiologically or psychologically, and that in addition they provide positive benefits to the child as well as to parents and teachers. So far the medical profession has utterly failed in this responsibility.[20]

Nevertheless, the war on children by the biological psychiatric establishment continues. The recent rapid rise in ADD diagnoses among the child populations is such that it has now reached epidemic proportions. What on earth has happened to our children in the last decade? Only ADD nerve beams, zapping our children from UFOs in outer space, could have suddenly and without warning thrust this insidious ailment upon all of the nation's children. Although not a problem in the 1950s, 1960s, or 1970s, in the 1980s and 1990s ADD and its companion, ADHD, have infected half of the nation's children and thousands of adults as well, who are also jittery and easily distracted and who are now diagnosed as having Adult Attention Deficit Hyperactivity Disorder (AADHD). The biologically-oriented experts insist it is genetic and there's nothing that can be done but sedate the sufferer into submission. This gets parents off the hook and improves the M.D.s' and drug companies' incomes.

Despite all claims to the contrary, the specific cause of the so-called ADD has not been determined, despite the large number of research studies labeling it a "genetic neurological disorder." As syndicated columnist John Rosemond wisely counseled, being recognized as "genetic" by several incompetently designed and seriously flawed studies in no way *proves* such a hypothesis.[21] These studies prove only that researcher bias and wishful thinking want to make it true. As Rosemond notes in his August 25, 1994, Knight-Ridder column:

> Despite millions of dollars' worth of research concerning the origins of this still mysterious syndrome, no one has isolated its cause. Even though thousands of parents yearly pay professionals to "test" their children for attention deficit disorder, there is no test, psychological or medical, that will accurately "bull's-eye" the diagnosis. A diagnosis is, therefore, an educated judgment call.
>
> Quite simply and quite factually, if there is no clear-cut evidence of disease, and if, furthermore, diagnosis cannot be scientifically confirmed, then it is impossible to make anything more than a guess as to cause.[22]

It is also quite clear that evidence of genetic influence is not proof. There is an even greater body of evidence suggesting that the ADD epidemic is primarily due to cultural and developmental, i.e., social factors, "relatively unique to the upbringing of children over the last thirty to forty years."

Rosemond also correctly notes that contrary to popular opinion, Ritalin—a central nervous system stimulant—does not work on only ADD children. Ritalin works on nearly everybody to increase their alertness and attention span. If, however, you're already alert and your attention span is normal, Ritalin will do very little. Outside observers would see little or no difference in your behavior. If you had a low attention span to begin with and then took the drug, however, an outside observer would see a change in your behavior because you were below normal to begin with. This, nevertheless, doesn't prove that a low attention span qualifies as a "disease," as the biopsychiatrists currently insist.

Before leaving the topic, attention must be called to a recent work, *The War against Children*, by Peter and Ginger Ross Breggin. The book covers this increasingly serious problem in great detail and also provides suggestions for ending the war being waged by biological psychiatry against children and giving them the proper love, attention, and care they need and deserve.[23]

NOTES

1. Ida Fogle, "The Business of Fixing People," *Alternative Press Review* (Winter 1994): 30–31.

2. Ibid., p. 30.

3. Ibid.

4. Ibid., p. 31.

5. Diane McGuinness, "Attention Deficit Disorder: The Emperor's Clothes, Animal 'Pharm,' and Other Fictions," in *The Limits of Biological Treatments for Psychological Distress*, eds. Seymour Fisher and Robert P. Greenberg (Hillsdale, N.J.: Lawrence Erlbaum Associates, 1989), p. 155.

6. D. P. Hinshaw, "On the Distinction between Attentional Deficits/ Hyperactivity and Conduct Problems/Aggression in Child Psychopathology," *Psychology Bulletin* 101 (1987): 444.

7. McGuinness, "Attention Deficit Disorder," p. 155.

8. J. Loney, J. Kramer, and R. S. Millich, "The Hyperactive Child Grows Up: Predictors of Symptoms, Delinquency, and Achievement at Follow-Ups," in *Psychosocial Aspects of Drug Treatment for Hyperactivity*, eds. K. D. Gadow and J. Loney (Boulder, Colo.: Westview Press, 1981), pp. 381–415; R. S. Millich and J. Loney, "The Role of Hyperactive and Aggressive Symptomatolgy in Predicting Adolescent Outcome among Hyperactive Children," *Journal of Pediatric Psychology* 4 (1979): 93–112; and C. E. Paternite and J. Loney, "Childhood Hyperkinesis: Relationships between Symptomatology and Home Environment," in *Hyperactive Children: The Social Ecology of Identification and Treatment*, eds. C. K. Whalen and B. Henker (New York: Academic Press, 1980), pp. 105–41.

9. M. A. Steward, C. S. de Blois, and C. Cummings, "Psychiatric Dis-

order in the Parents of Hyperactive Boys and Those with Conduct Disorder," *Journal of Child Psychology & Psychiatry* 21 (1980): 283–92.

10. G. J. August and M. A. Steward, "Familial Subtypes of Childhood Hyperactivity," *Journal of Nervous & Mental Disorders* 171 (1983): 362–68.

11. R. McGee, S. Williams, and P. A. Silva, "Factor Structure and Correlates of Inattention, Hyperactivity and Antisocial Behavior in a Large Sample of 9-Year-Old Children," *Journal of Consulting & Clinical Psychology* 53 (1985): 480–90.

12. McGuinness. "Attention Deficit Disorder," p. 160.

13. Diane McGuinness, *When Children Don't Learn* (New York: Basic Books, 1985), p. 160.

14. D. H. Sykes, V. I. Douglas, and G. Morganstern, "Sustained Attention in Hyperactive Children," *Journal of Child Psychology & Psychiatry* 14 (1973): 213–21.

15. G. Thorley, "Review of Follow-Up and Follow-Back Studies of Childhood Hyperactivity," *Psychology Bulletin* 96 (1984): 116–32.

16. R. A. Barkley and C. E. Cunningham, "Do Stimulant Drugs Improve the Academic Performance of Hyperkinetic Children?" *Clinical Pediatrics* 17 (1978): 85–92.

17. K. Kavale, "The Efficacy of Stimulant Drug Treatment for Hyperactivity: A Metaanalysis," *Journal of Learning Disabilities* 15 (1982): 280–89.

18. K. D. O'Leary et al., "Assessment of Hyperactivity: Observational and Rating Methodologies," in *Nutrition and Behavior*, ed. S. A. Miller (Philadelphia: Franklin Institute Press, 1981), pp. 291–97.

19. C. K. Whalen and B. Henker, "Psychostimulants and Children: A Review and Analysis," *Psychology Bulletin* 83 (1976): 1113–30.

20. McGuinness, "Attention Deficit Disorder," p. 184.

21. John Rosemond, "Little Is Certain about Attention Deficit Disorder," *Lexington (Kentucky) Herald-Leader*, 28 August 1994, p. E3.

22. Ibid.

23. Peter Breggin and Ginger Ross Breggin, *The War against Children* (New York: St. Martin's Press, 1994).

7

The MPD Fiasco:
Iatrogenesis Gone Berserk

The multiple personality disorder (MPD) syndrome has become a sensationalized and popular topic—dramatic and lucrative. Among the various dissociative phenomena MPD is perhaps the most fascinating. It is widely assumed in psychological and psychiatric circles that the pathology, i.e., the mental dissociation, is caused by severe abuse of the victim as a child in its formative stages. Beaten and mistreated by a warped or psychotic parent, the child concludes that if its main or primary personality is so evil and undeserving of love, then perhaps another completely different child or personality would be deserving of the needed and desired love and affection. Therefore, a new personality is born. Within the last decade cases of fugues and fugue states (temporary loss of memory and self-identity) and alternate personalities have grown like topsy within the clinical literature. The growth has been so rapid that investigators have become skeptical of many of the cases and have begun to question whether there was ever such a thing as MPD after all. Recently, such skeptics have discovered they were right in the first place: *There is no such thing as MPD!* Every case of MPD that has been carefully and thoroughly investigated since the 1960s was shown to be iatrogenic. It is now conclusively established—despite the raging protests of ego-committed psychiatrists and its inclusion in DSM-IV—that all so-called multiple personalities have been created by the therapist himself!

309

As far back as 1959, Rawcliffe argued most persuasively that not only are true cases of multiple personality quite rare, but that in nearly every so-called case of MPD, the therapist's own treatments and experiments were mainly responsible for the emergence of the subsidiary personalities.[1] Since the hysterical neurotic is normally so highly suggestible and hypnosis is the standard method of treatment, it is easy to see why many of the cases of MPD could be due simply to suggestion. They are artificial, therapist-hypnotist created personalities. As noted in the previous chapter, since so many therapists are now extremely sensitive to possible cases of child abuse, and since child abuse is the clearly recognized ("believed") cause of MPD, every case of early abuse —believed or verified—is now seen by the psychotherapeutic flock as the cause of multiple personality. And, it is well known if you look for something hard enough you are sure to find it!

The first secular description of pathological MPD is generally attributed to Paracelsus in 1646, who reported the case of a woman who was amnesic of an alter personality who stole her money.[2] Rare reports of such cases that appeared over the next two centuries generally ascribed pathology to the patient rather than the presence of a supernatural power. Nevertheless, the idea of demonic possession never really died and is still entertained as a causative factor by some psychologists and psychiatrists today.[3] In 1889, Pierre Janet emphasized the importance of trauma in the etiology of MPD.[4] At the turn of the century, the concept of dissociation was offered as the psychic defense mechanism that caused the personality split. Even when it was finally accepted as a true clinical entity it was considered to be extremely rare.

In 1816 S. L. Mitchell described the case of Mary Reynolds, a young English woman in her early twenties who fell into a deep sleep and upon awakening lost all prior memory and had to learn everything all over again. After a few months she had another attack of somnolence and upon arousal she was restored to her earlier self, but she could remember nothing of what had happened in between the two sleep states. For the next four years she underwent periodical transitions from one of the states to the other. The old and new personalities continued to alternate until her death.[5] This disorder was so rare no cases were reported between 1846 and 1877. After approximately 1905 most cases were reported as having more than two personalities and the condition became known as "multiple personality disorder." Morton Prince used hypnosis to study the alternates and his thinking had a great influence on later investigators—particularly his notion of a cerebral mechanism that caused the personality to disintegrate.[6] Nothing really new developed until Taylor and Martin identified twenty-eight cases in the literature between 1874 and 1900 and described three varieties: the mutually amnesic, the one-way amnesic, and the co-conscious types. They also argued that hypnosis could in no way account for the symptoms.[7]

In 1957 Thigpen and Cleckley published *The Three Faces of Eve*, and a diagnostic epidemic began. Eve's case set off a veritable deluge of diagnosis and popularization. Schreiber's *Sybil* appeared in 1973 and other, similar stories quickly followed.[8] Over three hundred cases were reported in the medical literature. Seventy-nine occurred between 1970 and 1981, but only eight cases were noted in the twenty-five-year period prior to this.[9] In 1980, in the DSM-III, Multiple Personality Disorder was listed as a diagnosis among the dissociative states. The disorder could be identified by the existence within the person of two or more distinct personalities, each of whom is dominant at a particular time and when dominant determines the individual's behavior. Each personality is complex and integrated and has its own unique behavior patterns and social relationships.

Predictably, these criteria were severely criticized as excessively vague and open to a wide variety of interpretations. The failure to provide a satisfactory description of "personality" in the context of the diagnostic criteria was also considered fatal. Annual workshops held by the American Psychiatric Association in combination with the dramatic portrayal of the sufferers in movies, on television, and in the popular press led to an increased number of patients showing up in the clinics. This was also the beginning of the end.

In 1987 Chodoff suggested that the increase in case reporting clearly reflected iatrogenic and cultural influences on suggestible patients.[10] This, when added to an upsurge of interest in child abuse, particularly satanic ritual abuse (SRA); hypnosis; and post-traumatic stress disorder also attracted therapists to the problem. Without fail, the popularization of all such sensationalistic phenomena, be it ghosts, UFOs, satanic cults, past lives, near-death experiences, and other such legendary events invariably produce a rapid and predictable proliferation of these occurrences in the general population. Such social-psychological phenomena have been observed and noted throughout the centuries. During the Middle Ages demon possession grew by leaps and bounds and the first few cases became thousands as the news spread from town to town. As for MPD, in 1984 Drs. Thigpen and Cleckley reported that over the twenty-five years following their book hundreds of patients, both self-diagnosed and those referred by other therapists, arrived in their office. Of all these cases, Thigpen and Cleckley found only one that was "undeniably a genuine multiple personality."[11]

Following Chodoff's lead, the entire edifice of MPD as a noniatrogenic disorder began to crumble. In 1985 Spanos, Weeks, and Bertrand threw a very large and disabling wrench into the therapeutic machinery with an experimental demonstration of just how easy it is to have normal individuals "role play" multiple personalities. Rather than being passive, ineffectual victims of unconscious processes that temporarily "take control" and "show up as new identities," Spanos and associates see these individuals as people who learn to play the role of an MPD patient. They follow the lead of their therapists and learn how to play the game perfectly in order to reap all the benefits for doing so—the admiration and esteem due a person with "a dramatic set of symptoms who overcomes numerous obstacles and eventually gains dignity, esteem, and much sympathetic attention from significant, high-status others."[12] It is also well known that many therapists argue that in any suspected case of MPD hypnotic procedures should be used to "bring forth" the other personalities. Allison and Schwarz, for example, state that clients are frequently reluctant to accept that they are multiple personalities and, under these circumstances, must be actively persuaded by the therapist to accept this diagnosis.[13] Various "experts" recommend hypnosis as the way to identify the number of indwelling identities and for communicating with them separately, in order to discover their individual characteristics. As Spanos and associates note,

Clinicians vary quite dramatically in the extent to which they deem it appropriate to encourage and legitimate enactments of multiple identity. It is little wonder, therefore, that some therapists are much more likely than others to "discover" cases of multiple personality, or that the recent upsurge in the number of such patients parallels increased interest in the disorder.

... From a social psychological perspective the amnesia displayed by multiple personality patients constitutes strategic enactment. This does not mean that such displays of forgetting are faked. It does suggest, however, that these patients maintain control over memory processes and enact displays of forgetting by exercising control in a goal-directed manner.[14]

Evidence also exists that posthypnotic suggestions to the primary personality intimating that it will gradually become aware of the other "hidden" personalities, or suggestions that encourage all the personalities to share their memories do work to increase the recall of previously "hidden" memories. Hypnosis alone wouldn't do this, but the "hypnosis" does provide an excuse for making the "memories" accessible.

What Spanos and coworkers have clarified is that although most patients who adopt an MPD role are not doing so to escape a murder charge (as in the case of the Hillside Strangler*), in the typical psychotherapy situation they do "go along" with the therapist's suggestions as a "socially acceptable" way of blaming someone else for shameful, disavowed, or unacceptable behavior. Young children do this often and will say "I didn't break the vase. The bad me did it—but he didn't mean to." It is also true that multiples are nearly always highly imaginative people with rich fantasy lives who, as children, created imaginary playmates. In addition, they are also easily hypnotized. They are highly prone to suggestion. In summary, multiples are people who are adept at playing a role whenever the situation makes it advantageous to do so. This also requires that one's background be interpreted in a manner to support the notion of "being a multiple," namely, imagining a childhood of incest or satanic ritual abuse. For people who have had a lot of practice in imagining themselves in different roles or in

---

*Ken Bianchi, the Hillside Strangler, was a murderer who faked MPD in order to avoid taking responsibility for the murders he had committed.

being different people, those who are good fantasizers, having alternate personalities is no problem at all.

In 1988 Paul Dell published a survey showing that 78 percent of therapists working with MPDs had encountered intense skepticism from fellow professionals regarding the authenticity of the disorder.[15] This was followed by a critical review of the diagnosis of MPD by Thomas Fahy, who argued convincingly that there is little or no evidence to support the reliability of the diagnosis and its prevalence. He also showed clearly that iatrogenic factors contributed to the development of the syndrome and that neither genetic nor physiological studies support the claim that MPD is a distinct psychiatric disorder.[16] In general, as Taylor and Martin stated in 1944, "Apparently most ready to accept multiple personality as real are (1) persons who are very naive and (2) persons who have worked with actual cases or near cases."[17]

It has also been emphasized that the psychotherapist could easily become an unwitting accomplice in molding the presentation, both by providing the patient with information, and by his selective reinforcement of the symptoms. The practice of interviewing the alternates at length and giving them names adds to the complexity of the alternate. In this fashion, each personality acquires a history, a function, and elaborate patterns of behavior. By selectively reinforcing one of the alternates an increase in the frequency of the appearance of that alternate has been reported.[18] This and similar studies show clearly that symptoms can be shaped iatrogenically. There is no doubt but that the disorder is most commonly reported during periods when the diagnosis is fashionable and in situations where patients have been treated, often over a lengthy period, in psychotherapy. Diagnosis increases to the extent that MPD is promoted as a high-status disorder, with consequent sick-role privileges (including the convenient excuse that one cannot be held responsible for his actions because he's sick, for example). The attempt to create a separate syndrome of MPD follows the precedent of hysteria in the nineteenth century when the diagnosis was conferred as a "halo of glory."[19] The diagnosis of hysteria may not only be a delusion but also a snare, and the warning is especially appropriate to MPD, where the hysterical symptom has been precipitously and uncritically inflated to a final diagnosis.

Curiously enough, in the *Harvard Newsletter* of September 1993, Dr. Paul R. McHugh, director of the Department of Psychiatry at Johns Hopkins stated, "Prompted by the unexpected flourishing of this extraordinary diagnosis, students often ask me whether multiple personality disorder (MPD) really exists. I usually reply that the symptoms attributed to it are as genuine as hysterical paralysis and seizures and teach us lessons already learned by psychiatrists more than a hundred years ago."[20] McHugh goes on to tell the story of Charcot, who argued he had discovered a new disease called "hystero-epilepsy." Joseph Babinski, one of Charcot's students, however, argued the point, claiming that his teacher had invented rather than discovered the disorder. Babinski eventually won the argument and he was even successful in persuading Charcot that doctors can induce a variety of physical and mental disorders, especially in young, inexperienced, and emotionally troubled women. There was no "hystero-epilepsy." As McHugh notes, "These patients were afflicted not by a disease but by an idea."

Charcot and Babinski then developed a two-stage treatment consisting of social isolation and countersuggestions which proved to be dramatically effective in eliminating the disorder. McHugh stresses that the rules discovered by Babinski and Charcot and now contained in the psychiatric textbooks have been overlooked. McHugh states, "MPD is an iatrogenic behavioral syndrome, promoted by suggestion and maintained by clinical attention, social consequences and group loyalties. It rests on ideas about the self that obscure reality and it responds to standard treatments."[21] McHugh goes on to say that MPD, like hystero-epilepsy, is created by therapists and the diagnosis did not become popular until several books and movies appeared.

McHugh also cites the work of Dr. Stephen E. Buie, director of the Dissociative Disorders Treatment Program in North Carolina:

> It may happen that an alter personality will reveal itself to you during this [assessment] process, but more likely it will not. So you may have to elicit an alter. . . . You can begin by indirect [*sic*] questioning such as, "Have you ever felt like another part of you does things that you can't control?" If she gives positive or ambiguous responses ask for specific examples. You are trying to develop a picture of what the alter personality is like. . . . At this point you may ask the host

personality, "Does this set of feelings have a name?" . . . Often the
host personality will not know. You can then focus upon a particular event or set of behaviors. "Can I talk to the part of you that is
taking those long drives in the country . . . Once patients have permitted a psychiatrist to "talk to the part . . . that is taking these
long drives," they are committed to the idea that they have MPD
and must act in ways consistent with this self-image.[22]

Agreeing with Spanos, McHugh sees the entire process as social
role playing. After the first alter emerges, the reality barrier is broken
and fantasizing is reinforced. Both patient and therapist now start
searching for additional alters surrounding the core personality. Frequently the original two or three alters will proliferate into twenty,
fifty, or even one hundred or more. A dramatic script also begins to
unfold: some of the alters will be of the opposite sex. One of the alters
may even be an animal. A dog or cat will be sought and it will also
know how to talk. Once the word has spread, the emergence of every
succeeding alter generates great interest among the hospital staff and
further implants the belief in other hidden alters. When this stage is
reached it is almost impossible for the patient to confess that he or she
is playing a game and to say to the therapist, "This is ridiculous, let's
stop this nonsense!"

It is especially difficult if the patient is told by the therapist that
the disorder is due to a horrible childhood sexual trauma—one so terrible it has been broken off, split away from the primary personality,
and is now hidden in the alters. Together the patient and the therapist
begin to search out the alters who remember the abuse and the abuser.
In McHugh's words, "commitment to the diagnosis of MPD is enhanced by the sense that a crime is being exposed and justice is being
done. The patient now has such a powerful vested interest in sustaining the MPD enterprise that it almost becomes an end in itself."[23]

Many patients did indeed suffer from traumatic experiences and
many may also be suffering from emotional disorders and difficulties,
but the patient's *real* problems should not be overlooked by attending
to the iatrogenically induced dramatic symptoms. In most cases once
the therapist has settled in on MPD treatment may become inter-
minable when therapists concentrate on fascinating symptoms. "It is

no wonder," McHugh notes, "that MPD is regarded as a chronic disorder that often requires long stretches of time in dissociative units."

McHugh's solution to the MPD problem is simple: Close all dissociative services; disperse the patients to general psychiatric units; and ignore the alters. Stop talking to them, taking notes on them, or discussing them in staff conferences. Attend to real and present problems rather than the fantasies.

When therapists direct attention away from the patient's alters and shift the therapeutic focus to other things such as problems in living, the patient's MPD behavior declines and the alters disappear.[24] A fascinating aspect of MPD iatrogenesis was demonstrated in a hospital ward in 1973. An MPD case with three different personalities was housed there, and the psychiatric staff interacted with each personality in a different manner. Once baseline behavior rates were established, the staff selectively reinforced, i.e., praised and rewarded, only one of the personalities. Thereafter the behaviors associated with the reinforced personality increased dramatically, whereas the others stayed the same. In later extinction trials, the reinforced personality also declined to the baseline level.[25]

Another brilliant psychiatrist is Dr. George Ganaway, who argues for a psychodynamic approach rather than the "currently popular but arguably simplistic trauma/dissociation theory as an explanation for MPD."[26] After being directly involved in the assessment and treatment of over 250 MPD patients in the last decade, Ganaway says that trying to carry out controlled studies with dissociative patients is very much like "trying to eat soup with a fork." The elusive and protean nature of their symptoms makes formal scientific inquiries almost impossible. Nevertheless, a large number of repeated clinical observations make it clear that (1) it has not been convincingly proven that childhood trauma *causes* MPD; (2) the entire scenario easily lends itself to iatrogenic influences in vulnerable individuals who already may have been through years of treatment under other diagnostic labels; (3) hypnotic techniques used in MPD diagnosis and to retrieve the alleged trauma memories is perpetuating the myth of the etiology and nature of MPD; (4) most MPDs are highly suggestible, fantasy-prone, have a dissociative character disorder and often turn the therapist into the ideal nurturer who will never abandon the patient, as long as the patient has one more trauma memory to uncover or one more hidden personality to reveal, (5) the resulting transference/countertransference quagmire leads to *stakes abreacticus*: the patient in trance, acts out for the therapist's fascination and approval an increasingly expansive repertoire of what both grow to believe are factual trauma memories involving layer after layer of often previously unknown personalities; (6) many therapists unwittingly encourage and reinforce the client's MPD symptoms—especially therapists who believe they are themselves survivors of childhood trauma; and (7) invasive hypnotic tactics and techniques increase the client's belief in his own multiplicity and an outpouring of reconstructed memories "that may, and I suspect frequently do, contain more fantasy than fact."

Ganaway candidly admits, "Multiple personality disorder may, in fact, be a valid clinical dissociative syndrome, but not necessarily based on what patients are telling us (or we are telling them) about it."[27] He also emphasizes that MPD patients are particularly adept at creating false memories since they rely so heavily on fantasy and magical thinking. Their alternate personalities often take the form of demons, angels, animals, God, or other entities that can exist in such places as enchanted forests or separate galaxies. It is also important to again note that in spite of the ubiquity of the reports of traumatic memories and tales of ritual abuse on the part of MPD patients, researchers have rarely corroborated these claims of childhood sexual abuse.[28]

The large pile of evidence showing clearly and unmistakably that MPD was a creation directly out of the mind of the psychiatrist led English psychologist Ray Aldridge-Morris to write an entire book exposing MPD as the result of a role assumed by the patient and encouraged by social reinforcement from an enthusiastic but misguided therapist who is responding to cultural pressure.[29] As a cultural phenomenon, it is interesting to note that the MPD diagnosis has many supporters in North America, but is viewed with skepticism everywhere else and is rarely, if ever, found in Japan or Britain.

More recently, the Canadian psychiatrist Merskey argued that because of the widespread publicity surrounding the concept, it is doubtful that any case of MPD can now arise that is not specifically promoted by suggestion or prior preparation by a therapist.[30] To determine if MPD was ever a spontaneous phenomenon, Merskey examined in detail case after case reported in the early literature giving particular attention to alternative diagnoses that could account for the phenomena as well as to the specific ways in which the first alternate personality merged. The earlier cases involved amnesia, striking fluctuations in mood, and sometimes cerebral organic disorder. The secondary personalities frequently appeared following hypnosis and several amnesiac patients were specifically trained to come up with new identities. Many others showed overt iatrogenesis. None of the reports fully excluded the possibility of artificial production. Merskey concludes his long and careful review with the statement that the diagnosis of MPD today represents a total misdirection of therapeutic effort and this misdirection seriously hinders the resolution of serious psychological problems in the lives of patients:

> No case has been found here in which MPD, as now conceived, is proven to have emerged through unconscious processes without any shaping or preparation by external factors such as physicians or the media. In respect of this argument, we may have reached a situation comparable to Heisenberg's principle of uncertainty: observation of the phenomena changes it. If this is true it means that no later case, probably since Prince, but at least since the film *The Three Faces of Eve*, can be taken to be veridical since none is likely to emerge without prior knowledge of the idea. . . .
>
> It is likely that MPD never occurs as a spontaneous persistent natural event in adults. The cases examined here have not shown any original conditions which are more autonomous than a fugue or a second identity promoted by overt fantasies or conscious awareness. The most that may be expected without iatrogenesis is that an overt inclination for another role could cause the adoption of different conscious patterns of life. . . . Without reinforcement, such secondary changes would ordinarily be expected to vanish.
>
> Suggestion, social encouragement, preparation by expectation, and the reward of attention can produce and sustain a second personality.
>
> Admittedly, if only those physicians who expect the disorder can see it, those who do not believe in it cannot see it. However, like

others, I was willing to entertain its existence and never found it myself before the dramatic rise in reported cases or since. Meanwhile it is not necessary to treat patients who have had terrible childhoods and who have conversion symptoms, by developing in them an additional belief in fresh personalities. Enthusiasm for the phenomenon is a means of increasing it.[31]

These paragraphs could just as well have been written referring to the alien abduction syndrome instead of the production of multiple personalities. Quite clearly, suggestion, social encouragement, preparation by expectation, and the reward of attention can produce and sustain the belief in an alien abduction as well as in MPD. Moreover, physicians and therapists who believe in and expect the disorder can see it, those who do not believe in it cannot see it.

Finally, in considering how patients, doctors, and other therapists come to believe in MPD or to present the popular pattern, Merskey offers four explanations as to how MPD is created: (1) the misinterpretation of organic or bipolar illness; (2) the conscious development of fantasies as a solution to emotional problems; (3) the development of hysterical amnesia, followed by retraining by the therapist; and (4) the creation by implicit demand of alters under hypnosis or by repeated interviews.

As noted earlier, Spanos emphasized the iatrogenic dimension within his social psychological conceptualization of MPD. In this model the patient is seen as actively involved in using the information available to him to create a social impression that is compatible with his objectives. Thus the individual learns to enact the MPD role, collecting impressions from movies, TV talk shows, and books where MPD victims are sympathetically portrayed. Spanos's most recent paper expands his earlier work to emphasize that the disease perspective of MPD is fundamentally flawed.[32] Spanos uses experimental, cross cultural, and historical findings to show that neither childhood trauma nor a history of psychopathology is necessary for people to develop multiple "selves." In the last twenty years in North America the idea of multiple personality has become a way for people to express their failures and frustrations as well as a covert tactic by which they can manipulate others and attain sympathy, succor, and other rewards.

According to Spanos, patients learn to play the role of a multiple and their therapists encourage them, tell them how to be good at it, and then legitimize it. Historically, MPD has been closely tied to hypnosis. Recently, however, the conventional ideas of hypnosis have been challenged, especially ideas about hypnotic amnesia which is rarely complete even among the highly hypnotizable subjects. Moreover, Spanos has shown that so-called hidden selves can be produced without resorting to hypnotic procedures. Past-life-regression experiences are also fantasy constructions and such "past lives" are very similar to the multiple identities of MPD patients. In summary, all of the evidence clearly shows that multiple identities are social creations that are easily elicited from many perfectly normal people.

Cross-cultural studies of spirit possession also support Spanos's contentions. The idea of spirit possession, that some alien spirit temporarily takes control of the body, occurs in most—but not all—cultures. In all of these cultures however, only a very small percentage is ever seen as "possessed." The number and frequency of possessions varies with the cultures. In the more advanced and highly civilized cultures, possession is less frequently encountered. In our own culture, glossolalia (speaking in tongues) and spirit mediumship (including channeling) are common examples of "believed" spirit possession. Of course, most mediums when subjected to careful study and investigation are found to be fraudulent.[33] In many other societies, Spanos notes, spirit possession occurs as part of a helping ritual; the spirits take over a human body to give aid and advice to help solve human problems. At times, ritual possession can involve several people who are possessed simultaneously. In many tribes, becoming a medium involves a long and extensive socialization process and when the individuals subject to demon possession become possessed it is fascinating to observe how sensitive such role enactments are to sociocultural changes. Possession is also often used as a form of political and social protest by many people and it may also become a form of social contagion.

Therapists sympathetic to the MPD diagnosis have always managed to find high rates of occurrence whereas others have not. MPD appears to be a "culture bound" syndrome. Such a diagnosis is rare in France, Great Britain, Russia, and India. As noted earlier, a 1990 sur-

vey in Japan failed to find a single case. In a Swiss study it was found
that 66 percent of MPD diagnoses were made by only six out of 655
therapists.[34] Spanos correctly argues that historical changes in the incidence rates of MPD, the substantial national differences in incidence,
and the large differences in the frequency with which different clinicians make the diagnosis cannot be accounted for in terms of a "disease" perspective. In other words, like demon possession, MPD seems
to be a social creation authored by therapists. It is also obvious that the
large majority of people so diagnosed do not enter therapy with the
symptoms of the disorder evident. The symptoms are "discovered" by
the clinicians who see MPD as a hidden syndrome which they discover
with their great clinical knowledge and skill.

Some of the nonsense that the MPD clinicians propagate as
"indicative of" or "signs" of the disorder boggle the mind. According
to one so-called authority, "a smooth complexion might indicate MPD
because the regular switching of alternate personalities prevents the
formation of wrinkles."[35] Headaches, depression, periods of missing
time, impaired concentration, hallucinations, fatigue, sexual dysfunction, and drug abuse are other symptoms. Obviously, such symptoms
are indicative of a lot of problems other than MPD! Once the diagnosis is suspected the MPD diagnoser goes after it with a vengeance, asking leading and explicit questions, calling for and suggesting alters
and hidden selves until the poor client gives in and supplies the therapist with what is demanded. Using hypnosis, the alters are, quite literally, dragged out of the patient. Spanos notes that the case of Ken
Bianchi—the notorious Hillside Strangler—is a classic example of
how the naive clinician elicits the alleged various "hidden personalities." Spanos also emphasizes the fact that the hypnotic interviews
used to diagnose MPD exactly mirror the Catholic exorcism procedures and accordingly obtain the obligatory "confession" of numbers
of indwelling "demons."

Advocacy of the MPD diagnosis has taken on the characteristics of
a social movement which Spanos argues is supported by MPD workshops, conferences, newsletters, and self-help therapy groups. Many
multiples now enjoy their MPD status and insist they will remain this
way. Some of the therapists are themselves former multiples.

Spanos concludes his argument with the view that the importance of the psychotherapists and their therapy—and related social supports in the creation and maintenance of MPD—cannot be overemphasized. This does not mean that MPD patients typically fake their multiplicity, but it does mean they see themselves the same way their therapist does. Multiplicity can occur in the absence of early child abuse and a major reason abuse has been linked with multiplicity is due to the fact that a large proportion of people seeking therapy—particularly women—are likely to report a history of child abuse. Since so many clinicians have been told this is a possible sign of MPD, more abused than nonabused patients are given "hypnotic" interviews and other diagnostic procedures that generate the MPD. In other words, "early abuse = MPD" becomes a self-fulfilling prophecy.

It is important to remember that some MPD patients do not recall having been abused in childhood until the therapist "discovers" their multiplicity. Then, after being pushed, the patients confabulate their abuse; they fantasize and think the memories are veridical. Again, it is important to remember that the evidence to support the theory that abuse causes dissociation and that the abuse memories are repressed does not exist. Memory is reconstructive and is congruent with current expectations. Hypnosis does not enhance the accuracy of recall.[36] Further, when MPD patients report they have no memories of being abused, therapists tend to disbelieve them and use leading and suggestive procedures to implant abuse memories where none exist. This is particularly true in cases of satanic ritual abuse. In a 1991 national survey of psychologists with regard to patients reporting ritual abuse, 70 percent reported they had never seen such patients. Only a small minority reported having seen large numbers. It would appear that the therapists with large numbers must be helping to shape their patients' memories. Anyone doubting this should read a 1992 report by Whitley. Several former patients from the same psychiatric clinic reported ritual abuse memories during therapy but later insisted they weren't true. The patients (some diagnosed as MPD) said their reports of early abuse were fantasies suggested and encouraged by their therapist and by other patients in their therapy groups. They were pressured to dream up reports of severe abuse and were told to believe they were memories as opposed to fantasies.[37]

The work of Spanos and many others leaves no doubt whatsoever as to the real cause of the MPD disorder. The disease theory is

> a local theory—and based on the idea that unhappiness and/or behavioral deviance in adulthood stems from particular traumatic events occurring in childhood. . . . Because of its emphasis on childhood antecedents and on the notion that "symptoms" reflect unconscious defenses, this approach tends to greatly deemphasize the social and strategic nature of multiple identity enactments. . . . It also deflects attention from the marked changes in symptomatology that have occurred in MPD over the years; changes that illustrate the role of social factors in shaping MPD displays. Since the 19th century, for example, the number of personalities per patient has jumped from two or three to often over 20, and sometimes into the hundreds. . . . Like other local theories the disease theory fails to provide a general account of multiplicity that takes into consideration its cross cultural and trans-historical manifestations.[38]

Before leaving the topic, a recent report by the noted hypnosis researcher Dr. Martin Orne and his colleague Dr. B. L. Bates is worthy of note. The authors draw a parallel between the clarification and understanding of hypnotic phenomena and that of MPD. Previously, MPD was a relatively benign condition whereas today MPD patients are severely disorganized and dangerously unpredictable. As in the case with hypnosis, the behavior and subjective experiences of MPD patients are "strongly influenced by the expectations and beliefs of both hypnotist and subject. In fact, hypnosis and MPD share a checkered past, marked by short periods of intense interest, during which outrageous and unsubstantiated claims were frequently made, followed by extended droughts of scientific and clinical attention."[39] One investigator has gone so far as to argue that MPD is due directly to the patient's abuse of self-hypnosis and such misuse is the primary mechanism of the disorder.[40] Orne and Bates remind us that neither hypnosis nor MPD can be studied directly. They have to be "inferred" on the basis of the patient's reports. Orne and Bates also note that the beliefs and expectations of what is going on during the hypnotic experience determines exactly what occurs. The failure of both the clinician and his patients to understand that MPD is "shaped by the culture and their own preconceptions underscores the insidious manner in which these forces exert their influence."[41]

Orne and Bates also note that clinicians believe in separate personalities in one body "because of the evidence." Evidence, in this instance however, is always the behavior of their patients, which does indeed differ dramatically from time to time. So does behavior differ radically when patients are subject to hypnotic age regression. A 1951 study by Orne clearly showed that hypnotic age-regression does not produce an individual who functions at the suggested age level either physiologically or psychologically. Instead, it produces an individual who has the "subjective experience of being younger" but who in fact retains all of his adult modes of cognitive and emotional functioning.[42] Studies of the performances of alter personalities shows the same phenomena. Despite many hysterical claims, in no way are any of these alters functionally autonomous entities. They are, rather, "symbolic caricatures" of some aspects of the patient's original self. Orne and Bates insist that recent attempts to establish the physiological independence of various alters are taking the same misguided path hypnosis researchers took forty years ago when they attempted to find physiological markers for "hypnosis." Thus far, all studies arguing for the physiological autonomy of alternate personalities have been found to be methodologically inadequate and lacking in adequate controls.[43]

These facts, when taken in addition to what is known about the reconstructive nature of memory and the ease with which memories may be created or altered, clearly indicate that all clinicians should be very careful in their treatment efforts not to exacerbate the client's presenting symptoms. Above all, the therapist should be aware not only of the iatrogenic nature of MPD but also that it is essentially a disorder of the self due to a problem of memory. Some patients have been abused and within the confines of psychotherapy they may and do report this. Nevertheless, it is not appropriate for the therapist to advise clients to seek legal retribution and revenge. The therapist should help his client deal with the feelings of victimization and anger. What should not be done is to recreate a dubious and traumatic past, vivifying negative memories, and attempting to expunge purely fictional and imaginary horrors. A better course is to help the clients put these hurts and harms behind them and to get on with their life. Therapy should focus on the meaning of remote memories rather than on their accuracy and on the present and the future which are amenable to change rather than a past which is both unreachable and unalterable.

In spite of the fact that it is now well known that MPD can be faked, this information has not trickled down into the current judicial system. In the spring of 1994 the Kentucky State Court of Appeals sided with a woman who claimed she was not responsible for her marital infidelity as a result of her multiple personality disorder. It was not *her* but one of her other personalities that had an affair. Because of her infidelity her ex-husband argued he should not be required to support her after their divorce. Two of the three appeal court judges sided with the woman while the third wrote a stinging dissent. Accusing the other two judges of embracing a legal standard "more in keeping with the 'psycho-babble' now prevalent on television talk shows than with sound jurisprudence," the dissenting judge also noted that the majority opinion also ignored statutory requirements that maintenance can be based on conduct in the marriage. He also stated, "While it may be accepted in some trendy circles that the victim is always to blame and no one guilty of misconduct should ever be held personally accountable for his or her actions, the law with the wisdom of human experience does not accept such a view." Had the other two judges been better informed about the true nature of MPD, they might have ruled otherwise.

This case, unfortunately, shows quite clearly the need for our legal system to be better informed about psychological matters and to rely less heavily on the out-of-date biases and uninformed opinions of too many of the nation's shrinks.

In time, if we are fortunate and are able to break the stranglehold such shrinks have on the North American public, MPD will join the other iatrogenic disorders (SRA, false memories, alien abductions, and so forth) on the garbage dump of medical history.

NOTES

1. D. Rawcliffe, *The Psychology of the Occult: Illusions and Delusions of the Supernatural and the Occult* (New York: Dover, 1959).

2. Sherrill Mulhern, "Satanism and Psychotherapy: A Rumor in Search of an Inquisition," in *The Satanism Scare*, eds. J. T. Richardson, Joel Best, and D. G. Bromley (Hawthorne, N.Y.: De Gruyter, 1991).

3. Some of those holding this view include M. Scott Peck, "A Psychiatrist's View of Exorcism," *Fate* 37, no. 9 (September 1984): 87–96; Ralph B. Allison and T. Schwartz, *Minds in Many Pieces* (New York: Rawson, 1980); Colin Ross, *Multiple Personality Disorder: Diagnosis, Clinical Features, and Treatment* (New York: John Wiley & Sons, 1989); and Edith Fiore, *The Unquiet Dead: A Psychologist Treats Spirit Possession* (New York: Doubleday & Co., 1987).

4. Pierre Janet, *Major Symptoms of Hysteria* (New York: Macmillan, 1920).

5. S. L. Mitchell, "A Double Consciousness or Duality of Person in the Same Individual," *Medical Repository* 3 (1816): 185–86.

6. Morton Prince, *The Dissociation of a Personality*, 2d ed. (London: Longmans Green, 1908).

7. W. S. Taylor and M. F. Martin, "Multiple Personality," *Journal of Abnormal Social Psychology* 39 (1944): 281–300.

8. See C. H. Thigpen and H. Cleckley, *The Three Faces of Eve* (London: Secker & Warburg, 1957); Flora Schreiber, *Sybil* (Chicago: Regnery, 1973); and H. Hanksworth and T. Schwarz, *The Five of Me* (New York: Pocket Books, 1977) among others.

9. Thomas A. Fahy, "The Diagnosis of Multiple Personality Disorder: A Critical Review," *British Journal of Psychiatry* 153 (1988): 597–606.

10. P. Chodoff, "More on Multiple Personality Disorder," *American Journal of Psychiatry* 144 (1987): 124.

11. C. H. Thigpen and H. M. Cleckley, "On the Incidence of Multiple Personality Disorder," *International Journal of Clinical & Experimental Hypnosis* 32 (1984): 63–66.

12. N. P. Spanos, J. R. Weeks, and L. D. Bertrand, "Multiple Personality: A Social Psychological Perspective," *Journal of Abnormal Psychology* 9 (1985): 362–76.

13. Allison and Schwarz, *Minds in Many Pieces*.

14. Spanos, Weeks, and Bertrand, "Multiple Personality," p. 374.

15. Paul F. Dell, "Professional Skepticism about Multiple Personality," *Journal of Nervous & Mental Disease* 176, no. 9 (1988): 528–30.

16. Fahy, "The Diagnosis of Multiple Personality Disorder."

17. W. S. Taylor and M. F. Martin, "Multiple Personality," *Journal of Abnormal & Social Psychology* 39 (1944): 281–300.

18. R. J. Kohlenberg, "Behavioristic Approach to Multiple Personality: A Case Study," *Behavior Therapy* 4 (1973): 137–40.

19. Fahy, "The Diagnosis of Multiple Personality Disorder," p. 604.

20. Paul R. McHugh, "Multiple Personality Disorder," *Harvard Newsletter* (September 1993): 4–6.

21. Ibid., p. 5.

22. Ibid., p. 6.

23. Ibid.

24. Fahy, "The Diagnosis of Multiple Personality Disorder," p. 600.

25. Kohlenberg, "Behavioristic Approach to Multiple Personality."

26. George K. Ganaway, "Critical Issues Task Force Report: Validity of Reports of Childhood Abuse," *International Society for Study of Multiple Personality & Dissociation News* 9, no. 6 (1991): 6.

27. George K. Ganaway, "Hypnosis, Dissociation and Multiple Personality Disorder: A Psychodynamic Clinician's Perspective," (Paper presented at MPD Symposium, 43rd Annual Convention of the Society of Experimental and Clinical Hypnosis, Washington, D.C., October, 1992).

28. Fred H. Frankel, "Adult Reconstruction of Childhood Events in the Multiple Personality Literature," *American Journal of Psychiatry* 150, no. 6 (June 1993): 954–58.

29. Ray Aldridge-Morris, *Multiple Personality Disorder: An Exercise in Deception* (London: Lawrence Erlbaum Associates, 1989).

30. H. Merskey, "The Manufacture of Personalities: The Production of Multiple Personality Disorder," *British Journal of Psychiatry* 160 (1992): 327–40.

31. Ibid., p. 337.

32. N. P. Spanos, "Multiple Identity Enactments and Multiple Personality Disorder: A Sociocognitive Perspective," *Psychological Bulletin* 116, no. 1 (July 1994): 143–65.

33. For example, Lamar M. Keene, *The Psychic Mafia: As Told to Allen Spraggett* (New York: Dell, 1977).

34. Spanos, "Multiple Identity Enactments."

35. Ibid., p. 144.

36. Robert A. Baker, *Hidden Memories* (Amherst, N.Y.: Prometheus Books, 1991).

37. G. Whitley, "Abuse of Trust," *D. Magazine* (January 1992): 36–39.

38. Spanos, "Multiple Identity Enactments," p. 160.

39. Martin T. Orne and Brad L. Bates, "Reflections on Multiple Personality Disorder: A View from the Looking Glass of Hypnosis Past," in *The Mosaic of Contemporary Psychiatry in Perspective*, eds. A. Kales, C. M. Pierce, and M. Greenblat (New York: Springer-Verlag, 1993), p. 248.

40. E. L. Bliss, "A Symptom Profile of Patients with Multiple Personalities with MMPI Results," *Journal of Nervous & Mental Disease* 172 (1984): 197–202.

41. Orne and Bates, "Reflections on Multiple Personality Disorder," p. 249.

42. Martin T. Orne, "The Mechanisms of Hypnotic Age Regression: An Experimental Study," *Journal of Abnormal & Social Psychology* 46 (1951): 213–25.

43. Orne and Bates, "Reflections on Multiple Personality Disorder," p. 254.

8

The Diagnostic and
Statistical Manual:
The Culmination of Psychiatry?

*Psychiatry is an unidentified technique applied to unspecified problems with
unpredictable outcomes . . . for which long and vigorous training is required.*
Victor Rainy[1]

Q: Is all human behavior diseased?
A: Yes, according to the American Psychiatric Association's DSM-IV

According to syndicated conservative George Will, things have
reached the point where a person has the right to "be a colossally ob-
noxious jerk on the job"[2] and can get away with it because the American Psychiatric Association and the *Diagnostic and Statistical Manual
of Mental Disorders* see such behavior as a mental disability for which
one can be treated and compensated. Will is commenting on the work
of D. E. Zuriff, a clinical psychologist whose article "Medicating Character" inveighs against the APA for now considering what was once
seen as irresponsibility, faults of behavior, and character flaws as illnesses or personality disorders akin to physical disabilities.[3] This is the
worst of all the various forms of iatrogenesis.

The "medicalizing" of all human behavior has now reached the
point that doctors as well as patients are becoming victims of the medical–pharmaceutical–insurance company complex that runs and man-

330

ages the multibillion dollar mental health industry. One of the industry's most important management tools was the DSM-III-R; in 1994 and beyond it is the DSM-IV, namely, *The Diagnostic and Statistical Manual of Mental Disorders* (third edition, revised, and fourth edition, respectively).* This manual establishes the criteria that psychiatrists, psychologists, counselors, and mental-health workers generally use for the diagnosis of the distressed. And diagnosis *is* the critical element because on it rests the basis for determining whether or not the therapist's treatment will be reimbursed by the insurer.

Nosology—the official naming of the mental disorders and the designating of what is or is not to be considered a disease—thus becomes of critical importance to all concerned: patient, therapist, insurer, and hospital. For example, several years ago homosexuality was considered a mental disease. Then the kindly psychiatric gods on psychiatry's Mount Olympus decided it wasn't, and it was dropped from the DSM in 1973. The DSM-IV merely continues the classification of insanity which was set in motion in 1952 by the publication of DSM-I. The original DSM listed only sixty types and subtypes of mental disorders. By 1980 these had swollen to more than two hundred and finally in 1987 so many different types of behavior were listed, the entire classification system grew so unwieldy it became necessary that special training courses be given before anyone could properly use the reference. In 1980 the creators of the DSM-III developed their own novel solution: the Multiaxial Diagnostic System. Five axes were designated, but information regarding how this number was determined is not available. The holy five, however, ensure that information for treatment, planning, prediction of outcome, and research is recorded.

The axes are concerned with:

Axis I   Clinical syndromes and additional codes, V codes.
Axis II   Personality disorders and developmental disorders.
Axis III Physical disorders and conditions

---

*Diagnostic and Statistical Manual of Mental Disorders III, 3d ed., rev. (Washington, D.C.: American Psychiatric Association, 1987); *Diagnostic and Statistical Manual of Mental Disorders IV*, 4th ed. (Washington, D.C.: American Psychiatric Association, 1994).

Axis IV   Severity of psychosocial stressors
Axis V   Assessment of global functioning

Axes I and II are used to describe the patient's current condition. When necessary, multiple diagnoses or diagnoses on both axes are made. Axis I lists the clinical syndromes present; if no mental disorder is present that fact is reflected. Axis II lists personality disorders or developmental disorders. It can also be used to record personality traits, repetitive defense mechanisms that impair the patient's ability to cope, or any premorbid personality disorders.

On Axis III the clinician lists all physical disorders or conditions. The physical condition may be causative (due to hyperthyroidism for example) or it may provide information important for treatment. Other notations regarding physical conditions and responses are made on this axis.

Axis IV contains the Severity of Psychosocial Scales—one for children and one for adults. The rating is based on the clinician's judgment as to the degree of stress present. Numerous factors are taken into account, for example, number of stressors, changes accompanying the subjects and the desirability of change.

On Axis V, the clinician estimates the patient's level of functioning at the time of the evaluation and the patient's highest level of functioning during the past year. The DSM-III-R has a Global Assessment of Functioning Scale (GAF Scale) for this purpose. The assignment codes are self-explanatory and take into consideration the psychological, social, and occupational functioning of the patient.

It should be obvious to anyone other than an idiot (or a clinician trapped in the system) that the entire unwieldy, unworkable, pseudoscientific, dismal mishmash is an affront to human sensitivity and intelligence. The draft criteria of DSM-IV alone run to approximately four hundred pages and require additional voluminous tomes, including training guides, case books, and such to make it either understandable or useable. The DSM-III-R contains 567 pages. One thing is certain: based upon the increase in size from DSM-I to DSM-IV, DSM-IV is truly a taxonomic disaster. DSM-V will probably consist of only one line on a single page: *All human behavior is pathological*!

The DSMs, collectively, have come under severe and repeated attack. Thomas Szasz in 1970 compared it to the *Malleus Maleficarum*, the book that defined who was and was not a witch during the Inquisition. The analogy is apt. Psychologist Dr. Mark A. Hubble has called the DSM "a fashion catalog of what's in and what's out" in the mind business. He also argues that the DSM-IV (1) totally fails to reflect fully the enormous influence of culture, ethnicity, and economic status in producing mental disorders—and in the conferring of diagnoses. Studies have shown that the wealthy receive more benign diagnoses while the poor are usually classified as more seriously ill; (2) consistently encourages stereotyped, catch-all labels, rather than in-depth understanding of each person's unique circumstances; (3) much too frequently becomes a political document (homosexuality, for example, was classed as a disease until 1973. The switch from disease to individual choice shows that "social agreement" rather than "scientific evidence" is the determiner); (4) ignores completely evidence from family therapy outcomes about real people in a social context; and (5) fails to help clinicians develop individual psychotherapy plans or to predict the outcome of their psychotherapy. Finally, Hubble notes that because most clinicians do not keep up with current research and are creatures of habit they wind up doing the kind of therapy they're most comfortable with, regardless of the diagnosis. Hubble is also caustically critical of some of the more common diagnostic categories such as "borderline personality disorder."[4] Psychiatrist Dr. Mitchell Wilson in a recent issue of the *American Journal of Psychiatry* also criticizes the DSM-IV on the grounds that it furthers "the medical look" and "the narrowing of the psychiatric gaze" by teaching psychiatrists to focus only on "the superficial and publicly visible" and to ignore personality, the development of character, and the unconscious mind.[5] Hubble says the DSM and its use has been "a road to hell paved with expert consensus" and both Hubble and Wilson agree that the DSM doesn't accurately reflect the nature of humanity's problems even though it is now more closely geared to the medications and drugs currently available as well as the classification codes insisted upon by the insurance companies.[6]

The new biopsychiatry evidenced in the DSM-IV is determined to wipe out all reference to the role of social factors in the etiology of mental illnesses. They have systematically ignored and suppressed the work of scientists like Courtney Harding, the principal investigator of the Vermont Longitudinal study, which showed schizophrenics have a higher recovery rate than previously expected when psychosocial rehabilitation is introduced. The biopsychiatrists ignore all such work and insist medication is the only hope. As Dr. Phil Brown notes, "In fact, unlike medicine where diagnosis typically leads the doctor to prescribe a medication with known effect, psychiatry often reverses this logic by making a diagnosis based on the patient's response to medication."[7] Brown also notes that in large measure the biopsychiatry revolution is one way of securing unity in a disunified profession as well as gaining professional dominance over the entire mental health field. This is particularly important today when psychology, social work, counseling, and family therapy have made serious inroads into the psychotherapy business. Psychiatric unity solidifies their claim that what they do is, indeed, hard scientific medicine and fully worthy of third party reimbursement.

Diagnosis forms the legal basis for the provision of benefits and quite often for involuntary commitment. If the DSM-IV is the culmination of psychiatry, as many of its proponents claim, Brown says, then we have to look at it also "in the context of all the errors and maltreatments of organized psychiatry—overreliance on drugs, abusive treatments such as psychosurgery, conscious and unconscious social control, replication and support of racism, sexism, and class bias."[8] Even though many people and facilities sincerely strive to help patients, such altruism is by no means universal.

Creators of the DSM-IV insist that all of the symptom clusters and categories are scientifically established. This is simply not true, as Mirowsky and Ross have clearly shown.[9] Just as the stellar constellations are mythical creations of human perception, so are the DSM's diagnostic groupings. They are, in fact, the grouping of elements that seem to form something distinct but which may have no real connection with each other. Another problem is that the categorical, biological state may not cause the symptoms on which a diagnosis is based. Moreover, even though the psychiatric literature is filled with DSM reliability studies of diagnoses on all the axes, hardly any research addresses the problem of how valid any of the diagnoses are. Gaining reliability among several different raters is easy if you teach all the people the wrong material, and get them to all agree on it. Armstrong notes that interrater reliability simply depends on those entering the psychology world sharing the same social biases to begin with, or being willing to be trained into those biases as the trade-off for membership in the judgment club. Those who differ and do not defer are simply said to have incomplete biopsychosocial background or training "and are thus inherently limited in their use of this diagnostic system." Chang and Bidder in a 1985 study stated, "Grouping patients according to selected properties rather than in terms of their total phenomenology is analogous to classifying a car by observing any four of the following eight properties: wheels, motors, headlights, radio, seats, body, windshield wipers, and exhaust systems. While an object with four of these properties might well be a car, it might also be an airplane, a helicopter, a derrick, or a tunnel driller."[10] J. Kovel, another critic, remarked that the medieval witch trials showed a much higher degree of interrater reliability than any of the DSM categories and we definitely would not impute any validity to those social diagnoses.[11] Kovel also notes that while validity requires that the variable or item be highly correlated with a known measure such as clinical diagnosis in medical records, biopsychiatry is satisfied with the fact that DSM-III-R and DSM-IV have been widely accepted by courts, prisons, clinics, and third party payers. This, according to the biopsychiatrists, is evidence of a "scientific breakthrough." Why? Because when the institutions accept the beliefs and practices of any scientific model, a form of scientific knowledge has been created. This is not, however, the way the rest of the scientific world defines validity.

When the validity of psychiatric diagnoses is studied the results are very clear: validity is almost nonexistent. For example, hallucinations show up in both schizophrenia and the affective disorders, yet clinicians will focus on a single symptom and ignore the rest. If one clinician concentrates on auditory hallucinations and the other on depression and anxiety, the diagnoses will differ. There is also considerable evidence that the use of the DSM is idiosyncratic. Clinicians resisted the official classification system to make their own work easier, to help their patients, and to criticize the official nomenclature and the system. Brown's staff routinely used humor and sarcasm and invented alternative diagnoses. They minimized and normalized certain behaviors by giving mild diagnoses to protect people from their employers and others. Whenever possible they evaded the formal procedures to cover their own mistakes and to protect patients from outside agencies. They also refused to do the dirty work for the homeless shelters, welfare departments, prison-prerelease workers, and other social agencies.[12]

In fact, the primary reason why the DSM system of diagnosing is not used is that it is, quite frankly, of no clinical value. Brown notes that one study carried out at a community mental health center found that the psychiatrists frequently criticized the official diagnostic system as rigid, inapplicable, or beside the point. Most often a specific diagnosis was chosen from a list of diagnoses that seemed to fit primarily for its administrative effect. The clinical social workers who used the official DSM categories said they did so primarily for insurance purposes because they are of little or no value for understanding and predicting their clients' behavior or for planning treatment. Most also felt that they merely were plastering medical labels on psychosocial problems and were of no help whatsoever in understanding problems. They admitted however that the DSM did provide a common language through which they could talk about mental disorders. In general, the official diagnoses are seen merely as labels and administrative pigeonholes that are totally irrelevant to the patients' symptoms and problems.

In practice, clinicians use shortcuts and have a basic distrust of any and all attempts to force-fit scientifically repeatable measures into a framework that is totally inapplicable and irrelevant. In other words, the DSM bears no resemblance to what therapists must deal with in the clinic, and in one 1988 survey, 35 percent of the psychiatrists sampled said they would stop using the DSM if they were not required to use it. Clinical psychologists were even more critical: 90 percent of them said their chief use of it was for insurance claim purposes only.[13] A survey of social workers found that 81 percent saw the DSM as important for insurance purposes and their top four categories of usefulness—insurance, agency, Medicaid, and legal requirements—had nothing intrinsically to do with clinical practice. Another survey discovered that psychologists prefer a social, interpersonal, and behavioral analysis to the DSM. Moreover, half of them rejected the idea that a universal classification system was of any value whatsoever.[14] Brown also clearly illuminates the biases—overt and covert—that drive the current crop of biopsychiatrists; their racial, sexual, and class biases as well as their diagnostic biases.

It is the goals of diagnosis that are more important for the clinician than his patient since the clinician is restricted by financial, bureaucratic, and professional pressures as well as the need to gain both certainty and control by naming the problem. Patients also want their problem named, but more important to them is the fact that they are understood and that they will be helped. Despite the existence of DSM-IV we can rest assured that clinicians will continue to ignore and bypass the codified diagnostic schema. Even when they do follow it, it is so unwieldy and complex many errors will be made. With all of the psychotherapeutic approaches and disagreements and internecine wars and skirmishes it is highly unlikely agreement will be obtained on anything having to do with the diagnosis and treatment of human mental disorders. Brown concludes his critique with the observation that "Criticism [of the reference] is stifled by a general impression fostered by DSM leaders that the 'old way' was merely a simplistic psychoanalysis or a radical antipsychiatry."[15] Ah, would that it were so simple!

Mirowsky's criticisms of the DSM and its makers are in full agreement with those of Brown. In Mirowsky's view, the boundaries of psychiatric diagnosis are arbitrary, like the lines of longitude and latitude superimposed on the earth. The neat, precise syndromes cited in the DSM "are not distinct and characteristic collections of symptoms and signs that immediately impress themselves on the minds of clinical observers."[16] They are official classifications laboriously negotiated over in endless committee meetings that have taken place over the last three decades. The results are "pushed" by the American Psychiatric Association and the National Institute of Mental Health and they are, accordingly, controlled and enforced by the disposition of grants and awards and reimbursements. In Mirowsky's view

the traditional categorical form of thinking inherited by psychiatry from medicine provides the poorest possible means of representing mental, emotional, and behavioral problems. Each diagnosis is an arbitrary subjective combination of problems. . . . Developing, promoting, and enforcing the use of official combinations does not make them any less arbitrary. It creates an illusion of objectivity and concreteness. The illusion may suit the institutional needs of insurance companies, government agencies, and the medical profession. The danger is that it discourages the development of non-diagnostic concepts and measures that are more efficient, flexible, and exact for scientific and clinical purposes.[17]

The summer of 1994 brought us the DSM-IV, 886 pages of a massive attempt to describe and classify every possible human mental disorder. It is a huge, pseudoscientific mess that costs $55 per copy. Every psychotherapist in the nation will be forced to buy and use it because insurance companies use it to determine reimbursement for psychotherapeutic services. Therapists, if they are to be paid, must list an official diagnostic label accompanied by the DSM-IV code number on their claims to government agencies or insurance companies. It is, in a word, therapeutic blackmail on the part of the American Psychiatric Association's monopoly over the definition of mental disorders. Shamefully, the book has no scientific merit and is no better—and thankfully—no worse than its predecessors. Stuart A. Kirk and Herb Kutchins, following up on their excellent 1992 book, *The Selling of DSM*, in a scathing review of the DSM-IV in the *National Psychologist* call it "a travesty." They also note, "For all the attention the book receives, few clinicians actually use it as a basis for psychotherapy. The book's inherent problem is that it applies no coherent standard of what constitutes a mental disorder."[18] They also note that it panders to insurers, drug companies and therapists by medicalizing what are basically social problems. It diagnoses so many ordinary kinds of behavior as psychiatric disorders, 50 percent of the American population is now mentally ill. Even poor spelling, grammar, and punctuation is now a disease: Code 315.2, "Disorder of Written Expression." Not only is this totally asinine, but to classify children who argue with adults; lose their tempers; refuse to obey rules; blame others; and act touchy, angry, or spiteful as mentally ill (Code 313.81, "Oppositional Defiant Disorder") is not only stupid but dangerous. If this nonsense is science, God help us all!

There is something weird and otherworldly about hearing mature and seemingly intelligent therapists attribute a mother's grief over her dead infant, marital conflict and difficulties, adolescent rebellion, premenstrual cramps, or a child's difficulties with algebra to a biological defect, a biochemical imbalance, a neurological deficit, or other unnamed organic disorder. Yet this is what the DSM (which should stand for Dense, Stupid and Moronic) sages have managed to do. The DSM revisions task force committee created a firestorm from women over the task force's attempt to insert Masochistic Personality Disorder into the revised DSM which would, in essence, put the blame for wife-beating on the wife's shoulders. Instead it was renamed the Self-Defeating Personality Disorder. As for the perfectly natural monthly feminine cycle, the Premenstrual Dysphoric Disorder has become the Late Luteal Phase Dysphonic Disorder in the DSM-IV.

Women and children have definitely been victimized by the psychiatric seers. In response to these labeling idiocies, in 1991 the therapists Kaye-Lee Pantony and Paula Caplan described the "Delusional Dominating Personality Disorder" (DDPD), an exclusively male disorder, of course. Fourteen criteria for DDPD are included. Among them are some classic bull's-eyes: "Inability to establish and maintain meaningful interpersonal relationships. . . . Inability to identify and express a range of feelings in oneself (typically accompanied by an inability to identify accurately the feelings of other people. . . . Tendency to use power, silence, withdrawal, and/or avoidance rather than negotiation in the face of interpersonal conflict or difficulties," and so on.[19] Pantony and Caplan even submitted their paper to the DSM chairman but, predictably, it was never considered. As Suzanne Fields in one of her syndicated columns recommends, a counter to this new psychiatric agenda that degrades and devalues women is needed, "a sort of equal opportunity ailment for men. . . . A few dysfunctional male problems that recur with some regularity suggest themselves: 'Beer absorption dysphoric disorder' (BADD), 'competition afflicting dysphoric disorder' (CADD), 'sexually aggressive dysphoric disorder' (SADD)." Fields's recommendations certainly seem as sound and reasonable as anything we find in DSM-IV.

As for seeing *all* behavior as diseased, however, truth is much stranger than fiction. As was mentioned previously, during the Civil War many physicians saw the black slave's desire to break his chains and run away as a form of mental illness (drapetomania). In our time psychiatrists James Hudson and Harrison Pope have conjured up a new mental disorder, the "affective spectrum disorder," which they argue affects nearly everyone. In their words, "If the model is validated, this family of disorders . . . would represent one of the most prevalent diseases in the population.[20] Of self-promotion and self-rationalization, it seems, there is no end.

NOTES

1. Victor Rainy, *Training Clinical Psychology* (Englewood Cliffs, N.J.: Prentice Hall, 1950).

2. George Will, "A Lousy Personality Could Count As a Disability," *Lexington Herald Leader*, 4 April 1996, p. A13.

3. D. E. Zuriff, "Medicating Character," *Public Interest* no. 123 (Spring 1996): 94–99.

4. Cited in Kent Christensen, "A Mind-Expanding Book," *Psychology Today* (November/December 1993): 17.

5. Mitchell Wilson, "DSM III and the Transformation of American Psychiatry: A History," *American Journal of Psychiatry* 150, no. 3 (1993): 399–410.

6. Christensen, "A Mind-Expanding Book."

7. Phil Brown, "The Name Game: Toward a Sociology of Diagnosis," *Journal of Mind & Behavior* 11, nos. 3 and 4 (Summer/Autumn 1990): 385–406.

8. Ibid., p. 389.

9. J. Mirowsky and C. E. Ross, "Psychiatric Diagnosis As Reified Measurement," *Journal of Health & Social Behavior* 30 (1989): 11–25.

10. M. M. Chang and G. Bidder, "Noncomparability of Research Results That Are Related to Psychiatric Diagnoses," *Comprehensive Psychiatry* 26 (1985): 202.

11. J. Kovel, "A Critique of DSM-III," *Research in Law, Deviance & Social Control* 9 (1988): 127–46.

12. Brown, "The Name Game."

13. H. Kutchins and S. A. Kirk, "The Business of Diagnosis: DSM III and Clinical Social Work," *Social Work* 33 (1988): 215–20.

14. D. Smith and W. A. Kraft, "DSM III: Do Psychiatrists Really Want An Alternative?" *American Psychologist* 38 (1983): 777–85.

15. Brown, "The Name Game," p. 404.

16. John Mirowsky, "Subjective Boundaries and Combinations in Psychiatric Diagnoses," *Journal of Mind & Behavior* 11, nos. 3 and 4 (Summer/Autumn 1990): 408.

17. Ibid., p. 420.

18. Stuart Kirk and Herb Kutchins, "DSM-IV: A Review," *National Psychologist* (September/October 1994): 12–13.

19. Kaye-Lee Pantony and Paula Caplan, "Delusional Dominating Personality Disorder: A Modest Proposal for Identifying Some Consequences of Rigid Masculine Socialization," *Canadian Psychology* 32, no. 2 (1991): 120–33.

20. James I. Hudson and Harrison G. Pope, Jr., "Affective Spectrum Disorder: Does Antidepressant Response Identify a Family of Disorders with a Common Pathophysiology?" *American Journal of Psychiatry* 147, no. 5 (May 1990): 552.

9

Medicated America:
The M.D. Pusher

Is cocaine habit forming? Of course not. I ought to know. I've been using it for years!

attributed to Tallulah Bankhead

Two other serious and far-reaching examples of "shrinkage" beside the major one of regarding all psychological problems as "diseases" are (1) the prescribing of drugs for psychological problems—toxic psychiatry—and (2) regarding recreational drug use as addictions and diseases that, again, can be overcome and cured by way of a "medical" approach. Taking a pill to cure pill taking is just a little ironic.

In his 1979 book, *Limits to Medicine*, medical historian Ivan Illich pointed out that while the United States price index rose about 74 percent between 1950 and 1971, the cost of medical care rose 330 percent. Public expenditure for health insurance increased tenfold during that time, private insurance benefits increased eightfold, and direct out-of-pocket payments about threefold.[1] Since then, health care costs have increased at a rapidly accelerating rate. Much worse, however, has been the increase in the pharmaceutical drug trade. According to Illich, the volume of the drug business in the United States has grown by a factor of one hundred during the current century: 20,000 tons of aspirin are consumed each year—almost 225 tablets per person. Central nervous system agents are the fastest growing sector of the drug market, making up 31 percent of total sales. Dependence on pre-scribed tranquilizers has risen by 290 percent since 1962 while liquor consumption rose only by 23 percent and the estimated consumption of illegal opiates only 50 percent.[2] Dr. Robert Mendelsohn accuses physicians of having "seeded the entire population with powerful drugs." What is even more deplorable, "Every year from 8 to 10 mil-lion Americans go to the doctor when they have a cold. About 95 per-cent of them come away with a prescription—half of which are for antibiotics," which, of course, do nothing at all to fight any viral-based disease such as a cold.[3]

Health care in the United States has now become a megabillion-dollar business. It is responsible for over 12 percent of the gross national product. Revenues from the health industry, which currently exceed $360 billion a year, are second only to those of the defense industry. In 1991 the United States spent $750 billion on health care. It has been estimated that by the year 2000, annual health care costs in the United States will have increased to at least 1.5 trillion dollars. It is not difficult, then, to see why this industry is so appealing to cor-porate investors.[4]

One result of the vast overconsumption of drugs is the astronomi-cal profits of the drug industry. A second result is the deterioration of public health. In 1978, for example, according to the FDA, 1.5 mil-lion Americans were hospitalized as a result of side effects from pre-scription drugs and 30 percent of all people hospitalized were further damaged by their medication. Every year, an estimated 140,000 Americans are killed because of prescription drug consumption while one in seven hospital beds are taken up by patients suffering from adverse drug reactions (including both overdoses and detrimental side effects). Many health officials grossly underestimate the extent of drug reactions and they also try to convince the unwary general public that drug-related illnesses are the consumer's and the physician's fault. To protect the drug industry from blame, many officials purposely ignore the fact that most drugs are harmful even if they are used "properly."[5]

It needs to be remembered that 50 percent of the drugs currently on the market today did not exist ten years ago. Therefore most doc-tors did not learn about them in medical schools. They are forced to rely primarily on the drug companies' sales staff who have neither formal medical or pharmacological training for their information about the new medications. These salesmen are unregulated by any state or federal agency. Their sales campaigns, however, have been notoriously successful. So successful, in fact, that we have an entire population that is overmedicated. Sadly enough, with the exception of marijuana, heroin, and cocaine, 85 percent of all the street drugs currently being abused are manufactured by "legitimate" drug companies and gross sales forecasts from such companies deliberately include profits made from illicit sales to drug peddlers.[6]

The pharmaceutical companies have not only curried the favors and won the allegiance of practicing physicians, but they have also enlisted the aid of influential academic physicians to the extent that they now *control the practice of medicine in the United States*. Not only do they set the standards of practice by hiring investigators to perform studies which establish the efficacy of their products and impugn those of their competitors, but the situation is now so bad that many physicians have been intimidated into using treatment regimes which they know do not work because they fear lawsuits. According to Dr. Alan Lewis, a distinguished medical professor at the University of California, this is particularly true in cancer chemotherapy. "Your family doctor is no longer free to choose the treatment modality he or she feels is best for you, but must follow the dictates established by physicians whose motives and alliances are such that their decisions may not be in your best interests."[7] If Lewis is correct, it seems that the medical establishment itself has now become a major threat to health and this sort of professional control over the practice of medicine has now become an epidemic.

While we like to believe that it is modern medicine that makes and keeps us healthy, this is a myth. Medical assistance or intervention is the least important of the factors that determine and keep us healthy. Not only are most of us born healthy, but if we are not subjected to an onslaught of accidents and environmental disasters, we remain healthy most of our lives. Both the mind and body are designed to defend themselves against disease and injury and to heal themselves. Our true need of medical assistance is actually rare. An unhealthy lifestyle (overeating, drinking, smoking) is the most prevalent cause of death in the United States (57 percent), followed by environment (21 percent), biological or hereditary factors (19 percent), and last, medical intervention (10 percent).[8] John and Sonja McKinlay have recently shown that medical intervention has accounted for only 1 to 3.5 percent of the increase in average lifespan in the United States since 1900.[9] These statistics suggest that our health and longevity depend primarily on how we live: disease is prevented, primarily, through improvements in lifestyle, hygiene and public sanitation, and proper and adequate nutrition.

We are also gradually beginning to realize that much allopathic medicine (which uses drugs to treat disease) can cause more harm to the patient than the illness it tries to treat. Of even greater significance is our growing recognition that too many of our new and most dramatic disorders are iatrogenic. Richard Taylor, an Australian M.D., states:

> In fact, because of the increasing complexity of medical technology and the increase in the variety of chemicals available for treatment iatrogenic disease is on the increase . . . unfortunately iatrogenic diseases may be self-perpetuating. Many iatrogenic complications require specific treatment, thus exposing the patient to the possibility of yet another iatrogenic disease, a patient may even experience an iatrogenic complication from a diagnostic test which was required to diagnose the initial iatrogenic disease. The situation in which an iatrogenic disease provokes a second iatrogenic complication could be termed second level iatrogenesis. In a hospital setting these situations are not uncommon. It is even possible for third and fourth level iatrogenesis to occur.[10]

Drs. H. Beaty and R. Petersdorf agree with Taylor and note that, "It should be pointed out that iatrogenic problems are cumulative, and in an effort to extricate himself from complications of diagnosis and therapy, the physician may compound the problem by having to employ maneuvers that are in themselves risky."[11] The problem is that the more medications, tests, and operations the patients endure; the more likely they are to acquire an iatrogenic disorder because of all the subspecialists involved who see only one part of the whole patient.

A second problem is that in their attempts to patch up all the symptoms of illness, the M.D.s often use dangerous drugs, radical and unnecessary surgery, and harmful radiation that often causes more harm than the original problem. Moreover, in addition to the creation of "new" illnesses, the treatments may mask the symptoms of the underlying causes of the presenting illness, making it much more difficult to detect and treat and thus, increasing its chronicity. While allopathic treatment is, of course, useful and life-saving in emergencies, its frequent ineffectiveness cannot be overemphasized.

A fascinating statistic, seldom cited and little known, is that during a one month physician's strike in Israel in 1973, the national death rate reached its lowest point in history. According to the Jerusalem Burial Society, the number of funerals dropped by almost half.[12] In 1976 in Bogota, the capital of Colombia, the doctors went on strike for fifty-two days. The *National Catholic Reporter* pointed out the death rate fell by 35 percent during that period. Identical events occurred in California and Great Britain during the late 1970s.[13]

THE SECOND DRUG CULTURE: PRESCRIPTIONS

The Medical profession has been oversold on the chemical solution, which is not to say that drugs might not be the right treatment for many for a short time or for a few for a long time. The problem is that too many people are taking too many drugs for too long. This is particularly true of the drugs that change the mood or alter the mind.

There is no opportunity in the system for the other side. Drug companies do not buy ads to tell doctors not to prescribe drugs. . . . No one buys ads or sends out salesmen to extol the virtues of marriage counseling for marital problems, family therapy for problems with the kids, . . . a good diet for the tired, a long talk for the fearful, a walk for the restless, a run for the overweight, a new hobby for the retired, a vocation for the widow. . . .

The chemical solution is what's sold, and it's been bought.[14]

Because today, in the 1990s, so many people are on medications of one sort or another, the stand-up comics have suggested our war on drugs should be waged against the physicians and drug companies rather than the Colombian Cartel. There is more than a grain of truth in this humor. There are few United States citizens over fifty years of age who are not on drugs of one sort or another, either over-the-counter type or those prescribed by their physicians. And the older we are it seems the more aches and pains we have and the more pills are required to get us comfortably through the days and nights.

While many people certainly benefit from drugs that lower their blood pressure, reduce the pain and discomfort of angina and arthritis, and treat other common ailments, they may also suffer from the adverse effects of medications—even those that can provide some relief. Nearly all the arthritis drugs, for example, while they may provide relief from the pain of arthritis, also can cause severe stomach pains and gastric distress. Other commonly prescribed medications, particularly the narcoleptics, can bring on other serious drug-induced disorders much worse than the condition for which the original drugs were prescribed! Tardive dyskinesia, for example, a drug-induced Parkinsonianlike condition that is, unfortunately, permanent, is a prime example. In older adults, these drugs can cause mental confusion and decreased motor coordination leading to falls and hip fractures, and progressive mental deterioration. Hard as it may be for most people to accept, in fact, for many older adults the best medicine may be *no medicine of any kind.*

In any event, whenever a medication is prescribed its effects on the patient should be carefully monitored—something that too many psychiatrists never do. Instead, many psychiatrists practice "wave therapy": after prescribing the medication, monitoring consists of waving to their patients as they hurriedly pass through the wards on their way out of the hospital. As every conscientious and dedicated physician knows, continual monitoring of every patient is necessary after drug treatment is started. Otherwise the doctor will never know if the desired therapeutic effects are occurring or if there are any adverse side effects or unwanted interactions with other drugs. All people taking medication of any sort should carefully monitor the drug's effect on every aspect of their behavior, mood, and feeling—independently of the physician's actions. You must never forget that *you* are responsible for your own health and welfare—not your physician!

If you are so naive as to believe that the first paragraphs of this section are exaggerations and alarmist propaganda, perhaps the following statistics will change your mind. Looking at older adults alone, each year there are approximately,

- 61,000 older adults with drug-induced Parkinsonian disorders;
- 32,000 with hip fractures, including 1,500 deaths attributed to drug-induced falls;
- 16,000 injurious car crashes caused by adverse drug reactions;
- 163,000 drug-induced or drug-worsened memory loss;
- 659,000 hospitalizations because of adverse drug reactions, including hundreds of thousands with drug-induced dizziness or fainting.
- Other drug reactions can also lead to death. Drugs such as digoxin, a heart medicine, causes 28,000 cases of life-threatening or fatal adverse reactions a year in hospitals alone, often because the prescribed dose is too high or the drug is given to people who do not need to be taking it in the first place. Newer drugs, such as the powerful sedative/tranquilizer Versed, can also be extremely dangerous. Used for so-called conscious sedation during oral surgery, or during diagnostic procedures such as gastroscopy, this drug has also caused dozens of preventable deaths. Most were in older people.[15]

Not only older people, but even much younger people need to be concerned. Even in our thirties the ability of the liver to metabolize and the efficiency of the kidneys to eliminate drugs begin to decline as does the heart's efficiency. Furthermore, adverse drug reactions can occur in anyone at anytime. In fact, many of the most frequently prescribed drugs can cause problems such as depression, sexual dysfunction, insomnia, memory loss, constipation, tardive dyskenesia, and hallucinations, among others, in people of any age. If one doesn't learn how to give up or keep prescribed drugs to a minimum at an early age, you are in danger of becoming over-medicated in your fifties, sixties, and seventies. You should also be concerned about older relatives and friends who need help to cope with the deluge of drugs most doctors are eager and willing to prescribe. About one out of three of the most commonly prescribed drugs for older adults (119 out of 364) *should never be used* (see Table 8.1).[16] The list of such drugs include Valium, Dalmane, and Halcion in the sleeping pill and tranquilizer group; antidepressants such as Elavil; painkillers and arthritis drugs like Darvocet or Darvon; heart drugs like Persantine, Lopid, and Catapres; gastrointestinal drugs such as Bentyl, Lomotil, and Tigan; and the very popular diabetic drug Diabinese.[17] Wolfe and Hope also stress that two-thirds of the prescriptions given—more than 429 million per year—fall into one of three categories: first, the drug isn't needed at all because the patient's problem is not one for which a drug is the proper solution; second, the drug is unnecessarily dangerous and a less dangerous drug would give the same benefit with a much lower risk; and, third, while it may be the correct drug the dose is unnecessarily high.

Another very common and very serious problem with prescribed drugs is what is known as the "illness-medication spiral." In this situation, whenever adverse reactions to one medication occur, the physician incorrectly interprets these symptoms as a new "illness" and prescribes yet another drug, instead of stopping or reducing the dosage of the first drug. Another related and deplorable medical practice is to prescribe one medication for the presenting symptoms, another to deal with the first drug's side effects, another to deal with the second drug's side effects, and so on ad infinitum. One teenager of my acquaintance who was under psychiatric care wound up taking eight different medications daily. Physicians who practice excessive polypharmacy should be prosecuted for malpractice.

Wolfe and Hope also note that if we broaden the definition of "drug abuse" to include victims of the choices of others—such as patients of doctors—then the *greatest epidemic of drug abuse in American society today is among our older people.* Like most other epidemics, it is preventable.

One significant cause of the epidemic among older patients is the fact that too many physicians, upon hearing about the symptoms of adverse drug reactions, dismiss them as merely attributes of "growing old" instead of being due to prescriptions. Such adverse drug reactions as depression, hallucinations, mental confusion, memory loss, cognitive impairment, sexual dysfunction, dizziness on standing, loss of appetite, constipation, and many others are common. In case you are inclined to

Table 8.1   Inappropriate Drugs for the Elderly

The panel of American Medical Association experts listed twenty-three drugs that it considered inappropriate, but Harvard researchers who studied drugs given to the elderly consider only the first twenty on the list inappropriate.

Name of Drug (Including Trade Names)	Possible Side Effects/Detrimental Aspects
Tranquilizers and Sleeping Aids	
Diazepam (Valium)	Addictive and too long-acting, causing possible drowsiness, confusion, and falls.
Chlordiazepoxide (Librium, Librax)	Too long-acting, might cause falls.
Flurazepam (Dalmane)	Too long-acting, might cause falls.
Meprobamate (Miltown, Deprol, Equagesic, Equanil)—Sometimes combined with an antidepressant or pain reliever.	Addictive, too long-acting, might cause falls.
Pentobarbital (Nembutal)	Addictive, long-acting.
Secobarbital (Seconal)	Addictive, long-acting.
Antidepressants	
Amitriptyline (Elavil, Endep, Etrafon, Limbitrol, Triavil)	Often causes inability to urinate, dizziness, and drowsiness in the elderly.
Arthritis Drugs	
Indomethacin (Indocin)	Can cause confusion, headaches. Might be appropriate in some elderly patients under certain conditions.
Phenylbutazone (Butazolidin)	Risk of bone marrow toxicity.
Pain Relievers	
Chlorpropramide (Diabinese)	Can cause dangerous fluid retention. Stays in the body a long time, and because of that, if an overdose occurs, it can take a long time to treat.
Diabetes Drugs	
Propoxyphene (Darvon Compound, Darvocet, Wygesic)	Addictive and little more effective than aspirin Has more side effects than morphine for patients who need a narcotic. Has been associated with seizures and heart problems.
Pentazocine (Talwin)	Addictive, has been associated with seizures and heart problems.

Name of Drug (Including Trade Names)	Possible Side Effects/Detrimental Aspects
Dementia Treatments	
Cyclandelate	Not shown effective.
Isoxsuprine	Not shown effective.
Blood Thinners	
Dipyridamole (Persantine)	Except in patients with artificial heart valves, not shown effective.
Muscle Relaxants, Spasm Relievers	
Cyclobenzaprine (Flexeril)	Can cause dizziness, fainting.
Orphenidrine (Norflex, Norgesic)	Can cause dizziness, fainting.
Methocarbamol (Robaxin)	Might cause dizziness or drowsiness.
Carisoprodol (Soma)	Potential for central nervous system toxicity is greater than potential benefit.
Antinausea, Antivomiting Drugs	
Trimethobenzamide (Tigan)	Might be less effective than other agents, might cause drowsiness, dizziness, and other reactions.
Antihypertensives	
Propranolol (Inderal)	Feeling slowed mentally and physically.
Methyldopa (Aldoril, Aldomet)	Feeling slowed mentally and physically.
Reserpine (Regroton, Hydropres)	Can cause depression.

Sxource: *Journal of the American Medical Association*, cited in an Associated Press release published in the *Lexington (Kentucky) Herald-Leader*, 27 July 1994. For additional, more detailed tables, see S. M. Wolfe and R. Hope, *Worst Pills, Best Pills II* (Washington, D.C.: Public Citizen's Health Research Group, 1993), especially chapter 2.

see this as a minor problem, a recent study estimated that in 1990, 66,000 Americans age sixty and older were hospitalized because of adverse reactions to drugs they were taking before their hospitalization.[18]

Another important—perhaps the primary reason for the over prescribing and misprescribing of drugs is the behavior of the drug companies and physicians. Despite the efforts of the Food and Drug Administration, the drug companies' drug testing policies and procedures, unfortunately, leave much to be desired. Not so with their marketing practices. Not only are their drugs heavily sold to physicians, often using false and misleading ad campaigns, but they push many new drugs that have few or no advantages over those currently in use. As for the doctors, too many physicians believe their job is to quiet the patient by writing a prescription. On the whole, doctors are woefully ignorant of both the drugs and the special problems of their patients.

One study of physicians treating Medicare patients found that 70 percent of the doctors who took an examination about their knowledge of prescribing for older adults failed to pass the test. The majority of doctors contacted for participation in the study refused to take the test. Their reason? They had "a lack of interest in the subject."[19]

If there is anything the modern physician is skilled at it is in writing prescriptions for pills. And there are good reasons for doing so. Nothing makes a patient angrier than going to a physician and coming away empty-handed, without free pill samples or a prescription or both. We are in every conceivable way a pill-popping, drug-consuming culture, constantly on the lookout for an easy-to-prescribe-and-take, instantly effective panacea. If we don't find it or fail to get our pills from one doctor, we will immediately seek out another who *will* supply us with the painkillers we seek. Little wonder the entire medical world is eternally on the lookout for the next new miracle drug that will cure instantaneously with little or no side effects. The search for such a system of therapy that is truly effective in giving the patient significant improvement and hopefully, in time, a permanent cure has been unending.

To trace the history of medication in all of the medical specialties would require an entire library.* Similarly, to track the history and development of psychotherapeutic drugs would require volumes. Entire books can and have been written on a single drug or a single therapeutic approach because medical measures designed to influence abnormal mental symptoms are legion. They can, however, be usefully divided into two major classes: physical and chemical.

---

*A recent, interesting survey of the general history of medicine to which the reader may refer, however, is John Mann's *Murder, Magic and Medicine* (New York: Oxford University Press, 1992).

Physical

The physical approaches that have been tried and discarded for mental problems in the present century alone are staggering: Hydrotherapy in the form of hot baths and cold baths; agitated water and still water; consuming large quantities of mineral water or purified water have all been tried. Physical stimulation in the form of massages; saunas; ice water baths or refrigeration; electricity applied to the various muscle groups or directly to the head and brain itself in the form of electroconvulsive shock; fever production via baths or electric cabinets; purgation; rest cures of various kinds including stimulus reduction and deprivation; exercise in excessive amounts to the point of exhaustion or none at all for protracted periods; sleep therapy using various narcotics (opiates, bromides, chloral, et al.); carbon dioxide, oxygen (too much or too little), nitrogen; and finally, brain surgery. Needless to say, none of these approaches has proved to be either highly useful or effective over time. Most have been abandoned as chemical methods proved to be easier to use, implement, and apply.

Chemical

It is highly unlikely that modern biological psychiatry would have made the progress it did had it not been for the fact that in 1913 Noguchi and Moore discovered that general paresis (paralysis accompanied by insanity) was due to the infiltration of the syphilitic spirillum into the brain tissue itself. This discovery was soon followed by "The Magic Bullet" (i.e., treatment by the drug salvarsan) as well as the mercury drugs and finally von Jauregg's malaria cure, which won him the Nobel Prize.

The discovery that fever therapy had a direct action on microorganisms in the brain led to experiments with fever production by baths, electric cabinets, and the injection of horse serum and typhoid vaccines. Similarly, efforts to influence the brain directly took the form of inhaling ether, nitrogen, and carbon dioxide in the hope that schizophrenic reactions would be eliminated. In addition, amphetamines, histamines, amytal, and pentothal—as well as all sorts of vitamins—were also administered. The idea behind the use of such chemicals was that the cerebral cortex would be influenced and the psychological conflicts (which were responsible for the malaise) would be reduced via psychotherapeutic "ventilation."

Sleep therapy had short-term, positive effects on some catatonics. Amytal was also temporarily effective in reducing the agitation of some manic patients. The concept behind the use of the gases—carbon dioxide, oxygen, and nitrogen—held that anoxia would affect brain-cell metabolism and would thus reverse the brain's malfunctions. Nitrous oxide (laughing gas) was also tried to put the patient in a "hypnoidal-like" state, based on the idea that in this state the unconscious of the stuporous or stubborn patients could be accessed.

Sedatives of every conceivable sort have also been used since the days of Hippocrates. Opiates, bromides, chloral hydrate, have all been used to quiet the patient and calm the physician. Nearly every endocrine gland in the body has had its hormones tried, in the hope that these extracts would somehow influence the disorders—particularly depression. Vitamins of every sort and in large quantities have also been experimentally administered.

Since all mental disorders and "diseases" were—and currently are — assumed to be due to disordered brain metabolism, then straightening out the faulty metabolism, most surely, will also straighten out the patient. In the early 1930s, Manfred Sakel, a Viennese physician, treated some schizoid drug addicts with insulin which produced hypoglycemia and eased the addict's withdrawal symptoms. Sakel then hypothesized that such insulin dosages might well help schizophrenic patients. After putting them into a comatose state and bringing on profound physical changes—sweating, convulsions, coma, and epileptic seizures—many of the patients showed a reduction in their delusions. Treatment results were so exciting that Sakel's method was tried in both Europe and in the United States. By 1937 experiments with other physical shock-producing methods were underway. Unfortunately, insulin shock turned out to be complicated, difficult, and dangerous (many patients died). Moreover, follow-up studies showed many relapses. Yet some schizophrenic patients were affected positively and interest in the "shock" treatment remained high.*

---

*Incredibly, the doctors don't really know why shock therapy seems to work. After shock treatment, many patients seem more alert, more active, and behave as if they had just awakened, refreshed, from a long sleep. However, shock treatment causes serious memory deficits and amnesia.

In 1935 Joseph Meduna, a Hungarian psychiatrist, obtained convulsions in a much safer and faster way using the stimulant Metrazol, which is marketed as Cardiozol. While Metrazol was safer and required less care than insulin, the use of electroshock (ECS) soon replaced both of the drug procedures. The use of "electric sleep" goes back to the use of shock on animals by Ledoc in 1902, followed up by Bini and Cerletti who experimented with dogs before turning to humans. Their work showed clearly that patients were less anxious, and by using curare to reduce spasms, the number of fractures was reduced, making electroconvulsive shock therapy significantly superior to all those methods using drugs. Since ECS seemed to be so effective in reducing depression, melancholia, and tension states, it soon became the treatment of choice for most psychiatrists. From the outset, however, it was very clear that ECS *did not cure the depressive state* nor were its results predictable. The more experience psychiatrists had with it, the clearer it became that any improvement obtained was only temporary. Nevertheless, after several years shock therapy became the standard treatment for severe clinical depression.

Some psychiatrists gave shock treatments repeatedly, as many as fifty to one hundred, in fact, over a period of two or three months. One paranoid patient in a state hospital received a total of 120 shock treatments within a six-month period. Not only are the effects of ECS unpredictable, but almost universally, severe memory impairment results. Recently, the number of shocks used by physicians has been drastically reduced because of the unpleasant and damaging side effects.

Amazingly, despite the fact that ECS is the treatment of choice for depressions, neither theoretical nor scientific support for it exists. Cerletti, the inventor of the procedure, believed a substance called agonine formed in the brain and altered the chemistry of the brain cells. This idea was, of course, pure fantasy.

Such speculation led quickly to the idea that the brain of the disturbed obviously had faulty or abnormal brain circuits. If the patient's thinking is faulty then the bad circuits must be in the frontal lobes, where thought occurs. Since so many bad organs can be fixed with surgery, then why not the brain? Accordingly, Moniz and Lima, two Portuguese physicians, performed leukotomies on a group of patients by cutting the nerve fibers in the motor area of the frontal lobe. Some improvement in mood occurred despite the lack of any improvement in intellectual performance. Next, Dr. Walter Freeman improved on the procedure by inserting an "ice pick" directly into the underside of the frontal lobe via the orbital plate (eyesocket) above the eye.

A more sophisticated technique consisted of cutting a hole in the skull inserting the tool and cutting the fronto-thalamic (nerve) fibers in the cerebral cortex. This lobotomy technique was used primarily for schizophrenics. While many manic patients were calmed, others were reduced to zombie-like status.

Many therapists, particularly the neurosurgeons, were completely revolted by such crude, theoryless assaults on the helpless patients. As a result, lobotomy was generally abandoned as a treatment method. Psychosurgery is now used only as a treatment of the last resort. However, it should never be used, since in nearly every case the damage done by such assaults on the brain is greater than the original existing disorder. In no way are such attacks in the name of medicine defensible. Incredibly, Moniz was awarded the Nobel Prize for Medicine in 1949. This would be equivalent to giving Attila the Hun, Adolf Hitler, Idi Amin, and Josef Stalin the Nobel Peace Prize.

Tranquilizers and Antidepressants: The Drug Revolution

In the 1950s the appearance of the major and minor tranquilizers and the antidepressants completely revolutionized hospital care of the so-called mentally ill. While the bromides and the barbiturates phenobarbital and veronal and hundreds of barbituric acid derivatives in the form of sedatives reduced anxiety, tension, and insomnia, they also clouded the normal and neurotic patients' consciousness. On psychotic patients, however, their effects were minimal. Rauwolfia, which was first extracted from the snake-root plant in the 1950s and marketed under the names of Reserpine and Serpasil, proved to be very effective for calming many patients.

In 1952, the French psychiatrists Delay and Deniker noted the effectiveness of Promethazine in reducing agitation, slowing motor activities, and improving the hospital environment. Thorazine, a product of the phenothiazines, was so effective it was quickly introduced into the wards of the state hospitals. Over the next few years over fifty million patients were treated with these drugs and over ten thousand research articles were written about their use. The fact that the phenothiazines quieted excited people, reduced resistance to psychotherapy, and replaced the patients' gibberish with intelligent speech was considered miraculous.

Buoyed up by their success, the drug companies developed new and improved phenothiazines which reduced excitement and agitation and "drew out" the apathetic, withdrawn patients. Soon, Miltown, Librium, Valium, and Haldol were developed and used for anxiety and minor neurotic states. Since depression was so common, the pharmaceutical industry soon came up with a number of drugs designed specifically to elevate one's mood: Marplan, Nardil, Elavil, Ritalin (which is also commonly used for its calming effects on preadolescents), and a number of amphetamines were all effectively used on minor depressions.

Since the manic-depressive state—now called the bipolar disorder—was so prevalent, the manic phase also had to be dealt with. As early as 1949 lithium carbonate was used to reduce the excitement in mental patients and today lithium salts are a recognized and standard treatment procedure for the bipolar disorder.

There can be no doubt that the development and widespread use of the narcoleptics revolutionized the hospital treatment of psychotics. In fact, it enabled the hospitals to reduce their population by allowing many patients to be sent home or released to half-way houses as long as they took their medication.

As for the medical attack on schizophrenia, in 1957 A. Hoffer used large doses of niacin or nicotinic acid for long periods, claiming improvement in acute cases but little change in the chronic. Hoffer and Osmond also used high doses of the megavitamins with schizophrenics and developed what has come to be known as orthomolecular psychiatry. They argued that metabolic deficiencies in the brain were behind the schizophrenic symptoms. Other psychiatrists, however, were not able to replicate Osmond and Hoffer's results. Another attack on schizophrenia took the form of using D-lysergic acid (LSD) to fight the emotional blocking of chronic schizophrenics. With low doses of LSD-25 they found the patient's so-called infantile bonds were loosened and verbal discussions were possible. High doses gave the patient an unusual mystical cosmic experience that, on occasions, proved to be helpful in maintaining contact with reality by providing examples of fantasy.

This knowledge about LSD's mystical qualities could not be kept secret and quickly was leaked to the college-age generation by Timothy Leary and other psychedelic revolutionaries whose experimental work and publications spawned the drug culture of the 1960s.

Mind-Influencing Drugs

Certainly it is common knowledge that we Americans have created a culture of addictions. Few United States citizens can get through the day without their periodic jolt of caffeine or nicotine and the thought of having to go without either one or both of these comforting companions strikes terror in our collective hearts.

After our coffee, colas, and cigarettes during our working hours, we head for our favorite bar to take in several ounces of alcohol during "happy hour" as soon as the work day is over. Then it's home to dinner with a bottle of good wine, an after dinner drink, cigars, and finally a nightcap. Whether we like to think so or not, we are already a drug culture and have been for a long time. When we speak of winning the "War on Drugs" we refer, of course, to only a few of our drugs of choice. The federal drug war is aimed only at drugs of which some people disapprove: LSD, the psychedelic downers, uppers, crack, opium and its derivatives, heroin, cocaine, and marijuana:, the drugs that are not, usually, prescribed by our friendly physician.

Interestingly enough, there is no war on tranquilizers or on Prozac, the medically approved substitute for cocaine. The medical means of dulling our minds to physical and psychological pain is in fact, encouraged by both the medical community and the public. Such encouragement has clearly worked: now one out of every six of our citizens is a regular user. According to the best estimates, the antianxiety drugs account for 250 to 300 million prescriptions a year which means over sixty doses for every man, woman, and child in the nation. In terms of "abuse" only alcohol, nicotine, and aspirin rank higher. Thirty percent of all women aged thirty to sixty attempt to solve their problems with mood-altering drugs. Based on hospital admissions, misuse of uppers and downers far outnumbers the abuse of illegal drugs. Tranquilizer abuse also accounts for 15 to 25 percent of annual hospital admissions. In spite of these facts, the friendly corner physician scribbles your panacea prescription not only because you want it but because the drug companies also want it. While helpful, perhaps, for the seriously disturbed, too often they are prescribed for hypochondriacs and the normal, healthy, middle-class "worried well."

Tranquilizers

Tranquilizers are categorized as major or minor. The distinction is a chemical one and has nothing to do with potency. Users of the minor tranquilizers see them as therapeutic, helping them get over life's rough spots. The major ones are prescribed only for the most serious psychiatric disorders.

All tranquilizers depress the central nervous system (CNS) and relax muscles. They can, therefore, decrease our reaction time and affect our judgment of distance, time, and space as well as affect our vision. So the operation of machinery, driving a car, and so forth can increase the chance of accidents. Street tranquilizers are even more dangerous, since they are not pure and therefore add to the unpredictability of an already unpredictable drug. The shelf-life of tranquilizers also varies; some pills become more potent with the passage of time, some less. Tranquilizers rank just behind aspirin and alcohol in drugs that cause damage to the stomach lining.

With heavy or prolonged use, both physical and psychological addiction is possible *no matter what the psychiatrists and drug companies maintain*. Moreover, withdrawal from tranquilizers is just as difficult as withdrawing from alcohol, opiates, or the barbiturates. Sedative users should use particular caution and withdraw only with medical supervision. No tranquilizer should be used over a long period of time and particular care should be taken even with the recommended and prescribed dosages.

Despite what the Medical Pill-Pushers (MPPs) may tell you, any and all tranquilizers cause more problems than they solve. Many less dangerous, less expensive and more successful alternatives to tranquilizers are available: relaxation techniques, meditation, massage, exercise techniques. All relieve muscle tension and many different cognitive therapeutic techniques are, in the long run, much more effective in solving the anxiety problem. With drugs, depression is merely suppressed—the problems that caused it remain unsolved. Despite what the MPPs may tell you, tranquilizers are only psychiatric bandages. They never have and never will solve our anxieties and depressions. One might as well get drunk or bang one's head with a baseball bat. Whether it be tranquilizers, booze, or head-banging, once the effects wear off, the original problem remains unalleviated.

In case you doubt these statements, let's look at four of the newer "wonder drugs" in the tranquilizer field: Valium, Xanax, Halcion, and Prozac. Valium, Xanax, and Halcion each had its moment in the psychiatric sun, its fifteen minutes in the "pill limelight," before fading away to be replaced by another drug. In the case of Prozac, the newest miracle drug, the final chapter is not yet written.

Valium

For the past twenty-five years, Valium has been the most popular pill for coping with anxiety. It was the leading minor tranquilizer in the late 1970s and 1980s with an estimated 50 to 60 million prescriptions written annually. Initially, both the drug's manufacturer and most MPPs touted it as safe and nonaddictive, with few or no side effects. Very quickly these attitudes changed. First, it was discovered that large doses were lethal but, even worse, when Valium was combined with alcohol or some other drug, even small doses could be deadly. Valium soon became known as a killer. In a well-known review of Valium's addictive properties, Drs. Maletsky and Klotter studied twenty-seven so-called scientific articles claiming Valium was free of addictive properties and found that "none had conducted sufficient controls to justify dismissing this question." Even more startling was their finding that in the twenty-seven studies "no trials of withdrawal with systematic observations were attempted."[20] More interesting was the report by Valium's maker, Roche Laboratories, that the drug was not only being misprescribed by physicians for lesser indications and without adequate supervision, but that it was being overused and misused by doctors, hospitals, patients, and pharmacists. Hughes and Brewin in *The Tranquilizing of America* cited the report, as well as research indicating the benzodiazepines (a type of minor tranquilizer) can and do cause brain damage and argued Valium should be eliminated. Nevertheless, the maker and many other dispensers continued to argue for the safety of such drugs. The manufacturer did, however, put out warnings that "the physician should periodically assess the usefulness of the drug for the individual patient" and that the drug was "usually not required for the treatment of anxiety associated with the stress of everyday life." Then, as profits began to fall, Roche, according to Hughes and Brewin, launched "a highly sophisticated sales campaign" to sell Valium not only to doctors but directly to the public by defining stress as "both the ordinary and extraordinary pressures of life that confront every individual"—and as *an illness* treatable with Valium.

In 1979 because of the rising national anxiety over the Valium habit, Senator Edward Kennedy sponsored a Senate hearing on the problem. The hearing made clear that Valium and similar drugs caused two major problems: physical dependency and sedation. People on benzodiazepines often found they couldn't stop taking drugs, and that they couldn't function well while they were on them. The drugs accumulated in the body and, over time, they made the user more and more sluggish, drowsy, and forgetful.

Xanax

These results launched the search for an even more effective drug and, in 1981, Valium's successor arrived: Xanax, a new class of the benzodiazepines that are completely eliminated from the body in less than half a day. Xanax was specifically developed to deal with "panic" attacks. Since the drug didn't accumulate, the belief was it wouldn't increase drowsiness or slow down the users as they continued to take it.

When Valium's patent expired in 1984, the generic competition undercut Valium's sales and the manufacturer cut its promotion. Upjohn, the manufacturer of Xanax, took advantage of the opportunity. By 1986 Xanax had overtaken Valium in number of prescriptions and by 1987 it was in fourth place on the national sales list of all pre-scription drugs. In 1991, Xanax accounted for nearly one-fifth of all of Upjohn's sales.

Unfortunately, Xanax is a powerful psychiatric drug that is most often prescribed for people without any psychiatric problem. Users may be suf-fering from a little stress, but who doesn't? The biggest problem with Xanax is that it has turned out to be even more addictive than Valium.

According to the January 1993 *Consumer Reports*, it has been found that Xanax is usually prescribed by physicians in general practice and, in a 1990 National Ambulatory Medical Care Survey, only 30 percent of Xanax prescriptions were written by psychiatrists, whereas nearly half were written by family, general, and internal medicine practition-ers. Of all the Xanax prescriptions, only 28 percent were written for people who were diagnosed with clinical anxiety or panic attacks. Another 21 percent were for people suffering from depression—some-thing Xanax will not affect. The rest were written for people without any psychiatric or behavioral problem at all.[21] The statistics clearly show that the drug was being used as an all-purpose stress reliever, even though the FDA-approved package insert states specifically that Xanax should not be given simply for the "stress of everyday life" and that it was developed as a short-term treatment for clear symptoms of anxiety or as a treatment for full-blown anxiety or panic disorders.

It is now well known that all benzodiazepines produce physical dependency if taken long enough. The brain "learns" over time to expect a certain level of the drug. If the drug is then taken away, the brain reacts with agitation, sleeplessness, and anxiety—the same symptoms that led people to take the drug in the first place. Quite fre-quently these symptoms are worse than the original ones; this is a phe-nomenon called "the rebound effect." Other clinical studies found that Xanax and other benzodiazepines that are rapidly eliminated produce a quicker and more severe rebound effect than Valium, which is elim-inated more slowly. According to *Consumer Reports,* a University of Pennsylvania study took patients who had been on benzodiazepines for a year or more and tried to take them off their medication. Fifty-seven percent of the patients on Xanax simply could not stop taking them, but only 27 percent of the Valium patients were that physically depen-dent. Other studies have shown similar results.[22]

Nor is Xanax a pleasant drug to take. Many users argue it makes them stupid, keeps them in a mental fog, and impairs memory. Many have referred to it as "a mind eraser." It can also have the paradoxical effect of causing rage and hostility rather than tranquility. Even though Upjohn states it should never be used for longer than four months, it is often used for considerably longer by many people, particularly those with panic disorders.[23] Even though Upjohn built Xanax's reputation on studies of people with panic attacks, it still isn't clear how much—if any—Xanax helps. Several of Upjohn's highly publicized studies produced highly ambiguous results. In one study there was no significant difference in the average number of panic attacks—or in functioning in work, home, and social life—between the people who had been taking Xanax and those who were taking placebos.[24] Also, people on the placebos avoided the rebound effect. Surprisingly, because the investment of time and money would be too much, Xanax has never been tested as a long-term treatment for chronic anxiety disorders. In summary, twenty years of studies using benzodiazepines to treat chronic anxiety have shown that patients who receive inactive placebo pills generally improved over time. In many cases, their anxiety decreased as much as that of the people who were on the real drugs. What this indicates is that chronic anxiety waxes and wanes over time, and that the drugs may have little effect after their initial benefit.

If you are in serious trouble with anxiety or going through a rough time because of death, divorce, and so on, you should seriously consider the nondrug approaches. Even if you suffer from panic attacks, agoraphobia, or chronic anxiety and have a serious problem which normally requires professional evaluation or treatment, don't think of drugs as the treatment of choice. Over the last few years it has become clear that the cognitive behavior therapy (CBT) approaches are much more effective than drugs. Although such treatment doesn't provide the immediate results that Xanax does, in the long run it is vastly more successful.

CBT works by teaching panic and anxiety victims a new way of thinking about and dealing with their physical symptoms. CBT consciously induces panic and/or anxiety symptoms and then teaches that nothing terrible happens. Gradually the patients' CNS and the musculature are reeducated. A recent study at the Center for Stress and Anxiety Disorders in Albany, New York, compared CBT with Xanax and placebos for a fifteen-week period. Xanax and CBT showed roughly equal reductions in general anxiety. Follow-ups two weeks after the study ended, however, showed that 87 percent of the CBT patients were completely free of panic attacks. Half of those in the Xanax group were still having the attacks even though they continued using the drug. In late 1991, CBT was endorsed by a panel of National Institute of Health experts as a superior and effective treatment for panic disorders.

Halcion

Although normally prescribed as a sleeping pill, Halcion (Triazolam—a benzodiazepine) is chemically quite similar to Xanax. M.D.s like to prescribe it as a sleeping pill because it is metabolized from the body very rapidly, which means that it will put you to sleep at night but by morning it has been eliminated and you won't be drowsy any more. Put on the market by Upjohn in 1982, by 1987 it was the most popular sleeping pill in the United States. Unfortunately, it turned out to have some very nasty side effects. The first major disadvantage to emerge was that people who used it for any length of time found if they tried to stop, their "rebound" insomnia was worse than the original. Second, many people who took it became aggressive, hostile, and paranoid. In fact, Halcion has been linked to more hostility reactions by the FDA than any other sleeping pill (relative to the number prescribed) in pharmaceutical history. Third, many people who took only one or two pills suffered from anterograde amnesia: on the morning after they took Halcion they got up, apparently fine and normal, but soon discovered they had no memory whatsoever of anything they had done. (The length of the memory lapses varied among patients.) Fourth, some people became so mentally out of control (they had bizarre and uncontrollable thoughts) they sank into severe depression and attempted suicide. In far too many instances the attempts were successful and Upjohn has faced a steady series of lawsuits ever since, most of which the company has lost. Because of its dangers Halcion was banned in the United Kingdom. In May 1992, an FDA advisory committee allowed Halcion to stay on the market in the United States, but recommended that the original recommended dose of 0.5 milligrams per day be reduced to 0.25 milligrams—especially for elderly people. The lower dose the committee believed would be less effective but it would also be less likely to cause side effects. They also recommended that the package inserts warning about rebound insomnia and hostility reactions be strengthened. Our recommendation is even stronger: *Don't take it at all!* There are many easier and more effective ways to deal with insomnia: relaxation exercises, physical exercise, cognitive strategies, and other much less harmful sedatives.

Fortunately, Halcion's sales are falling and a November 1992 decision by a Dallas jury that Halcion was partly responsible for driving a man to murder should, hopefully, help further the decline.

Prozac

Even though Xanax is still a best seller, it now has a very challenging competitor in the Eli Lilly Company's product fluoxetine hydrochloride, popularly known as Prozac. Developed as an antidepressant for oral administration, Prozac was introduced in 1987. Since that time, more than four million people worldwide have been treated with the drug, clinical trials have involved thirty-three thousand patients, and Prozac has been the subject of more than two thousand medical and scientific papers over the past twenty years.

Prozac enjoyed the fastest acceptance of any medicine ever put on the market. In its first two years 650,000 prescriptions per month were filled. The clinical trial program for Prozac has been one of the largest ever carried out for an antidepressant. The research data, on the whole, supports Prozac's safety and effectiveness when the drug is properly used.

There are however, reasons to be suspicious of Prozac's wonders. Although Prozac is generally safer than other antidepressants because it is less likely to be fatal if a patient takes an overdose, it hasn't lived up to its early press. Side effects, for example, include nausea, headache, dizziness, anxiety, insomnia, drowsiness, loss of appetite, tremor, rash, and impotence. These reactions have caused about 15 percent of users to stop taking it. Lilly argues that about twice as many patients stop taking other antidepressants because of side effects.

Nevertheless, the United States Food and Drug Administration received 16,583 reports of adverse reactions to Prozac between 1987 and 1991, more than the FDA had ever before received for a drug. This may have been due, however, to the amount of publicity the drug also received, as the FDA stated, "the volume of adverse reactions associated with Prozac is not unexpected for a product that is evidently used and that has been the focus of such intense public interest." The FDA also stated that the 858 adverse reaction reports of suicide attempts by people on Prozac "provide no way of distinguishing between the role of the patients' underlying medical condition and the role of the drug in causing these suicidal events."[25] Dr. Robert A. King, assistant professor of child psychiatry at the Yale Medical School and author of one of the studies suggesting a link between Prozac and suicide, has stated, "The moral of the story is that people who are on it must be followed closely, and people shouldn't be on it for trivial reasons."[26]

One individual who disagrees with Dr. King is Dr. Peter Kramer, a psychiatrist who, in 1993, published *Listening to Prozac*. Prozac, "a mood brightener" according to Kramer, works so well and has such few side effects, it "performs chemically what has, heretofore, been an intimate interpersonal function," i.e., psychotherapy. Kramer, however, has a sophisticated overview of the problem. He states emphatically, "To my mind psychotherapy remains the single most helpful technology for the treatment of minor depressions and anxiety. But the belief—espoused not infrequently by health care cost cutters in the managed care industry—that medication can obviate psychotherapy conceals, I believe, a cynical willingness to let people suffer."[27] Amphetamines, cocaine, heroin, opium, alcohol, and other street drugs which are used to elevate mood all ultimately result in a "crash," but this never happens with Prozac, according to Kramer. Moreover, Prozac is in no way addictive, he says, a statement that is highly questionable and highly unlikely. It is well known that people can quickly and easily become "addicted" to anything that makes them feel good;

that gives either physical or psychological pleasure.[28] Prozac is still much too new to tell about its possible addictive properties. If it is half as effective and pleasurable as Kramer and others maintain, it is difficult to see how it could not be highly addictive. If it works as a "mood brightener" as well as Kramer claims, then anytime one's mood begins to dull one should be highly tempted to pop the pill.

Do mood brighteners such as Prozac disconnect people from reality? Kramer argues they do not and since there are no adverse effects with Prozac there are no risks! Because the drug is frequently used for people who are not ill, the benefit is ambiguous. In Kramer's words,

> An addicting drug may make a well person happier but by virtue of the compulsion inherent in addiction it compromises autonomy. Illness also compromises autonomy so an addictive drug might be used in the treatment of illness and, on balance, meet the ethical guideline. This standard of autonomy makes us rethink what our objections might be to a mood brightener, *a drug that is by definition not addicting*. Prozac both elevates mood and increases emotional resilience—increases the ability to bear troubling emotions. [Emphasis added.][29]

Kramer admits, however, that Prozac, like all drugs, has side effects. As noted earlier, Prozac not uncommonly causes the same symptoms as the other antidepressants and

> it has been associated with damage of one sort or another to almost every body system and organ—from arrhythmia of the heart to inflammation of the liver to dysfunction of the thyroid gland. As antidepressants go Prozac is relatively safe, but no drug is risk free. . . . Concern over unforeseen or tardive effects is realistic because Prozac has been around too briefly for anyone to know its long-term effects.[30]

In her review of *Listening to Prozac* in the *Los Angeles Times,* Carol Tavris noted that Kramer raised enough concerns about the medication to write another book that might be called *Worrying About Prozac.*[31] Tavris comments that at one psychiatric conference she attended, a psychiatrist castigated his colleagues for prescribing medication "imbecilically," seeing eight to ten patients an hour, and failing to consider the limitations of drug treatment and its long-term consequences. Kramer admits we don't know very much about the brain, depression, or drug effects at the moment, nor do we know the long-term effects of Prozac, but this last fact he doesn't announce until the final page. Additionally, while Kramer mentions cognitive behavior therapy, he does so in a single paragraph and merely acknowledges that it is "lately much in vogue." Tavris's well-said response is, "You bet it is, because it works."

*   *   *

Hughes and Brewin in their excellent and neglected work, *The Tranquilizing of America*, asked the question: "How do we discriminate between drugs we take to cure our ailments and those we take for fun?" Location, perhaps?

> In today's home medicine chest, prescription and non-prescription drugs, whether the drug is Valium for anxiety, Ritalin for hyperactivity, or Contac for colds fill the shelves. The rationale, whether diagnostically sound or not, is that these drugs are helpful in curing ailments or relieving their uncomfortable symptoms. The drugs we take for fun or to enhance or alter our mood for social reasons [*Prozac perhaps?*]—to become "the life of the party," to match the beat of a rock concert, to relax from a hard day, or just to experiment—are placed elsewhere. The vodka is in the liquor cabinet, the beer in the refrigerator, the marijuana in a can, the cocaine in a plastic packet in a shoe. There is, in short, a separation, albeit sometimes blurred, between the drugs we take for medical reasons and those we take for social or recreational purposes. But with the development and widespread use of psychoactive medications for mood and mind control, the separation between the drugs we take to alleviate disease and those we take simply because we want to feel better or different is growing increasingly thin. . . . The physician, as the dispenser of these pills and potions, could become not only the healer of the "sick" but the arbiter of what the "healthy" feel, think, and do.[32]

Should we use drugs to control and adjust the human development and experience of normal, healthy people? Should we work toward the development of a "choose your mood" society? In science fiction writer Stanislaw Lem's *The Futurological Congress*, every human behavioral function is altered, controlled, monitored by specific drugs.* Do we want this kind of society ruled over by psychiatric drug company dictators? The biologically oriented psychiatrists would love it. Blood tests and spinal taps would tell them just what pills each patient needs. As Arnold Mandell enthused, "We will learn to think of ourselves, our personalities, as an orchestra of chemical voices in our heads."[33]

In 1971, psychiatrist Dr. Nathan Kline published a paper titled "The Future of Drugs and Drugs of the Future," which foresaw the use of drugs to cure us of our ailments and envisioned the use of drugs and drug technology to enhance the experience of life. Kline predicts that drugs will

1. prolong childhood and shorten adolescence—for learning purposes;
2. reduce or circumvent the need for sleep—more work hours per day;
3. provide quick-acting intoxicants with no bad side effects, such as hangovers;
4. bank and stoke sexual responses to increase pleasure and compatibility between the sexes;
5. control affect and aggression, i.e., prevent psychopathology;
6. control the genetic code to eliminate "ugly" physical pathologies;
7. prolong or shorten memory to enrich life—remember good things and forget bad;
8. enhance positive and negative learning experiences so we will learn faster and more efficiently;
9. provoke guilt "relevant to certain actions" (abuse or murder) to prevent their repetition and make punishment truly effective, or relieve guilt when necessary;
10. enhance or inhibit the juices which mediate the mothering behavior;

---

*(San Diego: Harvest Books, 1985).

11. extend time for pleasurable experiences and shorten it for unpleasant ones;

12. deepen our appreciation of the beauty that surrounds us and allow us to experience anew the awe of human existence.[34]

Kline argues drugs are no more artificial or unnatural than most trappings of culture. Moreover, chemicals that do the things listed above not only *should be developed* but also *should be used.* Not to do so Kline sees as scientific nihilism. "The real problem," Kline argues, "in the field of psychopharmaceuticals is not creating the new drugs but determining who should make the decisions as to when they should be used, on whom and by whom."[35]

Hughes and Brewin disagree entirely. They state, "In simple terms, if drugs can do everything for us, we do not need to do anything for ourselves, and we need not take any responsibility for ourselves or our society."[36] If we are all "sick" and are all victims then we are not, never have been, and never will be responsible, independent, or "free." As noted earlier, Matthew Dumont defines mental health as "freedom" and if we are kept in eternal thrall to psychotherapy and the psychiatrist's pills, true freedom will remain forever beyond our grasp.

Ever cognizant of this issue, Thomas Szasz asks "What, pray tell, is the specific disease that Prozac treats?" Is "I feel down today" a disease?[37] Never mind, if the drug companies can't find a disease for their pill, they'll invent one. Every day they attack the physicians with free samples of new and improved pills for everything the human mind can conjure up. Prozac, for example, is now "old hat." The "new hat" is now Pfizer's Zoloft, generically known as sertraline hydrochloride, approved by the FDA in December 1991. Since depression is such a universal condition in that just about everyone feels bad at times—and some feel worse than others on any given day—the drug companies have a great marketing opportunity. Winston Churchill once noted, "Most of the world's work is done by people who don't feel very good." Zoloft will take care of this immediately. It increases activity in the brain synapses, erases feelings of depression, and has no side effects such as dizziness, water retention, weight gain, depressed libido, etc. Racing to keep pace, Smith-Kline-Beecham has come up with another goody called Paxil which is also off and running in the profits race.

In 1990, the ten largest pharmaceutical companies had an average profit on sales of 15.5 percent, compared with an average of 4.6 percent for the *Fortune 500* companies. Zoloft had sales of $195 million in 1992 and is expected to reach $800 million by 1997. This is easily understandable when we note that one 150 milligram Zoloft tablet costs $3.05 wholesale. With the retail markup of approximately 25 percent, this comes to $114 a month and $1,368 yearly. But don't worry, the insurance companies will pay for it and they much prefer the pills to the talk therapies. Psychotherapy averages out at approximately $3,000 a year per patient, making pills cheaper on the average. Most insurance companies limit psychotherapy benefits but not drug therapy. This works against all therapists except the psychiatrists, and discourages patients who truly need the talk therapy.

However, this may be to the shrinks' advantage: with so many new drugs like Zoloft and Paxil to listen to, the nation's psychiatrists will soon be so busy listening to the new medications they will have no time left to listen to their patients. But this is just as it should be. The days of the doctor listening to his patient are gone forever. Gained, however, is great efficiency. Now the new psychiatrist can serve as many as eight to ten patients per hour or sixty-four to eighty in a normal eight-hour day. With a little streamlining and his nurses' help, the process could be automated and with both the disorders and the remedy coded (for example, insomnia–4, Halcion–6) perhaps as many as one or two hundred patients per day could be processed!

Previously, the question was asked "What is the specific disease that Prozac treats? Is 'I feel down' a disease?" Another, equally valid, can be added: "What disease, does Prozac cure?" To the latter, at least, it seems an answer has been found: Psychiatric greed.

*   *   *

Are these new drugs truly better than the ones already on the market? According to the FDA, of 348 new drugs brought onto the market in 1991, 308 of them or 84 percent were rated C- class, that is, they work better than a placebo but not better than other drugs already on the market. Then why the new drugs? A few may not have some of the side effects of the old, but the primary reason is cost and profit! The new drugs are always more expensive than the drugs they replace. The overall effect is an increase in health care costs that are both unnecessary and wasteful.[38]

Incredible as it may seem, opiates as well as cocaine were indiscriminately dispensed in the last century and before and, for the most part, people in Europe and the United States did not consider these drugs either dangerous or addictive. The average citizen used opiates regularly and no one—neither doctors nor users—thought anything of it. Until 1906, Coca-Cola contained a very potent dose of cocaine. The social historians Berridge and Edwards reported that the narcotic consumption in England during the middle of the nineteenth century averaged 127 narcotic doses per year for every man, woman, and child. The use of tinctured opiates for children (paregoric) was standard practice in both Britain and the United States. Berridge and Edwards also reported that only late into the nineteenth century did the medical profession see opiate abuse as a problem and that they, themselves, were at fault for pushing its usage.[39] Today, unfortunately, M.D.s are afraid to prescribe any opiates at all—no matter how much pain their patients feel—for fear of creating addicts or having the federal authorities on their backs. As Thomas Szasz has noted "people most in pain and in need of opiates are legally denied them and must obtain them illegally. God gave us opiates and the therapeutic state takes them away."[40]

Knowledgeable and responsible self-medication as a moral and social good is neither a medical disease nor an evil. In Szasz's view it is simply absurd that so many medications like penicillin, the minor tranquilizers, and opiates require an M.D.'s prescription,[41] especially when the insurance companies will not reimburse clients for "claims of illness" expenses such as over-the-counter painkillers unless a doctor has prescribed other medications.

Despite the fact that drug consumption in the United States today is incredibly high we are by no means the greatest abuser. Among modern nations this honor is held by France. With regard to painkillers and tranquilizers, French M.D.s give their patients all they want anytime they want them. They simply don't care, and the law agrees with them.[42]

Additional support for our argument that psychiatric pill pushers are doing more harm than good comes from recent articles by Dr. David H. Jacobs and by Seymour Fisher and Roger P. Greenberg. In a lengthy, in-depth review of the psychiatric use of drugs, Jacobs states, "The catastrophe of widespread and expanding medically-produced disease has failed to alarm psychiatry into taking stock of the determinants of the catastrophe—indeed the existence and magnitude of the tragedy is barely recognized within psychiatry."[43] Jacobs is severely critical of the pharmaceutical companies and their current procedures for testing and evaluating new drugs aimed at human consumption as well as the FDA's overly permissive approval of neuroleptic drugs whose long-term consequences are seldom if ever known. Jacobs also flays psychiatry for ignoring the fact that neuroleptics not only produce irreversible disorders but also have widespread pathophysiological effects in the brain and eventually produce emotional-behavioral impairments as well. He also concludes that, "the catastrophe of medically-created illness of unprecedented proportions on the part of psychiatry from the 1950s to the present . . . has not produced a critical self-examination within psychiatry of the ideological, conceptual, financial, professional, and systemic factors which in combination produced the catastrophe."[44] Jacobs also insists that the most important lesson that has been learned from the past forty years of psychopharmacological research is the potent and consistent effects of the placebo—which in most cases has proved to be almost as powerful as the drug being tested.

Fisher and Greenberg, in their article "Prescriptions for Happiness?" also zero in on the current biological approach to treating unhappiness and convincingly demonstrate that the so-called scientific studies underpinning claims of the effectiveness of drugs such as Prozac, Zoloft, and Paxil are seriously flawed.[45] They argue that at the moment no one actually knows how effective antidepressants really are. Fisher and Greenberg agree with Jacobs in that one thing that is known is the power of the placebo. Most people are unaware of the fact that placebos can create addictions as well as produce toxic effects such as rashes, apparent memory loss, fever, headaches, and more. The placebo literature stresses the fact that even these "sugar-pills" can act as powerful body-altering substances and they can and do influence a wide range of the body's systems. The authors argue that not only are most drug trials biased but the drug researchers typically recruit patients whose depression is not accompanied by any other type of physical or mental disorder—a situation that does not hold for depressed persons in the general population. Fisher and Greenberg also emphasize that even the patient's attitude toward the therapist is as biological in nature as a patient's response to an antidepressant drug. Modern biopsychiatry has, unfortunately, chosen to ignore and discount the psychological side of human beings and this is a tragic and catastrophic error. How effective are the psychiatrist's pills for unhappiness? Let us see.

NOTES

1. Ivan Illich, *The Limits to Medicine* (New York: Pantheon, 1979).

2. Ibid., p. 7.

3. Robert Mendelsohn, *Confessions of a Medical Heretic* (New York: Warner Books, 1980), p. 56.

4. Alan S. Levin, "Corruption in American Medicine," in *Dissent in Medicine—Nine Doctors Speak Out* (Chicago: The New Medical Foundation, Contemporary Books, 1985), pp. 78–80.

5. Food and Drug Administration, *Drug Review: Post Approval Risks 1976–1985* (Washington, D.C.: General Accounting Office Report, April 1990).

6. Levin, "Corruption in American Medicine," p. 82.

7. Ibid., pp. 80–84.

8. U.S. Department of Health and Human Services, *The Leading Causes of Death in the U.S. 1977* (Washington, D.C.: GPO, 1980).

9. J. B. Mickinlay and Sonja McKinlay, *Health and Society* (New York: Cambridge University Press, 1977), pp. 405–28.

10. Richard Taylor, *Medicine Out of Control: The Anatomy of a Malignant Technology* (Melbourne: Sun Books, 1979), pp. 46–47.

11. H. Beaty and R. Petersdorf, "Iatrogenic Factors in Infectious Diseases," *Annals of Internal Medicine* 65 (1966): 641.

12. Hans Ruesch, *Naked Empress or the Great Medical Fraud* (Massagno/Lugano, Switzerland: CIVIS Publications, 1992).

13. Cited in Ruesch, *Naked Empress*, p. 13.

14. Richard Hughes and Robert Brewin, *The Tranquilizing of America* (New York: Warner Books, 1980), pp. 248–49.

15. Paraphrased from S. M. Wolfe and Rose-Ellen Hope, *Worst Pills, Best Pills II* (Washington, D.C.: Public Citizen's Health Research Group, 1993), p. 3.

16. Ibid.

17. Ibid., p. 4.

18. R. H. Brook et al., "Appropriateness of Acute Medical Care for the Elderly," *Health Policy* 14 (1991): 225–42.

19. M. E. Ferry, P. Lanny, and L. Becker, "Physician's Knowledge of Prescribing for the Elderly," *Journal of the American Geriatrics Society* 33 (1985): 616–25.

20. Barry Maletsky and James Klotter, cited in *Overcoping with Valium* (FDA Consumer Report) (Washington, D.C.: U.S. Department of Health, Education, and Welfare Pub. No. 80–3100, December/January 1980).

21. "High Anxiety," *Consumer Reports* (January 1993): 19–24.

22. Ibid., p. 20.

23. Ibid., p. 21.

24. Ibid., p. 22.

25. Food and Drug Administration hearing on Prozac, Washington, D.C., September 20, 1991. See also Peter Breggin, *Talking Back to Prozac* (New York: St. Martin's Press, 1994), pp. 128–59.

26. Robert A. King et al., "Emergence of Self-Destructive Phenomena in Children and Adolescents during Fluoxetine Treatment," *Journal of American Child & Adolescent Psychiatry* 30 (January 1993): 179–86.

27. Peter Kramer, *Listening to Prozac: A Psychiatrist Explores Antidepressant Drugs and the Remaking of the Self* (New York: Viking, 1993), p. 292.

28. Stanton Peele, *The Diseasing of America: Addiction Treatment Out of Control* (Lexington, Mass.: Lexington Books, 1989), p. 3.

29. Kramer, *Listening to Prozac,* p. 295.

30. Ibid., p. 312.

31. Carol Tavris, "The Prozac Puzzle," *Louisville Courier Journal,* 3 July 1993, p. A15.

32. Hughes and Brewin, *The Tranquilizing of America,* pp. 314–15.

33. Cited in Hughes and Brewin, *The Tranquilizing of America,* p. 315.

34. Nathan Kline, "The Future of Drugs and Drugs of the Future," reprinted in Hughes and Brewin, *The Tranquilizing of America,* pp. 316–17.

35. Ibid., p. 322.

36. Hughes and Brewin, *The Tranquilizing of America,* p. 323.

37. Thomas Szasz, *Our Right to Drugs: The Case for a Free Market* (New York: Praeger, 1992), p. 129.

38. George C. Halvorson, *Strong Medicine* (New York: Random House, 1993), pp. 84–85.

39. V. Berridge and G. Edwards, *Opium and the People: Opium Use in 19th Century England* (New Haven, Conn.: Yale University Press, 1987), pp. 149–50.

40. Szasz, *Our Right to Drugs*, p. 143.

41. Ibid., p. 67.

42. Ibid., p. 92.

43. David H. Jacobs, "Psychiatric Drugging: Forty Years of Pseudo-Science, Self-Interest, and Indifference to Harm," *Journal of Mind & Behavior* 16 (1995): 421–70.

44. Ibid., p. 435.

45. Seymour Fisher and Roger P. Greenberg, "Prescriptions for Happiness?" *Psychology Today* 28 (September/October 1995): 32–37.

10

Depression: The Right to Feel Bad

Two hundred years ago, claiming the right to be happy was considered a revolutionary move, in the late twentieth century, claiming the right to be unhappy may be just as revolutionary. We need to reclaim depression from the exclusive clutches of popular psychology, in which happiness and feeling good remains the only valid modes of human experience.[1]

PATHOLOGIZING NORMAL EXPERIENCE

For many years now as we have moved more and more into our permanent role as "victims" and psychological casualties, we have finally succeeded in allowing the psychotherapists to convince us that we are all in need of their expertise. Their psychology, they tell us, can give us self-knowledge which, in combination with their knowledge, fully explains why we have all our problems and can solve them, setting us on the road to total mental health and human happiness. If you believe this nonsense then you suffer from what many observers call "the health neurosis": you have such a terrible fear of mental aberrations you're now neurotic about every aspect of your life and believe if you are not ecstatically happy every moment of every day then you are abnormal and need therapy. This absurdity led psychiatrist Adrian van Kamm to argue that the major goal of good psychotherapy today should be "liberation from the crippling influence of popularized psychological theories, from the tyrannies of anxious preoccupation with public image, and from the mistaken belief in the possibility of a 'scientific' manipulation of human existence towards an almost magical readjustment to wholeness."[2] Too many people, unfortunately, have been told they have a constitutional *right* to feel good all the time and not merely the right to *pursue* happiness but the right to *possess* and *own* it permanently!

Just in case you do not already know it, *you do not have any such rights nor have you ever had them.* You cannot pursue and catch happiness directly. It is always a by-product (not a "buy" product) of pursuing something else. If you have gained your ideas about mental health and depression from members of the psychotherapeutic community, odds are you have a warped and biased view of what is "normal." Clinicians tend to see the entire population as abnormal, sick, and depressed. Their views as to who is and is not healthy will differ markedly from most other people and other groups in our society.

Most so-called psychological depression is normal and only a very tiny part of depression is so severe that it requires the services of a professional. As Pat Love observed, "Given the state of the world, it would seen abnormal not to be depressed."[3] We read the first noble truth of Buddhism, "Life is suffering," and wonder if anyone alive would dare question it. If you are normal and mentally healthy, you are going to feel sad, depressed, and out of energy every now and then and question the value of life itself on numerous occasions. If you don't experience these occasions, you are definitely emotionally (mentally) abnormal or else the most fortunate person on the planet. Or, you are emotionally blank—totally incapable of experiencing the normal ups and downs of ordinary existence, which would deem you a psychopath.

If you fully understand that every human that has ever lived has also experienced grief, desolation, melancholy, doubt, and a loss of faith in a higher benevolent power or a benign presence in the universe, and that no one maintains emotional depression for very long, you should at least, philosophically, better understand the nature of human existence and begin to appreciate the fact that happiness and unhappiness lie on a continuum. Just about everyone who is rational and of normal intelligence has had encounters with serious depression; times in which they have gone into a blue funk and have had great difficulty in working out of it. Our emotional lives are cyclical, and there is no escape from this as long as we live. Without despair there can be no hope, and without gloom there can be no joy!

Economist Julian L. Simon published a book titled *Good Mood: The New Psychology of Overcoming Depression* in 1993. Simon says he was badly depressed for thirteen years—from early 1962 to early 1975. Except for working, playing, or making love Simon was continuously miserable, felt worthless, hoped to die, and avoided suicide only because he felt his kids needed him.[4] What Simon fails to realize is that hundreds—if not thousands—of people feel like this. In no way is or was he alone. Simon, however, is an intellectual, and was smart enough to realize people can improve their emotional life by changing their self-destructive thinking patterns. He also had enough smart, psychologically knowledgeable friends who convinced him that cognitive therapy (learning to control one's thinking) can be helpful to some people. Once Simon was convinced that he could control his own thinking, he began to put these ideas into practice. Simon did, however, add something novel and new: a computer therapist. Simon's book includes a therapeutic computer program that is both IBM and Apple Macintosh compatible and which allows the reader to plot his recovery from depression in step-by-step fashion. What is particularly amusing about Simon's book is his demonstration that, in many ways, the computer is a much better therapist than the average human shrink. The computer never wears out or suffers from fatigue. It never fails to pay attention to the client nor ever burns out from emotional overload. Neither does one encounter the usual transference and countertransference dilemmas. Most important of all, you can be sure no troublesome sexual problems will raise their ugly heads. Simon insists the Socratic dialogue can lift one onto a new plateau of thought and behavior that will make just about every negative aspect of normal human existence tolerable—unpleasant though they *still* may be. Simon also tells us that faith, hope, and religious conversion can also be helpful in a pinch.

The beauty and wisdom of Simon's advice is that not only can one endure bad feelings for years on end, but one can also lead a successful and productive life while feeling bad, and moreover, if you really put your mind to it, you can overcome and even conquer feelings of worthlessness and despair. The fact of the matter is depression will pass away! On occasion the very worst thing you can do is take these troubles to a therapist. Hemingway's suicide, Styron's near-suicide, and all of the other victims of the permanent side effects of lithium and the other antianxiety drugs are clear warnings of the possibilities that await you if you start a drug program. Much too often results from the drug therapy may be worse than your original problem.

Sensible psychotherapists are well aware that depression is a psychological disorder, not a physiological or biological one. Drugs only succeed in covering up the problem or delaying recovery. Competent therapists know very well that the vast majority of people get over their depressions without any help at all. Most people are able to renew their flagging spirits without help from anyone, particularly psychotherapists.[5] They find assistance instead in a trusted friend, lover, work, hobbies, and religion.

Unfortunately, instead of turning to a friend for comfort and relief from depression, many people run to the medical establishment, which immediately provides pills to ease the pain. However, downing antidepressants not only can have adverse side effects but they also make many people feel worse. The drugs also can become addictive and, in spite of the billions of prescriptions for them, the evidence for their effectiveness is scant. Additionally, it is difficult to measure their effectiveness, because at least 25 percent of all depressed patients recover spontaneously within one month and 50 percent in two or three months.[6] Carefully conducted research also casts a great deal of doubt as to the efficacy of the antidepressants.

Fisher and Greenberg, in their study *The Limits of Biological Treatments for Psychological Distress*, conclude there is little justification for the use of antidepressants because of the following facts:

1. Thirty to forty percent of the drug studies comparing antidepressants and placebos showed no differences between the drugs and the placebos.

2. "Substantial improvement" (i.e., feeling happier), the standard of effectiveness in the drug studies, averages out to only 25 percent.
3. Since there are no standard criteria for determining "improvement" and psychiatric measures are in terms of "gained weight," or "slept better," etc., rather than in psychological self-report and objective measures, true efficacy of antidepressants is unknowable.
4. Studies comparing the efficacy of medication and psychotherapy generally favor psychotherapy since "Psychotherapy had its main effect on mood, apathy, suicidal ideation, work, and interest, whereas medication mainly influenced sleep and appetite."

In summary they conclude, "Although drugs may help patients with their sleep disturbance, research shows they are often less efficient than psychotherapy in helping patients with depression and apathy and frequently ineffective in aiding patients in their social adjustment, interpersonal relationships or work performance."[7]

It is these last things, of course, which are the truly important measures of any and all therapeutic effectiveness. It should be clear that pills for unhappiness leave much to be desired.

Diagnosis

Getting your unhappiness (or as the shrinks describe it, "a dysthymic disorder"), from which an alleged five to six million Americans suffer, accurately diagnosed and properly treated is neither simple nor easy. A recent book, titled *On the Edge of Darkness*, reports conversations with well-known people who talk about their depressions. The book makes clear that good help for such problems is hard to come by. The author herself, early in her book, confesses, "I started seeing a therapist when I was seventeen. He was the first of a dozen. Each was helpful in his or her way; each assisted me through trying times, helped me toward greater self-knowledge, and in many cases offered true friendship. But of the twelve, eleven failed to diagnose or treat my disease."[8]

Most therapists make a clear distinction between the normal ups and downs of daily living which come and go and those moods which are considered "major depressions." In a "major depression" sufferers feel trapped in their sadness, are unable to control their emotions, and are unable to overcome or escape the mood of depression. Prominent feelings of hopelessness, gloom, sadness, and despondency are usually accompanied by an inability to take an interest in things that used to provide pleasure—hobbies, family, sex, work, food, etc. Sufferers also feel drained, exhausted, and overworked. Many times somatic difficulties also arise: indigestion, nausea, headaches, and pains of one sort or another. Insomnia and excessive sleepiness are both common. Anxiety in the form of dread or fear may also show up along with feelings of failure, inadequacy, and low self-esteem. Concentration and decision-making may also be difficult and thoughts of suicide are common, although only 1 percent or less commit suicide during the first year of "feeling bad."

Exactly what causes these symptoms is unknown, but biological psychiatrists are, of course, convinced the problem lies in the genes, or in the biology and the chemistry of the brain. If you go to them for help they will prescribe a regimen of medication, dependent upon the kind and number of symptoms you report. Most will also consult the DSM, which tells them that the client must experience a depressed mood for at least two weeks and have significant weight change, sleep problems, physical upset or agitation, low energy, guilt or worthlessness, problems concentrating, or repeated thoughts of death in order to be diagnosed as "clinically" depressed.

Kathy Cronkite, the author of *On the Edge of Darkness*, provides clinical guesstimates that 12 percent of the male population and 26 percent of the female population will experience a major depressive episode at some time in their lives, with the episode most frequently showing up between ages twenty and fifty. It can, however, occur at any time. For many clients the symptoms may disappear on their own after six months or a year whereas others—approximately 20 percent—may be depressed for longer than a year.[9]

There are, of course, other nonpsychological reasons for periodic depressions: infectious diseases, neurological diseases, cancer, vitamin deficiency, and so on. Medication can also cause depression. Some antibiotics, analgesics, heart and blood pressure drugs, steroids, hormones, and psychiatric drugs can affect one's mood in a negative way. In fact, just about anything and everything that makes us feel bad can bring on symptoms of dysthymia or neurotic depression. Some therapists argue "clinical or major depression" is due to genes, personality, temperament, and biology, whereas the milder forms can also be very upsetting over a long period of time but are more likely due to our faulty thinking and inadequate philosophy than to flawed genetics or diseased biology. Of course our biologically oriented psychiatrists see both types as curable with medication. Not being exceptionally skilled at diagnosis, many therapists will also confuse dysthymia with major depressions and bipolar disorders (mania then depression; i.e., vacillation or just the manic phase without the depression); anxiety disorder; borderline personality disorder; schizophrenia; and medication side effects. Since so many other behavioral disorders have depressive side effects, most therapists really don't know what to call the symptoms. If delusions and hallucinations plus rapid mood changes and loss of inhibitions occur, then the diagnosis is usually a bipolar disorder; what used to be called manic depression. To confuse the picture even further, some clinicians throw in the classification "cyclothymic disorder" which is a milder form of the bipolar disorder. Then, to add insult to injury, the DSM-IV has added, and considers as a disease, the "Late Luteal Phase Dysphonic Disorder," formerly known as the "Premenstrual Dysphoric Disorder," a depression associated with hormonal changes during the menstrual cycle—a pathologizing of a normal experience (PMS). The mere fact that this category was included and regarded as a "disease" speaks volumes about the absurdity of psychiatric thinking and the "diseasing" of America.

While speaking of absurdities and faulty thinking, we cannot omit examples of the unscientific views of some biopsychiatrists. John Kelsoe, M.D., for example, tells us:

> The outlook for psychiatric illness in general is very bright. We are in an era where the understanding of these behavioral disorders as brain disorders is exploding. The tools which we now have available to us to study the brain and to understand these things are changing at an incredible rate. . . . Distinguishing what things are characteristic of depression is not entirely clear right now, but we are

getting to the point where we will begin to be able to see functional brain differences in a scanner. . . . *If we understood what was really going wrong in the brain, we could devise drug treatments that are much more specific and potentially more effective.* [Emphasis added.][10]

A few lines later he gushes about the potential for genetically *correcting* depression, thus "proving" it is an illness. If Dr. Kelsoe really understood genetics and the difference between science and science-fiction, and if he had a better understanding of the nature of depression, he would realize what he has said is wishful thinking and is even further away in terms of scientific reality. Most important of all is the fact that psychological depression—like one's preference for classical over popular music—is in no way the result of or due to *faulty* genes. How in the name of science does one determine whether a gene *is* or *is not* faulty? Who writes the definition or decides the criteria for what is faulty? The assumption that thinking one way rather than another is due directly to faulty genes betrays a fundamental lack of biological understanding.

Like Kelsoe and other propagandists, biological psychiatry's aim is to prove that complex human behavior is merely a simple matter of genetics. Despite their efforts to blame everything from cancer to alcoholism to criminality on our genes, they misunderstand the scientific problem and completely ignore the complex interactions of genes with the environment at every level of human development. Like the eugenic "race improvement" theories of seventy-five years ago, this new genetic determinism serves a conservative social agenda reflecting our society's eagerness to blame ill-health and misfortune on the individual rather than on a sick and unsatisfactory society.

Biologists Avital and Jablonka have recently shown that many animals (including humans) transmit features of themselves from one generation to the next not simply by passing along their chromosomes, but by training their offspring to behave as they do. Because so many past observers were blinded by the concept of instinct and gene transmission they failed entirely to see the subtle and complex learning behavior taking place in young organisms whose physical and mental structures prepared them for the behavior-determining stimulation from their natural environments. Naturalists and biologists who are good observers have long known that behavior acquired through learning can be handed down through several generations, without the involvement of the DNA, which is mistakenly considered to be the source of the inherited information.

Moreover, differences in behavioral styles between one family line and another can provide an opportunity for the conventional forces of natural selection to operate. Thus, the best strategies or behaviors will survive and be passed on while the failures will be dropped. In other words, the behaviors will operate according to the very same principles that govern the survival and spread of genes. Useful styles will, accordingly, tend to expand through the population until many members are behaving in a very similar fashion. What is important here is that the behavioral variations have nothing to do with any underlying genetic variations. According to Avital and Jablonka, "the DNA-centric view of heredity is wrong. . . . It was useful and necessary for the development of genetics, but there is more to heredity than genes."[11] What is clear and important to recognize here is that socially acquired behavior can be and is transmitted through several generations and this behavior is independent of genotypic (DNA-based) variations. Natural selection can and does operate on an additional level. Thus, direct evolution of behavior becomes possible and affects the behavior patterns of the individuals who transmit them. Maternally transmitted behavior, for example, contributes to the evolution of maternal behavioral strategies, including the evolution of behavior associated with male-female conflict. Behavior patterns are usually cloned phenotypically (through education and training) not genotypically (through instinct). The implications of this for the belief that human behavior is unalterably and inevitably determined by our genes is staggering.

Moreover, as Hazleton emphasizes in her book, *The Right to Feel Bad*, the problem is the biopsychiatric view of human depression as an illness and the belief that the mind has to be diagnosed, treated, and cured like any other physical disease. The fact that depression is a *psychological* problem and not a disease is a fact that totally escapes the medically trained psychiatrist. Once the good "doctor" has labeled his client "depressive" there is nothing left except medication, electroshock, and hospitalization for curing the "sickness." Another idea that seems to escape the medical pathologizing of normal human experience is that most of the individual's problems with sadness, hopelessness, lack of faith, and discouragement are in no way pathological. Since psychiatry deals with pathology and abnormality and has a number of set procedures to deal with these things, then this is all that the pathologist knows to do. Most psychiatrists, particularly biopyschiatrists, are not well-equipped to deal with life's psychological and philosophical problems. They are far less able to provide you with the wisdom, sound practical advice and counsel needed than would be a close friend or a minister who has known you and your family for many years.

Our biggest social error—the one we have made as a society—has been to allow the medical profession to pathologize normal human behavior. Even further, we have allowed them to see human society itself as "sick" and, consequently, all of its members as necessarily pathological. Throughout history social critics have noted the pervasiveness of depression. *The Anatomy of Melancholy*, Robert Burton's seventeenth-century portrait of human nature, bemoaned the universality of depression and reminded readers that the Greeks and Romans found depression so common that scarcely one in a thousand was free of it. We have no reason whatsoever to believe that as a society we, today, are more depressed than people in other times. Our belief that this is an "age of depression" is not borne out by statistical estimates of the prevalence of depression: 7 to 15 percent of the general population. Our current conviction that it is now epidemic is based more on the statistics promulgated by psychiatrists, psychotherapists, and drug companies. If depression is more common and widespread today than it was in the past, it is because we have been talked into it and persuaded we are victims and, indeed, sick. As Hazleton notes, "When psychology offers itself as a full explanation of human unhappiness it becomes fraud, offering an impossible ideal as an achievable goal. The result is therapeutic megalomania—false expectations not only of cure but even of perfection through psychotherapy."[12]

What the psychotherapeutic state has done is convince us that we are so sick that we need help from the "experts," the kind of people who will reinforce and convince us of the idea that we *are* sick. We no longer have any faith in our friends or ourselves and if we do have any, a visit to your friendly shrink will destroy it. We have become victims of "health neurosis"; we are now so afraid of sickness—a fear fostered by psychiatry—we are now neurotic about our mental health. Nothing less than an unending state of euphoria, an everlasting state of "feeling good," will do anymore. Unless we feel good all the time and have complete control over our emotions and never suffer or feel depressed, we believe we need psychotherapy. And if you go to a therapist, he will agree with you. And if you choose a biopsychiatrist, you will be lucky if you manage to avoid medication, hospitalization, or both. If you are a little unlucky and don't respond quickly to the medication, you may well find yourself receiving electroconvulsive shock treatment whether you want it or not. In case you doubt this, recall the recent case of Lucille Austwick, an eighty-year-old nursing-home resident outside of Chicago mentioned previously. One of the nursing-home physicians had Lucille examined by a psychiatrist for depression. The shrink immediately chose to give Lucille electroconvulsive shock treatment because, in his words, "it is necessary in order to prevent further weight loss [she lost three pounds] and to save her life." Lucille refused. Nevertheless, the shrinks went to court to get an order allowing them to forcibly shock her. Through the efforts of Support Coalition International—an alliance of twenty-eight patients' rights advocacy and support groups—and her lawyers, she was able to avoid this mistreatment.[13]

In case the reader believes the case against the shrinks' desire to pathologize is overstated, let us look at another example. Anyone familiar with the current literature on depression is well aware that the books arguing depression is a serious psychological illness requiring treatment by psychiatric specialists outnumber by approximately ten to one those arguing for psychological, philosophical, or sociological treatment. In the former category one of the most flagrant examples of pathologizing is illustrated by the psychiatrist Ronald Fieve—a self-styled expert on depression and its treatment—who in his book, *Moodswing,* deplores the fact that he was unable to get his hands on Abraham Lincoln's bouts with depression in 1841:

> [Lincoln's] inability to attend the legislative sessions and the fear of
> his colleagues that he would attempt suicide would in modern times
> prompt most psychiatrists to arrange for inpatient hospitalization

and treatment. I would insist on hospitalization, observation for suicidal intent, antidepressant drugs, and later administration of lithium as the treatment of choice for such a condition.[14]

As Hazleton commented, "And all this for what? For a bad depression that lasted a sum total of one week! Lincoln was lucky that Fieve was not around in 1841. His psychiatric intervention would have deprived us of a brilliant and humane politician and we would all—including Fieve—be poorer for it"[15]

An unending drugged state of emotional equilibrium is neither ideal nor desirable. Only a shortsighted fool would ever consider it or want it for himself and only an even greater fool would ever consider foisting this off on someone else. Nevertheless this is what biological psychiatry prescribes every day for thousands of people in rapidly increasing numbers. For those who shake their head in wonderment that all these "MDeities" could be wrong, they need only read the literature written by people who have been through medical treatment and survived. Kathy Cronkite's book, *On the Edge of Darkness*, which was referred to earlier, is illuminating in this regard. Near the end of the book she says:

> I'll admit my own prejudice: I entered into this project with a strong belief in the chemical approach to the treatment of depression. . . . For me psychotherapy seemed a failure at treating my depression; medication a success. But after hearing so many different kinds of success stories, and interviewing numerous mental health experts, shades of gray emerged. I saw my success story from a new angle. Perhaps I needed the twenty years of therapy to clear away cobwebs of childhood misunderstandings and unfulfillments. Perhaps I needed to work on the various tangled issues I believe we all have by adulthood. Perhaps I needed the love and concern and expertise of those dozen different men and women who had helped me work through so much. Without them, perhaps I would never have been able to flip that internal switch that illuminated my problems and allowed me to confront them. For many people, the medication is necessary to bring the disease under control before they are able to work consistently with a therapist. For me much of that work was finished before medications were started.[16]

This tells us that Cronkite has no idea what brought about her relief of symptoms or those of anyone else she interviewed. Her next statements in this regard are truly insightful:

> For some patients, finding the right treatment is as easy as taking aspirin for a headache. For others, the search involves trial and error, sometimes over an extended period of time. Some are still looking. Some have given up. And more than a few are enraged at the medical community that they feel let them down.[17]

This last group has every right to be angry, especially if they have been assaulted with medication and electroshock and have been treated for a physiological disease that doesn't exist because their problem is essentially a psychological, philosophical, and existential one.

Cognitive therapy and group work have proved to be very helpful in dealing with depression because they teach people to monitor their thinking, i.e., their self-talk, which is usually erroneous. When they learn to stop the faulty self-talk and to gain support from caring others, most of the battle is won. After antidepressive medication there are frequent relapses, but there is less likelihood of this with cognitive therapy. Although the medical community will never admit it, they are not able to cope with depression on a practical level mostly because most depressions are not biological disorders. If people recover they do so of their own accord—often in spite of the therapists' efforts—especially if the therapists resort to lithium or electroshock or both.

The one thing that comes through most clearly in Cronkite's book is that the so-called authorities and alleged experts on depression don't know what they are doing. Every case is, for them, a crap shoot. Not only are they totally without a credible and viable theory or a factual, valid experimental base for their biological mythology, but their attempts to attribute the disorder to genetics and brain physiology are equally bankrupt. They are, quite simply, guessing when they face each individual sufferer. They try everything and anything, hoping something will work. As a class they may deserve an "A" for effort, but they deserve an "F" for stupidity and failure. If the poor depressives are fortunate they will recover spontaneously despite the treatment, leaving the therapist to congratulate himself on how successful his treatments were. The last thing on earth the therapist would ever admit is the fact that his efforts were futile.

Biologically oriented therapists will, of course, argue that all human depression is due to some neurochemical abnormality and the leading candidate today seems to be the neurotransmitter serotonin. Some theorists argue that hostile or violent behavior—even suicide—or attacks of anger in depressives is associated with low or abnormal levels of serotonin.[18] Reducing or blocking serotonin seems to increase aggressiveness and speculation has it that this promotes hostile thinking. Exactly how, no one has any idea. It is claimed that either abnormally high or abnormally low levels promote self-aggressiveness and suicide.[19] Also observed are the effects of some antidepressants, for example, Prozac, to reduce the ability of the presynaptic neuron to take back and store serotonin.[20] The result is a buildup of serotonin and increased neural activity. Cohen explains that, due to the medication, "compensatory changes occur in pre- and postsynaptic neurons, some therapeutic . . . but some not. In a few people, the drugs may produce a worsening of symptoms and heightened risk for suicide. A chronic, even treatment-resistant problem may then develop."[21]

Cohen believes that the psychological "environment" created by the parents is part of our "inheritance," and plays a large and influential role in our susceptibility to depression. However, he is wise enough to keep the belief in its proper place as but one of many influences and factors that is modified and manipulated over the developmental course of a lifetime. Cohen insists that it is "wrong in every sense of the word—incorrect, deceptive, and harmful—to think of the environment created by the parents as being not biological or not genetic."[22] He recognizes the difficulties of developing a credible neuropsychological or "brain" theory of depression and stresses the fact that we have a long way to go before the brain mechanisms underlying complex overt behaviors are ever understood.

Nevertheless, the propaganda machine for antidepressant drugs is currently in full swing and is succeeding in its efforts to convince the unwary and uninformed that relief from the terrors of clinical depression is only a pill or two away. For instance, Dr. Melvin Konner, a supporter of Prozac and biopsychiatry, says our medications are so good we have no excuse for not taking them. He uses the argument which states that if we blunt the pain we may fail to deal with the internal and external problems that are causing it as a noble but irrelevant sentiment. Why limit this to depression or obsessions? Konner asks:

> Why not let asthmatics wheeze instead of giving them bronchodilators, so they'll feel motivated to do something about the allergens in their environment? Why give acetaminophen or aspirin to the tens of millions of sufferers of chronic arthritis pain? Their pain is only natural, signaling them to slow down, and these drugs can certainly be harmful. One could go on but the point is very clear: It is only because we so belittle and devalue psychic pain that such critics even have a hearing.[23]

Really? Perhaps it could be that there are much more important and telling reasons: (1) the fact that depression is not a brain disease. Most depression is due to psychosocial experiences and emotional problems, not brain disorders and it is typically precipitated by losses and other stresses, not viruses and bacilli; (2) no causal relationship has ever been established between any specific complex behavior and specific biochemical brain states; (3) at present there is no biological theory of depression and the etiology of depression and all affective illnesses is unknown; (4) most depression develops in people with normal brain functioning who have been the victims of psychological stress and social conflict; and (5) the normal human brain when subjected to an artificially induced chemical imbalance as the result of the administration of an antidepressant will usually attempt to compensate and may, in all likelihood, produce behavioral results worse than the original problem the antidepressants were supposed to correct.[24]

What we clearly do not need at this time is additional propaganda on the part of the drug manufacturers, and their paid psychiatric mouthpieces, touting the wonders of a medication that may well prove in the long run to be as dangerously habit forming as crack cocaine.

Treating Depression

It should be obvious to everyone that we can change how we feel by altering the body's chemistry. Human beings have been doing this since the beginning of time by ingesting drugs of every conceivable type and variety. One of the most universal and historic has been alcohol, others include opium, cocaine, and marijuana. People have ingested all of these drugs and more because the drugs change the way they feel. We have, however, never before assumed that the way we felt before ingesting these substances was an illness or a disease. This, nevertheless, is exactly what we are doing in the case of the antidepressants. Moreover, in the case of *chemical* depression (if there is such a thing) we do not know whether chemical changes in the brain caused our depression or whether the chemical changes are a side-effect of or a reaction to our depression. The latter clearly seems more likely, because life's stresses and tragedies and our inability to cope with life's essential nastiness is the reason why so many people wind up in the therapist's office.

Assuming life's blows and tragedies are due to an alteration in brain chemistry is naive at best and stupid at worst. People are, first of all, emotional creatures and all mental health disorders are, at base, emotional. The death of someone we love is what makes us depressed and if, concomitantly, this causes a change in our brain chemistry, it was the tragedy that caused it, not vice versa. As Lesley Hazleton noted, "to look for a chemical imbalance in the brain and still pretend that everything else is fine constitutes a peculiar kind of blindness engendered by the obsession with cure. Chemistry can lessen severe depression, but it cannot prevent us getting depressed; nor should it. To imagine that it can is only another form of escapism."[25]

It is this peculiar sort of psychiatric blindness that has caused the biological believers to zero in on electroconvulsive shock (which causes memory loss and other psychological disasters), lithium (which because of the high toxicity is dangerous even when monitored), and the other highly touted antidepressants which are probably no more or less effective than placebos. Peter Breggin argues that their clinical impact is due primarily to four factors: (1) an enhanced placebo effect; (2) emotional blunting effects—alcohol does the same thing; (3) energizing or stimulant effects—cocaine and the amphetamines do the same; and (4) an artificial euphoria or contrasting apathy because of the drugs' effects on the brain.[26]

If, as therapists, we hope to permanently alter people's dysthymia, depressions, etc., we need to give them a useful, life-sustaining philosophy and practical, effective coping strategies that will help them deal with—and eventually overcome—emotional pain. This is exactly what competent and effective psychotherapists do when they encounter despairing clients.

If you are unaware of these things and read the media propaganda, you probably believe that

> well over 11 million people suffer from depression in a given year, that yearly two-thirds go undiagnosed and untreated. . . . Major depression is far more disabling than many medical disorders, including chronic lung disease, arthritis, and diabetes. . . . Clinical depression ranks second only to advanced coronary heart disease in number of days patients spend in the hospital or disabled at home.[27]

Exactly how these numbers were obtained is a good question. Obviously, if depression is undiagnosed and untreated it has not been reported. If it hasn't been reported, then it is unknown. If it is unknown, how can anyone know how prevalent it is? They can't. What we are told by these alarming statistics is that the medical personnel are trying to frighten the American public into running to the nearest M.D. for one more prescription. By stressing its costs to business the medical establishment ensures the nation's businessmen will back anything the propagandists dish out. This is but one more daily example of "disease-mongering" which takes a number of forms: manipulative ads, manufactured diseases, needless diagnostic tests, free screening clinics, and scare headlines and stories which hype minor illnesses as plagues. The result of disease-mongering—no matter what form it takes—is inevitably the same: healthy individuals are unalterably convinced they are either already ill or about to become so and if they do have any minor problems they are led to believe they are *seriously* ill and in need of professional help.

The depression-mongers are everywhere these days, constantly reminding us our lives are a mess which can be ameliorated or cured with a few bottles of Prozac. Tiring of this constant and ever present litany, in 1994 Jerry Adler, a *Newsweek* correspondent, penned a priceless bit of satire titled "A Dose of Virtual Prozac." In this essay, a very ordinary and normal writer, "Jerry A.," in his mid-forties, after listening to all the Prozac propaganda, becomes convinced something is terribly wrong with his life and that he is becoming more and more depressed. Such little things as failing to button his shirts all the way down and spending money on bottled water kept him awake nights. Upon telling his friends, they suggest Prozac, but since Christmas and New Year's are coming up he doesn't want to lose his appetite. To his everlasting joy, he discovers "Virtual Prozac."

> Yes, Virtual Prozac—the only medication guaranteed to have no side effects *and no direct effects either*. Virtual Prozac is the paradigm shift in a bottle—only without the bottle! Virtual Prozac cannot be bought at health-food stores, pharmacies or by mail order. It is not available in pill, capsule, liquid, or any other form. Virtual Prozac is the first antidepressant of the Information Age, the only one to harness the incredible healing power of the Placebo Effect. . . .
>
> Unlike ordinary antidepressants, Virtual Prozac does not affect your levels of serotonin, norepinephrine or any other substance you would have trouble pronouncing at a dinner party. Unlike conventional psychotherapy, it does not involve any depressing so-called insights into your behavior. Jerry A. achieved all the benefits of Virtual Prozac *without* having to go on national television to denounce his parents as child abusers. To make it work, you merely have to say to yourself, as Jerry A. did: *Look, you're 44 years old and you're still torturing yourself over the futility of existence. Why? Because it seemed more authentic that way. Because you thought it made you more interesting. . . . But now you're 44 years old. No one cares if you're authentic anymore. You don't have to be interesting to anyone. Stop worrying about your place in the universe for eternity and start looking for a place in Fire Island for August. Mia Farrow was the last woman in America who thought existential angst was romantic, and not even she believes it any longer. So give it up!*
>
> Of course, most people, hearing about this dramatic improvement in Jerry A.'s life, would say, sensibly enough, *what took him so long to figure this out?* Everyone else gave up on this stuff years ago and took up something productive, like golf—why should we feel sorry for him just because he can't let go of his adolescence? To which there is really no answer, except that different people reach this point in their lives at different times, and that society has finally

over the last few years given up on the myth of noble suffering. . . . Mental health, once the stigma of the smug bourgeoisie, has come out of the closet. And if Virtual Prozac helped Jerry A. resolve his spiritual crisis—just imagine what it can do for you! He sleeps for several hours at a time, eats a healthy diet plus anything else he can get his hands on and drinks only as much as he needs to. Setbacks in life that once would have seemed almost insurmountable, such as finding someone signed up ahead of him for the StairMaster, he now tolerates easily; instead of kicking the machine and throwing his towel around, he tries alternative strategies such as erasing the other person's name and writing in his own. He still occasionally feels the need to bite his knuckles until he draws blood when he remembers some of the dumb things he said to girls when he was in high school, but he's confident that by fine-tuning his dosage he will continue to gain improved impulse control. And despite all the terrible things that people who claim to be his friends have done to him and continue to do to him behind his back, he'll tell you that he's never felt better in his life than he has since he started taking Virtual Prozac.

And he's convinced the second week will be even better.[28]

What Adler suggests in fun should be seriously considered by anyone who is depressed: talk to your friends, stop brooding, learn to take a more active interest in life and in other human beings, make new friends, give up worrying about your past and blaming others for anything and everything that goes wrong in your life, work harder, give up your adolescence and the notion that existential angst and suffering is romantic—it isn't, it's both childish and silly.

All experienced and competent nonmedical psychotherapists are well aware of the fact that many of their severely depressed clients have managed to cope, to work their way through and out of their depression without having to resort to either drugs or electroshock. They are also very much aware of the fact that the vast majority of people overcome their depression on their own without either pills or talk. One fact about depression is now well established: we know that it is caused by many factors and thus it is extremely unlikely that any single type of therapy will serve all cases. Many therapists have noticed that clinically depressed patients improve markedly immediately after being admitted to a hospital without any treatment at all. The social support from the nurses, ward personnel, and friends is itself sufficient to cause a change in feelings and mood. This suggests that the social factor alone can be critical. Yet other experts on depression warn that while hospitalization may help in the short run, in the long run it will increase the depressives' resistance to doing things for themselves and hinder the insight that they must solve their problems through their own efforts. At the heart of the problem with depression is the fact that the public has swallowed the propaganda line that an instant cure is available and all one has to do is swallow the magic pill. They have been convinced that since depression is physical, organic, and genetic there's nothing else *to* do except see the shrink and swallow the pill. In fact, the antidepressants are in tune with the depression itself and reinforce the feeling of helplessness with which they are obsessed: "It's chemical and I'm helpless!" This attitude is diametrically opposed to any eventual cure. So what *should* you do?

First of all if you don't have an abiding philosophy toward life you should develop one. Second, you should stop mentally focusing on yourself and your problems and take an aggressive, active interest in the world outside yourself. Instead of exercising your self-concern like you worry a loose tooth with your tongue, let it alone and focus on other people and on improving your relations with them. Start with the people nearest and closest to you. If bad interpersonal relationships are the source of your depression, take positive active steps to improve them. If your efforts come to naught or it is impossible to change them, then move immediately to make new and more hospitable individual friends. Subject yourself to new and radically different experiences. Engage yourself in things you've never done before with people who are strangers. Make up your mind they will not be strangers very long. Do this by taking a personal interest in their lives, activities, and beliefs. The best and quickest way to forget your own misery and unhappiness is to immerse yourself in the affairs of others. You want to feel better about yourself? Then do something worthwhile to improve the world in some little way. If you feel you are so worthless you have to sacrifice your very life, don't waste it in a selfish, futile suicide. If you want to sacrifice your life, do it by dedicating yourself to a cause. The instant you have opened yourself to new friends and new experiences you will find a point of light in the visible darkness.

Changing your lifestyle can promote feeling good. Changing your diet and watching what and how much you eat can help create a good mood. Massages, hot baths, and showers can also boost your mood. Physical exercise is the best and safest antidepressant. If you must take something, make it vitamins and mineral supplements. A regular program of daily exercise such as brisk walking or jogging can promote "natural highs." Music, hiking, owning and caring for pets—all of these can help you break up your depressive moods and outlook. Also, there are a number of foods that contain amino acids which act as natural antidepressants. These are available in various forms at a number of food and health stores. These stores also sell a number of other herbs and natural products that are also mood enhancers.

If you are one of the sensitive souls who suffer from one of the recently popular seasonal affective depressive disorders (SADD), you should by all means take up "light therapy" and expose yourself to high intensity illumination in the wintertime. Also during the winter, outdoor activities like skiing and ice skating will do wonders for the blues. During the fall season travel and sightseeing can counteract the doldrums. Make sure you are outdoors and on the move in spring, renewing yourself along with nature. It also helps if you become a wildflower specialist or a birdwatcher. If holidays leave you depressed, spend your time helping others: visit hospitals, nursing homes, and orphanages. Feeding, clothing, cheering up the deprived, and improving the world just a little is a miraculous prescription for raising one's spirits and morale.

Learning to meditate and to relax can also help to bring on an inner sense of peace and well-being. If you are of a religious bent, prayer and placing your trust in a higher power can be helpful in getting rid of the blues. Making new friends and reinvigorating all your old friendships and acquaintances and systematically planning and executing and doing something for others is one of the most—if not the most—effective of all ways for destroying your depression. Talking out your problems with a trusted friend is, after all, what we mean by "psycho" or "talk" therapy. Improving your physical health also, invariably, will assist in improving your mental health. A good-feeling body helps to bring on a good-feeling mind. This does not mean, however, that you should gain this good feeling via drugs, i.e., alcohol, cocaine, or Prozac. An addiction—either psychological or physical—is counterproductive in the long run.

If you are absolutely convinced that you are totally incapable of helping yourself (which you should try first) and if you have no friends or are constitutionally unable to make any new ones and you feel you must seek out a psychotherapist, make sure the helper is someone who has a sincere and humane interest in you as a human being. A cold pill-pusher—who obviously has no personal interest in you whatsoever and shows it by reaching for his prescription pad after ten minutes in his office—will be of no help whatsoever. Avoid these people like the plague. Also, as noted earlier, never assume that the super salespeople of dysfunctionalism, with their emphases on "self-esteem," "childhood misfortunes," and all of the other recovery movement scams, can be of any help at all. As Martin Seligman recently noted,

> being a victim, blaming someone else or the system is a powerful and increasingly more widespread form of consolation. . . . Undeniably, depressed people have low self-esteem. But bolstering self-esteem without changing hopelessness, without changing passivity, accomplishes nothing. There are almost no findings that self-esteem causes anything at all. Rather self-esteem is caused by a whole panoply of successes and failures. . . . What needs improving is not self-esteem but improvement of our skills [for dealing] with the world.[29]

Seligman believes depression can be prevented by teaching people who are depressed or at risk for depression how to change their pessimistic outlook to one of optimism. Anyone who has serious "self-esteem hangups" should, by all means, consult Richard L. Franklin's sane little book *Overcoming the Myth of Self-Worth*. Franklin does a superb job of destroying the mythology surrounding the common problems of perfectionism, grandiosity, the dire need for approval, compulsions of all sorts, purposelessness, and neurotic depression. Franklin also reminds us that, "effective psychotherapy is ultimately a process of self-help. A counselor can guide the process, but the person seeking change must ultimately use the information he is given to revamp his dysfunctional thinking."[30]

This is very sound advice, which anyone who is depressed or suffering from any of these other problems brought on by faulty self-talk should keep in mind constantly. You must confront your mood disorder yourself and learn about its causes and then develop new patterns of thinking, new ways of behaving, and new and improved social skills. Never forget you have an inalienable right to feel bad, to experience both the highs and the lows of human existence, and to come to terms with yourself and your rightful place in the universal scheme of things. Avoiding life and drugging your feelings by resorting to alcohol, cocaine, the opiates, or the antidepressants is not, never has been, and never will be a desirable or effective answer to the everyday pain and stress of human existence. You have within yourself both the psychological and spiritual resources not only to survive, but to prevail and prosper. Any therapist who does not deliver this common-sense message and assist you in discovering these inner helpers is himself ill-informed, therapeutically incompetent, and unworthy of either your time or money.

Remember, a very large part of human depression is the only rational response possible to one's life situation in a society that has failed to deal adequately with or successfully meet basic human needs for large segments of our population. These "social" causes of human depression will be taken up in chapter 12.

NOTES

1. Lesley Hazleton, *The Right to Feel Bad: Coming to Terms with Normal Depression* (Garden City, N.Y.: Dial Press, 1984), pp. 36–37.
2. Adrian Van Kamm, "The Goals of Psychotherapy from the Existential Point of View," in *The Goals of Psychotherapy*, ed. A. R. Maher (Englewood Cliffs, N.J.: Appleton-Century-Crafts, 1967), p. 146.
3. Cited in Kathy Cronkite, *On the Edge of Darkness* (New York: Doubleday, 1994), p. 209.
4. Julian L. Simon, *Good Mood: The New Psychology of Overcoming Depression* (Chicago: Open Court, 1993).
5. Peter R. Breggin, *Toxic Psychiatry* (New York: St. Martin's Press, 1991), p. 171.
6. Ibid., p. 158.
7. Seymour Fisher and Roger Greenberg, eds., *The Limits of Biological*

Treatment for Psychological Distress (Hillsdale, N.J.: Lawrence Erlbaum Associates, 1989), pp. 13–21.

8. Cronkite, *On the Edge of Darkness*, p. 10.

9. Ibid., p. 7.

10. Cited in Cronkite, *On the Edge of Darkness*, pp. 299–300.

11. Eytan Avital and Eva Jablonka, "Social Learning and the Evolution of Behavior," *Animal Behavior* 48 (1994): 1195–99.

12. Hazleton, *The Right to Feel Bad*, p. 49.

13. "Lucille Austwick Sparks National Campaign," *Dendron*, no. 35 (Summer 1994): 1.

14. Ronald Fieve, *Moodswing* (New York: William Morrow, 1989), pp. 112–13.

15. Hazleton, *The Right to Feel Bad*, p. 36.

16. Cronkite, *On the Edge of Darkness*, p. 172.

17. Ibid.

18. One such example is David B. Cohen, *Out of the Blue: Depression and Human Nature* (New York: W. W. Norton, 1994).

19. M. Araton, L. Tothfalusi, and C. M. Banki, "Serotinin and Suicide," *Biological Psychiatry* 25 (1989): 196a–97a.

20. J. J. Mann and S. Kapur, "The Emergence of Suicidal Ideation and Behavior during Antidepressant Pharmacotherapy," *Archives of General Psychiatry* 48 (1991): 1027–33.

21. Cohen, *Out of the Blue*, p. 305.

22. Ibid., p. 240.

23. Melvin Konner, "Prozac: A 'Doctor's View," reprinted from *New York Times Magazine* in *Louisville Courier Journal*, 18 December 1994, pp. D1 and D4.

24. *Textbook of Psychiatry* (Washington, D.C.: American Psychiatric Association Press, 1988), p. 417.

25. Hazleton, *The Right to Feel Bad*, p. 179.

26. Breggin, *Toxic Psychiatry*, p. 170.

27. "Depression Costs $43 Billion a Year," reprinted from *New York Times* in *Lexington (Kentucky) Herald-Leader*, 3 December 1993, p. A11.

28. Jerry Adler, "A Dose of Virtual Prozac," *Newsweek* (February 7, 1994): 43.

29. Martin Seligman, "Presidential Address, Division 12 (Clinical Psychology)," (Speech given at the American Psychological Association Convention, Los Angeles, August 12–16, 1994).

30. Richard L. Franklin, *Overcoming the Myth of Self-Worth: Reason and Fallacy in What You Say to Yourself* (Appleton, Wisc.: Focus Press, 1993), p. 206.

11

Metapsychiatry:
Kooks, Quacks, Fundamentalists,
and True Believers

Psychiatry is a rudimentary medical art. It lacks easy access to proof of its proposals even as it deals with disorders of the most complex features of human life—mind and behavior. Yet, probably because of the earlier examples of Freud and Jung, a belief persists that psychiatrists are entitled to special privileges . . .[1]

METAPSYCHIATRY: THE PROMULGATION
AND PROMOTION OF THE IRRATIONAL

While most practicing psychiatrists today still retain philosophical and ethical connections to science and medicine, there are a few members of the profession who have severed their ties to the scientific, rational, materialistic aspects of the profession to take up a more superstitious, mystical, and pseudospiritual approach to the mental problems of others. These practitioners have created a new branch of psychiatry called "metapsychiatry," which seeks to bridge the gap between medical science and the occult.

As defined by Dr. S. R. Dean, metapsychiatry is the branch of psychiatry that deals with the *reality of psychic phenomena*. The term, according to Dean, was chosen because it is congruent with psychiatric terminology, it encompasses a wider area than parapsychology, it is related to

401

and harmonious with metaphysics, and is more palatable to psychiatrists than the term parapsychiatry. It is also closely related to mysticism and is strongly interdisciplinary, having synergistic relationships with philosophy, parapsychology, religion, and psychic phenomena. According to Dean, well over two hundred psychiatrists and other physicians belong to the American Metapsychiatric Association. Dean argues that "metapsychiatry" is a term born of necessity and it officially designates the interface between psychiatry and mysticism. And, he insists, it stands to reason that psychic research is a legitimate concern of psychiatry and that psychiatry is the specialty best qualified to investigate such phenomena, assess its validity, and expose fallacies in matters of the mind. That Dean dares argue that *psychiatry* is a *parapsychological research science* is not only pure nonsense since science and superstition are diametrically opposed, but the assumption itself is ridiculous. Nevertheless even parapsychologists, Dean notes, cannot agree as to exactly what *is* psychic and what *isn't*. The term encompasses beliefs ranging from witchcraft at one extreme and biofeedback at the other.

Paying homage to the mystic Dr. Richard Maurice Bucke, who in 1890 was the president of the American Medico-Psychological Association, the parent organization of the American Psychiatric Association, Dean notes that in 1894 Bucke predicted that psychic research would eventually become a major concern of psychiatry. Dean then argues that psychiatry should explore telepathy and extrasensory perception (ESP) for reasons of national security if for no other. Moreover, Dean says, even Freud and Jung were preoccupied with the occult. Dean believes this gives the nonsense respectability.

Dean, of course, is right about the psychoanalysts. The extent to which mysticism and superstition colored and influenced their thinking is not as well known as it should be. Freud, of course, was more wary of the occult's appeal than Jung and even went so far as to warn Jung not to be engulfed by "the black tide of mud—occultism." Whether it is appropriate to view Jung's thinking as "engulfed" is moot. Nevertheless it often colored his work and showed up in his concepts of racial memories, the collective unconscious, Eastern religion and other ascientific and unscientific ideas. Lately, of course, Jung's ideas have been adopted by the "New Age" thinkers.

In a fascinating collection of essays in metapsychiatry, *Psychiatry and Mysticism*, Dean compiled a number of essays sympathetic to his cause. He defines and defends the field and closes his introductory piece with a list of "Psychic Aphorisms," a number of which clearly define the nature of the belief system:

> Faith is not fantasy; it is a form of precognition that has divined for countless years what science is just beginning to understand;
>
> Science and mysticism are fraternal twins, long separated but now on the verge of reunion;
>
> Psychogeny recapitulates cosmogony, i.e., the developing mind includes an innate awareness of the origin and meaning of the universe;
>
> Evolution is not homogenous. . . . Mental evolution is far ahead of the physical;
>
> The ultraconscious state bridges the evolutionary gap and produces cosmic awareness;
>
> Psi power [such as ESP, psychokinesis, and such] is latent in all, and an experiential reality to many;
>
> Thought is a form of energy . . . thought fields, like the theoretical tachyon [a hypothetical, "faster than light," atomic particle], can interact, traverse space, and penetrate matter more or less instantaneously;
>
> Thought fields survive death and are analogous to soul and spirit;
>
> Thought fields are eternal; hence, past existence (reincarnation) is as valid a concept as future immortality;
>
> Psychic research is on a par with other important courses of study; it should be included in academic curricula and lead to degrees and doctorates;
>
> A new age is dawning—the Psychic Age—on the heels of the Atomic Age and Space Age.[2]

Nothing could be clearer than this. We have before us a believer! In the second essay Frances Braceland, former editor of the *American Journal of Psychiatry*, assures us that "psychiatry by becoming more humanistic need not in any way become less scientific" and manages to lend an element of dignity to the proceedings by quoting Roman philosopher and playwright Terence's famous remark, "Nothing that concerns man do I deem alien to me." Another contribution dealing with myth and mystique concludes with the statement, we have no more scientific evidence for the reality of Thanatos, orgone energy, UFO sightings, extrasensory perception, umbilical enlightenment, or other such phantasms than we have for the existence of devils, souls, or angels; however, we have uncontrovertible data that such beliefs have ever greatly influenced human behavior. And myths will continue to do so, since man seeks fulfillment of his yearnings for security (and with covert insistence, immortality) not only through his solipsistic sciences and social compacts, but through an eternal recourse to wishful mysticisms that to him represent the ultimate realities.

I, myself, therefore, make no claim to be immune to the need for the same quietly desperate yearnings . . .[3]

Most of the remainder of the book is comprised of essays which follow along similar lines. By far the most interesting, however, and the only skeptical paper in Dean's entire collection, is E. Fuller Torrey's "Psychic Healing and Psychotherapy." After looking at all the claims for psychic healing Torrey throws a wet blanket over most of these paranormal wonders:

Unfortunately, some of us are wedded rather happily to our cause-and-effect notions and I, for one, am not about to give them up on the basis of the research done in this field to date. I am willing, and think other psychiatrists should also be willing, to look at the research coming out of metapsychiatry with an open mind. We really cannot afford to do otherwise, since we have so little research data available on what constitutes the effectiveness of psychotherapy, the healing process which we claim to be using in our daily practices. . . . There has been practically no attempt within psychiatry to identify and examine the healing process of psychotherapy.[4]

Torrey also questions whether (1) psychic healing really occurs, (2) it can be explained by the natural laws of physics, chemistry, and biology, and (3) if new laws are required. Torrey argues that some of the so-called psychic healings can be explained by research already completed. He also insists that one of the principal reasons psychotherapists have not looked more deeply into the healing process is that doing so is threatening: "[T]o turn around and say that most of [the years of] learning [were] irrelevant to the psychotherapeutic healing process, that untrained therapists with the proper personality characteristics or those who can raise the patients' expectations high enough can be *better* healers than we are, is too much to admit."[5]

With regard to the possibility of healing that can't be explained using scientific natural laws, Torrey says it is too early to say it's impossible, but it is hardly likely. We are far far from exhausting natural explanations and turning to supernatural ones. Torrey's major criticism of the psychic healers is their reluctance to submit to controlled, scientific experiments. The fact that this has not been done is the reason why most psychologists and psychiatrists with a loyalty to both the spirit and practice of science reject metapsychiatry out of hand and in toto.

The opposition of organized science and scientifically grounded psychologists and psychiatrists—with the exception of a few like Torrey—however, has been scant. Therefore, it is hardly surprising that metapsychiatry has flourished and more and more psychiatrists have continued to argue for the validity of spirit and demon possession, the influence of previous lives on the present lives of their clients, contacts with and abductions by extraterrestrials, and other such occult and supernatural influences on human behavior.

Dr. Dean is also very concerned with the training of the next generation of psychiatrists. He is among whose who believe that psychiatrists of the future should study psychic phenomena. To determine the acceptability of the idea Dean, Phyter, and Dean surveyed 228 professional psychiatrists, all members of the American Psychiatric Association. After being assured that their replies would remain anonymous, 58 percent of the psychiatrists who responded (many of whom were heads of psychiatry departments and deans of medical schools) said that they believed, "an understanding of psychic phenomena" was important to future graduates of psychiatry! Forty-four percent admitted that they believed "psychic factors were important in the healing process."[6]

As a result, we have the recent forays into metapsychiatry by Dr. Ralph Allison and M. Scott Peck, who believe that many cases of multiple personality disorder are actually genuine cases of spirit or demon possession, and by Dr. Colin A. Ross, who believes in extrasensory perception and deplores its banishment from psychology and psychiatry. Ross sees strong links between childhood trauma, dissociation, and ESP in clinical populations and believes "[e]xtrasensory perception is a legitimate area of clinical study."[7] Ross also argues that Wayne Gretsky's skill as a hockey player is due to his ability to, believe it or not, control the puck with psychokinesis, that is, with his mind!

> He often seems to mesmerize the opposing team. The other players also enter an altered state momentarily, in which they are frozen and confused. . . . I think that Gretsky possesses a primordial skill that must have been used by ancient hunters to mesmerize game, or by warriors to put their opponents in trance. He is the supreme embodiment of this psychological skill in our culture.[8]

And, finally, we have Dr. Stanislav Grof, who has coined the term "psychoid events," strange phenomena "that lie in the twilight zone between consciousness and matter." Grof is perhaps the world's foremost authority on the psychotherapeutic uses of LSD and may be best known for his use of LSD, music, and suggestion to ease the dying pains of terminal cancer patients. This work led Grof into exploring alternate states of consciousness and the transpersonal realm of past lives, reincarnation, the Jungian collective unconscious, prenatal memories, and other occult and visionary experiences. Grof is also convinced that our racial memories and other unconscious aspects of our mental life are as important as—if not more important than—anything happening in our waking existence. Grof says he has experienced the transpersonal or spiritual phenomena first-hand in psychedelic sessions. He argues that electrical equipment fails during parapsychological experiments, and that some mediums didn't cheat and had *real* abilities. He also believes in recurrent spontaneous psychokinesis or poltergeist activity, UFO phenomena, intentional psychokinesis, ceremonial magic, and spiritual healing.[9]

ORGONOMY: WILHELM REICH AND THE LEGACY OF FREUD AND JUNG

Wilhelm Reich, a farmer's son, was born in 1897 and served in the Austrian army in World War I. After the war Reich moved to Vienna and entered the Faculty of Medicine at the University of Vienna. While there he began to read Freud and to correspond with members of Freud's circle. Even though he was only twenty-three years old, he was elected a member of Freud's Vienna Psychoanalytic Society in recognition of his talents (most members were middle-aged). Reich immediately seized upon Freud's libido theory and his concept of a specific sexual biological energy which serves as the basis of human personality. Failing to recognize the metaphorical nature of Freud's concepts. Reich took them all literally. Anxiety is due to a block in the flow of the libido. Neurotics, although they may achieve orgasm, cannot feel total pleasure and are forced to go on fruitlessly searching for satisfaction. For Reich, orgastic potency was everything. Unless one, in uninhibited fashion, surrendered to the flow of biological energy and discharged all of the repressed and dammed-up sexual excitation via orgasm, one would always be mentally unhealthy.

Early in Reich's career Freud began to move away from biology toward a theory of instincts, but Reich kept insisting on the literal truth of Freud's biology. As one would expect, the Psychoanalytic Society supported Freud and showed Reich and his ideas indifference and outright hostility. Working as a psychoanalyst, Reich established the Psychoanalytic Polyclinic which offered free treatment to the poor working people with Reich specializing in their problems and sexual behavior. From this it was but a short step to his political involvement with the Communist party to carry out his psychological and political convictions. Reich established the Socialist Society for Sex Consultation and Sexological Research, which dispensed advice on birth control, sexual and marital problems, and how to raise children. Since the clinic was open to the unmarried and adolescents, Vienna was scandalized and Reich was openly snubbed. Moving to Berlin in 1931, he set up a program called the German Association for Proletarian Sexual Politics with the help of the German Communist party. Here Reich's program advocated the abolition of antiabortion laws, distribution of free contraceptives, abolition of all legal distinctions between the married and unmarried, and programs aimed at doing away with prostitution and venereal diseases.

Although such things sound reasonable now, in pre-Nazi Germany they were regarded as anathema. Reich was wise enough to see that although the bourgeoisie Germans were preying on the poor, the Nazis were much much worse. Reich didn't like the Nazis and vice versa. Reich was not only a Jew but a Communist, and in Nazi eyes, a sexual pervert. So, in 1933 Reich went back to Vienna, where he was again rejected and his ideas were made fun of publicly. Because the psychoanalytic publishers would not publish his work, and due to his fear of the Nazi threat to Austria, Reich left Vienna and wandered across Europe, finally residing in Oslo (and even there his ideas got him in trouble), where he lived until he emigrated to America in 1939.[10]

It was in 1931 that Reich began to do the research for which he became both famous and infamous. After moving to middle-class Forest Hills, New York, some years later, Reich joined the New School for Social Research as associate professor of Medical Psychology and engaged in research so bizarre as to defy belief. One of the most persistent of all occult beliefs is the idea of a universal energy that pervades all things. Mesmer believed this energy was magnetism and Reich believed it was the orgone. Reich thought the body had a continuous bioelectric field that varied with different emotional states. He also believed in elementary life forms he called bions. Reich even believed that bions of a certain shape could cause cancer. These bions he called T-bacilli (T for *Tod* or death). Other bions he believed were luminescent, giving off a form of radiation that destroyed the T-bacilli. It was this radiation that Reich in 1940 called orgone energy.

To study orgone energy Reich had to trap it some way. He believed he could do this by using a sheet metal box lined on the outside with wood. Reich believed this worked because he alternated layers of organic materials with inorganic materials. For example, steel wool, glass insulation, or sheet metal might be layered with wool, cotton, or plywood. Reich attached a tube and funnellike arrangement to a closed orgone box, creating a "shooter" which he used to focus the accumulated energy on any area afflicted with T-bacilli, i.e., cancer. Reich believed such "orgone accumulators" worked because to astute observers it was clear that the insides of the boxes glowed. Although critics claimed the light was in the eye of the observer rather than in the box and was due primarily to suggestion, Reich countered by bringing Albert Einstein to his lab and convincing him that he too "saw the light."

Subjects, while sitting in the orgone box (with a tiny aperture for ventilation) to soak up the energy, experienced a rise in body temperature, as would be expected. Reich attributed the rise to orgone. One highly suggestible woman said sitting in the box gave her an orgasm. The publication of these weird discoveries under the guise of "scientific" research brought derision and hoots of laughter. When Reich published *The Cancer Biopathy* it became crystal clear to all oncologists that Reich was deranged, although on the surface his methods appeared to be scientific.

His writings and publications became more and more bizarre and irrational. Reich began to believe he could control the weather and constructed a device made up of metal tubes and sealed cables through which water flowed. Reich claimed the device was "powered" by a milligram of *orur*, radium that had been treated with orgone energy. Reich believed that this "Cloud Buster" could both attract rain clouds and as dissipate them.[11] Reich and his deluded followers actually believed that each time a drought ended it was due to their cloud-busting efforts. Though it may be hard to believe, Reich also claimed that he engaged in a duel at his laboratory in Rangeley, Maine, with a hostile invader from a UFO. The interplanetary battle was relived in February 1955, when a group of Reichian scientists claimed to have fought off invading UFOs outside Tucson, Arizona. The Reichians suffered one casualty as a heroic defender was injured by a blast of radiation. The invaders never returned.[12] According to Reich, the UFOs were powered by orgone energy and their crews consisted of beings he named CORE men, Cosmic Orgone Energy Men. Reich became increasingly paranoid and in 1956 he began to think that he, himself, was from outer space. He became convinced that his children were the founders of a new, superior, interplanetary race.

Reich's irresponsible claims that orgone energy could benefit those suffering from cancer soon brought in investigators from the Food and Drug Administration, who warned him against selling his orgone accumulator boxes across state lines. Reich ignored their warnings and the FDA charged him with contempt of court for ignoring the injunction. As a result the Reich Foundation was fined ten thousand dollars and Reich was sentenced to two years in jail. Just before he was due to be released from the Federal Correctional Institution in Danbury, Connecticut, in November 1957 Reich died of a heart attack.

It is understandable how Reich's gradual mental breakdown led him into the farther reaches of paranoia, but what is not comprehensible is how so many of his followers could abandon science and reason and take up his delusions. And take them up they have. One would have assumed we would have heard the last of Reichian nonsense with his demise. Instead, a number of psychiatrists and psychoanalysts have not only continued to promote Reich's insane beliefs that orgone energy could cure everything, whether biological or psychological, but in 1967 these faithful published their pseudoscientific *Journal of Orgonomy* and in 1968 one of Reich's students, psychiatrist Dr. Ellsworth Baker, founded the American College of Orgonomy (ACO) in Princeton, New Jersey. Composed primarily of psychiatrists who believe in and use "orgone therapy" on their unwary clients, the ACO also claims to do research and has managed to survive over the past thirty-seven years by soliciting funds from current or former patients. This, of course, is ethically improper. As Joel Carlinsky, one of orgonomy's most persistent and effective critics has observed,

> The A.C.O. has a very active outreach program to spread the word. They encourage gift subscriptions of their journal to university libraries. They have a speaker's bureau. They hold frequent conventions both here and abroad, and offer training programs and laboratory courses. Almost all of the people who get involved have had Orgone Therapy or go into Orgone Therapy subsequently; indeed, it is claimed that one cannot do successful work in Orgonomic biology, physics, or meteorology without having had psychiatric restructuring by Orgone Therapy. Their theories on . . . just about every . . . subject imaginable are totally at odds with those of estab-

lishment science. In spite of this (or because of it) they constantly reiterate the theme that Reich was the greatest genius in history and was persecuted as Christ was; that Orgonomists today are persecuted; that they have great knowledge and wisdom unknown to the rest of humanity (and that cannot be understood or appreciated by those who have not had Orgone Therapy); and that all social and environmental problems can be dealt with only by their enlightened leadership.[13]

There is little question that the coterie of M.D.s who support the College of Orgonomy, who read and write for the *Journal of Orgonomy* and who continue to administer orgone therapy—to mislead gullible individuals and hide behind the charisma of "medicine"—is all that keeps Reichian nonsense alive. Sad to say, a number of well-known and respected politicians and well-heeled businessmen have bought into this nonsense and have contributed and solicited funds to support its continued operations. Quackery is no respecter of either social or political position it seems. And it can only be defeated through exposure and ridicule.

PSYCHOTHERAPY AS A CULT

An almost totally neglected aspect of psychotherapy has been the large number of psychotherapists who have managed to violate every ethical rule and principle in the practice of their craft and wind up ruining their client's lives. Few clinical psychologists and fewer psychiatrists have studied psychotherapeutic cults. Most of the investigatory effort has come from sociologists, social psychologists, and social workers. Jane and Maurice Temerlin, Margaret T. Singer, Richard Ofshe, and M. D. Langone have been leaders in the effort to study the unethical techniques and practices psychotherapists have used to establish their cults and brainwash their clients.

In a seminal paper titled "Some Hazards of the Therapeutic Relationship," the Temerlins described precisely how charismatic psychotherapists are able to manipulate the therapeutic relationship and produce groups that function like the destructive religious cults of Jim

Jones and David Koresh.* Studying five charismatic psychotherapists who manipulated the therapeutic relationship to create a destructive religiouslike cult, the Temerlins showed that all of the therapists first established multiple relationships with their clients, that is, they brought their clients into their lives assigning them roles other than that of clients. Although still treating them as patients, the clients became employees, spouses, lovers, servants, debtors, students, and colleagues. Therapy then became progressively more destructive as the patients gradually became (although many were not aware of it at the time) "more dependent, submissive, confused, depressed, and less autonomous in the conduct of their lives."[14] In all five of the cults the Temerlins found that the ex-clients interviewed all idealized their therapists. Such idealization can, of course, make clients more vulnerable to exploitation by the therapist. All ethical therapists are alert to this transference problem and manage it before it becomes destructive. The cult therapists, however, saw the idealization as deserved and some of them stated it openly. Comments such as "I'm the best therapist in the world. Mine is the best training program in the world," or "I know what you need better than you do. Your wish to terminate therapy is just blind resistance," make it clear that the therapist is sicker than his clients and suffers from a bad case of megalomania.[15] Moreover, the cult therapists kept some of their clients on their string for ten years or more, destroyed the clients' self-confidence, and encouraged their total dependence. Using authoritarian techniques as time passed, the therapists forced the clients become increasingly submissive, anxious, and fearful. Difficult as it may be to believe, many of the client's fears were realistic: some clients who gathered enough courage to terminate were sued or physically assaulted or both. Many

---

*Religious cult leader Jim Jones headed the People's Temple Sect and founded his own city, Jonestown, in Guyana. In 1978 he was responsible for the massacre of nine hundred of his followers who lived there: Jones convinced them the world was about to end and therefore they should all commit suicide. David Koresh headed the Branch Davidians, a bizarre, offshoot sect of the Church of the Seventh Day Adventists, and established a military-type compound in Waco, Texas. Koresh and many of his followers died (several of whom committed suicide or were killed on Koresh's orders) in 1993 when Bureau of Alcohol, Tobacco, and Firearms officers stormed the compound in an attempt to capture Koresh and the many firearms he had cached there.

clients became progressively more infantile and many female clients were sexually seduced. Surrounded as they were by many adoring and dependent patients many of the therapists became grandiose, losing all touch with reality.

Surveying the techniques used by the therapists, the Temerlins noted four major categories: (1) techniques to increase dependence; (2) techniques to increase isolation; (3) techniques to reduce critical thinking; and (4) techniques to discourage termination of therapy. In the first group, therapists encouraged confession and then relieved the anxiety and guilt through reassurance and forgiveness. Increasing dependency by relieving the client's anxiety or guilt via the placebo effect or suggestion, as well as becoming sexually involved with the client also increased self-blame, guilt, and confusion. Vacillating unpredictably between expressions of love and acceptance and showing hostility, anger, and rejection had many clients frozen—unable to move closer or away. Encouraging the clients, as part of their therapy, not to make any personal decisions without consulting the therapist was also standard practice.

In the second approach, isolation, the therapists used communes, extended retreats, and long trips to isolate the clients from their friends and family. They also prescribed long periods of solitary meditation and blamed all the clients' problems on their friends and family, and recommended those people be avoided or rejected in the name of therapy. The therapists also encouraged fear-inducing fantasies, tried to develop "group-think" and a "we-versus-them" attitude and maligned all other forms of therapy and therapists.

To reduce the clients' critical thinking ability the therapists denigrated all intellectual activity as therapeutically counterproductive. All critical thinking was called "being negative" and the clients were encouraged to use the therapists' jargon. Ambiguity, nontestable concepts, and personal "put-downs" were also used to confuse and dominate. Also effective was redefining the clients' problems in terms that they could not personally verify by observation and experience.

To discourage termination of therapy and to keep the cash flowing, the therapists gradually reversed the therapist-client roles, getting the clients to put the therapists' needs ahead of their own. Any attempt to terminate was called "disloyalty" or "resistance." Lying to the clients about progress in therapy, calling all gains spurious, and saying gains would disappear if therapy were ended were also used. Creating new goals and browbeating the clients into continuing by saying "Since I'm the best there is, if you can't succeed with me you'd be a disaster with anyone else," were also common.

Over the years a number of psychotherapy cults arising from the distortion and corruption of long-term individual therapy or group psychotherapy have been identified, investigated, and destroyed. One of the best surveys of such activity was recently carried out by Singer, Temerlin, and Langone. While twenty-two psychotherapy cults were studied, the researchers focused particularly on a few that were typical of all the rest of the professionally led cults.

One group typical of those studied, the Center for Feeling Therapy, lasted for almost ten years. This cult consisted of 350 patients living near each other and sharing homes in the Hollywood district of Los Angeles. Although hundreds of other nonresident members were treated via correspondence, maximum therapeutic benefit came only to the residents. Therapist-leaders pushed a theory which argued that all of us are "reasonably insane" but can learn to become sane by putting aside all of our old images and attaining the "full experience of feelings" and "going 100 percent" in five areas: expression, feeling, activity, clarity, and contact. In the late 1980s, well over a hundred patients filed legal complaints of fraud, sexual misconduct, and abuse after undergoing "treatment" at the Center. So far, civil cases have settled for more than six million dollars on the behalf of former clients.

While at the Center clients were routinely abused and mistreated by licensed therapists who

1. Created a sense of powerlessness in their patients by stripping them of social support. They also used ridicule, physical exhaustion, physical punishment, and sexual harassment.
2. Used racial, religious, and ethnic slurs; threats of insanity and violence; and enforced states of physical and mental exhaustion.
3. Told patients they should hate and blame their parents for making them crazy, give up their children for adoption, and have abortions because they were too crazy to be parents.

4. Engaged in sexual intimacies with patients, beat and caused patients to be beaten by other patients, allowed and encouraged nonlicensed "therapists" to conduct unsupervised "therapy" sessions.
5. Collected donations for improving the Center from patients running into the thousands of dollars but used the money for private selfish ends.
6. Forced patients to stand naked in front of groups; made patients inspect genitals of other patients in front of groups.
7. Used humiliation techniques, for example, forcing patients who defied therapeutic wishes to wear diapers, sleep in a baby crib, and eat baby food.[16]

Another good example of a cult was found in 1971 by a forty-year-old, licensed clinical psychologist called Dr. Tim. His following lasted for over a decade. From his behavior and his statements it is now obvious Dr. Tim was psychotic. Dr. Tim told clients in his groups—which averaged forty members at a time—that he was "more enlightened than Jesus . . . and had created the ultimate therapy, combining Freud, Zen, Kundalini, Yoga, and LSD." The last, he said, was to "override their egos." Dr. Tim's therapeutic technique consisted of diagnosing every patient as having a severe mental illness that only he could cure. He told his clients that their parents—especially their mothers—caused their mental illness and should be rejected (except for financial support for their therapy). Patients were told only Dr. Tim and his group were their "family." Dr. Tim fed them LSD on a regular basis, and had their children raised by the group. He also promoted both homosexual and heterosexual contacts. He encouraged mutual masturbation among the men to "desensitize" them. Dr. Tim supervised these sessions and berated the men who were bewildered by his insisting this was therapeutically "good for them." Dr. Tim had sexual liaisons with many of the women, several men, and certain teenage girls whose single parents were in the group. Dr. Tim owned all the property and cars and forced patients to turn over their property and possessions. Many patients were forced to do menial labor as Dr. Tim's personal servants. In 1984 Dr. Tim died of cancer. Incredibly, a small number of his ex-patients still live near each other and praise him and his work, although they are still socially isolated and disturbed. Most ex-members claim that they have been irreparably damaged, but there's nothing they can do.[17]

Difficult as it may be to believe, in years past a number of ex-felons and parolees have started psychotherapeutic cults of their own. Using the tactics and techniques picked up from their group therapy experiences in prison, they have managed to hook a large number of unwary clients by promising psychological wonders they, of course, are totally incapable of delivering.[18] You must remember that many states have no laws regulating the practice of psychotherapy and you are left on your own to decide who should deal with your troubles.

Although nonprofessional therapy cults have existed in the past and have done considerable damage, their threat to public health and sanity is nowhere as large as is the threat from the professionals such as those just detailed who are themselves mentally sick or have gone morally sour.

RELIGIOUS PSYCHOTHERAPISTS: THE THREAT OF FUNDAMENTALISM

Sick and dangerous as the "cult shrinks" may be, they have not done as much physical and moral harm or caused as many wide and deep psychological wounds as have the large number of religiously inspired psychotherapists who are out to save people's sanity as well as their sinful souls. Such "pseudoshrinks" or "soul saviors" are more dangerous to the public's mental health than a truckload of cobras or plague-infected rats are to their physical health. They are particularly dangerous because of the religious cover they use to sow their poisons and infections.

One of the most chilling essays of modern times is titled "I Beg You, Do Not Torment Me." Written by Bonnie Henderson Schell, a recovered mental patient, this essay describes some of the monstrous therapeutic practices of a number of organized religious groups in the nation today.

Schell, after having witnessed the infamous exorcism telecast by the "20/20" news program on April 5, 1991, remarked to another ex-patient how barbarous such a telecast was, deceiving the public by representing the teenager's suffering as part of a cosmic battle between good and evil. The ex-patient she spoke to told her about his own recent experience: After visiting an independent evangelical church one Sunday wearing his "Psychiatric Survivor" button, he was forcibly taken to a meeting that evening where he was held down and banged on the forehead with a heavy redwood cross and was forced to verbally renounce Satan, praise Jesus Christ, and to pray. When Schell consulted an anthropologist who specialized in evangelists and expressed shock that an exorcism ritual from 1614 was being used by supposedly sane people in 1991, the anthropologist laughed and told her to go to a local grocery or drug store and take a look at the various "spiritual warfare" novels. These books are everywhere and are perennial best sellers in the Christian bookstores that dot the nation. They deal with a world of incessant war between the angels of good and the spirits of darkness. Readers of these novels believe in both the good and bad angels and feel a war is being waged for their immortal souls. If they are Christians they are under attack.

The size and pervasiveness of the "Christian" literature is massive and amazingly profitable. A large part is devoted to mental health and invariably, urges the reader to seek biblical or ministerial salvation. In the 1700s and before, mental disorders were the exclusive province of the clergy. They wish this were true today and if they had their way it would be. Many clerics are deeply convinced any and all mental disorders are due directly to demonic influence and intervention. These individuals and religious institutions are part of what is known as the Deliverance Ministry—a loosely organized group of fanatics who believe that anyone not filled with the Holy Spirit is subject to hosting a demonic presence. This evangelical model looks at modern behavioral disorders and places the blame not on parents, genes, environment, or disease, but—believe it or not—*on the occult practices of one's relatives dating back at least four or five centuries*. Mind boggling as this may be, it is confirmed by books such as C. Fred Dickason's *Demon Possession and the Christian*.[19]

Dickason warns his readers that good angels can be corrupted by Satan and the only way to know what is pure is to consult one of the

Deliverance Ministers. Failure to realize one's full potential is evil and an indicator of demonic possession. Other such authors see sudden mood changes, aggression and expressions of hostility, sexual immorality, perversion, blasphemy, and any involvement with fortune-telling or the occult as indicators of demonic possession. Anyone living in a geographic area where a Judeo-Christian influence is missing, anyone failing to instantly benefit from medication or psychotherapy, anyone resisting Christian religious thought or practices subject to demonic possession. We are told demonic possession is much more prevalent among American Indians, Orientals, and other foreign nationals, and that all mental disorders are the result of sin.[20]

While many of these church-inspired psychoevangelists have embraced the psychiatric position, others see it as the work of Satan himself. They believe psychology and psychiatry are competition for the body and soul of human beings, which belong to the fundamentalists, not to satanic psychiatrists. Both the Deliverance Ministry and institutionalized psychiatry, however, want complete power and control over social misfits and the mentally disabled:

> Neither fundamentalist Christianity nor institutional psychiatry has much tolerance or respect for individual differences, for "odd-balls," or for troublemakers who persist in questioning its motives or ethical practices. Thus, many Deliverance Ministers and mental-health-system providers enter other peoples' lives of suffering not as healers but as authorities claiming to know what is in someone else's best interest, and they each claim the power to impose solutions on another's body and mind.[21]

Bad as the ministry and psychiatry are alone, when they are combined in the person of a religious psychotherapist you can be sure the resulting therapy can be, in many instances, doubly damaging. Newton Joseph, a California counselor, has long been critical of such religious psychotherapists and sees such people doing more harm than good. Joseph argues that these psychotherapists "pander feelings of guilt, shame, dependency, powerlessness, self-hate, and compliance to invisible and visible authority figures. . . . It only proves one can have a degree in psychology and still be irrational, superstitious, and unaware of one's own conditioning."[22] He also argues that Christianity's emphasis on the primacy of the human-to-God bond has made it extremely difficult for human beings to develop the supportive human-to-human bonds required for adaptive interpersonal and social functioning. Christianity keeps the individual in an infantile emotional state and promotes fear, guilt, submissiveness, low self-esteem, and dependence—all of which are antitherapeutic. Joseph also insists that none of the religious therapists is willing to deal with these negative aspects of religion because each fears it would cost clients and income. Another reason for the unwillingness is that many such therapists also believe in mythical gods, life after death, past lives, demon possession, and other New Age concepts. Their approach, in general, is to help their clients learn to "get used" to their problems rather than solve them. Such clinicians often pretend they are concerned only with health and not with ethical belief systems when, in reality, most of the interventions they make are heavily value-laden. Such therapists wind up promoting the very pathology they are supposed to be treating.[23]

Over the last few years psychologist Dr. Edmund D. Cohen has devoted his time and attention to studying the psychological problems of the born-again Christians. Their psychological problems are so numerous and varied that

> A specialized, parochial, mental health treatment industry for the twice-born has arisen. It has become the most active and fastest developing segment of the contemporary conservative church subculture. Among born-agains all over North America, the traditional coping strategies of denial, secrecy, and keeping up a good front are collapsing . . . The same psychological effects that made the conservative church movement strong and cohesive during the seventies and eighties now so overtax those who are caught up in it that a breaking point has been reached.[24]

Cohen too was a born-again Christian before he became disaffected and broke with his clique. Cohen notes that the approaches to mental health treatment embodying fundamentalist theology came to the fore in the 1970s. Science was seen as totally irrelevant to the Bible's view of humanity and both psychology and psychiatry were rejected. As far

as biblical counselors were concerned all psychological problems are
spiritual problems and if the sufferer gets closer to Jesus all will be
well. Unfortunately this point of view doesn't work. Cohen found that

> [b]ehind their facade of euphoric calm, people marinated in the Bible
> and surrounded by the born-again church subculture tend to be
> *depressed* and suffer from a sort of *generalized emotional distress* partaking
> of anxiety, worry, and fear. To put it in the smallest possible nutshell:
> for the prescribed prayer and devotions to achieve their intended
> altered state of mind, much effort must be expended to suppress
> thoughts and feelings considered inappropriate for a saved person.
> Pro-social or neutral interests and desires that conflict with the reli-
> gious agenda come to arouse as much guilt as genuinely anti-social
> ones for the Bible-believers. . . . The Bible-believer makes himself or
> herself depressed. Being constantly at war with one's natural and nor-
> mal emotions wears a person out. [Emphasis in original.][25]

Strangely enough, few psychiatrists and psychologists have spoken
out against this mixing of biblical belief and natural science, which
leads Cohen to remark that "The mixing of biblical devotions and psychology presents the same problems as the mixing of Genesis and pale-
ontology to get so-called creation science."[26] If we are ever to ground
mental health on a scientific base, the conflict between scientific data
and religious doctrine is inevitable. At the moment however, one could
legitimately argue that the differences between the pseudoscience of
biological psychiatry and the tenets of the Deliverance Ministry are
minimal. This may well explain the reluctance of mainstream mental
health practitioners to protest too strongly. After all, the church shrinks
have the same insurance companies, hold equal degrees, and are licensed
by the same professional societies. Moreover, they are doing no more
harm than anyone else. Keeping quiet and laying low may be advisable.

Before closing this chapter, again, the public should be very cautious in going to any of these charismatic "true believers" for relief from
psychic pain. It is very easy for such passionate advocates of the spiritual world to slip from the bounds of reason and common sense and
embrace megalomania and sainthood, persuaded it is the Creator's will
that they save the world. It is a very short step indeed from charisma to
culthood. Cults exist even within the confines of the Catholic Church,

as the recent exposé of the activities of Opus Dei has made clear.[27] It is also important to remember, "[t]here may be as many as two thousand religious groups in North America that can be classified as cults . . . If only 1 percent of those two thousand resort to killing, that's still a serious threat."[28] If you have doubts about what you might be getting into, you should contact the Cult Awareness Network which has affiliates nationwide. Its national office is at 2421 West Pratt Boulevard, Suite 1173, Chicago, Illinois 60645, (312) 267-7777. If you, at any time, feel that you are being taken advantage of and subjected to mind control of any sort—by either religious or therapeutic figures—you should read *Combating Cult Mind Control** by Steven Hassan and take the steps he recommends. Also required reading is Michael Langone's *Recovery from Cults*.† Both of these books provide relief and solace for any and all victims of these vicious and virulent evils.

NOTES

1. Paul R. McHugh, "Psychiatric Misadventures," *American Scholar* 6, no. 4 (1992): 497–510.
2. Stanley R. Dean, ed., *Metapsychiatry: The Confluence of Psychiatry and Mysticism* (Chicago: Nelson-Hall, 1975), p. 15.
3. Ibid., p. 34.
4. Ibid., p. 240.
5. Ibid., p. 244.
6. Stanley R. Dean, C. O. Phyter, and Michael L. Dean, "Should Psychic Studies Be Included in Psychiatric Education?: An Opinion Survey," *American Journal of Psychology* 137, no. 10 (1980); 1247–49.
7. Colin A. Ross, *Multiple Personality Disorder: Diagnosis, Clinical Features, and Treatment* (New York: John Wiley & Sons, 1989), p. 185.
8. Ibid., p. 187.
9. See the following works by Dr. Stanislav Grof for more detailed descriptions of his beliefs: *The Adventure of Self-Discovery* (Albany: State University of New York Press, 1988); *LSD Psychotherapy* (Alenda, Calif.: Hunter

---

*Steven Hassan, *Combatting Cult Mind Control* (Rochester, Vt.: Park Street Press, 1990).

†Michael D. Langone, *Recovery from Cults: Help for Victims of Psychological and Spiritual Abuse* (N.Y.: W. W. Norton Co., 1993).

House, 1980, reprinted 1994); *The Holotropic Mind: The Three Levels of Human Consciousness and How They Shape Our Lives* (San Francisco: Harper San Francisco, 1993); and *The Stormy Search for the Self*, coauthored by his wife, Christina Grof (New York: G. P. Putnam & Sons, 1990).

10. Myron Sharaf, *Fury on Earth: A Biography of Wilhelm Reich* (New York: St. Martin's Press, 1983).

11. Ibid.

12. Richard Morrock, "Pseudo-Psychotherapy," *Skeptic* 2, no. 3 (1994): 95.

13. Joel Carlinsky, "Ekigones of Orgonomy," *Skeptic* 2, no. 3 (1994): 91.

14. Jane W. Temerlin and Maurice K. Temerlin, "Some Hazards of the Therapeutic Relationship," *Cultic Studies Journal* 3, no. 2 (1986): 234.

15. Ibid., pp. 235–36.

16. Margaret T. Singer, Maurice K. Temerlin, and Michael Langone, "Psychotherapy Cults," *Cultic Studies Journal* 7, no. 2 (1990): 101–25.

17. Ibid.

18. Ibid.

19. C. Fred Dickason, *Demon Possession and the Christian* (Wheaton, Ill.: Crossway Books, 1988). See also Charles Swindoll, *Demonism: How to Win against the Devil* (Nashville: Word, 1981); Rodger Bufford, *Counseling and the Demonic* (Nashville: Word, 1989); and Thomas White, *Believer's Guide to Spiritual Warfare: Wising up to Satan's Influence in Your World* (Ann Arbor: Vine Books, 1990).

20. Bufford, *Counseling and the Demonic.*

21. Bonnie H. Schell, "I Beg You, Do Not Torment Me," *The Humanist* (May/June 1992): 16.

22. Newton Joseph, "Religious Psychotherapists," *Free Inquiry* 13, no. 3 (Summer 1993): 24–25.

23. Wendell Watters, *Deadly Doctrine: Health, Illness and Christian God-Talk* (Amherst, N.Y.: Prometheus Books, 1992), pp. 2–3.

24. Edmund D. Cohen, "And Now, Psychiatric Wards for 'Born-Again' Christians Only," *Free Inquiry* 13, no. 3 (1993): 26.

25. Ibid., p. 27.

26. Ibid., p. 29.

27. For information on Opus Dei, refer to the following articles, all of which appear in *Free Inquiry* 15, no. 1 (Winter 1994/1995): Mario Mendez-Acosta, "Opus Dei, A Threat to Liberty," pp. 13–15; Jesus P. Fuertes, "The Masked, Dangerous Cult," pp. 16–19; Klaus Steigleder, "Opus Dei: An Insider's View," pp. 20–24; and Tammy DiNicola, "Joining Opus Dei," pp. 25–26.

28. James A. Haught, "And Now, the Solar Temple," *Free Inquiry* 15, no. 1 (Winter 1994/1995): 31.

12

Caring for Ourselves and Others

*There are many paths of psychospiritual growth, all of them exploring the
delicate harmonies between helplessness and independence, skepticism and
faith, reason and emotion, self and other, human beings and nature, and, in
religious terms, between all life forms and God. Professional therapy of any
kind can be but a slender reed, and one that cannot possibly claim to be the
only staff to be used along the path.*[1]

Despite what you've read thus far, there are some competent and caring psychotherapists out there who, in a pinch, can provide some useful advice. Before turning to these individuals, however, you should
make a sincere effort to resolve your own troubles and solve your problems without the help of a shrink. You might as well face it: you alone
are responsible for your physical and mental health and well-being. All
that a doctor or advisor can do is make recommendations, give advice,
and if you are already ailing, prescribe medications. Whether you follow this advice or whether you take these medications *is up to you.* It is
your choice and your responsibility: no one can force you to go to an
M.D. or a psychotherapist and no one can force you to take either the
medication or the advice. Many of these physicians and therapists may
think they are God and have the power to force their advice and opinions upon you, but they do not. Their advice and opinions are just
that: neither commandments nor law! You are free to take them or

423

leave them. Fortunately, most of the time you will be better off taking rather than leaving them. But never, under any circumstances, should you surrender your freedom to make the final decisions about your physical or mental health.

As for your mental health, make sure that whoever you consult about your mental status is at least as sane and rational as you are. If you are suffering from an intense grief reaction, the last thing on earth you need is some arrogant ass telling you he's going to reengineer your genes and make you well sometime in the twenty-first or twenty-second century, or that he'll put a brand new bandage on your mental carcinoma by giving you Prozac or a tranquilizer. You'd be better off drinking a quart of bourbon. In either case, when you sober up, your problem will still be untouched, but you'll have either an addiction or a hangover. The hangover is better and cheaper. One thing you definitely do not need is the advice of some fool who is too dense to see that your problem is existential, not biological. Such idiots deserve neither your time nor money. Moreover, they're not really interested in you and your problem. They're much more interested in how quickly they can get your check to the bank and the starting time of their golf foursome. Shrinks, please remember, should be your last resort. You should first make an effort to solve your dilemmas yourself. But how?

CARING FOR ONESELF

First of all, remember that your mental disorder—if you really have one—is most likely *an emotional disorder*: socially and environmentally engendered; due to bad luck, injustice, and mistreatment, or to faulty learning and thinking and a lack of adequate coping strategies and techniques. It cannot and will not be corrected or straightened out by a pill! The majority of therapists are well aware that most of their clients, if they do manage to get well, do so with or without the therapist's help or advice. Nature does the work and the shrink takes the credit in most instances. Although your therapist would rather that you didn't know it, there's a great deal that you can do on your own to solve your problem, whatever it happens to be.

When we have a problem or a burden most of us want someone

with whom to share it. We don't want to face our fears and terrors alone. You don't have to. You can and should talk to someone else: a friend, a relative, a minister or priest, or even the bartender. Yet many feel they don't have any friends, or they are ashamed or afraid of ridicule or rejection. They believe that because they pay a shrink he has to listen and sympathize. But do you really want to buy love and sympathy? Wouldn't you prefer *the real thing*?

As was discussed previously, the quickest and best way to have friendships is to be a friend to others. Deliberately and systematically set out to make friends if you don't already have them. While you may not have "friends," almost everyone has "acquaintances." You can begin here and make friends out of your acquaintances. Get out of your world and into theirs. Talk to them about themselves, their health, job, problems, family, interests, likes and dislikes, hobbies, etc. If you don't know how to do this, read Dale Carnegie's *How to Win Friends and Influence People** and put his principles into practice. It is impossible to have too many friends, and the more you make the merrier. The more you get out of your life and problems and into someone else's the better off you'll be. Set a goal of making a new friend every day or at least four or five a week. If you already have friends and acquaintances, talk to them and share your feelings. The most important thing is to get out of yourself and into someone else's life so you can see your problem in perspective.

Join social groups and clubs. Take up a new hobby, even one that you may not be terribly interested in at the outset. The more you participate and share experiences with others, the greater you will find your interest and attachment. Shared experiences are the basis for emotional attachment and growth. New interests, hobbies, and experiences are the ways in which we grow emotionally and, thus, as human beings. There are hundreds of untouched, unknown, and undiscovered joys and pleasures all around you at all times. Learn to draw, paint, carve, dance, skate, sew, ski, sing, swim, cook, play an instrument, collect, travel, write poetry and prose, meditate, and garden. Once you have learned these things, you can teach and share them with others.

---

*Dale Carnegie, *How to Win Friends and Influence People* (New York: Simon & Schuster, rev. ed. 1981).

Once you escape the prison of your own misery which you have, mostly, made for yourself, you will find to your amazement it's not so bad after all.

Give up all drug habits. *All*. This includes alcohol, nicotine, and caffeine, including coffee, beer, colas, tea, and chocolates, if they *are* really addictions and *are* interfering with your lifestyle of healthy habits such as eating, sleeping, exercising, and so forth. If they give you pleasure and satisfaction and you are not abusing them, enjoy! Most of our modern addictions, however, can be given up. Remember, our ancestors survived without them and you can too. Don't deny or deprive yourself of little pleasures that make life worth living *unnecessarily*, however.

Another thing that you can do to improve your life both generally and specifically is to get involved in both local and national social issues. If you don't know what they are, find out. Millions of people are being mistreated, discriminated against, victimized, neglected, overlooked, etc. every day. Commit yourself to making this world a better place and then take some specific action. It may be as little at the outset as cleaning the trash out of the gutter and putting it in the garbage can or giving a pint of blood to the blood bank or visiting shut-ins at the nursing home or reading books for the blind. You will be amazed at the number of things that need doing if you only open your eyes and look at the world around you.

For God's sake, *read*! Watching the tube is all right, but you need to be an *active*, not merely a passive, participant in the world. Nearly every town, hamlet, city, or county has a local library, usually with bookmobiles. City libraries have just about everything—not only books, but CDs, audio and video tapes, lectures, games, hobby and interest group activities, children's activities, etc., all free for the asking. Failure to utilize these treasures of educational (as well as motivational and psychological) value is a *true* American tragedy. Read poetry, philosophy, history. Read about people like yourself with your problems and troubles and pains and tragedies—people who have suffered like you—people who have been screwed, blued, and tattooed ten times more and a thousand times worse than you will ever be. Tragedy, injustice, and horror are part of the human condition and they always have been. The very best stories and films in any genre are those that involve our deepest emotions and universal themes of truth, justice, tragedy, love, and death. Never sell life short! The only meaning life has is the meaning you give it and the best, happiest, and most successful lives are those that are dedicated and devoted to other human beings and human values: to our families, community, religions, country, to science, medicine, knowledge, or some worthwhile cause. Familiarize yourself with the creeds, beliefs, and religions of others. Visit a Buddhist group or a synagogue, for example, and learn to understand their point of view. Read philosophy if you aren't religiously inclined. If no philosophy or religion satisfies you, then create your own. After all, the quarrel you have with the creator is private— it is yours *and yours alone*, and you should never let anyone else dictate to you how you will handle this relationship. If anyone insists *he* has the right to determine how and what you shall believe, make sure you return the favor: insist you have the right to tell *him* what *he* should believe! Never forget: the essence of mental health is *freedom*. Anyone who wants to take this away from you is not operating in your best interest! He is an enemy! Shun him!

Always remember, there are no experts on how and why we exist. All of us have to find this out for ourselves over a lifetime. Never trust or listen to those who claim to know what is best for you. As one wag put it: the unwritten title of every book is "How to Be More Like Me." This is a thousand times truer for the mouthings of most psychotherapists. They will, of course, do everything in their power to convince you their lives are infinitely more successful than yours and therefore, you should listen and heed and hopefully also succeed. Don't fall for this con job! They may or may not have more troubles and problems than you'll ever have. Look up the suicide rates for psychiatrists, psychologists, and clergymen if you doubt these words.

Most important of all: keep yourself knowledgeable and informed about your mental problem. If you haven't already, take college courses in normal and abnormal psychology and find out what is known about normal human behavior. Learn how your body and mind work. Specialize your reading as far as your personal problem is concerned. And be sure to take everything you read with a very large, agricultural-size block of salt. Read critically. Above all, read the books that have been referred to in the preceding chapters.

CHOOSING A THERAPIST—IF YOU MUST

As a last resort, after all your efforts to help yourself have been exhausted, after your friends, relatives, and local bartenders have been unable to help, if you still feel a professional is required—and, I repeat, this should be only as a last resort—then you want to make sure you find a shrink who is both competent and caring. Never, under any circumstances, fall for newspaper or magazine ads for hypno-, psycho-, or pharmacotherapists promising immediate magical cures. If you do, you will, more than likely, live to regret it.

Finding competent and caring medical help of any variety is by no means easy. A recent issue of *Consumer Reports* (CR) devoted its lead story to helping consumers obtain the best medical care possible.[2] In researching the issue, CR surveyed more than seventy thousand subscribers and asked about their medical care experiences. While most people were satisfied with their care in general, they did indicate some sources of unhappiness and dissatisfaction. Significant numbers faulted their doctors' communication skills, stating that their doctors weren't open to questions, didn't ask their patients' opinions about their ailments, and didn't give advice on making healthy life changes or on prevention techniques. At least a quarter of the time physicians failed to discuss the side effects of the drugs they prescribed—even those with fatal side effects. The survey also found that the patients of those doctors who didn't communicate well were less likely to follow the physician's instructions.

These recent results merely add to what was already known about physician behavior in the past. Since the days of Hippocrates, doctors have been advised by their mentors not to discuss with the patient either the disease or its treatment. This knowledge is for the "holy physician" only. When the American Medical Association was founded and its first code of ethics published in 1847, physicians were advised *not* to share their knowledge and expertise. This secrecy enhanced their authority and increased their patients' dependence upon them. This, in turn, enhanced the physicians' social status and prevented the patients from trying to doctor themselves and, by so doing, deprive the physicians of their deserved income. As CR reported, "If you try to take an active role in your medical care, bear in mind that you'll be bucking centuries-old habits and traditions."[3] One of the nineteenth century medical manuals advised physicians to use Latin terms and to write all their prescriptions in Latin as well to confuse their patients. As reported chapter 3 of this book, it is clear that most nineteenth- and twentieth-century physicians had no interest whatsoever in any- thing their patients had to say. The doctor alone was the supreme authority—the Deity himself—an omniscient expert who knew what was best. It wasn't until the 1970s that the idea of the patient having a say or playing any role whatsoever in the treatment process came to the fore. It is still considered the most abominable of heresies in many medical quarters. CR also noted that,

> In one small survey, physicians described the "best" patient as one who respects the doctor's time, seems to understand what the doctor says, and is compliant. Those who asked questions were apt to make the doctors impatient. Another survey, reported in the *Journal of the American Medical Association* in 1989 found the majority of physi- cians said they would withhold the truth if they decided it was in the patient's best interest. This, despite overwhelming evidence that patients want to be fully informed—and *need* to be informed if they are to make the decisions they need to make.[4]

What is both tragic and depressing about this is that in the years immediately ahead there will be even less time or desire for the harried physician to take a personal interest in his patients due to increasing pressure from managed-care and insurance companies for the physician or therapist to keep the cost of care as low as possible. The more patients the physician treats and the faster and more efficiently they are treated, the higher the profits for the care companies and insurers.

In such instances only the patient suffers. As the CR article notes, "Some 70 percent of correct diagnoses depend solely on what you tell your doctor . . . but unless you're fast and direct your whole story may never be heard."[5] A 1984 analysis of seventy-four medical interviews showed how quickly physicians assert their control. On average, the doctors in the study interrupted their patients *eighteen seconds* after they had begun to speak. From there the doctor took charge of the visit asking questions that demanded a one-word answer and essentially halting the patient's flow of information. Only one of the interrupted speakers went on to express his full set of concerns. Never forget, modern medicine is "doctor-centered" not "patient-centered." A radical change in physician arrogance and attitude is demanded before any joint patient-doctor cooperation and interaction will ever come about.

As the patient who is paying the bill, it is both your duty and your responsibility to speak up and insist on your right to both physician time and information. Don't be bullied when you see the doctor. Mention at the outset the number of problems you wish to discuss and state clearly your wish to be heard without interruption. If the doctor hasn't got time for you, move on to another doctor. Although this information applies to any and all physicians, more specific recommendations are needed for psychiatrists, psychologists, and psychotherapists. You must diagnose the behavior of shrinks in order to pick one that will not be a waste of time and money.

Eileen Walkenstein has provided some useful questions you should ask yourself about any particular psychotherapeutic candidate. If, after observing the candidate's behavior, attitude, and stance, you can say yes to all the questions listed below, chances are good that you have met a caring and competent advisor. There is no guarantee, but it is at least a promising start. Walkenstein's ten questions are paraphrased here:

1. Does the therapist look you in the eye?
2. Does the therapist answer your questions directly, without hemmings and hawings? (If the therapist makes you feel foolish for asking *any* direct questions, then your answer is no.)
3. Does the therapist say: "I don't know" or "I'm not sure"?
4. Does the therapist refuse to give you any kind of drugs, no matter how much you plead?
5. Does the therapist *move*, facially and bodily? (If the therapist sits there like a stone, he probably wants to turn you into one!)

6. Does the therapist show emotions?
7. Is the therapist's office free from diplomas hanging all over, big desks to separate you, and couches to hide behind?
8. Does the therapist see you for an appointment soon after your first call? (Clue: if he is too busy seeing too many patients, he might get you mixed up with one or several others, and how, from that morass, would you ever decipher your own identity?)
9. Does the therapist listen to you and refrain from coming up with an analysis to impress you with his omniscience, or with diagnoses of the life-sentence variety?
10. Is your first response to the therapist, whether on the phone or in person, warm and positive?

If you can say yes to all ten, chances are your diagnosis would come up okay and that you are dealing with more of a human being than a "diagnoser."[6]

Even this is no guarantee, however, that the therapist you get is worth your time and money. But if all of these tests are passed with flying colors, the odds are good that you do have a human being with a rational, humanistic outlook offering assistance, and there is a much better chance of the encounters proving to be of value. You will, nevertheless, probably be much better off talking to someone whom you do not have to pay—someone who is willing to be your friend for free.

Many people are pushed into the hands of authority figures (priests, doctors, therapists, etc.) by mindless obedience, the inability to trust their own skills and abilities, and fear. If you happen to be one of these, you need to learn how to become less vulnerable to those who would take advantage of you. You need to learn how to resist those with influence and authority. Whether we like it or not, all of us are subject to the tremendous power of social suggestion and crowd influence. It is, in fact, quite easy for us to fall prey to the so-called experts. Even the strong can be seduced into "going along with" domineering, forceful, and overbearing authority figures. You must be on your guard at all times.

THE FALLACY OF BIOCHEMICAL CAUSATION

Psychotherapy is a window on the damage done to children by uncaring thoughtless, hostile, or disturbed parents, and the damage done to everyone by a social system that encourages mindless competition and implicitly embraces the philosophy of social Darwinism.[7]

True, there *are* a large number of deviant, crazy people in our society. It is far from unfair to state that those given the responsibility for dealing with these disturbed have done little or nothing to "cure" them of their disturbances or reduce their number over the years. The primary stumbling block has been the "medical model" and the critical error has been in looking at all deviant behavior as a "mental disease" in the brain of the person. Fisher, Mehr, and Truckenbrod long ago argued instead that most behavioral disorders are expressions of the failure of society's institutions and systems.[8] They are, of course, correct.

The biggest problem of so-called mental health and mental illness in our society today is the same as it has been for the past thirty years: a total misconception and misunderstanding of the nature of the *social* problem. According to the "experts," the medical doctors and the psychiatrists, all behavior considered abnormal or deviant is the result of a disease process—the expression of a bodily organic disease no different from any other disease. Therefore, schizophrenia or depression or acute anxiety can and *must* be placed in the same categories of diseases as cancer and pneumonia and treated in the same way by a medical doctor, i.e., someone who is an expert in the body and in those medicines that can be prescribed to cure it. Once we have locked mental disease into the same bin with the traditional *physical* diseases we can apply the standard hospital–M.D.–pill system.

We have known for quite some time, however, that diagnosing and labeling is a total waste of time and effort. It is an exercise in absurdity. In 1958, Hollingshead and Redlich showed that the treatment actually provided in hospitals, clinics, and the therapists' offices is based more on race and socioeconomic status than on diagnostic categories. These findings are as true and applicable today as they were in the 1960s.

Difficult as the task is when the best possible care and concern is religiously devoted to those who suffer from profound and chronic mental disabilities, it is the height of irony to discover that the effective treatments and procedures—things that do work—are being ignored and derailed by a biological-psychiatric steamroller hell-bent on drugging the nation and playing genetic science-fiction games with people's lives. This social soul-sickness on the part of the psychiatric–pharmaceutical–insurance industries currently making billions from the public's misery certainly has nothing whatsoever in the form of a plan—or even a dim, distant dream of a plan—to take active steps to improve society and thereby *promote* mental health and social well-being. What fool would even for a moment, contemplate sabotaging or slowing down the biggest gravy train in human history? Remember, Eli Lilly's profits on Prozac alone are in the billions of dollars. Yet, if you are on the side of either humanity or the good of society this train must come to a sudden and screeching halt. We cannot, as a society, continue to drive people into hopelessness and despair. In George Albee's words, "changing the incidence of emotional disorders will require large scale political and social changes affecting the rates of injustice, powerlessness, and exploitation, none of which is affected by individual psychotherapy."[9] Albee goes on to argue individual psychotherapy is futile. At the rate we are going, "we might end up with more mental disorders, serious and otherwise, than there are people in the United States."[10] He also notes that not only are the kinds of disorders proliferating as the DSM gets bigger and bigger as more and more of the ordinary human problems in living are labeled "mental illnesses," i.e., social-clinical judgments for which therapists can collect insurance payments. Albee rightly is outraged at our fixation on individual psychotherapy for "segments of the middle and upper classes while the most serious mental and emotional disorders are more prevalent among the very poor."[11] How can we take such people seriously in a world where

> millions die of the infectious diseases of childhood and the spectre of mass starvation haunts much of humankind[?] Fifteen million of the world's children die each year of preventable conditions like infant diarrhea from polluted water, infectious diseases and starvation. Four hundred million women live in regions where the soil is defi-

cient in iodine and as a result give birth to retarded children. The rate of epilepsy is high in the third world from too much lead and too little iron. Millions of children live with preventable handicaps—the underdeveloped malnourished bodies and minds ... Thirty-seven million Americans have no health insurance of any sort, most of those who do have union negotiated insurance, have no (or very limited) mental health coverage.[12]

As emphasized throughout this book, the training our shrinks receive leaves them totally unsuited for any kind of work except one-to-one psychotherapy with middle-class people like themselves. While it *is* true that some clinical psychologists and some psychiatrists may work in comprehensive care centers or other public mental health facilities, once their training is finished they move on to private practice with upper-class neurotics like themselves to deal with neurotic, anxiety, and interpersonal relationship problems. The real problems of poverty, unemployment, hopelessness, exploitation, powerlessness, discrimination, poor housing, etc., Albee notes, though more urgent, are not even therapeutically perceived as being of any relevance to "mental health." Poor people's taxes do, however, help fund psychotherapy for the affluent. Psychotherapy, Albee makes clear, is rarely available to the poor, is not sought after by blue collar workers, and is never aimed at rectifying social injustices. This raises an ethical issue: "Limiting psychotherapy to the affluent does nothing to advance the cause of social justice and may actually dull sensitivity to injustice. . . . Only with radical social changes leading to a just society will there be a reduction in the incidence of emotional problems."[13]

Shrinks, as a group, however, are *against* social change, not for it. If they were to wholeheartedly throw their effort into preventing people from ever becoming emotionally disturbed in the first place and if their efforts at primary prevention were successful, then all shrinks would be out of a job! In Albee's words, "While psychotherapy uncovers the individual damage inflicted by all of these social problems, treating the victims does nothing to correct the basic causes. Only when the findings of psychotherapists are translated into well-formulated preventive actions to correct or change the social and economic structure will it have made a significant contribution to prevention."[14]

Albee pessimistically observes that in today's society with so many lonely and alienated people, the breakdown of families, and the decline of orthodox religions, the desire for charismatic guides and gurus who can serve as surrogate parents will continue to be great. As for parents, the biological psychiatrists with their emphasis on the genetic-biological nature of all mental disorders and their credo that "all mental disorders are 'medical disorders' " certainly frees parents from all sense of guilt as they join the American Mental Health Fund, which denies the role of parenting in mental disorders. Only a fool would argue that bad childhood experiences, physical, emotional, sexual abuse, and neglect play no role whatsoever in our adult behavior and outlook. These things, like the plagues of cholera and smallpox, are what we need to take action against. We can adopt the approaches used in the field of public health and although most mental disorders are not diseases,

> the traditional methods of primary prevention apply: (1) discovering and controlling the noxious agents (like bad parenting and the stresses of sexism, racism, exploitation, etc.); (2) strengthening the resistance of the susceptible (like empowerment, social coping skills, political action to improve self-esteem of the disadvantaged, and developing social support networks); and (3) preventing transmission (controlling child physical and sexual abuse, neglect, exploitation and emotional damage). Primary prevention efforts, being proactive, generally require social and political action.[15]

Designating every human problem in living as an illness or disease, and seeing all mental illness as a medical problem treatable by drugs fits right into the conservative agenda designed to protect the status quo and to oppose any efforts aimed at prevention, i.e., the improvement of society and the establishment. Instead of laying all of our mental problems on the doorstep of genetics we should be fighting for a social learning model of mental and emotional disturbances and for ridding ourselves of that destructive and debilitating notion known as the medical model.

Albee is by no means alone in his clarion call for scientific common sense. David Jacobs has also railed against biological psychiatric nonsense. Jacobs sees three common sources of error in psychiatric reasoning about psychopathology. First, we should realize that we have no biological existence apart from our species' normal social environment in which learning is such a crucial determiner of our future behavior. Not only are actual genetic disorders very uncommon, but the naive notion that complex behavioral patterns including behavioral abnormalities such as panic or depression are due to unchanging and permanent genetic heritage can only be characterized as "a gross misunderstanding of evolutionary genetic thought."[16] Second, the idea that people are genetically predisposed or vulnerable to psychopathology completely ignores the human environmental impact and power in the etiology of what is currently labeled psychopathology. Third, in the process of regarding some behaviors pathological and others less so, there has been a wholesale confusion on the part of the psychiatric establishment and a gross failure to distinguish between causal forms of explanation and explanation based upon connections of meaning and significance. Disturbing behavior is most often the failure to solve life's problems and to gain hope in the face of overwhelming reality.

Only rarely these days do we manage to encounter professional psychotherapists who have a broader vision of a just and better social order and who have taken steps to make their vision a reality.

One outstanding example of a therapist with such a vision notes:

> Hardly even considered anymore is the simple notion that psychosis might be one of the unfortunate permutations and conditions of being human; rather than the comforting notion that psychosis is only a rare disease, psychosis maybe the natural consequence of the way anyone has lived. Perhaps the medicalization of insanity has created for all of us a false sense of security. . . . Believing that psychosis begins and ends with idiosyncrasies of the brain nullifies it as a human tragedy, and contributes to the steadily deteriorating conditions of care that today face almost all of the chronically mentally ill.[17]

Recognizing that more than 70 percent of the mentally ill are released after treatment and go home, still in need of further care which they do not receive, Dr. Edward M. Podvoll developed a home-care healing program using the patient's own inner resources instead of drugs. Seeing modern treatment as handicapped by cost effective-

ness, insurance regulations, and fear of malpractice allegations and recognizing that all three work against the development of therapist-
patient intimacy, Podvoll developed a "new-but-old" approach to dealing with the psychotic. Through his creation of a sane, compassionate,
and healing environment, he has been able to help even the most psychotic of individuals work through madness to full recovery. Podvoll's
excursions into the nature and development of madness and the subsequent mental workings out of deranged thinking is both fascinating
and illuminating. The creation and structuring of therapeutic teams,
the organizing and arranging of daily activities and exercises, breaking
drug dependence, the working concepts of family teams, and a therapeutic home and a healing community are all shown to be very effective ways of restoring sanity. Such procedures can be implemented in
almost any home environment.

If you must seek counseling, various reputable, successful programs are available. Dr. Podvoll's Windhorse Project in Boulder, Colorado; Burch House in Littleton, Colorado; and Spring Lake Ranch in
Cuttingsville, Vermont, are just a few. None of these depends upon
highly paid professionals and all work with people in crisis in direct,
personal, and practical ways. Most so-called mental patients are better
off without the interference and "help" of the biopsychiatrists since
such "counselors" do not know psychotherapy or cognitive therapy
and, because of their training, are in no way people-oriented.

In fact, most patients would do better if they avoided biopsychiatry altogether and joined one of the psychiatric survivor networks such
as the National Association of Psychiatric Survivors, which has its
headquarters in Sioux Falls, South Dakota (P.O. Box 618, Sioux Falls,
South Dakota 57101). The Re-Evaluation Co-Counseling groups
headquartered in Seattle as well as the Chicago-based Recovery organization have also proved helpful to those who do not want to fall into
the "shrinkage" trap. If you are interested in supporting a patient-centered psychotherapy you should, by all means, join or at least lend your
support to the National Association for Rights Protection and Advocacy, 587 Marshall Avenue, St. Paul, Minnesota 55102, (612) 224-
7761 and their newsletter *The Rights Tenet*. You might also get in
touch with the National Empowerment Center, 20 Ballard Road,

Lawrence, Massachusetts 01843-1018, (800)-POWER-2-U. If you have also been a victim of Prozac, Zoloft, or Paxil then you may wish to contact The Prozac Survivors Support Group Inc., 3080 Peach Avenue, No. 104, Clovis, California 93612, (209) 291-8661. If you are concerned with the drugging of every child in the nation under the ruse of an "Attention Deficit Disorder" you may also wish to contact Children First! Center for the Study of Psychiatry, 4628 Chestnut Street, Bethesda, Maryland 20814 sponsored by Peter and Ginger Ross Breggin. You are also advised to subscribe to the psychiatric survivor journal *Dendron*, P.O. Box 19284, Eugene, Oregon 97440, (503) 341-0100.

Despite a relative lack of progress against biological psychiatry in this nation, advances have occurred in Europe over the last decade. There has been a steady move toward community care and toward more control for the users of mental health care services. Impetus for change has come from independent groups and national mental health groups. There has also been a shift away from the disease or illness model toward a concept of functional disability. According to Bob Grove,

> [t]he concept of disability management is about enabling someone to lead a normal life, and this requires a multidisciplinary approach which will deal with areas in which the medical professionals have no claim to expertise—housing, employment, social and political activity. The medical profession is not necessarily in a leadership role, but rather one of a number of professional groups who provide timely specialized intervention. . . . Current critiques of mental health care are marginalizing psychiatry and forcing a painful rethink about the nature and extent of the medical role.[18]

As part of this "new look," greater emphasis is now given to work and employment as an essential step away from the culture of dependency. The result has been a dramatic increase in waged employment for people disabled by poor mental health. In both Germany and Italy self-help cooperatives and "social firms" now provide economic integration and independence. Some of these firms also supply housing. Although developed but seldom used in the United States, both the United Kingdom and the Netherlands are using the "clubhouse" model which combines the idea of a self-help group with a structured program leading to job skills and permanent employment. While large-scale mental institutions still exist, there is a steady move to the provision of community-based services and the rights of mental patients are gaining increasing recognition by European legal systems. After-care for the chronically disabled is still a major problem and people still "fall through the cracks" because the skills of the professionals are spread too thin. It must be faced that community care is not a cheap option in terms of either time or money.

Looking at recent political developments in the United States and the recent development of conservative mean-spiritedness toward the poor, the minorities, and the deviant, it seems highly unlikely there will be any major support given to anything in the way of social change. In fact,"proper treatment" seems increasingly unlikely because of the emphasis on cost containment, factory-like processing of patients through the mental health clinics, and the insurance companies' careful monitoring of every charge and payment, which results in the denial for extended care.

Because of the rapid takeover of psychological practice by managed-care companies, many clinical psychologists are ready to quit. A late 1994 nationwide survey by the Practice Directorate of the American Psychological Association revealed that clinical psychologists are vulnerable to decisions made in a vacuum by policy makers and managed-care executives who are ignorant of what is required to properly treat the mentally disturbed. Managed care executives expect a "cure" in six or seven sessions just like the pill pushers achieve. Clinicians now feel they have no control over either their practice or their profession. They have had the "medical model" forced upon them, and they are expected to make the diagnosis most likely to assure insurance coverage. A typical dilemma: the therapist jeopardizes the patient's insurance coverage if she says the patient is improving, but she also jeopardizes coverage if she notes that the patient is worsening, since the insurer then questions the effectiveness of the treatment. Managed care makes everyone do more work for less money and the system denies services to those who need them most. In such a situation, practicing psychotherapy simply isn't worth the time and trouble.

Ironically, at a time when biological psychiatry is dominating the treatment of people, the research evidence is mounting higher and higher in support of the effectiveness of social and community therapy and the cognitive psychological approach to all of the major disorders. Moreover, the use of psychosocial approaches such as family therapy, early intervention, coping strategies, and training in illness self-management have now been shown to reduce relapse rates and disabilities. Additionally, cognitive behavior therapies based on the work of A. T. Beck and associates and Albert Ellis are not only experimentally well-supported, but clinically effective.[19] Studies of normal and schizophrenic thinking processes, formation of beliefs, schizophrenic thought content, and learning how to reason and deal with patients' delusions and delusional perceptions and moods have all resulted in significant patient improvement. Nonconfrontational and collaborative techniques must find their way into current therapeutic practice. Patients, after all, are human beings, not enemies, objects, or hopeless things of disdain to be medicated and ignored.

We cannot, under any circumstances, continue to disregard the importance of social factors and the cultural context in mental disorders. Theorists both here and abroad are well aware that claims for the location of a gene for schizophrenia and manic-depressive disorders, using DNA markers, have been followed repeatedly by the retraction of such claims in the face of heaps of contrary evidence.[20]

Most thoughtful therapists are painfully aware that culture is the major determinant of personality and mental health and that if the society into which one is born does not meet the developmental needs of most of its citizens, psychiatric and behavioral disorders are inevitable. Years ago Hansell set forth what he called essential "attachments" that every individual adult must make if he or she is to maintain mental equilibrium in any society. Failure to make any one of these attachments, which range from the obvious (food and air) to the more obscure (intimacy, society, and meaning), will precipitate a stress reaction that will bring on an emotional crisis.[21] If such a crisis is not resolved, then pathological behaviors result. Recognition of these fundamental needs makes clear that the only rational philosophy and the only sensible approach to any workable mental health system should be a public health and prevention-based model. If Hansell's human needs could be met for every member of our society, there would be far less need for either psychotherapy or psychotherapists. Today, unfortunately, the current mental health system fails to understand the social implications of the symptoms it treats and fails to concern itself with the psychopathological breeding grounds from which their clients emerge. Alvin Pam has argued that psychotherapy would have a greater impact if mental health workers moved from hospitals, clinics, and prisons to therapeutic nurseries, day-care centers, and schools, concentrating their efforts on the children. Moreover, therapists should become involved at the political level in such controversial areas as welfare reform, family planning, foster care policy, child support, divorce custody, and children's rights. It is a moral obligation for anyone calling himself a therapist![22]

Yet, even at the personal adult level it is possible to deliver effective and compassionate psychotherapeutic assistance to people in distress. Success is highly unlikely, however, if one belongs to the new psychiatry or believes in genetic and biological causation or chemical imbalance, or is a pill pusher. Dennis Biddle, in his essay "Of Demons and Drugs: The Fallacy of Biochemical Causation" says with brilliant clarity:

> If the most you're willing to do toward dealing with your emotional health is take a pill, then you may as well forget about things like having a satisfying and meaningful life. Any problem, emotional or otherwise, puts the human spirit to the supreme test. Are you going to find a way to solve the problem and keep it solved, or are you going to run to a Great Wahoo and ask them to make it better? It is most important to learn to ride out emotional storms, both to survive them, and also to gain the confidence that you know something about steering your own ship. What a person with a psychological problem needs most is emotional support, increased awareness of their choices, and the encouragement to tackle their fate with their bare hands.[23]

It should now be crystal clear that there's no salvation in the psychiatrist's pill and the devout should remember religion's painful message: God helps those who help themselves. It's high time we face the truth: if we're to survive, if we are to be saved, it's up to us to take full responsibility and save ourselves. No one else can or will do it for us!

NOTES

1. Peter Breggin, *Toxic Psychiatry* (New York: St. Martin's Press, 1991), p. 375.

2. "Health Care Issue," *Consumer Reports*, (February 1995): 81–88.

3. Ibid., p. 81.

4. Ibid., p. 82.

5. Ibid., 87.

6. Paraphrased from Eileen Walkenstein, *Don't Shrink to Fit: A Confrontation with Dehumanization in Psychiatry and Psychology* (New York: Grove Press, 1977), pp. 112–13.

7. George Albee, "The Futility of Psychotherapy," *Journal of Mind & Behavior* 11, nos. 3 and 4 (Summer/Autumn 1990), p. 377.

8. Walter Fisher, Joseph Mehr, and Philip Truckenbrod, *Power, Greed and Stupidity in the Mental Health Racket* (Philadelphia: Westminster Press, 1973).

9. Albee, "The Futility of Psychotherapy," p. 370.

10. Ibid., p. 371.

11. Ibid., p. 374.

12. Ibid., pp. 374–75.

13. George W. Albee, "Does Including Psychotherapy in Health Insurance Represent a Subsidy to the Rich from the Poor?" *American Psychologist* 32 (1977): 719–21.

14. Albee, "The Futility of Psychotherapy," p. 377.

15. Ibid., p. 380.

16. David Jacobs, "Environmental Failure—Oppression is the Only Cause of Psychopathology," *Journal of Mind & Behavior* 15, nos. 1 and 2 (Winter/Spring 1994): 9.

17. Edward M. Podvoll, *The Seduction of Madness* (New York: HarperCollins, 1990), p. 2.

18. Bob Grove, "Reform of Mental Health Care in Europe," *British Journal of Psychiatry* 165 (1994): 431–32.

19. A. T. Beck et al., *Cognitive Therapy of Depression* (New York: Guilford Press, 1979); and Albert Ellis, *Reason and Emotion in Psychotherapy* (New York: Lyle Stuart, 1962).

20. John Horgan, "Eugenics Revisited," *Scientific American* (June 1993): 122–31. See also Ruth Hubbard and Elijah Wald, *Exploding the Gene Myth* (Boston: Beacon Press, 1993).

21. Novus Hansell, "Introduction to the Screening–Linking–Planning

Conference Method," unpublished manuscript cited in *Power, Greed and Stupidity in the Mental Health Racket*, by W. Fisher, J. Mehr, and P. Truckenbrod (Philadelphia: Westminster Press, 1973), pp. 158–59.

22. Alvin Pam, "The New Schizophrenia: Diagnosis and Dynamics of the Homeless Mentally Ill," *Journal of Mind & Behavior* 15, no. 3 (Winter 1994): 199–221.

23. Dennis Biddle, "Of Demons and Drugs: The Fallacy of Biochemical Causation," unpublished paper, December 1994.

Afterword

Because of the widespread use of ineffective, unscientific, and even dangerous mental health treatments and practices, within the last two years a number of scientifically oriented psychologists and psychiatrists have begun to lobby state legislatures to enact new laws to protect the consumer of mental health services under what is now known as the Truth and Responsibility in Mental Health Practices Act (TRMHP). One of the leaders of this movement is psychologist and lawyer Dr. R. Christopher Barden. According to Barden, much of the growth in untested and dangerous mental health practices is due to "inappropriate financial reimbursements by state, federal, and private insurance systems."[1] The present reimbursement systems make no effort to distinguish between effective, scientifically valid treatments and invalid, dangerous, and unethical practices.

In a similar manner, Barden argues, unprofessional treatments now also are clogging and contaminating the American legal system. Unscientific testimony by mental health practitioners has reached epidemic proportions within the civil, family, and criminal justice systems. This deceptive "junk science" testimony, Barden avers, is dangerous to both individual and family liberty and is destroying the integrity of America's legal system.

What the TRMHP is asking for is nothing more than common

444

sense—a quality that has been missing from the mental health arena for much too long. First of all, the act merely asks that all psychotherapists would be required to *tell the truth* to all of their patients about the safety and effectiveness of their proposed and alternative treatments. Second, all psychotherapists will be required to *tell the truth* to state, federal, and private insurance systems about the safety and effectiveness of the treatments offered to patients. Treatment methods that are "too vague and abstract to be scientifically tested" are simply too vague and abstract to be paid for with taxpayer dollars. Third, all psychotherapists and social scientists will be required to *tell the whole, scientific truth* in all American courts of law. So-called experts using worthless psychological tests and dubious "clinical opinions" regarding "doll play," "interpretations of drawings," "facilitated communication," and "hypnotic testimony" have sent scores of innocent citizens to prison and have defrauded judges and juries into believing such procedures are uncontroversial and based on findings from responsible scientific research. This act would require that states enact and enforce legislation that would mandate an affirmative duty for all "expert" witnesses to tell the truth including full disclosure of limitations on the validity and reliability of the witnesses' methods and conclusions.

Careful research conducted across several decades has not only shown that "clinical judgment and experience" in the mental health professions is, in general, of little practical value and lacks both validity and reliability, but it can also be dangerous as well. One of the most famous of all studies comparing clinical versus actuarial (experimental and statistical) judgment has shown that clinicians "have considerable difficulties distinguishing valid and invalid variables" (in other words, fact and fiction are easily confused) and that "clinical judgments based on interviews tend to be of low or negligible accuracy."[2] Finally, objective evidence is, uniformly, vastly superior to any and all subjective impressions.

Who in their right minds could possibly object to or oppose any law maximizing truth, responsibility, and accountability in the mental health system? Why, hundreds of clinical psychologists, psychiatrists, and social workers, of course, as well as those whose unscientific, unreliable, and unethical practices are seriously threatened. Because of the vast numbers of psychotherapists making up the membership of the American Psychological Association, the APA Practice Directorate has been working closely with the state psychological associations and state licensing boards to block all TRMHP acts and actions, justifying their efforts on the grounds that:

> In essence, such a bill, if enacted, would create a series of duplicative, inappropriate and unduly onerous regulations. According to the directorate analysis, the typical legislation based on the model act would require all forms of therapy to meet ambiguous standards of effectiveness before they could be used with most patients, require "cookbook" approaches to complex psychotherapy procedures that might be unsuitable for some patients and inappropriately restrict psychologists' ability to serve as expert witnesses.[3]

In other words, do not hold us to the normal and usual standards of truth, fair play, and honesty in the American marketplace, American legal system, or the world of science. Do not ask nor expect us to meet such inappropriately high and unapplicably reasonable standards. Psychotherapy, you should know, is much too subjective, much too mysterious and ineffable an art to ever be tested scientifically.

Whether or not the future will see any improvement in either the delivery or the effectiveness of mental health services for people suffering from emotional disorders remains to be seen. Neither pills nor pseudoscience has, in the long run, given us much to cheer about. Nor is there, unfortunately, any known or effective treatment techniques or procedures for "shrinkage." If you can possibly avoid it—in its many and various forms—by all means do so. Once again, *caveat emptor*—let the buyer beware! Long-term, intensive, emotional re-education via tender loving care and kindness administered in a warm, humane, supportive social milieu seems to be the only thing that is truly effective for depression, eating disorders, anxiety and panic attacks, and the schizophrenias. But this asks much more of most psychotherapists than they are ready, willing, or able to give and very few, it seems, pay any attention to the therapists' first commandment: *first do no harm*. In their zeal and eagerness to make you well they may do you incalculable damage. *Caveat emptor!* Anyone in *this* market had best be wary!

NOTES

1. R. Christopher Barden, "Model Legislation Package," Barden Exhibit, 23 March 1995 (Plymouth, Mich.: National Association for Consumer Protection in Mental Health Practices, 1995), pp. 1–59.

2. R. M. Dawes, D. Faust, and P. E. Meehl, "Clinical versus Actuarial Judgment," *Science* 243 (1989): 1668–74.

3. American Psychological Association, *Practitioner Update* 3, no. 1 (April 1995): 1.

Suggested Readings

THE LITERATURE OF VICTIMIZATION

Protests and complaints against abuses of the psychotherapeutic state have gone on/for years. An entire literary genre of autobiographical material by mental patients condemning their treatment at the hands of incompetent and uncaring therapists has been available for some time. Some of the most damning of therapeutic cruelty and mistreatment recorded during the past fifty years include the following:

Brandt, Anthony. *The Reality Police: The Experience of Insanity in America.* New York: William Morrow, 1975.

Collins, William J. *Out of the Depths.* New York: Doubleday, 1971.

Dahl, Robert G. *Breakdown.* Indianapolis: Bobbs-Merrill, 1959.

Donaldson, Kenneth. *Insanity Inside Out.* New York: Crown, 1976. Donaldson, who was committed against his will to the Florida State Hospital at Chattahoochee, where he remained for fifteen years, is the first American psychiatric patient ever to win damages against his physicians, as well as the first to have his case heard by the United States Supreme Court. His book brings to the fore the issue of patients' civil rights.

Etten, Howard J. *Memoirs of a Mental Case.* New York: Vantage, 1972.

Farmer, Francis. *Will There Really Be a Morning?* New York: Putnam, 1972.

Geller, Jeffrey L. and Maxine Harris. *Women of the Asylum: Voices from behind the Walls, 1840–1945.* New York: Anchor Books, 1994. This book, which is certain to arouse the reader's ire, contains twenty-six first-person accounts of women who were placed in mental institutions against their will, usually by male family members, because they held views or behaved in ways that deviated from the norm of their day.

Gotkin, Janet and Paul. *Too Much Anger, Too Many Tears: A Personal Triumph over Psychiatry*. New York: Quadrangle, 1975.

Hellmuth, Charles F. *Maniac: Anatomy of a Mental Illness*. Philadelphia: Dorrance, 1977.

Knauth, Percy. *A Season in Hell*. New York: Harper, 1956.

Lane, Edward X. *I Was a Mental Statistic*. New York: Carlton, 1963.

Larkin, Joy. *Strangers No More—Diary of a Schizo*. New York: Vantage, 1979.

Lelchuk, Alan. *Shrinking*. New York: Little Brown, 1978.

Marks, Jan. *Doctor Purgatory*. New York: Citadel, 1959.

McNeill, Elizabeth. *Nine and a Half Weeks*. New York: Dutton, 1978.

Moore, William L. *The Maid in Chains*. New York: Exposition, 1955.

Nelson, Robert Q. *Mental*. Chichester, England: Quentin Nelson, 1970.

O'Brien, Barbara. *Operators and Things: The Inner Life of a Schizophrenic*. London: Elek Books, 1960.

Peterson, Dale. *A Mad People's History of Madness*. Pittsburgh: University of Pittsburgh Press, 1982. This bibliography of writings by mad and mental patients prior to 1982 lists over five hundred separate items.

Rebeta-Burdett, Joyce. *The Cracker Factory*. New York: Macmillan, 1977.

Roberts, Marty. *Sojourn in a Palace for Peculiars*. New York: Carlton, 1970.

Rodgers, Hope. *Time and the Human Robot*. Vinton, Iowa: Ink Spot Press, 1975.

Russell, James W. *The Stranger in the Mirror*. New York: Harper, 1968.

Simpson, Jane. *The Last Days of My Life*. London: Allen & Unwin, 1959.

Stebel, S. T. *The Shoe Leather Treatment*. Los Angeles: J. P. Tarcher, 1980.

Sugar, Frank E. *Mindrape*. New York: Exposition, 1978.

Tew, Raya E. *How Not to Kill a Cockroach*. New York: Vantage, 1978.

Vonnegut, Mark. *The Eden Express*. New York: Praeger, 1975.

Wellon, Arthur. *Five Years in Mental Hospitals: An Autobiographical Essay*. New York: Exposition, 1967.

PROFESSIONAL OPPOSITION TO THE TYRANNY OF THE PSYCHOTHERAPEUTIC STATE

Some of the most powerful and impressive antitherapeutic tracts that have been written in the last twenty years are by professional therapists themselves. All such lists should begin with the work of Thomas Szasz, who has been a pioneer in pointing out the evils of psychiatric oppression. All of his books are recommended, but his most important works include the following:

Szasz, Thomas S. *The Myth of Mental Illness: Foundations of a Theory of Personal Conduct.* New York: Hoeber-Harper, 1961.

————. *The Myth of Psychotherapy: Mental Healing As Religion, Rhetoric, and Repression.* New York: Anchor Press, 1978.

————. *The Manufacture of Madness.* New York: Harper & Row, 1970.

————. *Schizophrenia: The Sacred Symbol of Psychiatry.* New York: Basic Books, 1976.

————. *Law, Liberty, and Psychiatry.* New York: Macmillan, 1963.

————. *The Theology of Medicine.* New York: Harper & Row, 1977.

————. *Our Right to Drugs: The Case for a Free Market.* New York: Praeger, 1992.

Additional works of considerable importance which have appeared since 1970 are listed below:

Aftel, Mandy and Robin T. Lakoff. *When Talk Is Not Cheap: Or, How to Find the Right Therapist When You Don't Know Where to Begin.* New York: Warner Books, 1985.

Armstrong, Louise. *And They Call It Help: The Psychiatric Policing of America's Children.* Reading, Mass.: Wesley Publishing, 1993.

Braginsky, Benjamin, Dorothy Braginsky, and Kenneth Ring. *Methods of Madness: The Mental Hospitals As a Last Resort.* New York: Holt, Rinehart & Winston, 1969.

Breggin, Peter. *Toxic Psychiatry: Why Therapy, Empathy, and Love Must Replace Drugs, Electroshock, and Biochemical Theories of the "New" Psychiatry.* New York: St. Martin's Press, 1991.

Breggin, Peter R. and Ginger R. Breggin. *Talking Back to Prozac: What Doctors Aren't Telling You about Today's Most Controversial Drug.* New York: St. Martin's Press, 1994.

————. *The War against Children: How the Drug Programs and Theories of the Psychiatric Establishment Are Threatening America's Children with a Medical Cure for Violence.* New York: St. Martin's Press, 1994.

Campbell, T. W. *Beware the Talking Cure: Psychotherapy May Be Hazardous to Your Mental Health.* Boca Raton, Fla.: Upton Books, 1994.

Chamberlin, Judi. *On Our Own: Patient-Controlled Alternatives to the Mental Health System*. New York: McGraw-Hill, 1979.

Cohen, David, ed. *Challenging the Therapeutic State: Critical Perspectives on Psychiatry and the Mental Health System*. New York: Institute of Mind and Behavior, 1990.

———. *Challenging the Therapeutic State, Part Two: Further Disquisitions on the Mental Health System*. New York: Institute of Mind and Behavior, 1994.

Dawes, Robyn M. *House of Cards: Psychology and Psychotherapy Built on Myth*. New York: Free Press, 1994.

Ennis, Bruce J. *Prisoners of Psychiatry: Mental Patients, Psychiatrists, and the Law*. New York: Harcourt Brace Jovanovich, 1972.

Farber, Seth. *Madness, Heresy, and the Rumor of Angels: The Revolt against the Mental Health System*. Chicago: Open Court, 1993.

Fisher, Seymour, and R. P. Greenberg, eds. *The Scientific Evaluation of Freud's Therapy*. New York: Basic Books, 1979.

———. *The Limits of Biological Treatment for Psychological Distress: Comparisons with Psychotherapy and Placebo*. Hillsdale, N.J.: Lawrence Erlbaum Associates, 1989.

Frank, Leonard Roy, ed. *Madness Network News Reader*. San Francisco: Glide Publications, 1974.

Friedberg, John. *Shock Treatment Is Not Good for Your Brain*. San Francisco: Glide Publications, 1976.

Gambrill, Eileen. *Critical Thinking in Clinical Practice: Improving the Accuracy of Judgments and Decisions about Clients*. San Francisco: Jossey-Bass, 1990. Aimed at helping psychologists and psychiatrists offer better service to their clients, Gambrill's book is primarily a manual on critical thinking, decision-making, and logical reasoning.

Glenn, Michael, and Richard Kunnes. *Repression or Revolution? Therapy in the United States Today*. New York: Harper & Row, 1973.

Hall, David. *The Politics of Schizophrenia: Psychiatric Oppression in the United States*. Lanham, Md.: University Press of America, 1983.

Hamstra, Bruce. *How Therapists Diagnose: Seeing through the Psychiatric Eye*. New York: St. Martin's Press, 1994.

Healy, David. *The Suspended Revolution: Psychiatry and Psychotherapy Re-Examined*. London: Faber & Faber Ltd., 1990.

Ingleby, David, ed. *Critical Psychiatry, the Politics of Mental Health*. New York: Pantheon, 1981.

Kiernan, Thomas. *Shrinks, Etc.: A Consumer's Guide to Psychotherapies*. New York: Dial, 1974.

Lewontin, R. C., Steven Rose, and Leon J. Kamin. *Not in Our Genes: Biology, Ideology, and Human Nature.* New York: Pantheon, 1984.

Masson, Jeffrey. *Against Therapy.* New York: Atheneum, 1988.

————. *Final Analysis: The Making and Unmaking of a Psychoanalyst.* New York: HarperCollins, 1991.

Noble, June and William. *The Psychiatric Fix: Psychiatry's Alarming Power over Our Lives.* New York: Delacorte Press, 1981.

Peele, Stanton. *Diseasing of America: Addiction Treatment Out of Control.* Lexington, Mass.: Lexington Books, 1989.

Podvall, Edward M. *The Seduction of Madness: Revolutionary Insights into the World of Psychosis and a Compassionate Approach to Recovery at Home.* New York: HarperCollins, 1990.

Portland, Frank K. *The Anti-Psychiatry Bibliography and Resource Guide,* 2d ed. Vancouver: Press Gang, 1979.

Robertiello, Richard C. and Gerald Schoenewolf. *101 Common Therapeutic Blunders: Countertransference and Conterresistance in Psychotherapy.* Northvale, N.J. and London: Jason Aronson, Inc., 1987.

Sarbin, Theodore, and James C. Mancuso. *Schizophrenia: Medical Diagnosis or Moral Verdict?* New York: Pergamon, 1982.

Schef, Thomas J. *Labeling Madness.* Englewood Cliffs, N.J.: Prentice-Hall, 1975.

Sykes, Charles J. *A Nation of Victims: The Decay of the American Character.* New York: St. Martin's Press, 1992.

Tennov, Dorothy. *Psychotherapy: The Hazardous Cure.* New York: Abelard-Schuman, 1975.

Thornton, E. M. *The Freudian Fallacy: An Alternative View of Freudian Theory.* New York: Dial, 1984.

Torrey, E. Fuller. *The Death of Psychiatry.* New York: Penguin, 1975.

————. *Witchdoctors and Psychiatrists: The Common Roots of Psychotherapy and Its Future.* New York: Harper & Row, 1986.

Valenstein, Eliot S. *Great and Desperate Cures: The Rise and Decline of Psychosurgery and Other Radical Treatments for Mental Illness.* New York: Basic Books, 1986.

Walkenstein, Eileen. *Don't Shrink to Fit: A Confrontation with Dehumanization in Psychiatry and Psychology.* New York: Grove Press, 1975. Walkenstein is a Veterans' Administration-trained humanistic psychiatrist active in starting and leading growth centers both in the United States and abroad. Chapter titles of this book alone provide an excellent preview of its content: "Human Beings Can't Be Diagnosed," "A Psychiatric Diagnosis Is a Jail Sentence," and "Diagnosing the Shrink." A splendid read.

Wood, Garth. *The Myth of Neurosis: Overcoming the Illness Excuse.* New York: Harper & Row, 1989.

Zilbergeld, Bernie. *The Shrinking of America: Myths of Psychological Change.* Boston: Little, Brown & Co., 1983.

GUIDES TO HELPING YOURSELF AND AVOIDING THERAPY ENTIRELY

There are, amazingly, even some useful and worthy things in the "self-help" section of every book store. Some of the better offerings are listed here:

Bernard, Michael E. *Staying Rational in an Irrational World: Albert Ellis and Rational Emotive Therapy.* New York: Carol Publishing Group, 1991.

Ellis, Albert. *Reason and Emotion in Psychotherapy.* Secaucus, N.J.: Lyle Stuart/Citadel Press, 1962.

Ellis, Albert, with R. Grieger. *Handbook of Rational Emotive Therapy.* New York: Springer Publishing, 1977.

Johnstone, Lucy. *Users and Abusers of Psychiatry: A Critical Look at Traditional Psychiatric Practice.* London and New York: Routledge, 1989.

Padus, Emrika. *The Complete Guide to Your Emotions and Your Health.* Emmaus, Pa.: Rodale Press, 1992, distributed by St. Martin's Press. This excellent guidebook deals specifically with how to build "emotional hardiness" and control, how to develop a positive, optimistic view of life, how to rid yourself of negative emotions, how to minimize life's key stressors, and much more. It is, in my opinion, the single best book you can buy and read if you are interested in promoting mental health.

Seligman, Martin E. P. *What You Can Change and What You Can't: The Complete Guide to Successful Self-Improvement.* New York: A. A. Knopf, 1994. "Therapy that reviews childhood endlessly, that does not focus on how to cope in the here and now, that views a better future as incidental to undoing the past has a century-long history of being ineffective" (p. 241).

Simon, Sidney B. *Getting Unstuck: Breaking through Your Barriers to Change.* New York: Warner Books, 1988.

Simon, Sidney B. and Suzanne. *Forgiveness: How to Make Peace with Your Past and Get on with Your Life.* New York: Warner Books, 1990.

Viorst, Judith. *Necessary Losses: The Loves, Illusions, Dependencies, and Impossible*

Expectations That All of Us Have to Give up in Order to Grow. New York: Simon & Schuster, 1986 and Ballantine/Fawcett Crest, 1987.

Weiner-Davis, Michelle. *Fire Your Shrink: Do-It-Yourself Strategies for Changing Your Life and Everyone in It*. New York: Simon & Schuster, 1995.

Zois, Christ, and Patricia Fogarty. *Think Like a Shrink: Solve Your Problems with Short-Term Therapy Techniques*. New York: Warner Books, 1993.

To discuss each critique in turn would require another book longer than the present one. Nevertheless, some of the insights and conclusions from these volumes are worth repeating. With regard to "psychiatric power" Anthony Brandt notes that psychiatric power degrades both its victim and the abusers and vitiates whatever therapeutic effectiveness psychiatry may actually have. As for craziness, Brandt—along with others—argues that it is the name we give to behavior we don't understand and can't or won't deal with and the ability or possibility of going "crazy" exists in everyone.

In the 1989 Fisher and Greenberg volume concerned with biological treatments, the authors conclude with the following statement:

the results of somatic treatment approaches for "psychiatric disorder" should be viewed with caution and perhaps, even more appropriately, with a fair amount of skepticism. We have been personally startled to read research reports that seemed ostensibly to indicate a quite limited advantage for a particular drug as compared to a placebo, but then to find such reports hailed in another context as proof that the drug is highly effective... the entire structure of somatic treatments is more fragile and limited in potency than publicly acknowledged.[1]

Dawes, in his book *House of Cards*, also calls attention to a large number of commonly held "myths" within psychology that have little or no supporting data and/or scientific justification for their existence. Some of the most pernicious include the following: (1) the belief that self-esteem is an essential precursor to being a productive human being; (2) the belief that events in one's childhood determine one's fate as an adult; (3) the belief that you have to love yourself before you can love someone else; (4) the belief that greater clinical experience makes for a better therapist, and that clinical prediction is better than statistical prediction. Dawes also notes that the Rorschach tests are bogus, many so-called psychiatric expert witnesses are frauds, and current licensing procedures for both psychiatrists and psychologists are fraudulent and a waste of time.

In general, most of the critics would strongly endorse the statement that psychotherapy is a poorly applied "art" created by a medical/professional elite which has managed to sell it to middle-class America as a "health function" that will cure whatever it is that ails them mentally. While some individual therapists have, at times, been helpful to their clients, in the long-run and on an overall basis, the primary thrust of psychotherapy has been political and its effects have been oppressive. The concern has focussed much more on increasing the therapists' power than on curing patients. The client has been adjusted, normalized, calmed, and shown the error of not only his ways but also his feelings, ideas, and passions. Is he happy? Is he free? Is he liberated? Don't be absurd!

Regarding psychotherapy, critic Jeffrey Masson is uncompromising. In his view psychotherapy cannot be reformed in its parts or as a whole because the activity, fundamentally, is harmful. He says, "Recognizing the lies, the flaws, . . . the potential for harm, the imbalance in power, the arrogance, the condescension, the pretensions may be the first step in the eventual abolition of psychotherapy that I believe is one day in the future inevitable and desirable."[2] These words, written in 1988, are today sad and ironic in view of the lack of progress thus far. Antipsychiatry (as a body of writings, practice style, philosophy, or social movement) has been pronounced dead or irrelevant, however, even by historians.

> The acceptance by world mental health professions of American psychiatry's official nosology, followed by epidemiological studies which uncovered fifty million cases of "diagnosable mental disorders" in the United States alone, confirm the primacy of that profession's influence in the mental health system. In turn, the system represents the culmination of the therapeutic state of the advanced psychiatric society.[3]

In one of the important essays in Cohen's *Challenging the Therapeutic State,* Dr. Ken Barney states that in spite of three decades of trenchant critique and rights advocacy nothing has had any effect on either the language or the basic operations of the mental health system. As Barney observes, "Oppressive and dehumanizing practices continue unchanged; social and psychological services remain circumscribed or have become diminished; biomedical reductionism retains its great appeal."[4] Despite the weakness of psychiatric theory and the uncertainty of the biopsychiatrists' medical approach, their arrogance and megalomanic air of competence has continued unabated. In this regard they have been aided and abetted by an uncritical media who trumpet every new drug as a panacea and rarely or never report retractions, disconfirming studies, or concessions of failure.

Barney notes that most criticisms fail to consider the role of sociopolitical factors and fail to recognize that social control does not require medicalization. While the current system of psychiatric labeling is convenient it is, in no way, a necessity. Psychologists are as good as psychiatrists in judging "dangerousness to self and others" as well as the need for treatment. They are also just as effective in the courtroom and professional hospital administrators can and do run hospitals and clinics. As for drugs, they are already prescribed by nonpsychiatric physicians, nurses, and specially trained psychologists. In other words, mental health services would continue whether psychiatry exists or not. The psychological viewpoint can and should prevail, and in the long-run probably will, despite the current dominance of biopsychiatry and the medical model. Certainly, as the amount and range of human suffering continue to increase there will be an increased need for psychotherapy, but as anyone who can see beyond the end of his nose is well aware, psychotherapy can do little to change the fundamental sources of misery in our society today. Poverty, violence, alienation, and despair are far beyond the reach of professionals who are primarily concerned with self-service and serving their profession and who give only lip service (or less) to basic human needs.

NOTES

1. Seymour Fisher and Roger P. Greenberg, eds., *The Scientific Evaluation of Freud's Therapy* (New York: Basic Books, 1979), p. 309.

2. Jeffrey Masson, *Against Therapy* (New York: Atheneum, 1988), p. 254.

3. David Cohen, *Challenging the Therapeutic State, Part Two* (New York: Institute of Mind and Behavior, 1994), p. i.

4. Ken Barney, "Limitations of the Critique of the Medical Model," in Cohen, *Challenging the Therapeutic State, Part Two,* p. 20.

Index

Hudson, James I., on affective spectrum disorder, 340; on studies of repressed memories of childhood sexual abuse, 268–69

Hughes, Richard, 368, 370

humanistic psychology, 118

hydrotherapy, 98

hyperactivity, 303

hypnosis, 128, 129, 272; in Kentucky UFO case, 287, 290, 293–94; and memory, 260, 261, 268; and multiple personality disorder, 311, 324; procedures of, 263; and psychotherapists' understanding of, 269

hypnotic age regression, 262–63, 325

hypothermia therapy, 240

hysteria, 97

iatrogenesis, 249–95 (chapter 5)

Illich, Ivan, on U.S. health care trends, 342–43

implicit memory account, 257

incubi, 94–95

Ingram, Paul, 257, 270

insulin, as a psychotherapeutic treatment, 354

insurance companies, 83

International Psychoanalytic Congress, 133

introversion (in Jung's thought), 142–43

involuntary commitment law, 190

"Ishakower Effect," 291

Jablonka, Eva, on learned vs. gene-based behavior, 384–85

Jacobs, David H., on biology and psychiatry, 435–36; on the efficacy of major psychiatric drugs, 373–74

Jacobs, Douglas, on depression, 57

Jacobs, Mary Jo, 168

Jacobson, Neil, on efficacy of professional training in psychotherapy, 63–64; on eye movement and desensitization reprocessing, 83

James I, 94

James, William, 109, 111

Janet, Pierre, 310

Janov, Arthur, 135

Jefferson, James, on obsessive-compulsive disorder, 55

Jenkins, Philip, on alleged occult survivors, 277

Jesilow, Paul, on psychiatric Medicaid fraud, 166–67

Jesus, 91–92

Johnson, Catherine, on U.S. use of psychotherapy, 64

Johnson, F. H., on hallucinations, 229

Joint Commission on Accreditation of Health Care Organizations, on the American hospital industry, 195–96

Jones, Ernest, on Freud's "behavioral eccentricities," 125–26; on megalomania, 186–87

Jones, Jim, 412fn

Joseph, Newton, on religious psychotherapists, 418–19

Journal of Orgonomy, 410

Juhasz, J. B., study of suggestion by, 203

Jung, Carl, 74, 141–44, 163; animosity toward Freud of, 143; antecedents to the thought of, 127; on the megalomania of doctors, 187–88; and Nazism, 143, 144; and the occult, 402; theory of, 141–42; therapy of, 143

Kaminer, Wendy, on the codependency and recovery movement, 69

Kamm, Adrian van, on liberation from popularized psychological theories, 377–78

Karolinska Institute, 234

Karon, Bertram, on drug treatment of

Malleus Maleficarum, 93
malpractice, Harvard study of, 172–73
managed care, and psychotherapy, 439
Mancuso, James, on the lack of a biological basis for schizophrenia, 201, 207–208; on mental health drugs, 212
Mandell, Arnold, 369
Manhattan State Hospital, 111
Marbs, Isaac, on obsessive-compulsive disorder, 55
Markowitz, Laura M., on sex with clients, 163
marriage therapists, 29
Martin, M. F., 311, 314
Maslow, Abraham, 118
Masserman, Jules, 164–65
Masson, Jeff, on John Rosen, 157–59; on Albert Honig, 159–61; on psychotherapy, 154–56; on the harmfulness of psychotherapy, 456
Masters, William, 147
masturbation, 113, 114–15
Mavromatis, Andreas, 291
McCulloch, Warren S., and sodium cyanide treatment, 240
McGuinness, Diane, criticism of attention deficit disorders by, 301–303; on drug treatment for attention deficit disorder, 305
McHugh, Paul R., on multiple personality disorder as iatrogenic, 315, 317
McKinlay, John and Sonja, on causes of increased lifespan, 345
Medawar, Peter, on psychoanalytic glibness, 133–34
medicaid fraud, 166–67
medical negligence, 196
medicine, role in increased lifespan of, 345
megalomania, 186–87; of doctors, 187–88
Melton, J. Gordon, on Satanism, 273

memories, false, *see* false memories
memory, 253, 256–57; change of over time, 258–59; hidden, 272; and hypnosis, 260; reliability of, 261; of traumatic events, 258
Mendelsohn, Robert, on U.S. drug prescription culture, 343
Menninger, Karl, and criminology, 140
mental health, of Americans, 52–53; definition of, 16; history of, 79–80; in the United States, study by National Institute of Mental Health on, 65–66; violent therapeutic treatment of, 103
mental health industry, 76–80
mental hospitals, abuses in, 189–91, 192–96; first, 92; history of, 99–102. *See also* hospitals
"mental hygiene" movement, 111
mental illness, biological basis of, 80–81; effective ways to reduce, 435; fallacy of organic nature of, 432–41; rates of, 433–34; Plato on, 91
Merskey, H., on evidence that multiple personality disorder is induced, 318–20; on source of multiple personality disorder, 320
mesmerism, influence on Freud of, 127
metapsychiatry, 401–21 (chapter 11); definition of, 401–402
Methylphenidate, *see* Ritalin
Metrazol, 355
Meyer, Adolf, 108, 111, 112; on schizophrenia, 224
Meyerson, Abraham, 117
Middlebrook, Diane Wood, on Anne Sexton, 177
Millett, Kate, treatment of, 173–74
Mintz, Sandy, 161
Mirowsky, J., on the inappropriate precision of the *Diagnostic and Statistical Manual of Mental Disorders,* 337–38
misdiagnosis, benevolent, 40–42

Mitchell, S. L., 310

Mitchell, S. Weir, 98–99

Modrow, John, on being labeled a schizophrenic, 228–29; on neuroleptic drugs, 233–34; on psychological causes of hallucinations, 229; on schizophrenia, 222–43; on schizophrenia as a generational phenomenon, 222–24; on schizophrenia as a way of coping with loss of self-esteem, 227; on sleep deprivation in schizophrenics, 227–28

Moniz, Antonio Egas, 355

Moreno, J. L., 118

Morgan, Robert F., and "balloon therapy," 22–23

Morrissette, Karen, on mental health fraud, 192–93

Morrow, Mary, 179

mortality rates, public, effect of doctors' strikes on, 346

Mosher, L. R., on use of neuroleptics in first episodes of schizophrenia, 214–15

MPD, see multiple personality disorder

Mulhern, Sherrill, on psychotherapy and Satanism, 278–79

Multiaxial Diagnostic System (of the *Diagnostic and Statistical Manual of Mental Disorders*), 331

multiple personality disorder, 309–26 (chapter 7); absence in Japan and Britain of, 318; cultural nature of, 321–22; national nature of, 318; history of, 310–12; and hypnosis, 324; lack of evidence supporting, 314; nature as iatrogenic of, 311–12, 315, 317

muscle relaxants, prescribed for the elderly (table), 351

music, 105

Mutual UFO Network, 290

Myers-Briggs Type Indicator, 142–43

Nabokov, Vladimir, on psychoanalysts, 140–41

Nader, K., study of memories by, 264

Nagel, Ernest, on the scientific basis of psychoanalysis, 133

Namka, Lynne, 70

Napoleon, on Gall, 97

Narrow, William, on Americans' mental health, 53

National Association of Psychiatric Survivors, 437

National Alliance for the Mentally Ill, attempt to revoke Breggin's medical license by, 217

National Ambulatory Medical Care Survey, 362

National Institute of Health, on cognitive behavior therapy, 364; and the *Diagnostic and Statistical Manual of Mental Disorders*, 337; on drugs in mental health treatment, 144; study on U.S. mental health by, 65–66

National Institute on Alcohol Abuse and Alcoholism, 70

National Medical Enterprises, Inc., 191–94

National Training Laboratory, 118

Nazism, 143, 144, 408

negligence, medical, 196

neuroleptics, alternatives to treatment with, 216; definition of, 17, 212; lack of antischizophrenia properties of, 233–34; studies of damage done by treatment with, 215; use of, to treat first episodes of schizophrenia, 214–15

neurosis, myth of, 33

New York Office of Professional Medical Misconduct, disciplining of doctors by, 172

niacin, 357

nicotinic acid, 357

Smith, M. Brewster, on psychiatrists in public service, 80

Smith, Michelle, 271, 274

Social Science Research Council, 136

Socialist Society for Sex Consultation and Sexological Research, 407

Sock, Benjamin, 139

sodium cyanide treatment, 240

Spanos, N. P., on induced nature of multiple personality disorder, 312–13, 320–21, 322–23; on theory of childhood origin of multiple personality disorder, 324

Spencer, Herbert, on mental processes and evolution, 97

"spinning," 104

Spitz, R.A., on nineteenth-century medical treatments, 115

Sprenger, James, 93

Sprinkle, Leo, 287, 290

Spurzheim, Johann Caspar, 97

St. Luke's Hospital, 101

Stafford, Mona, 286–87, 290, 291–93

Stanovich, Keith A., 135

starvation therapy, 240

Stone, Alan A., 178

Stratford, Lauren, 274, 276–77

Styron, William, and accounts of Halcion's effects, 174–75; on drugs in psychotherapeutic treatment, 174, 175

succubi, 94–95

suggestion, 203, 206

suicide, as a result of psychotherapeutic sexual abuse, 169; as a result of electroshock therapy, 173; as a result of Halcion, 364

Sullivan, Henry Stack, on schizophrenia, 226

survivors, psychiatric, 437

Sybil, 311

Sykes, Charles, on John Bradshaw, 70; on the "Therapeutic Culture," 74, 75

Szasz, Thomas, on classes of psychiatric treatment, 21; on the definition of disease, 21; on the *Diagnostic and Statistical Manual of Mental Disorders*, 333; on the medicalization of all human problems, 74; on opiates, 372; on Prozac, 370; on the psychiatric industry, 206; on psychotherapy, 21; on the requirement of prescriptions for some common medications, 372

taraxein hypothesis (for the cause of schizophrenia), 233

tardive diskinesia, definition of, 214; prevalence of, 214, 215

Tavris, Carol, on Kramer book about Prozac, 367–68

Taylor, Richard, on iatrogenic disease, 345

Taylor, W. S., 311, 314

TD, *see* tardive diskinesia

team approach, to psychotherapy, 117–18

Temerlin, Janet and Maurice, on cultish psychotherapy, 411–14

Temerlin, Maurice, study of psychotherapeutic cults by, 414–15

Terence (playwright), 403

Terr, Lenore, on forgetting sexual abuse, 255; on memory of traumatic events, 258

theosophy, 110

"Therapeutic Culture," 74, 75

"Therapeutic State," origins of, 51. See *also* Psychotherapeutic State

Thigpen, C. H., 311, 312

Thomas, Elaine, 286, 291–93

Thoraxine, 356

Thorley, G., 304

Thornton, E. M., on Freud, 124, 125, 126; on psychoanalysis and the first years of life, 129